Corporate Risk Mitigation Through Socially Responsible Governance

Rana Yassir Hussain
University of Education, Lahore, Pakistan

Sikandar Ali Qalati
School of Business, Liaocheng University, Shandong, China

Haroon Hussain
Malik Firoz Khan Noon Business School, University of Sargodha, Pakistan

Published in the United States of America by
IGI Global
701 E. Chocolate Avenue
Hershey PA, USA 17033
Tel: 717-533-8845
Fax: 717-533-8661
E-mail: cust@igi-global.com
Web site: https://www.igi-global.com

Copyright © 2025 by IGI Global. All rights reserved. No part of this publication may be reproduced, stored or distributed in any form or by any means, electronic or mechanical, including photocopying, without written permission from the publisher.
Product or company names used in this set are for identification purposes only. Inclusion of the names of the products or companies does not indicate a claim of ownership by IGI Global of the trademark or registered trademark.

Library of Congress Cataloging-in-Publication Data

CIP Data Pending
ISBN:979-8-3693-5733-0
eISBN:979-8-3693-5734-7

Vice President of Editorial: Melissa Wagner
Managing Editor of Acquisitions: Mikaela Felty
Managing Editor of Book Development: Jocelynn Hessler
Production Manager: Mike Brehm
Cover Design: Phillip Shickler

British Cataloguing in Publication Data
A Cataloguing in Publication record for this book is available from the British Library.

All work contributed to this book is new, previously-unpublished material.
The views expressed in this book are those of the authors, but not necessarily of the publisher.

Table of Contents

Preface xiv

Chapter 1
Sustainable Financing and Supply Chain Financial Risk Management:
Sustainable Financial Instruments and Risk-Free Resilient Supply Chains 1
    Naveed Mushtaq, University of Sargodha, Pakistan
    Mohsin Altaf, Global Banking School, Manchester, UK
    Muhammad Bilal Mustafa, Birmingham City University, UK

Chapter 2
Corporate Social Responsibility and Organizational Performance
Mediated by Customers Satisfaction: Corporate Social Responsibility and
Organizational Performance 31
    Ali Shaibu, Islamic University College, Ghana
    Geoffrey Norman Tumwine, Kyambogo University, Uganda
    Mohammed Kassim, Islamic University College, Ghana
    Anas Sandow Seidu, University of Business and Integrated Development
        Studies, Ghana
    Hajara Mohammed, Islamic Finance Research Institute, Ghana

Chapter 3
Effect of Informal and Out-of-Court Resolutions on the Post-Bankruptcy
Performance of Companies: Empirical Evidence From India 61
    Santosh Kumar, Christ University, India
    S. Parameswaran, Christ University, India

Chapter 4
Corporate Disclosure and Transparency as a Tool of Socially Responsible
Risk Management 91
    Hammad Hassan Mirza, University of Sargodha, Pakistan
    Haroon Hussain, University of Sargodha, Pakistan
    Rana Yassir Hussain, University of Education, Lahore, Pakistan
    Muhammad Waqar Ahmed, University of Sargodha, Pakistan
    Muhammad Adil, University of Education, Lahore, Pakistan

Chapter 5
The Auditor's Guide to Corporate Social Responsibility: Enhancing Ethical Practices 105
> Shujah ur Rahman, University of Education, Lahore, Pakistan
> Nyla Saleem, School of Humanities and Social Sciences, Pakistan
> Yasir Habib, Institute of Energy Policy and Research, Malaysia
> Saba Sattar, Government Technical Training Institute for Women, Pakistan

Chapter 6
The Impact of Artificial Intelligence on Achieving Corporate Social Responsibility 115
> Yasir Aleem, The University of Sargodha, Pakistan
> Saifullah Hassan, The University of Sargodha, Pakistan

Chapter 7
Theoretical and Conceptual Approach of Corporate Governance and CSR Activities in Financial Decision Making 131
> Rabia Arshad, The University of Faisalabad, Pakistan
> Faiq Mahmood, Government College University, Faisalabad, Pakistan
> Maryam Saleem, The University of Faisalabad, Pakistan

Chapter 8
Risk and Uncertainty Factors in Managerial Economics 153
> Saqib Muneer, University of Ha'il, Saudi Arabia

Chapter 9
The Roll Of Managerial Economics In Business Development 177
> Saqib Muneer, University of Ha'il, Saudi Arabia

Chapter 10
The Impact of Financial Policies and COVID-19 on Sustainable Performance 201
> Rashid Mehmood, University of Education, Lahore, Pakistan
> Ilyas Ahmad, University of Education, Lahore, Pakistan
> Shujah Ur Rahman, University of Education, Lahore, Pakistan
> Sohail Rizwan, Fatima Jinnah Women University, Rawalpindi, Pakistan
> Saba Sattar, Government Technical Training Institute for Women, Pakistan

Chapter 11
The Role of Corporate Governance in Bank Risk-Taking 215
    Rashid Mehmood, University of Education, Lahore, Pakistan
    Ilyas Ahmad, University of Education, Lahore, Pakistan
    Shujah Ur Rahman, University of Education, Lahore, Pakistan
    Saba Sattar, Government Technical Training Institute for Women, Pakistan

Chapter 12
An Exploratory Study of the Complex Interplay Between Society and
Finance: Ways of Empowerment and Elements of Precarity 227
    Muhammad Sohail Ahmad, University of Education, Pakistan, Pakistan
    Taskeen Fatima, University of Education, Pakistan, Pakistan

Chapter 13
Female Governance in COVID-19: Complex Nexis of Psychology, Society,
and Governance in Educational Sector of Pakistan 239
    Asma Kanwal, University of Education, Lahore, Pakistan
    Tahir Mehmood, Suncheon National University, South Korea

Compilation of References 253

About the Contributors 297

Index 299

Detailed Table of Contents

Preface xiv

Chapter 1
Sustainable Financing and Supply Chain Financial Risk Management:
Sustainable Financial Instruments and Risk-Free Resilient Supply Chains 1
    Naveed Mushtaq, University of Sargodha, Pakistan
    Mohsin Altaf, Global Banking School, Manchester, UK
    Muhammad Bilal Mustafa, Birmingham City University, UK

Sustainable financing has emerged as a novel approach to ensuring that supply chains have access to the funds they need promptly, even in the face of volatile economic situations. Sustainable, flexible, and environmentally friendly supply chains may be established with the use of financial tools like social bond frameworks, green bonds, and sustainability-linked credit platforms. We also go over the problems with sustainable finance, possible solutions, and upcoming projects and studies in this area. In conclusion, we emphasize the fundamental ideas that guide company-level management decisions, giving the company a rare chance to be a pioneer in sustainable development while preserving its competitive edge in a rapidly evolving global market.

Chapter 2

Corporate Social Responsibility and Organizational Performance Mediated by Customers Satisfaction: Corporate Social Responsibility and Organizational Performance 31

    Ali Shaibu, Islamic University College, Ghana
    Geoffrey Norman Tumwine, Kyambogo University, Uganda
    Mohammed Kassim, Islamic University College, Ghana
    Anas Sandow Seidu, University of Business and Integrated Development Studies, Ghana
    Hajara Mohammed, Islamic Finance Research Institute, Ghana

Institutions in Ghana nowadays are beginning to realize the significance of corporate social responsibility (CSR) and its relevance to the society. Many studies today have linked corporate social responsibility activities to customer satisfaction and organizational performance. The main objective of this paper is to determine the mediating role of customer satisfaction on the relationship between corporate social responsibility activities and organizational performance in some organizations in Ghana. A cross sectional design was employed, the sample size was 246 and the respondents were selected on a convenient basis from different organizations. Data were analyzed using the structural equation model and partial least squares. Findings from this study indicated that the more an organization embarks on CSR activities the more the customers will be satisfied with the organization thereby increasing to organizational performance. The study also shows that customer satisfaction has positive influence on organizational performance.

Chapter 3

Effect of Informal and Out-of-Court Resolutions on the Post-Bankruptcy Performance of Companies: Empirical Evidence From India 61

    Santosh Kumar, Christ University, India
    S. Parameswaran, Christ University, India

The need for seeking a timely & cheaper resolution of distressed companies has always been the top priority for creditors & corporate debtors alike. In this regard the current study analyses the role of informal & out of court settlement on the Post-Bankruptcy financial performance of Companies. This is a sample study of insolvent companies approved for out of court settlement under section 12 A of IBC in India. In this study the effect of financial, operational & portfolio restructuring actions under out of court settlement are analysed during pre & post bankruptcy period. The outcome of this research provides strong evidence of changes due to restructuring actions.

Chapter 4
Corporate Disclosure and Transparency as a Tool of Socially Responsible
Risk Management 91
    Hammad Hassan Mirza, University of Sargodha, Pakistan
    Haroon Hussain, University of Sargodha, Pakistan
    Rana Yassir Hussain, University of Education, Lahore, Pakistan
    Muhammad Waqar Ahmed, University of Sargodha, Pakistan
    Muhammad Adil, University of Education, Lahore, Pakistan

The issue of access to information becomes more critical when it comes to the modern corporate world. The importance of easily accessible information, as and when needed, in corporate governance has been widely recognized in the literature. Transparency in corporate practices can help in attracting capital and maintaining confidence in the capital markets. The demand for transparency and disclosure is driven by investors who continuously demand better reporting and greater access to information because such information is material to their investment decisions. Disclosure facilitates corporate governance by enabling shareholders to monitor the actions of management and hold them accountable. However, the relationship between disclosure and corporate governance practices especially when it comes to risk management is complex. Increase in disclosure without assurances that the information can be effectively used by shareholders may not necessarily result in improved governance practices.

Chapter 5
The Auditor's Guide to Corporate Social Responsibility: Enhancing Ethical Practices 105
> Shujah ur Rahman, University of Education, Lahore, Pakistan
> Nyla Saleem, School of Humanities and Social Sciences, Pakistan
> Yasir Habib, Institute of Energy Policy and Research, Malaysia
> Saba Sattar, Government Technical Training Institute for Women, Pakistan

Auditors are essential in guiding companies toward responsible and sustainable business practices. Their expertise in assessing and verifying CSR initiatives is crucial for ensuring that organizations meet the expectations of stakeholders, comply with regulatory standards, and contribute positively to society and the environment. As CSR continues to gain prominence in corporate strategy, the role of auditors will remain integral to fostering ethical business practices and driving meaningful change. To ensure accountability and transparency, auditors must verify that CSR disclosures are accurate and comply with frameworks set by organizations such as the Global Reporting Initiative (GRI) and the Sustainability Accounting Standards Board (SASB). The importance of technology and innovation in the auditing process cannot be overstated. Auditors can boost stakeholders' trust and confidence in the company's ethical and sustainable operations by employing advance technology to ensure the quality of CSR reports.

Chapter 6
The Impact of Artificial Intelligence on Achieving Corporate Social Responsibility 115
> Yasir Aleem, The University of Sargodha, Pakistan
> Saifullah Hassan, The University of Sargodha, Pakistan

The emergence of the concept of social responsibility in the early decades of 20th centuries, the businesses or companies started to strengthen the relationship with stakeholders including employees, customers, and communities. The Artificial Intelligence can help the corporations to measure the demanding CSR's initiatives, related to the specific population, community, or a country, including but not limited to the community engagement, employee well-being, human rights, education and skills development, promotion of health, climate change and advancement to the access of technology and literacy in remote and deserving communities. This chapter will address the role of Artificial Intelligence in addressing the CSR's followed by the corporations. Further, the chapter will discuss the gap analysis between the risk attached to the ethical use of AI in data analysis. Lastly, the chapter will scrutinize the impact of AI to provide robust backing to the corporations.

Chapter 7
Theoretical and Conceptual Approach of Corporate Governance and CSR Activities in Financial Decision Making 131
    Rabia Arshad, The University of Faisalabad, Pakistan
    Faiq Mahmood, Government College University, Faisalabad, Pakistan
    Maryam Saleem, The University of Faisalabad, Pakistan

In today's business world, corporate social responsibility (CSR) and corporate governance have become essential components. They have a big impact on financial decision-making processes in addition to organizational behavior. The objective of this chapter is to offer a thorough theoretical and conceptual framework for comprehending how financial decision-making, CSR initiatives, and corporate governance interact inside businesses. Foundations of Corporate Governance Theoretically explain about how agency theory clarifies how shareholders and management interact as principals and agents, highlighting how important it is to have aligned interests to reduce agency conflicts. Examine how this theory emphasizes the wider societal impact of company actions by promoting the consideration of multiple stakeholder interests beyond shareholders and Analyze how this theory affects governance frameworks and decision-making procedures by emphasizing how dependent organizations are on outside resources.

Chapter 8
Risk and Uncertainty Factors in Managerial Economics 153
    Saqib Muneer, University of Ha'il, Saudi Arabia

The concept of risk in managerial economics encompasses various unexpected events such as natural disasters, risk, economic challenges, uncertainty or product failures that lead to undesirable outcomes. Risk arises from incomplete information about future events, which makes the results unpredictable. The inherent uncertainty of the future because of the unpredictable nature of the universe, further complicates the understanding and management of risk. Scientific uncertainty, defined as any deviation from complete determinism, illustrates the difficulty in clearly defining risk. Sometimes managerial economics explores risk through its two primary dimensions, highlighting its complexity and the challenges it presents to decision-makers.

Chapter 9
The Roll Of Managerial Economics In Business Development 177
Saqib Muneer, University of Ha'il, Saudi Arabia

This study aims to explore the relationship between family involvement in a business and the managerial factors that influence the success of recent business developments. The research is guided by three key questions focusing on the connection between family involvement and managerial factors, how these factors are managed in family firms, and the differences in management approaches between family and non-family firms. Utilizing the Johansen-Juselius cointegration method, the study examines the end-of-day relationship between financial development and economic strategies in Chinese firms. Findings suggest that managerial quality, as signaled through reputation and past performance, plays a critical role in securing government support and resource allocation, ultimately influencing the economic strategy in China.

Chapter 10
The Impact of Financial Policies and COVID-19 on Sustainable Performance 201
Rashid Mehmood, University of Education, Lahore, Pakistan
Ilyas Ahmad, University of Education, Lahore, Pakistan
Shujah Ur Rahman, University of Education, Lahore, Pakistan
Sohail Rizwan, Fatima Jinnah Women University, Rawalpindi, Pakistan
Saba Sattar, Government Technical Training Institute for Women, Pakistan

This study is basically the impact of corporate finance on the firm performance. Two major pillars of the corporate finance are capital structure and dividend policy which play vital role for long term financial success of a firm. We investigate the influence of financial policies such as capital structure and dividend policy on firm sustainable performance. The study also captures the role of COVID-19 as control variable in influencing the sustainable performance. The analysis is done on panel data of 150 non-financial firms listed on Pakistan Stock Exchange from 2010 to 2023. Our findings show that capital structure has significant and negative effect on sustainable performance, while there is positive correlation between dividend policy and firm sustainable performance.

Chapter 11
The Role of Corporate Governance in Bank Risk-Taking 215
    Rashid Mehmood, University of Education, Lahore, Pakistan
    Ilyas Ahmad, University of Education, Lahore, Pakistan
    Shujah Ur Rahman, University of Education, Lahore, Pakistan
    Saba Sattar, Government Technical Training Institute for Women, Pakistan

Bank credit risk is the significant factor that needs to be managed effectively. For better management of credit risk in banks, an effective corporate governance is an important factor. We examine the effect of corporate governance on bank risk taking. We use the data of 85 banks of South Asian countries while taking data from time period of 2010-2023. We apply the generalized method of moments (GMM) to analyze the results. We find that the corporate governance such as gender diversity, CEO duality and board meetings have significant negative effect on bank credit risk.

Chapter 12
An Exploratory Study of the Complex Interplay Between Society and
Finance: Ways of Empowerment and Elements of Precarity............................. 227
    Muhammad Sohail Ahmad, University of Education, Pakistan, Pakistan
    Taskeen Fatima, University of Education, Pakistan, Pakistan

This study aims to evaluate the relationship between society and finance using Butler's theory of precarity. People are the workforce of society and they are divided into multiple institutions like family, education, religion, healthcare finance etc. The study addresses how these institutions especially that of finance work to empower society and vice versa. The study uses Butler's theory of precarity to highlight the elements that lead to social and financial precarity. Moreover, how precarity in one of the two factors i-e; finance and society leads to the same in the other. The study concludes that not only are the marginalized or differentiated groups precarious, but when financial or social precarity prevails, every single life becomes a victim.

Chapter 13
Female Governance in COVID-19: Complex Nexis of Psychology, Society,
and Governance in Educational Sector of Pakistan 239
    Asma Kanwal, University of Education, Lahore, Pakistan
    Tahir Mehmood, Suncheon National University, South Korea

This chapter shines a light on the critical role of women's governance during COVID-19, the Complex nexus of psychology, society, and Governance. The COVID-19 pandemic has dramatically transformed the educational landscape worldwide, Presenting unprecedented challenges and pressure. This pandemic is, no doubt, a threat to humanity (Poon & Peiris, 2020). Female leaders in education sectors across various countries have been instrumental in shaping responses to the pandemic, often demonstrating a unique blend of empathy, resilience, and strategic foresight. This chapter delves into the complex nexus of psychology society and governance, exploring how women's governance has influenced the educational sectors during COVID-19, the societal perceptions and pressures faced by these leaders, and the psychological ramifications of their roles. The COVID-19 pandemic also brought unprecedented challenges to educational systems worldwide, exposing and exacerbating existing inequalities.

Compilation of References 253

About the Contributors 297

Index 299

Preface

In an era defined by unprecedented challenges and rapid transformations, the interplay between corporate governance, corporate social responsibility (CSR), and risk management has never been more crucial. We, the editors—Rana Hussain, Sikandar Ali Qalati, and Dr. Hussain—invite you to explore our meticulously curated collection, *Corporate Risk Mitigation Through Socially Responsible Governance*. This volume is not merely a compilation of scholarly articles; it is a clarion call for students, educators, practitioners, and policymakers to reimagine the frameworks that govern corporate behavior, particularly in the wake of the COVID-19 pandemic.

The pandemic exposed vulnerabilities within both financial and non-financial sectors, underscoring the urgent need for resilient governance structures that prioritize not just profitability but also social and environmental stewardship. As we navigate the complexities of a post-COVID world, this book presents innovative perspectives on how effective corporate governance and robust CSR initiatives can serve as the backbone of sustainable economic growth—especially in developing countries, where the stakes are particularly high and the need for strategic foresight is imperative.

In this publication, we explore the evolving landscape of corporate governance and CSR, emphasizing their intertwined roles in risk management. The onset of COVID-19 necessitated swift adaptations in governance structures, highlighting the potential for these practices to mitigate risk and drive positive societal impact. Here, we provide a platform for diverse voices from emerging economies, showcasing promising practices and strategies that can be adopted globally. The insights offered not only illuminate the challenges but also celebrate the opportunities for enhancing corporate accountability and transparency.

Our goal is to equip readers with an in-depth understanding of how various mechanisms—board diversity, ownership structures, audit quality, and CSR activities—interact to influence risk-taking behavior and financial stability. By analyzing these dynamics through advanced statistical techniques and comprehensive case studies, we aim to contribute to the broader discourse on how businesses can operate ethically while securing their long-term viability.

This book is particularly relevant for those involved in finance, corporate governance, risk management, and social responsibility. It speaks to researchers, educators, and practitioners alike, providing a vital resource for anyone looking to understand the intricate balance between achieving financial success and fostering social good.

We urge you to recognize the importance of this moment. The lessons learned during this transformative period offer invaluable insights for shaping future corporate practices. The discourse around governance and CSR has shifted; it is no longer just about compliance but about creating a legacy of responsible leadership that prioritizes the welfare of stakeholders and the planet.

As you turn these pages, we invite you to think critically about the implications of these studies. Consider how you can contribute to building a more resilient and socially responsible corporate landscape. Together, we can forge a path toward a future where businesses not only survive but thrive, ensuring economic prosperity while making meaningful contributions to society.

As we embark on this exploration of *Corporate Risk Mitigation Through Socially Responsible Governance*, we present an insightful array of chapters that collectively illuminate the multifaceted nature of corporate governance and its crucial role in risk management. Each chapter delves into key themes and practices that can drive sustainable success in an evolving business landscape.

Chapter 1: Sustainable Financing and Supply Chain Financial Risk Management introduces the innovative landscape of sustainable financing as a pivotal mechanism for fostering resilient supply chains. This chapter emphasizes the importance of financial instruments—such as social bonds and green financing—that ensure timely access to funds, even amidst economic volatility. It further discusses the challenges of sustainable finance and potential solutions, ultimately framing sustainable practices as not just ethical imperatives but as competitive advantages in a rapidly changing market.

Chapter 2: Corporate Social Responsibility and Organizational Performance Mediated by Customer Satisfaction investigates the impact of CSR activities on customer satisfaction and organizational performance in Ghanaian institutions. Through robust data analysis, this chapter reveals a clear correlation: organizations that engage meaningfully in CSR initiatives see heightened customer satisfaction, which in turn boosts overall performance. This underscores the significance of CSR as a strategic pillar for enhancing organizational success.

Chapter 3: Effect of Informal & Out-of-Court Resolution on Post-Bankruptcy Performance of Companies offers empirical evidence from India on how informal resolution strategies can facilitate better post-bankruptcy outcomes for companies. By analyzing restructuring actions during the pre- and post-bankruptcy phases, this chapter provides critical insights into the financial recovery processes, emphasizing the efficacy of informal settlements in navigating financial distress.

Chapter 4: Corporate Disclosure and Transparency as a Tool of Socially Responsible Risk Management explores the vital role of transparency in corporate governance. It posits that accessible information empowers stakeholders and fosters investor confidence, while also allowing for better management accountability. However, it cautions against the pitfalls of increased disclosure without effective utilization, urging a balanced approach to transparency that genuinely enhances governance practices.

Chapter 5: The Auditor's Guide to Corporate Social Responsibility highlights the indispensable role of auditors in promoting ethical corporate practices. This chapter discusses how auditors can ensure compliance with CSR frameworks and verify the accuracy of CSR disclosures. By leveraging technology and innovation, auditors can enhance stakeholder trust, thereby supporting companies in their quest for responsible and sustainable operations.

Chapter 6: The Impact of Artificial Intelligence on Achieving Corporate Social Responsibility investigates how AI can be harnessed to advance CSR initiatives. This chapter outlines AI's capacity to address various societal challenges—from employee well-being to climate change—while also scrutinizing the ethical implications and risks associated with AI in data analysis. It advocates for a robust ethical framework to maximize AI's benefits in corporate social responsibility.

Chapter 7: Theoretical and Conceptual Approach of Corporate Governance and CSR Activities in Financial Decision-Making provides a comprehensive framework for understanding how CSR and corporate governance intersect within financial decision-making. It highlights the relevance of agency theory in aligning interests between shareholders and management, emphasizing the broader societal impacts of corporate actions and the importance of considering multiple stakeholders in governance frameworks.

Chapter 8: Risk and Uncertainty Factors in Managerial Economics delves into the complexities of risk management in the realm of managerial economics. This chapter discusses how various unforeseen events—ranging from natural disasters to economic shifts—can create uncertainty and complicate decision-making. It encourages a nuanced understanding of risk that takes into account both known and unknown variables.

Chapter 9: The Role of Managerial Economics in Business Development examines the influence of family involvement in businesses, particularly within the context of managerial factors driving success in family firms. By employing advanced analytical methods, this chapter reveals how managerial quality can secure essential resources and support from government bodies, thereby shaping economic strategies in China.

Chapter 10: The Impact of Financial Policies and COVID-19 on Sustainable Performance analyzes how corporate financial policies, particularly capital structure and dividend policy, influence sustainable performance in non-financial firms. The study underscores the significant, albeit negative, relationship between capital structure and sustainable performance, while also revealing the positive correlation between dividend policies and organizational success, especially during the COVID-19 pandemic.

Chapter 11: The Role of Corporate Governance in Bank Risk-Taking investigates the crucial interplay between corporate governance practices and credit risk management in banks. Through rigorous analysis of data from South Asian banks, this chapter finds that elements such as gender diversity on boards and governance structure significantly mitigate credit risk, reinforcing the importance of sound governance practices in the financial sector.

Chapter 12: An Exploratory Study of the Complex Interplay Between Society and Finance employs Butler's theory of precarity to explore the interconnectedness of social and financial dynamics. This chapter sheds light on how precarious conditions within one domain—be it financial or social—can have cascading effects on the other, thus emphasizing the need for holistic approaches to addressing systemic vulnerabilities.

Chapter 13: Female Governance in COVID-19 focuses on the pivotal role of women leaders in education during the COVID-19 crisis. This chapter explores the psychological and societal challenges faced by female governance figures, highlighting their unique contributions in navigating unprecedented educational disruptions. It advocates for recognizing and amplifying women's leadership as a crucial factor in fostering resilience within educational systems.

As you navigate through these chapters, we hope you find a rich tapestry of ideas and practices that inspire a deeper commitment to socially responsible governance and risk mitigation in your own endeavors. Together, we can cultivate a more sustainable, equitable, and resilient corporate landscape.

As we conclude this preface to *Corporate Risk Mitigation Through Socially Responsible Governance*, we reflect on the vital themes interwoven throughout our collection. This volume represents a collective endeavor to not only address the pressing challenges of our time but also to propose actionable frameworks that empower organizations to thrive while prioritizing social and environmental responsibilities.

The chapters within this book serve as a testament to the resilience and adaptability required in today's corporate landscape. They underscore the notion that effective corporate governance and robust CSR initiatives are not merely supplementary practices but fundamental components that can drive sustainable growth. Each contribution offers unique insights and innovative strategies that illuminate the path toward a more responsible and ethical corporate ethos.

In navigating the complexities of a post-COVID world, we recognize that the lessons learned during this pandemic extend beyond immediate responses; they call for a transformative reimagining of corporate practices. The urgency for businesses to integrate social responsibility into their core operations has never been clearer. As we face the intertwined challenges of economic recovery, social inequality, and environmental degradation, it is imperative that corporate leaders, policymakers, and stakeholders collectively foster an ecosystem where ethical governance and sustainability take precedence.

We encourage readers to engage critically with the insights presented in this volume. The knowledge contained herein is not just theoretical; it is intended as a practical guide for implementing change within organizations, influencing policy decisions, and inspiring a new generation of leaders who prioritize the greater good. Let this book serve as a catalyst for dialogue and action, prompting each of you to consider how your roles—whether as researchers, practitioners, or educators—can contribute to a more equitable and sustainable future.

As we embark on this journey together, may we remain steadfast in our commitment to responsible governance that not only seeks profitability but also fosters a legacy of positive impact. Together, we can redefine success in the corporate realm, ensuring that our organizations not only survive but thrive, creating lasting benefits for all stakeholders and the planet alike. Thank you for joining us in this important discourse, and we look forward to seeing how these insights resonate in your endeavors.

Chapter 1
Sustainable Financing and Supply Chain Financial Risk Management:
Sustainable Financial Instruments and Risk-Free Resilient Supply Chains

Naveed Mushtaq
https://orcid.org/0000-0002-9067-1953
University of Sargodha, Pakistan

Mohsin Altaf
Global Banking School, Manchester, UK

Muhammad Bilal Mustafa
https://orcid.org/0000-0001-9374-9958
Birmingham City University, UK

ABSTRACT

Sustainable financing has emerged as a novel approach to ensuring that supply chains have access to the funds they need promptly, even in the face of volatile economic situations. Sustainable, flexible, and environmentally friendly supply chains may be established with the use of financial tools like social bond frameworks, green bonds, and sustainability-linked credit platforms. We also go over the problems with sustainable finance, possible solutions, and upcoming projects and studies in this area. In conclusion, we emphasize the fundamental ideas that guide company-

DOI: 10.4018/979-8-3693-5733-0.ch001

level management decisions, giving the company a rare chance to be a pioneer in sustainable development while preserving its competitive edge in a rapidly evolving global market.

INTRODUCTION

Just picture yourself when there is an earthquake at a manufacturing plant that is owned by a critical supplier or if a certain route critical in shipping has been hindered by a big storm. Catastrophes are a scourge to supply networks as they lead to manufacturing difficulties, and shipment delays and hence result in low returns due to these natural calamities. The earthquake and Tsunami that occurred in Japan at the beginning of the year 2011 rippled across the globe to affect numerous global supply chains. For example, in the automobile and electronics business, one can see that the organization could be greatly impacted by the disaster. Due to this disaster, certain key components were scarce; this in a way affected production in many companies by causing delivered prices to increase. In a similar vein, customary global supply networks were also discovered to be fragile during the COVID-19 pandemic as shortages and delays caused by lockdowns and restrictions emerged. Supply chains must be sufficiently resilient to absorb shocks like those instigated by the pandemic whether it is the access to resources/cos enablers, individual components, or the final product(s) at the delivery point.

Yet another big challenge is the instability of the economy in the region. Unlike fixed costs which remain relatively constant regardless of the sales and the type of operation, fluctuations in various aspects such as currencies, trade wars, or changes in consumer demands create unpredictable and unstable parameters in the cycle of production and distribution of goods and services. Global supply chain operations suffered due to tariffs and trade barriers that the U.S.-China trade war exerted on global industries, resulting in increased costs and hindrances in planning and execution. Given the costs associated with such a move, firms had no option but to come to grips with the reality of being outcompeted while facing high costs or passing the extra costs to consumers.

Sustainable Finance has recently appeared as a new style of financing the supply chains to meet their timely demand of finances at times of uncertain economic conditions.

Sustainable finance has just emerged as a new approach to increase the supply chain's efficiency and meet the demands during the uncertain economic climate. Therefore, Companies need to develop smart financial capabilities tied to sustainable financing sources to handle the market's ups and downs along with long-term payoffs. Such moves help businesses stay afloat when markets get choppy.

Big catastrophes aren't the biggest danger. Productivity was cut short due to bottlenecks, and operational risks such as cyber assaults, supplier failure, and labor strikes increased expenses. Production lines could be halted and delivery dates impacted if suppliers go bankrupt, have quality control problems, or have transportation problems. Supply chain activities are now at risk from sophisticated cyber assaults that might damage software or data, steal information, or disturb communication. The striking workers pose a major threat to the supplies of goods and materials as they go on strike for several days and this is often unpredictable. These dangers explain why there is a necessity to have great backup strategies and variability of sourcing procedures. These risks require an integrated approach where both structural balance and operational autonomy should be achieved.

The risks inherent in supply chains and to which they are exposed require the creation of new protection measures that would ensure that supply chains remain viable. Businesses, therefore, require a more proactive approach that involves utilizing modern tools such as technology and data to forecast and address disruptions effectively. There are methods like supply chain diversification, live monitoring, as well as prognostication approaches that can help in risk identification and developing effective risk mitigation plans that can easily minimize the effects of the mentioned risks. Supply chain diversity can be defined as sourcing parts and materials from several different locations and suppliers so that it is not necessary to rely solely on a single supplier. The IoT gadgets and advanced software are employed in real-time tracking and monitoring of shipments through supply chain networks. It enables one to have a quick look at any disruption that may occur in the process. With the help of historical data, predictive analytics can find out potential threats that might happen and how to avoid them. As highlighted by Sarkis et al. in their 2020 study, financing for sustainability is a critical element for these strategies because it provides the needed capital to fund resilience and flexibility for adaptation to various environments.

One exciting element of supply chain management is the use of digital twins. Analogous to virtual prototypes of physical products, digital twins are the digital replicas of supply chain structures where hypotheses can be tested and predictions made without having an impact on the actual supply chain. By creating a digital twin of the supply chain, companies can model potential disruptions and weigh various contingencies before implementing them in the real-world environment. These are a few of the benefits that make this innovative method revolutionary to risk management because the planning is more precise, and the understanding of the underlying supply chain is superior.

Another aspect of supply chain collaboration is risk management which is also critical. Firms can enhance their supply chain networks through the support of logistics providers, suppliers, and manufacturers that hold substantial mutual partnerships. In essence, if several users are following the same transportation plans, inventory levels, and production schedules, then integrated planning systems can improve efficiency and response time. Sustainability financing might assist these collaborations by giving long-term stability that all of the stakeholders in the supply chain require. They might include investing in common technology, developing similar types of risk assessments, and synchronizing reaction strategies.

Today, the concept of supply chain resilience encompasses not only strictly financial and operational measures but also driving the sustainable culture inside the industry. Companies that practice sustainability are more capable of handling disruptions. There are responsible activities such as reducing carbon footprints, ensuring decent work, and purchasing materials responsibly. Sustainable financing appears to be capable of supporting such efforts as the usage of green technology, improved working conditions, and sustainable materials. As a result of limiting possible adverse effects, it helps to enhance consumer confidence in the brand and their commitment to it putting it in a favorable position in a competitive market.

Sustainability-linked loans constitute another unsecured financing solution linked with the high temporal growth of organizations' sustainable performance. These loans are supposed to help borrowers attain sustainability goals and these may involve minimizing the emissions of gases or increasing the efficiency of usage of resources. SLK makes organizations adopt sustainability into supply chain management and other business strategic plans because the financial returns are pegged to the sustainability indicators. It is not only the strengthening of the supply chain but also the direct associations between financial rewards and sustainable lifestyle in the future, in the future.

Furthermore, a variety of individuals and organizations collaborate as a consortium to address various supply chain risks. These include manufacturers, suppliers, financial institutions, and technology providers. With shared funding (for knowledge, skills, and money), the consortium members can fund resilience projects such as digital transformation, diversification of supply chains, and catastrophes. Besides improving supply chain operation effectiveness, these cooperative initiatives increase supply chain robustness regarding externalities such as disasters or political issues. The supply chain as a whole benefit from these endeavors and becomes more resilient.

This chapter's main goal is to look at how sustainable funding can be used to lower risk in the supply chain and suggest ways to make supply chains more secure. So, the first part of the chapter will talk about the different risks that today's global supply chains face, such as natural disasters, unstable finances, operating delays, and the weaknesses that global events like the COVID-19 pandemic show.

Sustainable financing gives businesses the money they need to make long-term plans that make the supply chain better able to handle problems and adapt to changing conditions. This means spending money on a diverse supply chain, tools for constant tracking, predictive analytics, and digital twin technologies. These technologies have enabled companies to simulate their ideas and visualize the hitches online before really going into action.

This chapter also discusses the importance of working relationships between manufacturing units, raw material vendors, intermediate suppliers, banks, and technology-providing companies. It advises supporting group initiatives to pay for projects that boost resilience—digitalization, supply chain diversification, and catastrophe readiness—by means of long-term financing. These combined efforts help supply networks become more immune to outside source challenges.

This section also addresses the value of sustainability-linked loans (SLLs) in enabling environmentally friendly supply chain management. By linking rewards to how well businesses perform on sustainability criteria, these loans inspire businesses to meet goals including decreasing greenhouse gas emissions or improving resource utilization. By providing financial incentives combined with environmentally beneficial activities, SLLs help businesses adopt better and more ecologically friendly supply chain strategies. Finally, this chapter seeks to provide companies with a firm foundation from which to create successful, long-standing supply networks. This chapter seeks to provide companies with the information and strategies they need to control and reduce supply chain risks by concentrating on sustainable financing as a main driver. This method not only keeps the finances of the supply chain stable but also supports a responsible and long-lasting way of managing the global supply chain.

NAVIGATING SUPPLY CHAIN RISKS

When one tries to probe deeper into the heart of supply chain risks it quickly dawns on anyone that firms are vulnerable to a plethora of risks. Six sources can be distinguished through which these threats may emerge, and all of them can lead to significant disruptions. By giving simple examples, we elucidate the consequences these disruptions inflict, thus underlining the imperative to make efforts to mitigate risk. In this part, various risk types are discussed under separate sub-sections, with detailed discussion and examples offered for each type.

Territorial Catastrophes

Natural disasters are arguably one of the worst risks that supply networks have to deal with as they are among the most unpredictable and destructive risks that supply networks are exposed to. Some examples of natural disasters that can cause significant damage to infrastructure and affect industries and transportation networks include hurricanes, earthquakes, floods, and tsunamis. Such natural disasters can also lead to loss of property and the environment in general.

Violent Earthquakes and Tsunamis

In reality, after the earthquake and tsunami in Japan in 2011, people all over the world could experience the consequences of an earthquake. Not only did the calamity devastate the lives of the victims, but it also disrupted the supply chains of countries across the globe. The hardest impact was felt in the automobile sector which largely relied on Japanese suppliers for essential parts. This was mainly because they were the main supplier of many factories in the region. Besides, businesses must have processes that help them to cope with such shocks like this one because the tremendous losses that occurred when manufacturing lines were halted completely demonstrate it.

Both Hurricanes and Floods

Additionally, supply networks are vulnerable to hurricane damage. The logistical and transportation networks along the Gulf Coast were severely disrupted by Hurricane Katrina in 2005, leading to significant economic losses. Oil and gas supplies were negatively impacted, and the Gulf Coast experienced difficulties as a result. The 2011 floods in Thailand also affected the global electronics sector. The reason behind this is that hard discs are abundant in Thailand. Production halted and prices spiked due to the floods. This shows how vulnerable supply networks are to catastrophic events.

Dynamic Changes in the Economy

As a consequence of the state of the economy, supply networks are put in a position where they are vulnerable to enormous risks. There are many examples of this, some of which include shifts in trade policies, variations in the value of currencies, and inflation.

Wage Trade

Trade tensions particularly the ongoing trade war between the US and China are another aspect of economic risk. Tariffs and other trade restrictions create challenges that force the supply chains to devise new strategies. This disrupted the supply chain because a large number of companies had to look for new suppliers, rewrite contracts, and incur additional expenses. The tariffs increased the price of bringing in parts from China and this proved to be a huge problem for many organizations including Apple. Due to this, manufacturers experienced increased production costs and were forced to relocate some operations in their supply chain to other countries.

The Volatility of Currency

Moreover, fluctuations in the currency pose risks to the supply chain as this affects the prices of various imported commodities and raw materials. A good example to illustrate this is the fact that the British pound hugely devalued after the Brexit referendum in 2016, which translated to higher import costs for firms based in the UK. Therefore, firms had to change their pricing framework and supply chain management to effectively manage the shocks due to exchange rates.

Risks to the Financial System

Supply chains are particularly vulnerable to financial concerns, which in turn make it harder for companies to maintain efficient operations and get the resources they need.

The Risk of Credit

Credit risk occurs when either the suppliers or the customers do not pay their bills when they are supposed to. For instance, crucial components may be unexpectedly scarce if a supplier declares bankruptcy, and cash flow issues may arise if a large customer fails to pay. The 2008 financial crisis exposed the credit risk vulnerability of supply chains. Many companies' vulnerabilities were exposed when they were hit with tighter credit standards and increasing default rates.

Concerns Regarding Cash Flow Liquidity risk refers to the likelihood that a company will be able to satisfy its short-term financial commitments. Because they are marked by a decrease in cash inflows while fixed expenses remain intact, supply chain disruptions like delayed shipments or industrial halts can put a strain on liquidity. The COVID-19 outbreak exacerbated liquidity issues for many businesses. Cash flow became a major issue due to falling revenues and ongoing expenditures

Adjustments Made to the Interest Rate

Changes in interest rates may impact the cost of borrowing money as well as the cost of investing that borrowed money. The cost of financing inventories and capital expenditures within the context of supply chains could rise if interest rates were to climb. Because of this, it will become more costly to grow or keep current operations running. However, lower interest rates could encourage investment but also make it harder for businesses to get loans. Remembering this is something everyone should do.

The Uncertainty of the Financial Sector

There are several diverse ways in which fluctuations in the financial markets can affect the stability of supply chain relationships. Some examples of these variations include volatility in the prices of commodities, shares, stocks, and exchange rates. For instance, there can be specific transport costs where changes to the price of gasoline can affect ferrying costs, while variations in the price of metals can affect the raw materials bill. Both of these factors are critical in determining the total cost of Acrylic in the final design. For enterprises to sustain their low-cost model of operation must eliminate these risks.

The Volatility of the Financial Economy

Organizational risks can be equally devastating as acts of god or economic crisis, albeit not as fancy. Some examples of these are failures from the supplier's side, hacker attacks, or strikes.

Risks Involved in Operations

A supplier might be struggling financially or might not have enough funds to continue operations, the supplier might be having problems with the quality of their products or service delivery, or the supplier may be facing challenges with the delivery of products or services. If there is an issue with one of the links, it can impact on the other linked items and cause some to be delivered late and therefore lead to other costs being obtained. For example, the global impact of the 2016 bankruptcy of Hanjin Shipping Company is an excellent illustration. It immobilized cargo vessels and distorted the sea transport network globally, which was bad news for many organizations that depended on such vessels.

Attacks on the Internet

Nowadays, cyberattacks pose a growing concern due to the prevalence of digital technologies. Because supply networks are becoming more reliant on technology developments, the probability of cyberattacks has grown. Threat actors can compromise supply chain software, wreak havoc on communication networks, and steal sensitive information. A large global shipping company Maersk, not only had to stop its operations in 2017 but paid a huge cost in millions of euros due to a cyber-attack. This lets the many large-scale operating businesses globally rethink and develop contingency plans. This case highlighted the necessity for strict measures to stop any kind of cyber threat that may hinder the operations of any supply chain.

Strikes by Workers

Labor strikes are an obstacle in the way to supply chains and disruptions can significantly disrupt supply systems. When workers go on strike, production and shipments might be suspended or delayed, causing a chain reaction across the supply chain. As an example, the West Coast port protests in the United States in 2014 disrupted the operation of exporting and importing commodities, resulting in shortages and increased costs. Effective labor relations and contingency measures are essential for mitigating the impact of such disruptions.

Taking Preventative Measures for Risk Management

A more proactive approach to risk management is the best option due to the varying nature of the threats and their unpredictability. Risk assessment frameworks should be carefully designed for the timely detection of these threats, systems weaknesses, and the magnitude of their impact.

Frameworks for the Assessment of Risk

To develop a risk assessment farmwork the entire supply chain starting from raw material supplier to end consumer should be mapped. This would help in the development of a smart risk-mitigating strategy by identifying the interrelationships, failures nodes, and weaknesses that might exist in the supply chain.

For example, following the 2011 earthquake in Japan, Toyota implemented a comprehensive risk management system. This system involved identifying alternate vendors and developing thorough recovery

Geolocation and Big Data Analytics Provide Accurate Prognoses to a Certain Point

Another fact is that corporations have the potential to enhance their risk management capabilities with the help of operational monitoring as well as big data analytics. Automated tracking systems enable the supply chain management to track items for real-time visibility as they are handled. This helps businesses to respond promptly to any disruptions that may occur in the supply chain system. Using historical information and an analytical method that involves machine learning, predictive analytics is also used to determine future risks and necessary precautions. Analyzing supply chains and applying predictive analytics to them by companies like IBM enables the companies to plan supply chain disruptions and adjust the logistics in advance to minimize their vulnerability and remedy the frequency of interruptions they encounter.

The Idea of Using a Digital Twin

The use of the twin functions is an aspect of supply chain management that can be considered remarkable and highly significant. Digital twins refer to the real-life supply chains modeled in digital systems that allow businesses to arrange different instances and predict their performance outcomes without causing any disruptions to the existing functioning supply chains.

Risk Management: Planning for Different Cases and Experiments

A Supply chain digital twin enshrouds the effect of likely disruptions and helps to assess the effectiveness of some strategies for sequestering disruptions in a risk-free environment. This new strategy allows more accuracy in planning and brings a deeper insight into the supply chain management dynamics. For instance, through digital twins, Unilever can model out different logistics and product manufacturing possibilities, and this eventually leads to a huge negative-to-positive ratio in the supply chain both in terms of productivity and minimization of disruption.

Sustainability Issues Within Supply Chains.

. Some major issues that require sustainable financing include:

1. **Zero Carbon:** Global Supply chains have a huge impact on the environment, and this is one reason that global supply chains are moving from traditional to low carbon or zero carbon emission technologies. But such renewable energy resources that are cost efficient and eco-friendly, require heavy investment. Sustainable Financing is one best way out.
2. **Resource Efficiency**: Different resources such as raw materials, water, and energy is an important input in any supply chain. Therefore, optimization of these resources through recycling and waste reduction is possible with state of innovative infrastructure and advance recycling processes. It is pertinent to mention here that innovative recycling solutions require investments.

3. **Circular Economy Implementation**: Moving towards a circular economy, where products and materials are reused and recycled, demands substantial investment in redesigning processes and developing new technologies. Sustainable financing can support these transitions.
4. **Sustainable Sourcing**: It is usually necessary to provide funds for auditing supply chains, establishing fair trade procedures, and certifying suppliers in order to guarantee that raw materials are obtained in an ethical and green manner.
5. **Resilience to Climate Change**: It is possible to invest in resilience-enhancing infrastructure enhancements and risk management measures with the support of sustainable financing.
6. **Social Responsibility and Fair Labor Practices**: The supply chain as a whole need's investments in facilities education, and monitoring to guarantee social fairness, safe working conditions, and fair compensation. Sustainable finance has the potential to bolster these aims of social sustainability.
7. **Green Logistics**: Traditional logistics uses different means and modes that are high in carbon emission. Similarly traditional packaging has polluted the environment. Today logistic solutions demand carbon free transportation and more ecofriendly packaging material which require investment for such innovative solutions development and adoption.
8. **Transparency and Traceability**: Use of advance information technology-based systems that can operate in real time for timely availability of the data to track and report sustainability metrics within the supply chain demands investment for the development of such systems.
9. **Innovation in Sustainable Technologies**: Ensuring a long-term supply chain sustainability is crucial and it requires huge investment in R&D for new technological developments. One best solution is sustainable financing that can provide funds on such a large scale for innovation purposes.

EXPOSING SUSTAINABLE SOURCES FOR SUPPLY CHAIN FINANCING FOR THE MANAGEMENT OF RISKS AND RESILIENCE

The value chain within the larger supply chain farmwork is composed of raw material vendors, production units, intermediate suppliers, logistic providers, etc. which ensure the smooth running of the entire supply chain for timely delivery of the product and revision to the end consumers. Unfortunately, each of these value chain entities is highly exposed to unknown threats of natural calamity, political turmoil, and technological changes, that might cause serious delays due to the propagation of the threat throughout the value chain. Hence, more innovative solutions are required to strengthen these value chains. Sustainable financing has therefore been considered a twinkly star, a game-changing opportunity to eliminate the financial risk associated with the supply chain. These green sources may include funding through environmental, social, and governance (ESG) concerns to enhance financial choices. Such a financial strategy could help in marinating long-term risk protection. By devoting investments towards more eco-friendly approaches and technologies, companies could accomplish their environmental targets.

Below we will explore the use of such financial instruments as sustainability-linked loan platforms, social bond frameworks, and Green Bond allocations to establish sustainable, adaptable, and ecologically sound supply chains. Furthermore, we describe the challenges of sustainable funding, how they can be addressed, and what future research and initiatives are expected in this sphere.

Meaning of Sustainable Financing

The term sustainable finance refers to sound decision-making on how to allocate finance while putting into consideration the ESG factors. This approach utilizes several funding forms to strengthen projects with social and ecological benefits. SLLs, social bonds, and green bonds are the three most significant strands of sustainable finance. Each of these parts has its special role in sustainable development.

This is evidenced by the evolution of sustainable fundraising over the years where more people are developing an appreciation towards sustainable fundraising. Environmental sustainability was the initial focus when it began with some projects such as the European Investment Bank that issued green bonds in 2007. It was an early endeavor of its kind. As a result of a more comprehensive understanding of sustainability, the focus has evolved to include social and governance aspects. Sustainable financing is presently a rapidly growing market that is attracting a diverse range of players, such as financial institutions, businesses, governments, and NGOs are all considered stakeholders.

Sustainability in finance is essential to supply chain resilience because it links financial incentives with larger social, environmental, and governance objectives. By integrating sustainability into their financial strategy, companies can enhance their risk management procedures, build more resilient and flexible supply chains, and help reach global sustainability goals.

o **Mechanisms of Sustainable Financing**
- **Green Bonds:** Green bonds provide a strong form of sustainable finance capital that can dramatically increase the resilience and sustainability of supply chains. The funds raised through these bonds are used for environmental projects that lead the companies toward Renewable

Energy, Increase the Efficacy of Energy, and also manage water thematically. Such projects, from the perspective of businesses, can help manage risks and uncertainty arising from environmental regulation, resource scarcity, and climate change. Besides, green bonds provide leverage in developing infrastructure and practices that could face major risks such as natural disasters or supply chain disruption. The green bond issuance process also requires stringent levels of transparency and accountability- to ensure that the projects financed indeed address sustainability objectives. Therefore, green bonds in supply chain financing not only solve the problem of the environment but also reduce risks from other directions, unprecedentedly close to establishing a long-term stable and reliable supply chain output.

- **Social Bonds: Sustainability-linked loans (SLLs)** are an important and rapidly growing method of sustainable finance that can significantly increase the resilience and stability of supply chains by incorporating sustainability performance goals into loan agreements. Green or social bonds earmark funds for certain types of projects, whereas SLLs link the financial terms of a loan to the borrower's achievement on a range of sustainability criteria - reducing carbon emissions, improving energy efficiency, or supporting social impact initiatives. It gives companies the flexibility to build sustainability into their larger business strategies, so you get this multiplicative effect from making improvements in operations conserved. SLLs incentivize companies to reach sustainability goals and impact other risks such as environmental regulations, resource shortage, and social instability, leading to better supply chains.

- **Sustainability-Linked Loans**: Sustainability-linked loans are then a versatile instrument of sustainable financing with the ability to improve the robustness and reliability of the supply chain by incorporating sustainability performance covenants in loans. While green or social bonds involve allocating funds for specific types of projects, SLLs link the loan's financial structure to subsequently improve the borrower's sustainability indicators on criteria like carbon footprint, energy performance, or social outreach. It entails the integration of sustainability into strategic management, enabling organizations to make wide-ranging changes to all their activities. The Sustainability-Linked Loan Principles state that encouraging companies to achieve challenging sustainability targets, which SLLs do, reduces the exposure to the consequences of environmental legislation, resource dependencies, and social unrest to make supply chains stronger. In addition, the fact that these loans are performance-based contributes to the ongoing efficiency and growth of sustainability solutions because businesses and organizations must work diligently to ensure that they are capable of meeting certain long-term goals. It helps in maintaining focus on sustaining the goals even when market conditions are poor or the business is experiencing some challenges.

SLLs also contribute to boosting confidence among investors and improving the image of the company since organizations are obliged to disclose much information compared to the approaches used earlier. They maintain that as organizations show their efforts towards sustainability through performance or other tangible indicators, there will be likely to be enhanced trust-based relationships between the organizations and their suppliers, customers, and investors. Therefore, extending SLLs into supply chain financing serves the double bottom line of considering environmental and social issues as well as ensuring supply chain robustness against various forms of risk for durable, sustainable, and competitive development. Therefore, obtaining SLLs within its supply chains also provides a solution to environmental and social problems, shifting risks into credit facilities and contributing to the objectives of harmonizing with the chain of food staples and their resilience and competitiveness. Furthermore, social connections enable the establishment of a framework for response through planning to further shocks like economic loss of growth and social unrest. Social bonds, on the other hand, share a rather significant responsibility of disclosure and reporting given the fact that the financed projects have to prove that they make a positive impact on social sustainability goals. Thus, including social bonds in the concept of supply chain finance is the solution not only to significant social problems but also to making the whole supply chain less sensitive to various risks and, as a result, more stable in the long-run development.

ESG Investing: Sustainable financing is a crucial aspect of financing supply chains by integrating ESG initiatives into supply chain investment processes to substantially improve supply chain sustainability. Different from conventional investment strategies, ESG investing concerns assess companies on factors like their impacts on the environment, social policies, and governance systems. It also promotes sustainable and ethical business practices, thus enhancing risk and value management performance and sustainable future growth. It means that investors should prioritize funding businesses with good ESG outcomes as it assists them in managing risks tied to environmental pollution, social instability, and corporate mismanagement. This results in more efficient and integrated supply chains hence making them more resilient. For instance, firms that place a greater emphasis on environmental responsibility will not be plagued by fines regulatory violations, and excessive demands for resources as much as firms that emphasize social responsibility will not suffer from labor unrest and boycotts from the community as much.

Good governance practice also enhances the management structure of companies and increases their accountability hence greatly minimizing incidences of fraud.

Furthermore, ESG investing provides an ongoing process of progress and responsibility because firms feel compelled to upgrade their ESG rating to secure more finance. This generates a virtuous circle as companies with improved ESG bring better financial results and investors' confidence. Therefore, the consideration of ESG criteria for SC financing is solving significant environmental, social, and governance challenges while simultaneously bolstering various risks, and establishing long-term sustainability, robustness, and competitiveness of the supply chain.

- **Impact Investing**: It is the process of investing in financial instruments to create both, social and environmental benefits and also earn some financial gains. Mission-related investors intentionally look for opportunities in equities, bonds, and funds to achieve social and environmental objectives like eradicating poverty, increasing access to health, supporting renewable energy, and others. Unlike conventional charity, this model of social investment aims at achieving a profitable impact through financial investment. Some examples are funding micro-credit lending institutions that target business persons and borrowers who are excluded from formal banking institutions or funding renewable energy initiatives that aim at providing power to remote places.
- **Blended Finance:** Blended finance is therefore defined as the integration of development finance and philanthropic capital with commercial sources of funding to support investment in emerging and frontier economies. It involves the mobilization of public and private finance for the development of sustainable projects, this management minimizes risks attached to some projects making them almost unprofitable or risky for private financiers on their own. Potential sources of blended finance can be grants, concessional loans, guarantees as well as equity investments. Blended finance can mobilize large amounts of private capital for sustainable projects by minimizing the potions of risks that private financiers bear.

Sustainable Supply Chain Finance: Sustainable supply chain finance on the other hand is flexible financing solutions used to improve the sustainability of a supply chain. It can also involve extending favorable credit terms to suppliers based on criteria or policies that promote the use of environmentally friendly and socially responsible procedures in the supply chain. For example, a certain firm may offer suppliers better terms such as early payment discounts or low interest rates in exchange for minimum carbon emissions or better working conditions. This is good for sustainability and also good for building better relationships with the suppliers and makes the supply chain companies more resilient.

Green Mortgages and Loans: Green credit products also improve the stability and cross-industry sustainability of supply chains while supporting green practices of firms and households. These financial products provide modifications of loan interest rates and other beneficial credit conditions to borrowers using energy-efficient and renewable approaches. Through promoting the usage of renewable energy, use of sustainable materials, and environmentally friendly technologies, green mortgages, and loans assist in lowering operations costs and utilization of un-renewable resources. It also helps to manage risks associated with fossil fuel costs and other disruptions in globally connected supply networks.

In addition, green mortgages and loans facilitate sustainable financial year plans and strengthen the supply chains. For instance, a manufacturing firm using green loan funds to put in solar lighting, company's manufacturing equipment will use solar energy instead of consuming energy, this means that their energy costs will be low and they have a small carbon footprint. This helps to minimize reliance on outside energy sources, thereby making the company less susceptible to interruptions in power and high operating costs. Focusing on green building, energy-efficient types of machinery, and other sustainable measures, companies build up their resilience to bounce back to normalcy especially after a shock event hence improving the resiliency of the supply chain.

- **Green Sukuk: Green** Sukuk are financial securities that are Shariah compliant for financing environmentally friendly projects. These instruments are compliant with Islamic finance and are designed to guarantee that the generated revenues are spent on green development, say in terms of energy from renewable resources, sustainable agriculture, or even water management. The increase in Green Sukuk is evident in the expansion of market interest in sustainable finance in Islamic finance markets and opens up a new way for the financing of green activities. Thus, by directing investments in these green initiatives, companies can balance their cost structures and minimize their reliance on the tirade of non-renewable resources. While this shift helps to reduce the impacts on the environment, it also helps make supply chains less dependent upon high-priced energy and other resources. This results in more stable and sustainable supply chains with less vulnerability to economic shock and slight changes in the environment.

One example of this is the Malaysian government in early 2017 which launched the world's first green sukuk to fund large-scale solar power plants. In the case of Malaysia, green sukuk helped to finance these renewable energy projects and in the process, decreased their dependence on fossil fuels, reduced their emissions, and provided a stable source of energy. Not only did this reduce the energy expenses of the companies involved, but it also made the energy supply more efficient and less prone to interruption. Green sukuk provided companies with opportunities to invest in these projects, thus improving the stability of the supply chain by locking into a reliable and renewable source of energy hence making them relatively immune to energy shocks or changes to the carbon cap outlined by various governments. Through green sukuk, it establishes how such financial innovations can help create stronger supply-chain networks that are ready to brave any environmental and economic turbulence.

- **Green Insurance:** Green insurance as one of the sustainable financial tools helps manage risks in supply chains by incentivizing eco-responsible actions. It is a type of insurance that protects against various kinds of environmental exposures like natural calamities, climatic changes, and changes in the rules and regulations concerning the conservation of the environment. Since green insurance guarantees recovery on the back of green investments and sustainable operation, organizations are motivated to implement cost-cutting measures, minimize emissions, and incorporate sustainable practices that support the conserved ecosystems. This not only protects businesses from loss as a result of disruptions in the environment but also promotes sustainability and the building of a sustainable supply chain over the long term.

For instance, a manufacturing firm based in an area vulnerable to floods may use green insurance to address losses arising from natural disasters such as floods. By constructing economical building structures to flood-resistant levels and incorporating sustainability features in the water management systems, such as rainwater and permeable pavements, the company can lower its risks from floods. The green insurance policy would then offer financial backing for the restoration or replacement of the faulty structures to sustain its operations with fewer service interruptions.

Concisely, green insurance, as a sustainable financial product, offers not only environmental risk coverage but also encourages businesses and industries to be more resilient within the supply chain with sustainable actions. Nonetheless, green insurance furthers the insurance industry's strategic goal of promoting the development of insurance-based risk management incentives that will strengthen supply chains against climate and other environmental risks.

- **Benefits of Sustainable Financing**

As will be demonstrated, sustainable financing has many advantages for supply chains, especially in the realm of risk management. These impacts relate to the issues of risks, operations, stakeholders, and competitive advantage and, therefore, have become one of the strategic tools of modern supply chain management.

Risk Mitigation

In this sense of risk minimization, sustainable financing is indeed an advantage in the framework of anti-risk. This approach not only makes businesses less opaque but also helps them distribute their financial risks and potentially respond to interferences more effectively. For example, green bonds and sustainability-related loans have rather stringent reporting requirements, in addition to performance benchmarks linked to the ESG factors. This level of inspection ensures that businesses are taken to task as well as ensuring that they adhere to sustainable inspection standards. It thereby reduces their risks of incurring penalties from the regulatory authorities as well as having their reputations dragged in the mud.

Since threats accompany scarcity, maybe sustainable funding could help to reduce their impact. As natural resources are getting more depleted, organizations need to consider resource efficiency as key to guaranteeing more efficient resource availability in the long run. Some of the industries that rely largely on a particular type of input are manufacturing and technology industries. They will find this particularly important for those companies that have already transformed themselves into digital businesses. Where such operations are to occur in areas where water scarcity could be a concern then there must be a guarantee for water availability and stability. Some examples include companies that invested in water conservation technology and equipment.

Operational Resilience

As mentioned earlier, sustainable funding is an important input in creating structures needed to create supply networks that can respond to different pressures and shocks. With environmental threats, which have escalated of late, and geopolitical conflicts which have also increased over the years the ability to rebound is essential. Companies can also avoid supply disruptions and fluctuations in the price of fossils by embracing the use of solar or wind energy sources. Corporations can go on operating at any given period in the event of an emergency through the provision of a consistent source of energy supply.

Other advantages include: Cost reduction and Increased competitiveness since sustainability can enhance operational capacities and minimize waste. Energy can be conserved through the use of efficient technologies or sustainable procurement processes, which in turn leads to enhanced business performance and reduced operating costs. Sustainability leaders are proving that companies with strong sustainability plans can weather the pandemic better.

However, sustainable finance also assists in expanding technological improvement and innovation. Firms may increase organizational performance and the ability to respond to disruption by funding sustainable technology innovation. This will give them the chance to develop new goods and processes. In line with this, according to the Ellen MacArthur Foundation (2019), the use of new materials and the integration of circular economy solutions can enhance the stability of industrial networks and reduce the dependence on conventional supply chains.

Stakeholder Engagement

Another pro that comes with sustainable financing is the chance to involve stakeholders like consumers, investors, and government. With the help of these groups, there is an opportunity to build more trust and gain customer loyalty which will positively affect the company's reputation and the brand. As an example, firms engaged in issuing green or social bonds are normally praised for their corporate sustainability which may help draw investors and consumers with a sensitized social conscience. One good example of this is the option to issue green bonds for financing different environmental initiatives by Apple. It was not only helpful in achieving Apple's sustainability objectives but also provided benefits to the company from the investor's and consumers' perspectives, which enhanced Apple's image of being one of the top corporations in terms of responsibility.

Sustainable finance also implies that information about the firm becomes publicly available and that ensures compliance with laws and regulations to avoid troubles with penalties and fines. An example of this is the European Union's Sustainable Finance Action Plan whose purpose is to fuse sustainability into risk management along with capital allocation towards sustainable investments. Some of the regulatory frameworks that may help a business minimize compliance risks while seizing opportunities offered by a specific regulation include:

Another potential outcome of implementing sustainable forms of finance is that it may foster cooperation opportunities. Partnering with NGOs and other stakeholders such as governments can be vital in that businesses are likely to benefit from the abundant knowledge and resources in sustainability. Supply chain disclosure, fairness to workers and shareholders, and environmental conservation could reasonably be managed by collective action bolstered by sustainable finance.

Strategic Advantage

Through sustainable financing, companies may be able to achieve a competitive edge and become leaders in sustainability. Management can ensure that the firms stand out from the competitors, get the best talents, and venture into uncharted territories. Establishments that actively pursue Sustainability will capture and retain people seeking employment with socially conscious organizations. It is argued that this can result in a workforce that is not only motivated, but also more productive by a large measure.

In addition, organizations that can use sustainable funding to finance new sustainable goods and services can tap into new markets of green and sustainable goods and services to meet new demand. This can encourage revenue growth and the firm's market position strength. Firms involved in the development and supply of electricity technologies and related EV systems through sustainable financing are well-placed to benefit from this trend. For instance, a recent trend that has received a lot of attention is the increased uptake of Electric Vehicles (EVs).

FORGING A SUSTAINABLE PATH TO RESILIENCE

Introduction: Sustainability and resilience are two fundamental concepts in the modern world that can be explained as two sides of the same coin.

In the general context of developing strategies in modern businesses, no better bond has become the foundation for organizations' sustainability and longevity than that of sustainability and resilience. Corporate social responsibility, an embrace of sustainable environmental practices, and the promotion of ethical business management not only correspond to the call for corporate responsibility across the globe but also become a critical factor for organizational adaptation to a broad range of threats, including those associated with supply chain risks and fluctuations in legislation and demand.

Defining Sustainability and Resilience

Sustainability is the incorporation of environmental, social, and governance considerations into company operations and policy. It refers to practices that aim to eliminate negative environmental consequences, maintain strong corporate ethics, and have a positive influence on the community. Resilience describes the ability of a company to successfully prepare for, respond to, and recover from disruptions or shocks that influence its fundamental activities and business.

Risk Mitigation and Adaptation: Businesses can empower themselves through the implementation of environmentally sound procedures to offset possible challenges provided by ecological factors, legislative changes in regulations, and societal trends. For example, firms that use sources of clean electricity reduce their sensitivity to energy price risk and interruptions caused by a lack of resources, which influences the supply chain. Similarly, sustainable sourcing ensures that supply chains are varied, which means they are not controlled by geopolitical conflicts or market volatility.

Operational Continuity and Efficiency: Governance of sustainability helps to ensure the company's continued existence and operational efficiency. Organizations that consume fewer resources and employ waste reduction measures not only save money in the short term but also make better use of scarce resources in the long run. Implementing circular economy methods, such as recycling and reuse, results in little or no waste creation while using resources efficiently and effectively in the face of resource shortages or changing regulatory structures.

Adaptive Capacity and Innovation: Sustainability promotes an atmosphere of creativity and adaptability within enterprises. Organizations that adopt environmentally conscious technologies and procedures frequently create innovative approaches to solve developing social and ecological problems. For example, advances in green farming or renewable energy solutions not only help the environment but also provide new business possibilities and advantages over rivals.

The Role of Sustainability in Building Stakeholder Trust

Beyond operational benefits, sustainability enhances stakeholder trust and brand reputation. Transparent reporting on ESG performance and sustainability initiatives builds credibility with investors, customers, employees, and communities. Stakeholders increasingly favor companies that demonstrate a commitment to ethical business practices, environmental stewardship, and social responsibility. By fostering trust and transparency, organizations strengthen relationships with stakeholders, mitigate reputational risks, and attract investment capital.

1. IKEA: Sustainability Profile and Leading in Circular Economy

IKEA is well-known for its corporate responsibility and improving people and planet's quality, mainly in the case of the circular economy and lowering the ecological footprint in every facet of operations and product life cycle.

Investment in Renewable Energy: IKEA has intervened in paying particular attention to renewable energy solutions where it has developed several wind and solar power plants. IKEA saves energy price risk and uncertainty definitely because the company generates renewable energy and minimizes greenhouse gas emissions. This strategic investment improves operational flexibility and helps with IKEA's global ambition of creating its electricity in operation.

Circular Economy Initiatives: IKEA embraces the principles of the circular economy by designing products for longevity, repairability, and recyclability. Through initiatives such as furniture take-back programs and the use of sustainably sourced materials, IKEA promotes resource efficiency and waste reduction. By closing the loop on product lifecycles, IKEA minimizes environmental impact, conserves natural resources, and enhances resilience against resource scarcity and regulatory changes.

Sustainable Supply Chain Management: IKEA collaborates with suppliers worldwide to promote sustainable forestry practices, responsible sourcing of materials, and ethical labor standards. By integrating sustainability criteria into supplier relationships, IKEA ensures supply chain transparency, reduces risks associated with non-compliance and reputational damage, and strengthens resilience against supply disruptions.

2. Toyota: Driving Innovation in Sustainable Mobility

Toyota is a global leader in sustainable mobility solutions, leveraging innovation to reduce environmental impact and enhance operational resilience.

Advancement in Hybrid and Electric Vehicles: Toyota has pioneered the development of hybrid electric vehicles (HEVs) and continues to invest in research and development of fuel-efficient technologies. By promoting HEVs and expanding its lineup of electric vehicles (EVs), Toyota addresses consumer demand for cleaner transportation options and reduces dependence on fossil fuels. This strategic focus on sustainable mobility enhances Toyota's resilience against fluctuating fuel prices and regulatory shifts towards stricter emissions standards.

Environmental Management and Manufacturing Practices: Toyota integrates sustainability into its manufacturing processes through initiatives such as energy-efficient facilities, waste reduction programs, and water conservation efforts. By optimizing resource use and minimizing environmental impact, Toyota improves operational efficiency, lowers production costs, and strengthens resilience against environmental regulations and resource scarcity.

Corporate Social Responsibility (CSR) and Stakeholder Engagement: Toyota's commitment to CSR extends beyond environmental stewardship to include community engagement, employee welfare, and ethical business practices. The company actively engages with stakeholders to address social and environmental challenges, aligning with global sustainability goals such as the United Nations Sustainable Development Goals (SDGs). By fostering trust and collaboration with stakeholders, Toyota enhances its brand reputation, attracts socially responsible investors, and builds resilience against reputational risks.

3. Patagonia: Environmental Stewardship and Ethical Supply Chains

Patagonia is renowned for its commitment to environmental sustainability, ethical sourcing, and corporate activism, making it a compelling case study for integrating sustainability into business strategy.

Environmental Sustainability and Carbon Neutrality: Patagonia has set ambitious goals to minimize its environmental footprint, aiming for carbon neutrality across its operations. The company invests in renewable energy sources, energy-efficient technologies, and offsets to reduce greenhouse gas emissions. By achieving carbon neutrality, Patagonia not only mitigates environmental impact but also enhances operational resilience against climate-related risks and regulatory pressures.

Ethical Sourcing and Supply Chain Transparency: Patagonia prioritizes ethical sourcing and supply chain transparency, ensuring that its products are made under fair labor conditions and with minimal environmental impact. The company collaborates closely with suppliers to uphold high social and environmental standards, fostering resilience against reputational risks and supply chain disruptions. Patagonia's commitment to transparency and accountability strengthens stakeholder trust and attracts consumers who value sustainability and ethical practices.

Innovative Product Design and Circular Economy Initiatives: Patagonia promotes product durability, repairability, and reuse through initiatives like the Worn Wear program, which encourages customers to repair and recycle their clothing. By embracing the principles of the circular economy, Patagonia reduces waste, conserves resources, and extends the lifecycle of its products. This approach not only aligns with environmental sustainability goals but also drives operational efficiencies and cost savings, enhancing resilience in a competitive market.

Corporate Activism and Community Engagement: Patagonia is renowned for its corporate activism and advocacy on environmental and social issues. The company uses its platform to support environmental conservation efforts, advocate for policy changes, and engage with communities affected by environmental degradation. By leveraging its brand influence for positive change, Patagonia strengthens stakeholder relationships, enhances its brand reputation, and builds resilience against regulatory challenges and societal pressures.

THE STRATEGIC IMPERATIVE OF SUSTAINABLE FINANCING: PAVING THE WAY TO RESILIENCE AND INNOVATION

CPC in the modern world has gone beyond being a question of trend and has become a global necessity for organizations all over the world. This imperative is but equally based on ethical concern as well as practical returns that it holds to the organizations that seek to achieve improvement in their levels of resilience and innovation as well as to deliver sustainable value. Sustainable finance involves various structures of financing structures and solutions for development such as; green bonds, sustainability-linked financing, and impact financing that incorporate ESG factors. Through such mechanisms, businesses can not only mobilize funds for funding sustainable endeavours but at the same time, underwrite sustainability as a permanent fixture of their core operating models and thus, enhance their structural competitiveness in a world that is becoming progressively complex and changeful.

Green Bonds: It is referred to as financing environmental solutions and can be further subdivided into several categories. For instance, sustainable bonds are an integral part of sustainable financing that is especially conducive to the investment of projects that can have beneficial effects on the environment. These bonds are used to support projects like renewable energy, energy-efficient structures, environmentally friendly transport systems, and water management programs. Green bond sales target investors seeking to invest in socially responsible goals and provide opportunities for enterprises to attract funds for such activities.

Sustainability-Linked Loans: Offering Carrots for the Elephants

The other innovative area in sustainable finance is sustainability-linked loans where steps taken by the borrower towards sustainability define loan repayment terms. Stating a fact that significantly deviating from conventional loans, sustainability-linked loans offer targets based on monetary incentives including – lower interest rates or longer payback periods to achieve sustainability goals. Possible evaluation criteria include greenhouse gas emission reduction, increase in energy efficiency, better water management, and enhanced quantifiable social impact factors.

Impact Investments: Achieving Positive Social and Environmental Impacts

On top of financial, this type of investing also seeks to deliver measurable social and environmental returns from investment in companies, organizations, or funds. Education, low-income housing, healthcare, renewable energy and efficiency, and sustainable agriculture are some of the topics that have benefited from this funding. Organizations that work towards the goal of alleviating poverty, empowering communities, gender equality, or environmental conservation are some of the types of efforts that influence impact investors.

One example of impact investment could be to support a firm developing 'green' technology needed in a local area to enhance the environment create jobs and increase GDP. Impact investments have two primary objectives: directing capital towards solutions that are sustainable and realizing viable and replicable business models to tackle large global concerns. Sustainability and inclusive growth are highly supported by impact investors who mobilize capital to provide resources to both environmental and social concerns through achieving SDGs.

- **Enhance Resilience:** Controlling climate change, resource shortage, and new regulation issues can however be controlled through investing in green business infrastructure and undertaking sustainable activities that promote conservation. To be less sensitive to market shocks, companies can leverage green bond financing for efficiency technology, and reduce variable price elements, such as electricity costs.

- **Drive Innovation:** As sustainable finance promotes novel solutions to implement environmentally friendly procedures, products, and company models, it is about creative solutions. Sustainable product design or implementation of the concepts of circular economy further innovation that will help reduce resource waste, enhance the usage of resources, and respond to the evolving customer needs for more environmentally friendly products.

- **Improve Stakeholder Relations:** Sustainable financing reporting and disclosure, to include information believed and expected by stakeholders with interests in the operations of firms such as investors, customers, employees, and communities, can be used to instill confidence and credibility among the various stakeholder groups. Corporate entities can gain brand equity and be endorsed by investors and consumers who appreciate sustainability policies and responsible management of environmental, social, and governance factors.

Finally, sustainable financing could be considered as the change of the financial strategy as well as the shift in the perception of how businesses can become sustainable and strong. Green bonds, sustainability-linked loans, and impact investments are instruments that can spur innovative solutions that enable the creation of sustainable value while achieving financial targets. One of the key themes that orientate management decisions at the business level is sustainable financing as a component of profitability and responsibility, which provides the organization with a unique opportunity to act as leaders of sustainable development while maintaining their competitive advantage in a world that has increasingly changed for a short period.

References

Apple. (2020). Apple's Environmental Progress Report. Retrieved from https://www.apple.com/environment/pdf/Apple_Environmental_Progress_Report_2020.pdf

Baker, M. (2017). NotPetya cyber-attack cost TNT at least $300m. Retrieved from https://www.bbc.com/news/technology-40870928

Baker, M., Bergstresser, D., Serafeim, G., & Wurgler, J. (2018). Financing the Response to Climate Change: The Pricing and Ownership of U.S. Green Bonds. NBER Working Paper No. 25194.

Bennett, M., & James, P. (2017). *The Green Bottom Line: Environmental Accounting for Management*. Routledge. DOI: 10.4324/9781351283328

Bloomberg, N. E. F. (2020). Electric Vehicle Outlook 2020. Retrieved from https://about.bnef.com/electric-vehicle-outlook/

Bugg-Levine, A., & Emerson, J. (2011). *Impact Investing: Transforming How We Make Money While Making a Difference*. Jossey-Bass.

Chopra, S., & Meindl, P. (2020). *Supply Chain Management: Strategy, Planning, and Operation*. Pearson.

Christopher, M. (2016). *Logistics & Supply Chain Management*. Pearson.

Christopher, M., & Peck, H. (2004). Building the Resilient Supply Chain. *International Journal of Logistics Management*, 15(2), 1–14. DOI: 10.1108/09574090410700275

Climate Bonds Initiative. (2020). 2019 Green Bond Market Summary. Retrieved from https://www.climatebonds.net/resources/reports/2019-green-bond-market-summary

Climate Bonds Initiative. (n.d.). Green Bonds. Retrieved from https://www.climatebonds.net/resources/green-bonds

Danone. (2020). Danone issues a €2bn sustainability-linked bond to support climate goals. Retrieved from https://www.danone.com/media/press-releases-list/2020/green-bond-2020.html

Doherty, B., Haugh, H., & Lyon, F. (2014). Social Enterprises as Hybrid Organizations: A Review and Research Agenda. *International Journal of Management Reviews*, 16(4), 417–436. DOI: 10.1111/ijmr.12028

Eccles, R. G., Ioannou, I., & Serafeim, G. (2014). The Impact of Corporate Sustainability on Organizational Processes and Performance. *Management Science*, 60(11), 2835–2857. DOI: 10.1287/mnsc.2014.1984

Ellen MacArthur Foundation. (2019). Completing the Picture: How the Circular Economy Tackles Climate Change. Retrieved from https://www.ellenmacarthur foundation.org/assets/downloads/Completing_The_Picture_How_The_Circular _Economy-_Tackles_Climate_Change_V3_26_September.pdf

European Commission. (2018). Action Plan: Financing Sustainable Growth. Retrieved from https://ec.eu.eu/info/publications/180308-action-plan-sustainable-growth_en

European Commission. (2018). Action Plan: Financing Sustainable Growth. Retrieved from https://ec.europa.eu/info/publications/180308-action-plan-sustainable -growth_en

Friede, G., Busch, T., & Bassen, A. (2015). ESG and financial performance: Aggregated evidence from more than 2000 empirical studies. *Journal of Sustainable Finance & Investment*, 5(4), 210–233. DOI: 10.1080/20430795.2015.1118917

Fruth, M., & Teuteberg, F. (2017). Digitization in Maritime Logistics—What is there and what is missing? *Cogent Business & Management*, 4(1), 1411066. DOI: 10.1080/23311975.2017.1411066

Gianfrate, G., & Peri, M. (2019). The Green Advantage: Exploring the Convenience of Issuing Green Bonds. *Journal of Cleaner Production*, 219, 127–135. DOI: 10.1016/j.jclepro.2019.02.022

Global Impact Investing Network. (n.d.). What is Impact Investing? Retrieved from https://thegiin.org/impact-investing/what-is-impact-investing

Gourinchas, P. O., & Obstfeld, M. (2012). Stories of the Twentieth Century for the Twenty-First. *American Economic Journal. Macroeconomics*, 4(1), 226–265. DOI: 10.1257/mac.4.1.226

Gurney, J., Humphries, D., & Newton, D. (2020). Brexit and the Automotive Industry: A Supply Chain Perspective. *The Journal of Supply Chain Management*, 56(3), 45–61.

Haraguchi, M., & Lall, U. (2015). Flood risks and impacts: A case study of Thailand's floods in 2011 and research questions for supply chain decision making. *International Journal of Disaster Risk Reduction*, 14, 256–272. DOI: 10.1016/j.ijdrr.2014.09.005

Hirsch, J., Parry, I., Coady, D., & Shang, B. (2020). The fiscal and welfare impacts of reforming energy subsidies in emerging market and developing economies. *IMF Economic Review*, 68(3), 586–635.

Höhne, N., Khosla, S., Fekete, H., & Gilbert, A. (2012). Mapping of Green Finance Delivered by IDFC

IKEA Group. (2020). Sustainability Report FY20. Retrieved from https://www.ikea.com/us/en/this-is-ikea/sustainability-report-pub0159a43b

Ivanov, D. (2020). *Predicting the impacts of epidemic outbreaks on global supply chains: A simulation-based analysis on the coronavirus outbreak (COVID-19/SARS-CoV-2) case*. Transportation Research Part E: Logistics and Transportation Review.

Ivanov, D. (2020). Predicting the impacts of epidemic outbreaks on global supply chains: A simulation-based analysis on the coronavirus outbreak (COVID-19/SARS-CoV-2) case. Transportation Research Part E: Logistics and Transportation Review.

Ivanov, D., & Das, A. (2020). *Coronavirus (COVID-19/SARS-CoV-2) and supply chain resilience: A research note*. International Journal of Integrated Supply Management.

Jin, Y. (2017). The impact of the Hanjin Shipping bankruptcy on global supply chains. *International Journal of Physical Distribution & Logistics Management*, 47(6), 500–518.

Kölbel, J. F., Heeb, F., Paetzold, F., & Busch, T. (2020). Can Sustainable Investing Save the World? Reviewing the Mechanisms of Investor Impact. *Organization & Environment*, 33(4), 554–574. DOI: 10.1177/1086026620919202

Kovács, G., & Spens, K. M. (2007). Humanitarian logistics in disaster relief operations. *International Journal of Physical Distribution & Logistics Management*, 37(2), 99–114. DOI: 10.1108/09600030710734820

Marquis, C., Toffel, M. W., & Zhou, Y. (2014). Scrutiny, Norms, and Selective Disclosure: A Global Study of Greenwashing. *Organization Science*, 25(2), 483–504. DOI: 10.1287/orsc.2015.1039

McKinsey & Company. (2020). How COVID-19 has Pushed Companies over the Technology Tipping Point—and Transformed Business Forever. Retrieved from https://www.mckinsey.com/business-functions/strategy-and-corporate-finance/our-insights/how-covid-19-has-pushed-companies-over-the-technology-tipping-point-and-transformed-business-forever

Negri, E., Fumagalli, L., & Macchi, M. (2017). A review of the roles of digital twin in CPS-based production systems. *Procedia Manufacturing*, 11, 939–948. DOI: 10.1016/j.promfg.2017.07.198

Pagell, M., & Shevchenko, A. (2014). Why research in sustainable supply chain management should have no future. *The Journal of Supply Chain Management*, 50(1), 44–55. DOI: 10.1111/jscm.12037

Patagonia. (n.d.). Our Footprint. Retrieved from https://www.patagonia.com/our-footprint.html

Porter, M. E., & Kramer, M. R. (2011). Creating Shared Value. *Harvard Business Review*, 89(1/2), 62–77.

Sarkis, J.. (2020). Sustainable supply chain management and the transition towards a circular economy: Evidence and some applications. *Omega*.

Sheffi, Y. (2021). *The Power of Resilience: How the Best Companies Manage the Unexpected*. MIT Press.

Sodhi, M. S., & Tang, C. S. (2012). *Managing supply chain risk*. Springer Science & Business Media.

Tang, C. S., & Musa, S. N. (2011). Identifying risk issues and research advancements in supply chain risk management. *International Journal of Production Economics*, 133(1), 25–34. DOI: 10.1016/j.ijpe.2010.06.013

Tang, D. Y., & Zhang, Y. (2020). Do shareholders benefit from green bonds? *Journal of Corporate Finance*, 61, 101427. DOI: 10.1016/j.jcorpfin.2018.12.001

Toyota. (n.d.). Toyota Global Vision. Retrieved from https://global.toyota/en/vision

Unilever. (n.d.). Sustainable Living. Retrieved from https://www.unilever.com/sustainable-living/

Chapter 2
Corporate Social Responsibility and Organizational Performance Mediated by Customers Satisfaction:
Corporate Social Responsibility and Organizational Performance

Ali Shaibu
Islamic University College, Ghana

Geoffrey Norman Tumwine
Kyambogo University, Uganda

Mohammed Kassim
Islamic University College, Ghana

Anas Sandow Seidu
University of Business and Integrated Development Studies, Ghana

Hajara Mohammed
Islamic Finance Research Institute, Ghana

ABSTRACT

Institutions in Ghana nowadays are beginning to realize the significance of corporate social responsibility (CSR) and its relevance to the society. Many studies today

DOI: 10.4018/979-8-3693-5733-0.ch002

have linked corporate social responsibility activities to customer satisfaction and organizational performance. The main objective of this paper is to determine the mediating role of customer satisfaction on the relationship between corporate social responsibility activities and organizational performance in some organizations in Ghana. A cross sectional design was employed, the sample size was 246 and the respondents were selected on a convenient basis from different organizations. Data were analyzed using the structural equation model and partial least squares. Findings from this study indicated that the more an organization embarks on CSR activities the more the customers will be satisfied with the organization thereby increasing to organizational performance. The study also shows that customer satisfaction has positive influence on organizational performance.

INTRODUCTION

During the last decade, financial performance was the major standard to assess firm's value. Institutions were ranked based on their profit margins. The main focal point of every organization was to maximize the shareholders wealth and nothing else. Corporate social responsibility was not part of corporate strategies and had no seat in the budget of most institution.

In recent time, however, the understanding and perception about corporate social responsibility has changed outstandingly (Aasad, 2010). Today, the achievement of many companies is measured by their social contribution to the society (Latif et al., 2015; Raman, M. et al., 2012). Companies have realized the importance of corporate social responsibility and how it can impact positively on the well-being of the society. In other parts of the world, scoring and rating system is being developed by agencies like the stock exchange and the security and exchange commission (SEC) to measure companies' with corporate social responsibility actions aside the financial performance of the companies. A country like China has made it compulsory to include corporate social responsibility rating in their corporate report and to the extent that, they publish the score to the general public (Welford, 2005, p.1). This confirms the importance of corporate social responsibility in our modern day business and management style.

In Ghana, there were international firms engaged in large scale manufacturing, communication, banking and oil and gas exploration that were predominantly practicing CSR practices. There initial goal was capacity building, employee skill improvements and helping the government. However, as this concept expanded the local firms were also made part of CSR campaign to achieve the sustainable development goals. Ghana is undergoing rapid development in public infrastructure and industrial growth. Environmental and social concerns are key areas to look for in such dynamic situations. Therefore, this study becomes more valid in the context of Ghana. It also serves to develop a model that proposes intervention of customer satisfaction in our study as one of primary stakeholders

In recent times, many research conducted have linked corporate social responsibility to customer satisfaction and loyalty. Some studies have associated corporate social responsibility and customer satisfaction and concluded that, they are positively correlated (Sambala, G. L., 2015).

As customer loyalty is considered a very important objective for a firm's survival and development, building a loyal customer base has not only become a major goal of organization, but it is also an important basis for creating a maintainable competitive advantage within the industry (Shabbir et al., 2018; Chung et al., 2015). Understanding customer satisfaction and loyalty maintenance is considered to be a key component in delivering long-term corporate profitability. Customer satisfaction and loyalty can be increased over the lifetime of a customer through his/her retention.

This study contributes to the existing body of knowledge on CSR practices in several ways; a) It addresses this issue in an emerging market whereas most of the previous literature focus on developed economies, b) this study is conducted in the post pandemic scenario as the world has changed a lot after this and c) this study incorporates the role mediating role of customer satisfaction which is unexplored previously. Earlier research has established that corporate social responsibility has significant impact on consumers' attitudes, purchase intentions, consumer-company identification, satisfaction, and loyalty. Initial research shows that customers take a firm's commitment to corporate social responsibility activities under consideration when assessing companies and their products (Oberseder et al., 2014). It is broadly accepted that customer satisfaction leads to customer retainment, purchase intentions and word-of-mouth (Westin & Parmler, 2020). Becker-Olsen and Hills (2006) have reported that consumers take into consideration corporate social responsibility activities and initiatives of companies before making purchasing decision (Becker-Olsen, Cudmore & Hill, 2006; He & Li, 2011; Sen et al., 2010). Thus, it is expected that corporate social responsibility would influence customer satisfaction and loyalty which in the long run affect organizational performance positively.

Studies conducted in the past has linked CSR and organizational performance and concluded that there is positive relation between them, researchers like Mittal et al (2008) investigated the relationship between CSR and organizational profitability and concluded that there exist a positive relationship between them. Cheruiyot (2010) carried out a research to establish the relationship between CSR and organizational performance and he too concluded that, there is a significant positive relation between them, another research conducted on Chinese cooperation by Li X., (2009) presents results which show that, there is a significant positive relationship among them.

Nevertheless, corporate social Responsibility and organizational performance has not been examined thoroughly and there appear to be scanty literature in that area. Therefore the main aim of this paper is to bridge the gap in literature by determining the mediating role of customer satisfaction on the relationship between CSR and organizational performance in some organizations in Ghana.

MATERIALS AND METHODS

Relationship Between CSR Activities and Organizational Performance.

To date, many research works have been conducted to establish the importance of corporate social responsibility (CSR) and financial performance. Different works conducted have different opinions about the impact of corporate social responsibility (CSR) on financial performance and some have revealed that there is a positive impact while others suggested otherwise (Mumtaz & Pirzada, 2014)

According to Wagner, S. 2019, they explained that there are variations with respect to the results of impact of corporate social responsibility (CSR) on financial performance and to resolve it, they must adopt the theory of contingency. Olitzky, M. (2013) also added that the relationship between Corporate social responsibility and financial performance most of the time depend on the reputation of the Organization and its operation in society. Some renowned researchers also suggested that there is a positive relationship between corporate social responsibility (CSR) and financial performance when resource base view approach is being considered (Yang & Baasandorj, 2017). According to Choi and Yu (2014) they explained in their work that, perceived corporate social responsibility (CSR) has a significant impact on the organizational performance whiles Brammer et al. (2012) reported a negative relationship between corporate social responsibility (CSR) and organizational performance and explained that organizations are at disadvantage when it comes to competition because of too much spending of financial resources on corporate social responsibility (CSR).

McWilliams et al. (2006) also suggested that, corporate social responsibility (CSR) and financial performance has no relationship between them. Post et al, (2011) in his study found out that there are various impact of corporate social responsibility such as decision making, internationalization strategy, research & development and share price which leads to firm performance. Renowned research scholars like Gallardo-Vázquez and Sanchez-Hernandez (2014) and Larrán Jorge et al. (2015) revealed that, there is a strong positive relationship between corporate social responsibility (CSR) and organizational performance. Recent works on corporate social responsibility (CSR) by Lee et al., (2013) explained that operational-related corporate social responsibility (CSR) practices can bring financial performance. In this view, the following hypothesis is proposed on the relationship between CSR and organizational performance:

H1: Perceived CSR activities have a positive effect on organizational performance

CSR Activities and it Relationship with Customer Satisfaction

The idea of corporate social responsibility (CSR) has been extensively used and widely debated by different categories of people across the globe including business men, investors, government officials and the general public. It has been an age-old practice in the world of business and thus, it has become a center of attraction and a serious area of debate for those in the field of academia, professional and the practitioners. Yet, despite its significance and importance, and so many millions of research that was carried out, the term corporate social responsibility (CSR) still lacks a general and acceptable definition (Green & Peloza, 2011). There are many variety of theoretical perspective and definitions that throw more light on the CSR phenomenon (McWilliams, Siegel & Wright, 2006; Vlachos, 2012). Among the most popular definitions are the ones proposed by Carroll (2016) and cited in his work and the World Bank definition. Carroll (1979, p. 500) defined corporate social responsibility (CSR) as "a construct that encompasses the economic, legal, ethical, and discretionary expectations that society has of organization at a given point in time". Carroll went further to explain that firms are supposed to perform their responsibilities not for their sake but for the sake of the society as a whole.

The World Bank also defines corporate social responsibility (CSR) as "the commitment of business to contribute to sustainable economic development working with employees, their families, the local community, and society to improve their quality of life, in ways that are both good for business and good for development" (Carroll & Shabana, 2010). Kotler and Lee (2005) also defined CSR "as a commitment to improve societal well-being through discretionary business practices and contributions of corporate resources".

In recent times, most literatures suggest that, CSR has different dimensions, but the most popular and classified ones are those presented by Carroll (2016) which emphasizes on the four (4) main principles of CSR dimensions. These are economics, legal, ethical and philanthropic dimension. Carroll in his argument suggested that the four main dimensions are interrelated to each other and organizations should at all times try to achieve all the four dimensions. Thus a socially responsible firms "should strive to make a profit, obey the laws, be ethical and be a good corporate citizen" (1991, p. 43). Even though some researchers proposed other dimensions, they all correspond with Carroll's proposed dimensions. For instance, Lantos (2001;

2002), explained the three dimension of CSR as ethical, altruistic and strategic, but two of their dimensions are directly linked with Carroll's dimensions. Mohamed and Sawandi (2007) also explained that CSR activities can be put in five main dimension; environmental activities, welfare and charity activities, community activities, products or services activities and natural disaster related activities. They concluded that, the implementation of the above CSR activities will have positive impact on customer satisfaction which will lead to customer loyalty and ultimately organizational performance. A review of the empirical literature suggests that there has been an extensive research studies on CSR, however, findings till date remain mixed. Research works on the impact of CSR on financial performance was established to be positive in some studies (e.g., Arıkan, & Güner, S. 2013) whiles in other works it was proven to be negative (e.g., Aupperle, Carroll & Hatfield, 1985; Mc Guire, Sundgren & Schneeweis, 1988).

However, some researchers also focus their attention on the effect of corporate social responsibility (CSR) on some stakeholder group, especially workers and customers. In this context, many research works done has looked at whether corporate social responsibility (CSR) activities enhanced organizational performance through job satisfaction (Story & Neves, 2015) or organizational trust (Valentine & Godkin, 2016) whiles other related studies looks at the effect of CSR on customer satisfaction (CS) (Afiffah & Asnan, 2015; He & Li, 2011; Luo & Bhattacharya, 2006) and loyalty (Stanisavljević, M. (2017); Marin, Ruiz & Rubio, 2009; Salmones, Crespo & del Bosque, 2005; Stanaland, Lwin & Murphy, 2011). Moreover, other related works on link between corporate social responsibility (CSR) and customer satisfaction by El-Garaihy, Mobarak and Albahussain (2014) has shown positive relationship. Researchers like Maignan, Ferrell & Ferrell (2005); Daub and Ergenzinger, (2005), are of the view that, customers are part of the stakeholders of the company and they do not only consider the economic value of consumption but also consider the company's social performance and how well they relate to the society.

Pérez, Salmones and Bosque (2013a:222), suggested that, "Customers are likely to drive a better perceived value and higher satisfaction from a product when it is offered by a socially responsible firm". Luo and Bhattacharya (2006) further explained in their study that, customers are likely to be highly satisfied if the companies they purchase from or patronize from are socially responsible. A research carried out by them on 500 companies revealed that, there is a direct link between corporate social responsibility (CSR) and customer satisfaction (CS). It further revealed that, customer satisfaction mediates the relationship between CSR and firm's market value (Luo & Bhattacharya, 2006). On the other hand, He and Li (2011), in their works on the mobile telecommunication sector also revealed that there is a direct relationship between corporate social responsibility (CSR) and customer satisfaction (CS). We therefore hypothesize that:

H2: CSR strategy implementation would have a positive effect on customer satisfaction

Relationship Between Customer Satisfaction and Organizational Performance.

To date, previous literatures suggested that, customer satisfaction (CS) is one of the conventional strategy that influences financial performance of many firms. The main brain behind this strategy is that, the more the customers are satisfied, the more they tend to demonstrate some level of loyalty which in its turn leads to an increase in financial performance of the organization. Well established organizations sees their customers as their key asset of their business. They consider customer satisfaction as primary goal of the organization (Dossi & Patelli, 2010). Customers who are well satisfied are more likely to continue engaging with the organization with less cost for the firm in maintaining these relationship (Srivastava, Shervani, & Fahey, 1998) and most of the time is more costly to acquire a new customer compared to maintaining an already existing one (Naumann, 1995; Bergman & Klefsjoe, 2003).Satisfied customers are more likely to be loyal and loyal customers are more profitable.

Customer satisfaction is an imperative key strategic tool for organizational performance especially in the service sector due to an increase in competition. A lot of works has examined the relationship between customer satisfaction and performance of the organization (Anderson et al., 2018; Al-Hawari & Warid; 2006). However the results of many research work conducted suggested that customer satisfaction is significantly associated with current and future financial performance. Researchers such as Nelson, Rust, Zahorik, Rose, Batalden, and Siemanski (1992) suggested in their works that, there is a positive relationship between customer satisfaction and all profitability measures such as earnings, net revenues, and return on assets. Many of the empirical research in the last two decades and last decade shows that, customer satisfaction was positively related organizational performance. In the works of Anderson et al. (1994) on Swiss companies, he reported that, there is a positive relationship between customer satisfaction and profitability. They again found out that, customer satisfaction and Return on Asset has positive correlation. Westin & Parmler (2020) also added that customer satisfaction and future financial performance are highly positively correlated. Banker et al. (2000) also found that there is a positive correlation between customer satisfaction and financial performance. Based on the above assertion, we propose the following hypothesis:

H3: There is a positive relation between customer satisfaction and organizational performance.

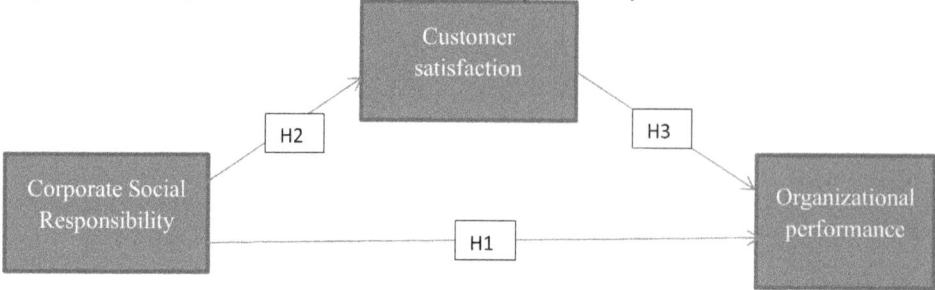

Figure 1. Conceptual model and hypotheses of the study

METHODOLOGY

With reference to the literature review above, both the conceptual model of the paper (Fig.1) and the related hypotheses are formulated. The aim of this paper is to determine the mediating role of customer satisfaction (CS) on the relationship between CSR and organizational performance in some organizations in Ghana. Convenient sampling method was employed to select respondent from the company's customers listed on Ghana Stock Exchange (GSE) who we can have easy access to, (Usakli & Baloglu, 2011). The data were collected from April 2019 to June 2019. Five hundred (500) respondents were selected; however, 246 responses were received from the respondent and after the initial screening and data cleaning.

The questionnaire entailed closed ended questions for the constructs, five-point Likert scales, and socio-demographic data. Scales for the study were adapted from Swaen and Chumpitaz (2008) to measure CSR whiles customer's constructs measured by multiple items selected from existing literature. The measuring Scale for customer satisfaction were adapted from Chiou and Droge (2006), whiles the measuring scale for organizational performance were adapted from Maignan et al. (1999, 2001). Five-point Likert scales ranging from (1=strongly disagree, 5=strongly agree) were used to measure each item on the construct.

RESULTS AND DISCUSSIONS

Confirmatory Factor Analysis (CFA)

CFA is a statistical technique used to verify the factor structure of a set of observed variables. Since we are testing for the common method variance in our study, the Harmann's Single –Factor test was adopted and exploratory factor analysis (EFA) was used for the test. Initially 21 items were entered but 8 was later removed leaving 12 items. This account for about 73.90% of the variance in the sample (See Table 1).

Table 1. KMO and Bartlett's Test

KMO and Bartlett's Test		
Kaiser-Meyer-Olkin Measure of Sampling Adequacy.		.739
Bartlett's Test of Sphericity	Approx. Chi-Square	608.937
	Df	36
	Sig.	.000

Reliability and Validity of Scales

Exploratory Factor Analysis (EFA) was used through SPSS to measure the underlying dimensions associated with 13 items. Bartlett's Test of Sphericity was used to measure the construct validity whiles the Kaiser-Meyer-Olkin (KMO) was used to measure the Sampling Adequacy of individual variables. Note that the overall of the KMO should be 0.6 or even more for the factor analysis (özdamar, 2017). According to the above results, it revealed that, both are significant and it is suitable for the factor analysis (See Table 1). The cumulative variance in the table shows 73.90%, which exceeds the minimum acceptance level of 60% (özdamar, 2017), The table again indicates that Bartlett's Test of Sphericity is sufficient for the correlation between the variables, its shows 608.937 and significant (P> 0.000). Whiles the factor loadings of all the construct exceeded 0.5 (Hair, Ringle & Sarstedt, 2011; Ringle, Wende, & Becker, 2015). This values represent an evidence that, there is convergent and discriminant validity (See Table 3).

Demographics Characteristics of Respondents

Below were some demographics gathered for this work; age, gender, level of education, industry, ownership, number of employees, and their results are presented below in Table 2.

Table 2. Demographics of respondents

Variable		Category Frequency	Percentage %
Gender	Male	158	61
	Female	102	39
Age (years)	18 - 25	54	22
	26 – 33	97	39.4
	34 – 41	68	27.6
	42 +	27	11.0
Level of education	Basic level	7	2.8
	High Sch.	35	14.2
	Diploma	41	16.7
	Undergraduate	62	25.2
	Graduate	88	35.8
	Others	13	5.3
Industry	Banking & Finance	68	27.5
	Manufacturing	51	20.7
	Trading	39	15.9
	Beverage & Food Manuf.	15	6.1
	Telecommunication	9	3.7
	Chemical & Pharm.	15	6.1
	Diversified	6	2.4
	Others	43	17.5
Ownership	Private Limited	180	73.2
	Public Limited	36	14.6
	Government	30	12.2
No. of Employees	Lessthan1000	180	73.2
	1000 – 5000	50	20.3
	5000 – 10000	11	4.5
	10000 – 20000	3	1.2
	Morethan20000	2	0.8

Response from the above Table 2 shows that 158 respondents representing 61% are males; and 102 respondents representing 39% are females. About 22% of the respondent were between the age of 18 and 25 years;39.4% were between the age of 26 and 33 years;27.6% of the respondent were between the age of 34 and 41 years; and 11.0% were above 42 years of age. In terms of education, about 2.8% of the respondent have Basic level education; 14.2% of the respondent have High level education; 16.7% of the respondent have Diploma level education; 25.2% of the respondent have Bachelor's degree; 35.8% of the respondent have Post Graduate degree; 5.3% of the respondent have other level of education. About 27.5% of the respondent comes from the Banking and Finance industry; 20.7% of the respondent were from the Manufacturing industry ; 15.9% of the respondent were from the Trading industry ; 6.1% of the respondent were from the Beverage and Food Manufacturing industry ;3.7% of the respondent were from the Telecommunication industry,6.1% of the respondent were from the Chemical and pharmaceutical industry, 2.4% of the respondent were from diversified industry whiles 17.5 are those from other industries. In terms of Ownership, 73.2% of the respondents were from the Private limited companies; 14.6% of the respondents were from the Public limited companies whiles 12.2% of the respondents were from the Government Sector. About 73.2% of the respondent were from companies that has less than 1000 employees; 20.3% of the respondent were from companies that has between 1000 - 5000 employees; 4.5 of the respondent were from companies that has between 5000 -10000 employees; 1.2% of the respondent were from companies that has between 10000 -20000 employees whiles 0.8% of the respondent were from companies that has employees above 20000.

Measurement Model Reliability and Validity

Construct reliability is measure of reliability that is used to evaluate the degree to which different test items that probe the same construct produce similar results. This is measured through item loadings with an acceptable region of 0.70 and again using Cronbach's Alpha level of an acceptable figure of 0.70 (Ringle et al., 2015; Hair et al, 2011, p.144). From the table below, the construct shows that the item loadings are all higher than the 0.70 recommended.

Table 3. Item loading and construct reliability

ITEMS	FL	CA	rho_A	CR	AVE
CSAT1	0.833	0.810	0.858	0.885	0.719
CSAT2	0.881				
CSAT3	0.829				
CSR1	0.837	0.929	0.933	0.944	0.736
CSR2	0.849				
CSR3	0.874				
CSR4	0.865				
CSR5	0.866				
CSR6	0.858				
OP1	0.912	0.881	0.881	0.927	0.808
OP2	0.898				
OP3	0.886				

Notes: CSAT- Customer Satisfaction, CSR- Corporate Social Responsibility, OP –Organizational Performance, FL –Item Loadings, CA – Cronbach's Alpha, CR- Composite Reliability, AVE –Average Variance Extracted.

ITEMS FL CA rho_A CR AVE

Notes: CSAT- Customer Satisfaction, CSR- Corporate Social Responsibility, OP –Organizational Performance, FL –Item Loadings, CA – Cronbach's Alpha, CR- Composite Reliability, AVE –Average Variance Extracted.

All the variables in Table 3 depict that, the Cronbach's Alpha is above 0.70, and this indicates that all the constructs in the table has higher reliability in terms of measurement. According to Fornell and Larcker (1981), they explained in their works that, construct validity assesses the degree to which a measurement represent and logically connects the observed phenomenon to the construct through the fundamental theory, while according to Ringles et al. (2015), assessment is done through convergent validity and discriminant validity. From the Table 3, The AVEs and the CR has fulfilled the minimum requirement of 0.5 and 0.70 respectively (Fornell & Larcker, 1981; Ringle et al., 2015).This shows that the convergent validity is clearly adequate.

Table 4. Discriminant Validity

	CSAT	CSR	OP
CSAT	0.848		
CSR	0.083	0.858	
OP	0.095	0.766	0.899

Table 4 above shows the discriminant analysis with regards to the scales used in this study. Discriminant analysis requires a factor to correlate higher than with any other construct on its scale (Messick, 1988). All the scales in Table 4 shows the constructs loading higher than any other factor on their scales. Customer Satisfaction on its scale had a value of about (0.84) which is higher than any other construct on that scale. Corporate Social Responsibility had a value of (0.85) and Customer Loyalty is (0.89) which are all higher than any other factors on their scales.

Outcome of Structural Model

The structural equation modeling (SEM) was employed to test the proposed relationships. SEM is superior in tackling causal and structural paths among latent variables. It is better approach in theory testing and also helpful in developing structural diagram that summarizes a whole set of relationship in a summarized figure. It is also pretty much suitable for primary data analysis. The assessment of the structural model was done through the regression weights, t-values, p-values for significance of t-statistics (Chin, 2010; Ringle et al., 2015). The outcome of the structural model with regards to the testing the research hypotheses are all present in the in Table 5 below.

Figure 2. Structural model

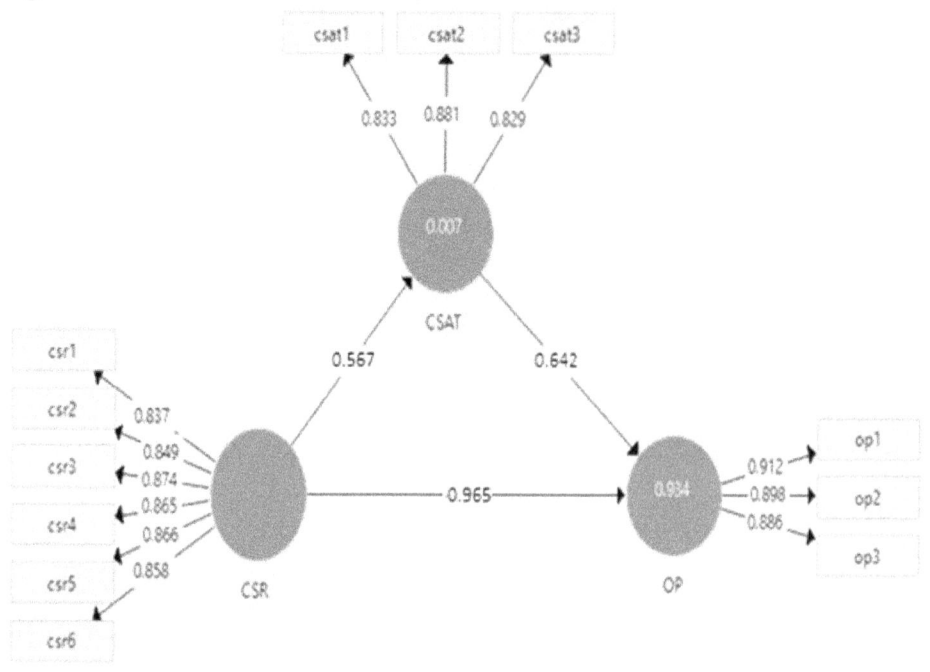

Table 5. Hypothesis Test

Paths	Beta	Standard Deviation	t-values	p-values	95% CI	
CSR -> OP	0.965	0.004	214.712	0.000	0.956	0.973
CSR -> CSAT	0.567	0.065	8.723	0.021	0.514	0.586
CSAT -> OP	0.642	0.016	40.125	0.008	0.591	0.663

Note: * significant at 0.05, *** significant at 0.001; CSR – Corporate social responsibility, – CSAT— Customer satisfaction, OP – Organizational Performance.

A hypothesis test was done using the Smart PLS software on two models (See Table 5). The first model tested the relationship between Corporate Social Responsibility activities and organizational performance. Corporate Social Responsibility activities had a significant and positive effect on organizational performance. OP ($\beta = 0.965$; t= 214.712; p < 0.000). This led to the acceptance of H1. This means that Corporate Social Responsibility activities have greater positive influence on organizational performance. Also, the Beta value shows that, when Corporate Social Responsibility activities increase by 1%, organizational performance increases by 96.5%.

Again, we tested the relationship between Corporate Social Responsibility activities and customer satisfaction. Corporate Social Responsibility activities had a significant and positive effect on Customer satisfaction. CSAT ($\beta = 0.567$; t= 8.723; p < 0.021). And this led to the acceptance of H2. The Beta scores mean that, when Corporate Social Responsibility activities increases by 1%, Customer satisfaction increase by 56.7%. Thus when an organization carryout Corporate Social Responsibility activities, customers of the said organization tend to be satisfied with the organization.

Finally, in the second model, we tested the relationship between Customer Satisfaction and organizational performance. Customer Satisfaction had a significant and positive effect on organizational performance, OP ($\beta = 0.642$; t= 40.125; p < 0.008); this led to the acceptance of H3. The Beta scores mean that, when Customer Satisfaction increases by 1%, organizational performance increase by 64.2%. Thus when customer of an organization becomes more satisfied with the output of the organization, they tend to be more committed to the company, thereby paying more for product and service which will lead to profitability.

Mediation Analysis

In conducting mediation test, there is the need for the establishment of mediation effect. Finding out such effects, Baron and Kenny (1986) mediation conditions were used as a guideline for the testing of all significant parameters. All regression analysis in the study were estimated. Customer satisfaction (CSAT) which is the initial mediator was regressed on corporate social responsibility (CSR) (independent variable) and it showed a significant effect (CSR → CSAT, $\beta=0.567$, p=0.021). Secondly, Organizational Performance (OP) (dependent variable) was regressed on corporate social responsibility (CSR) (independent variable) and this showed a significant effect. (CSR → OP, $\beta=0.966$, p=0.000), Thirdly, Organizational Performance (OP) (dependent variable) was regressed on corporate social responsibility (CSR) (independent variable) and customer satisfaction (CSAT) (mediator) and the effect was significant. (CSR →CSAT→OP, $\beta=0.965$, p=0.000), finally, Organizational Performance (OP) (dependent variable) was regressed on customer satisfaction (CSAT) (independent variable) and this showed a significant effect (CSAT → OP, $\beta=0.642$, p=0.008) .The outcome of the regressions are shown on Table 6. The assumption of Baron and Kenny (1986) was that, the mediation test would be possible, if all the three relationship are significant. The table below depict that, all the three relationship test are significant.

Table 6. Mediation Analysis Table

Paths	Beta	Standard Deviation	t-values	p-values	95% CI	
CSR -> CSAT	0.567	0.065	8.723	**0.021**	0.514	0.586
CSR -> OP(without mediator)	0.966	0.005	214.036	**0.000**	0.957	0.974
CSR -> OP(with mediator)	0.965	0.004	214.712	**0.000**	0.956	0.973
CSAT -> OP	0.642	0.016	40.125	**0.008**	0.591	0.663
CSR -> CSAT -> OP (specific indirect)	0.364	0.022	16.546	**0.034**	0.423	0.489

Note: * significant at 0.05, *** significant at 0.001; CSR – Corporate social responsibility, – CSAT— Customer satisfaction, OP – Organizational Performance.

With regards to this type of relationship, if corporate social responsibility (CSR) on Organizational Performance (OP) is more in the model two than in the model three, then that type of mediation is considered to be partial. Total mediation stands if corporate social responsibility (CSR) has no effect when the Customer Satisfaction (CSAT) is hold constant. In spite of the fact that the t-values in the third model has (214.712) and second models has (214.036), the significant level for model two (p-value = 0.000) was higher than that of model 3 (p-value = 0.000). The outcome depicts partial mediation.

After establishing that Customer Satisfaction partially mediates the relationship between corporate social responsibility and Organizational Performance, a standardize analysis was applied to the structural model to provide a broad-based representation of H2 and H3. Initially, the path coefficients for the relationships between corporate social responsibility and the Organizational Performance was examined. The effect of CSR on OP was positive and statistically significant ($\beta=0.966$, p-value=0.000) with a t-value > (214.036) which is > 2.

Subsequently was the introduction of the mediating variable. The second objectives and third objectives of this paper were to identify the mediating role of Customer satisfaction and the relationship between customer satisfaction and organizational performance. The result shows that Customer satisfaction partially mediated the relationship between CSR activities and OP as both the indirect effect with mediator (CSR → CSAT→ OP, path 1: $\beta= 0.965$, p=0.000; path 2: $\beta=0.642$, p=0.008) and the direct effect without mediator (CSR→OP, $\beta=0.966$, p=0.000) were significant. The results implied that CSR influences OP even without CSAT. Yet, CSAT improves the relationship between CSR and OP since it has positive relationship with organizational performance ($\beta=0.642$, p=0.008). This provides support for H2 and H3. Table 6 shows a summary of the mediation test.

Again, establishing the mediation effect, the variation accounted for (VAF) condition by Hair et al., (2013, P.224) will be considered. So to calculate the VAF;

VAF = (p12 * p23) / (p13 + p12 * p23).
i) If 0 < VAF < 0.20, then No Mediation.
ii) If 0.20 < VAF < 0.80, then Partial Mediation.
iii) If VAF > 0.80, then Full Mediation.
Therefore:
Total effect = 0.965+0.364= **1.329**
Indirect effect = **0.364**

Table 7. Mediation Analysis: CSAT as Mediator

Independent Variable	Direct Effect	Indirect Effect	Total Effect	VAF Range	Mediation
CSR	0.965	0.364	1.329	0.2738	Partial

Dependent variable: OP

DISCUSSION

First and foremost, this study reveals that carrying out Corporate Social Responsibility activities leads to Organizational performance. Corporate Social Responsibility activities contributes more significantly to organizational performance; followed by the mediating role of customer satisfaction which contribute marginal (See Table 6). This findings is significant as it shows that the more companies embarks on Corporate Social Responsibility activities, the more the customers will become more satisfied and subsequently pay more for products and services which will lead to performance of the organization. This finding supports earlier findings by (Piercy and Lane, 2009; Matzler & Hinterhuber, 1998; Anderson, Fornell, and Rust 1997; Hussain et al., 2020). Further, the scenario becomes more evident in post pandemic period (Khaskheli et al., 2023).

Secondly, with regards to the hypotheses in this study, the findings shows that all the hypotheses stated were accepted thus hypothesis H1, H2 and H3 were all supported by the research findings. The first hypothesis H1, revealed a positive relationship between Corporate Social Responsibility activities and Organizational Performance. This findings indicates that, the more a company embarks on Corporate Social Responsibility activities, (thus donate in the forms of charity, provide quality product and services, provide platforms for equal treated for both physically challenged and disabled customers), the more the company will become more successful socially and financially which will lead to organizational performance. Thus when organizations embarks on CSR activities there is the likelihood that because of the organization's social intervention, the organizations gets higher sales which will lead to financial performance.

The second hypothesis H2, revealed a positive relationship between Corporate Social Responsibility activities and customer Satisfaction. This finding indicates that, the more a company embarks on Corporate Social Responsibility activities (thus attending to the complaints of customers, respect and protect the natural environment of the customer), the more the customers becomes satisfied with the company. Thus, when an organization embarks on Corporate Social Responsibility activities the likelihood that the customers would be more satisfied is very high. And once customers are satisfied about the organization, they become apostles and share positive word of mouth communication about the company to friends, relatives and acquaintances thereby increasing the possibility of sustained growth and profitability for the firm.

The third hypothesis H3, revealed a positive relationship between customer satisfaction and organizational performance. This finding also indicates that, the more customers are satisfied with the company(thus providing them with quality product and services, establishing recreational facilities) the more they become loyal to that company there by spending more on their products and services. Every business would wish to have loyal customer base to support its profitability and growth as well as sustained competitive advantage. One way of achieving this is by ensuring that customers are satisfied with the company's offering or activities. Customer satisfaction thus is a prerequisite for attaining profitability. This supports the position of Mohsan et al. (2011) that customer satisfaction is positively associated with repurchase intentions, customer loyalty and profitability.

Mediating Role of CSAT on CSR and OP

The objective tend to investigate the mediating role of CSAT on the relationship between CSR and OP. To realize the above objective, the researcher initially examines the direct effect of CSR activities as a whole on OP. It was not surprising that CSR activities positively and significantly influenced OP ($p>0.000$). This results empirically can easily be interpreted that the more Ghanaian organizations engage in robust CSR practices the more customers will be buy from them and the higher the level of profitability therefore leading to Organizational Performance. This conclusion is consistent with previous studies (Anderson, Fornell and Mazvancheryl 2004; Bolton and Drew 1991; Fornell et al. 2006).

With regards to the mediation effect, the researcher considered the suggestion and the guidelines of Baron and Kenny (1986). From the above study, CSAT was established to have a mediating effect on the relationship between CSR activities and OP. with regards to the type of mediation, the results depict that CSAT partially and significantly mediates the relationship between CSR activities and OP (p<0.000). This indicates that CSR activities alone can influence OP even without CSAT. However, CSR activities with increase in CSAT can creates better organizational performance. Confirming the above results, findings of (Luo & Bhattacharya, 2006; Hussain et al., 2021; Xuezhou et al., 2022), which indicates that CSR activities on its own provides less significance but considering customers satisfaction can lead to a better organizational performance.

The Influence of CSAT on OP

The final objective of the paper tend to look the influence of CSAT on OP. The findings shows that CSAT influence through CSR activities could positively and significantly influence OP (p<0.008). This results can easily be explained that when customers are highly satisfied with organizational social interventions, they tend to purchase more from that organization since they know what the organization use their money for and how they help in the community, this will increase their sales therefore lead to profitability, which in subsequent lead to performance. The above findings is similar to the findings of many scholars in different studies within marketing literature (Bergman & Klefsjoe, 2003; Anderson et al., 1994; Al-Hawari & Warid, 2006; Hussain et l., 2023).

CONCLUSION AND IMPLICATIONS

CONCLUSION

This study focused on role of customer satisfaction on the relationship between corporate social responsibility activities and organizational performance in some organizations in Ghana. Findings with regards to the effect of Corporate Social Responsibility activities on organizational performance revealed that, organizations that takes into consideration Corporate Social Responsibility activities and initiatives as part of their organization strategic tool makes a lot of profit, since investors takes into consideration companies that embark on social intervention programme before they make their investment. The investment will lead to expansion and subsequent lead to growth of the organization which will later lead to performance.

This study also revealed that, CSR activities influences customer satisfaction positively and significantly. The findings shows that consumers' takes into consideration Corporate Social Responsibility activities and initiatives of companies before making purchasing decision. They tend to be more satisfied with companies who embark on Corporate Social Responsibility activities. This means that, it is important for companies to invest in Corporate Social Responsibility activities and again communicate to their customers what they do for the society, so that consumers will be satisfied and be loyal to them and pay more for product and services.

Finally, the study revealed that, customer satisfaction influences organizational performance positively and significantly. The findings shows that the more customers are satisfied with companies who embark on CSR activities, the more they will engage with that company by buying more from them. For instance the case of Vodafone Ghana where the company embarks on CSR activities by giving back to the community in the form of paying hospital bills for the sick, giving scholarship to needy students and so on. The customer pay more to the company because they know what they benefit from the company. Their customer base to increase within that period. This will simply lead to organizational performance since the more the customer base increase the more sales you make. That will lead to profitability.

Implications

This research contributes to industry and research related area on Corporate Social Responsibility. Firstly, it allows practitioners, professionals and researchers to explore the response of customers with regards to Corporate Social Responsibility activities from developing country context. Secondly, at the industry level, the results of the study shows that, companies will become better when they carry out Corporate Social Responsibility activities and that can lead to profitability. Board of Directors, managerial team and CEO's as a matter of fact are encouraged to embark on Corporate Social Responsibility activities because it will create company image in the minds of customers and lead to customer satisfaction and loyalty which subsequently will lead to profitability.

The results from the above study is in accordance with the theoretical expectations. However every scientific research work comes with its own limitations which this one is no exception. The future direction of the research need to be set straight. This research primarily concentrated only on some company's listed on the Ghana stock Exchange. Which of course is a limited and one cannot make a general conclusion. However, this open the gate for future research consideration which should give opportunity for other sectors like the hospitals and other institution to be assessed.

References

Aasad, A. (2010).The role of brand equity in the effects of corporate social responsibility on consumer loyalty. Unpublished master's diss., Universiti Sains Malaysia, Malaysia.

Afifah, N., & Asnan, A. (2015). The impact of corporate social responsibility, service experience and intercultural competence on customer company identification, customer satisfaction and customer loyalty (case study: PDAM Tirta Khatulistiwa Pontianak West Kalimantan). *Procedia: Social and Behavioral Sciences*, 211, 277–284. DOI: 10.1016/j.sbspro.2015.11.035

Al-Hawari, M., & Ward, T., (2006).The effect of automated service quality on Australian bank's financial performance and the mediating role of customer satisfaction, marketing intelligence and planning, 24(2), 127-147.

Al-Hawari, M., & Ward, T. (2006). The effect of automated service quality on Australian banks' financial performance and the mediating role of customer satisfaction. *Marketing Intelligence & Planning*, 24(2), 127–147. DOI: 10.1108/02634500610653991

Anderson, E. W. (1998). Customer satisfaction and word of mouth. *Journal of Service Research*, 1(1), 5–17. DOI: 10.1177/109467059800100102

Anderson, E. W., Fornell, C., & Rust, R. T. (1997). Customer satisfaction, productivity, and profitability: Differences between goods and services. *Marketing Science*, 16(2), 129–145. DOI: 10.1287/mksc.16.2.129

Anderson, E. W., & Sullivan, M. W. (1993). The antecedents and consequences of customer satisfaction for firms. *Marketing Science*, 12(2), 125–143. DOI: 10.1287/mksc.12.2.125

Anderson, R. L., DAHLQUIST, S. H., & GARVER, M. S. (2018). MILLENNIALS'PURCHASING RESPONSE TO CSR BEHAVIOR. *Marketing Management Journal, 28*(1).

Anderson, Eugene W., Fornell, C., and Mazvancheryl S., K. (2004). Customer Satisfaction and Shareholder Value, *Journal of Marketing*, 68, 172-85.

Anserson, E. W., & Mittal, V. (2000). Strengthening the satisfaction-profit chain. *Journal of Service Research*, 3(2), 107–120. DOI: 10.1177/109467050032001

Arıkan, E., & Güner, S. (2013). The impact of corporate social responsibility, service quality and customer-company identification on customers. *Procedia: Social and Behavioral Sciences*, 99, 304–313. DOI: 10.1016/j.sbspro.2013.10.498

Aupperle, K., Carroll, A., & Hatfield, J. (1985). An empirical examination of the relationship between corporate social responsibility and profitability. *Academy of Management Journal*, 28(2), 446–463. DOI: 10.2307/256210

Aydin, S., & Özer, G. (2005). The analysis of antecedents of consumer loyalty in the Turkish mobile telecommunication market. *European Journal of Marketing*, 39(7/8), 910–925. DOI: 10.1108/03090560510601833

Banker, R. D., Potter, G., & Srinivasan, D. (2000). An empirical investigation of an incentive plan that includes non-financial performance measures. *The Accounting Review*, 75(1), 65–92. DOI: 10.2308/accr.2000.75.1.65

Baron, R. M., & Kenny, D. A. (1986). The moderator-mediator variable distinction in social psychological research: Conceptual, strategic, and statistical considerations. *Journal of Personality and Social Psychology*, 51(6), 1173–1179. DOI: 10.1037/0022-3514.51.6.1173

Becker-Olsen, K. L., Cudmore, B. A., & Hill, R. P. (2006). The impact of perceived corporate social responsibility on consumer behavior. *Journal of Business Research*, 59(1), 46–53. DOI: 10.1016/j.jbusres.2005.01.001

Bergman, B., & Klefsjoe, B., (2003).Quality: From customer needs to customer satisfaction (2nded.). Lund: Student literature

Bergman, B., & Klefsjoe, B. (2003). *Quality:Fromcustomerneedstocustomersatisfaction(2nded.).* Studentlitteratur.

Bilawal Khaskheli, M., Wang, S., Hussain, R. Y., Jahanzeb Butt, M., Yan, X., & Majid, S. (2023). Global law, policy, and governance for effective prevention and control of COVID-19: A comparative analysis of the law and policy of Pakistan, China, and Russia. *Frontiers in Public Health*, 10, 1035536. DOI: 10.3389/fpubh.2022.1035536

Bolton, R. N., & Drew, J. H. (1991). A Longitudinal Analysis of the Impact of Service Changes on Customer Attitudes. *Journal of Marketing*, 55(1), 1–9. DOI: 10.1177/002224299105500101

Bontis, N., Booker, L. D., & Serenko, A. (2007). The mediating effect of organizational reputation on customer loyalty and service recommendation in the banking industry. *Management Decision*, 45(9), 1425–1445. DOI: 10.1108/00251740710828681

Brammer, S., Jackson, G., & Matten, D. (2012). Corporate social responsibility and institutional theory: New perspectives on private governance. *Socio-economic Review*, 10(1), 3–28. DOI: 10.1093/ser/mwr030

Carroll, A. B. (1991). Corporate social performance measurement: A comment on methods for evaluating an elusive construct. In Post, L. E. (Ed.), *Research in corporate social performance and policy, 12, 385-401*. JAI Press.

Carroll, A. B. (2016). Carroll's pyramid of CSR: taking another look. *International journal of corporate social responsibility, 1*(1), 1-8.

Carroll, A. B., & Shabana, K. M. (2010). The business case for corporate social responsibility: A review of concepts, research and practice. *International Journal of Management Reviews*, 12(1), 2010. DOI: 10.1111/j.1468-2370.2009.00275.x

Cheruiyot, F. K. (2010)., The relationship between corporate social responsibility and financial performance of companies listed at the Nairobi Stocks Exchange, *Unpublished MBA Thesis*, University of Nairobi.

Chin, W. (2010). How to write up and report PLS analyses. In C. W. W. EspositoVinzi V, Henseler, J. & Wang, H. (Eds.), *Handbook of partial least squares: concepts, methods and applications* (pp. 655 – 690). Heidelberg: Springer. DOI: 10.1007/978-3-540-32827-8_29

Chiou, J. S., & Droge, C. (2006). Service quality, trust, specific asset investment, and expertise: Direct and indirect effects in a satisfaction-loyalty framework. *Journal of the Academy of Marketing Science*, 34(4), 613–627. DOI: 10.1177/0092070306286934

Choi, Y., & Yu, Y. (2014). The influence of perceived corporate sustainability practices on employees and organizational performance. *Sustainability (Basel)*, 6(1), 348–364. DOI: 10.3390/su6010348

Chung, K. H., Yu, J. E., Choi, M. G., & Shin, J. I. (2015). The effects of CSR on customer satisfaction and loyalty in China: The moderating role of corporate image. *Journal of Economics. Business and Management*, 3(5), 542–547. DOI: 10.7763/JOEBM.2015.V3.243

Daub, C. H., & Ergenzinger, R. (2005). Enabling sustainable management through a new multi-disciplinary concept of customer satisfaction. *European Journal of Marketing*, 39(9/10), 998–1012. DOI: 10.1108/03090560510610680

Dick, A., & Basu, K. (1994). Customer loyalty: Toward an integrated conceptual framework. *Journal of the Academy of Marketing Science*, 22(2), 99–113. DOI: 10.1177/0092070394222001

Dossi, A., & Patelli, L. (2010). You learn from what you measure: Financial and non-financial performance measures in multinational companies. *Long Range Planning*, 43(4), 498–526. DOI: 10.1016/j.lrp.2010.01.002

Du, S., Bhattacharya, C. B., & Sen, S. (2010). Maximizing business returns to corporate social responsibility (CSR): The role of CSR communication. *International Journal of Management Reviews*, 12(1), 8–19. DOI: 10.1111/j.1468-2370.2009.00276.x

El-Garaihy, W., Mobarak, A., & Albahussain, S. (2014). Measuring the Impact of Corporate Social Responsibility Practices on Competitive Advantage: A Mediation Role of Reputation and Customer Satisfaction. *International Journal of Business and Management*, 9(5), 109–124. DOI: 10.5539/ijbm.v9n5p109

Fombrun, C., & Shanley, M. (1990). What's in a name? Reputation building and corporate strategy. *Academy of Management Journal*, 33(2), 233–258. DOI: 10.2307/256324

Fornell, C. (1992). A national customer satisfaction barometer: The Swedish experience. *Journal of Marketing*, 56(1), 6–21. DOI: 10.1177/002224299205600103

Fornell, C, & Larcker, D. F. (1981). Evaluating structural equation models with unobservable

Fornell, S., Mithas, S., Morgeson, F. V.III, & Krishnan, M. S. (2006). Customer Satisfaction and Stock Prices: High Returns, Low Risk. *Journal of Marketing*, 70(1), 3–14. DOI: 10.1509/jmkg.70.1.003.qxd

Gallardo-Vázquez, D., & Sanchez-Hernandez, M. I. (2014). Measuring Corporate Social Responsibility for competitive success at a regional level. *Journal of Cleaner Production*, 72, 1422. DOI: 10.1016/j.jclepro.2014.02.051

Garaya, L., & Font, X. (2011). Doing good to do well? Corporate social responsibility reasons, practices and impacts in small and medium accommodation enterprises'. *International Journal of Hospitality Management*, 30, 1–9.

Green, T., & Peloza, J. (2011). How does corporate social responsibility create value for customers? *Journal of Consumer Marketing*, 28(1), 48–56. DOI: 10.1108/07363761111101949

Guo, J., Sun, L., & Li, X. (2009). Corporate social responsibility assessment of Chinese corporation. *International Journal of Business and Management*, 4(4), 54–57. DOI: 10.5539/ijbm.v4n4p54

Hair, J., Ringle, C. M., & Sarstedt, M. (2011). PLS-SEM: Indeed a Silver Bullet. *Journal of Marketing Theory and Practice*, 19(2), 139–151. DOI: 10.2753/MTP1069-6679190202

Hansen, S. D., Dunford, B. B., Boss, A. D., & Angermeier, I. (2011). Corporate social responsibility and the benefits of employee trust: A cross disciplinary perspective. *Journal of Business Ethics*, 102(1), 29–45. DOI: 10.1007/s10551-011-0903-0

He, H., & Li, Y. (2011). CSR and service brand: The mediating effect of brand identification and moderating effect of service quality. *Journal of Business Ethics*, 100(4), 673–688. DOI: 10.1007/s10551-010-0703-y

Hilman, A. J., & Keim, G. D. (2001). Shareholder Value, Stakeholder Management, Social Issues: What's the Bottom Line. *Strategic Management Journal*, 22(2), 125–139. DOI: 10.1002/1097-0266(200101)22:2<125::AID-SMJ150>3.0.CO;2-H

Hsu, K. (2012). The advertising effects of Corporate Social Responsibility on corporate reputation and brand equity: Evidence from the life insurance industry in Taiwan. *Journal of Business Ethics*, 109(2), 189–201. DOI: 10.1007/s10551-011-1118-0

Hussain, R. Y., Bajaj, N. K., Kumari, S., & Al-Faryan, M. A. S. (2023). Does economic policy uncertainty affect foreign remittances? Linear and non-linear ARDL approach in BRIC economies. *Cogent Economics & Finance*, 11(1), 2183642. DOI: 10.1080/23322039.2023.2183642

Hussain, R. Y., Wen, X., Butt, R. S., Hussain, H., Ali Qalati, S., & Abbas, I. (2020). Are growth led financing decisions causing insolvency in listed firms of Pakistan? *Zagreb International Review of Economics & Business*, 23(2), 89–115. DOI: 10.2478/zireb-2020-0015

Hussain, R. Y., Xuezhou, W., Hussain, H., Saad, M., & Qalati, S. A. (2021). Corporate board vigilance and insolvency risk: A mediated moderation model of debt maturity and fixed collaterals. *International Journal of Management and Economics*, 57(1), 14–33. DOI: 10.2478/ijme-2020-0032

Husted, B. W. (2000). Contingency theory of corporate social performance. *Business & Society*, 39(1), 24–48. DOI: 10.1177/000765030003900104

Ittner, C., & Larcker, D. F. (1998). Are non-financial measures leading indicators of financial performance? An analyses of customer satisfaction. *Journal of Accounting Research*, 36(supplement), 1–35. DOI: 10.2307/2491304

Kotler, P., & Lee, N. (2005). *Corporate Social Responsibility: Doing the Most Good for Your Company and Your Cause*. John Wiley & Sons, Inc.

Lantos, G. P. (2001). The boundaries of strategic corporate social responsibility. *Journal of Consumer Marketing*, 18(7), 595–630. DOI: 10.1108/07363760110410281

Lantos, G. P. (2002). The ethicality of altruistic corporate social responsibility. *Journal of Consumer Marketing*, 19(3), 205–230. DOI: 10.1108/07363760210426049

Larrán Jorge, M., Herrera Madueño, J., Martínez-Martínez, D., & Lechuga Sancho, M. P. (2015). Competitiveness and environmental performance in Spanish small and medium enterprises: Is there a direct link? *Journal of Cleaner Production*, 101, 26–37. DOI: 10.1016/j.jclepro.2015.04.016

Latif, W., Islam, M. A., Mohamad, M., Sikder, M. A. H., & Ahmed, I. (2015). A conceptual framework of brand image on customer-based brand equity in the hospitality industry at Bangladesh: Tourism management and advertisement as moderators. *Journal of Scientific Research and Development*, 2(11), 1–16.

Lee, S., Seo, K., & Sharma, A. (2013). Corporate social responsibility and firm performance in the airline industry: The moderating role of oil prices. *Tourism Management*, 38, 20–30. DOI: 10.1016/j.tourman.2013.02.002

Luo, X., & Bhattacharya, C. B. (2006). Corporate social responsibility, customer satisfaction, and market value. *Journal of Marketing*, 70(4), 1–18. DOI: 10.1509/jmkg.70.4.001

Maignan, I., Ferrell, O. C., & Ferrell, L. (2005). A stakeholder model for implementing social responsibility in marketing. *European Journal of Marketing*, 39(9/10), 956–977. DOI: 10.1108/03090560510610662

Maignan, I., Ferrell, O. C., & Hult, G. T. M. (1999). Corporate citizenship: Cultural antecedents and business benefits. *Journal of the Academy of Marketing Science*, 27(4), 455–469. DOI: 10.1177/0092070399274005

Margolis, J. D., & Walsh, J. P. (2003). Misery Loves Companies: Rethinking Social Initiatives by Business. *Administrative Science Quarterly*, 48(2), 268–305. DOI: 10.2307/3556659

Marin, L., Ruiz, S., & Rubio, A. (2009). The role of identity salience in the effects of corporate social responsibility on consumer behavior. *Journal of Business Research*, 84(1), 65–78.

Matzler, K., & Hinterhuber, H. H. (1998). How to make product development projects more successful by integrating Kano's model of customer satisfaction into quality function deployment. *Technovation*, 18(1), 25–38. DOI: 10.1016/S0166-4972(97)00072-2

McGuire, J., Sundgren, A., & Schneeweis, T. (1988). Corporate social responsibility and firm financial performance. *Academy of Management Journal*, 31(4), 854–872. DOI: 10.2307/256342

McWilliams, A., Siegel, D. S., & Wright, P. M. (2006). Corporate social responsibility: Strategic implications. *Journal of Management Studies*, 43(1), 1–18. DOI: 10.1111/j.1467-6486.2006.00580.x

Messick, S. (1988). Validity. In Linn, R. L. (Ed.), *Educational Measurement* (3rd ed.). Macmillan.

Mittal, R. K., Sinha, N., & Singh, A. (2008). An Analysis of Linkage between Economic Value Added and Corporate Social Responsibility. *Management Decision*. 46 (9), 1437-1443 available on line. www.emeraldinsight.com/journals.htm?articleid =1747817 accessed.

Mohamed, M. B., & Sawandi, N. B. (2007). Corporate Social Responsibility (CSR) activities in mobile telecommunication industry: case study of Malaysia. *Paper presented at theEuropean Critical Accounting Conference*

Mohr, L., Webb, D., & Harris, K. (2001). Do consumers expect companies to be socially responsible? The impact of corporate social responsibility on buying behavior. *The Journal of Consumer Affairs*, 35(1), 45–72. DOI: 10.1111/j.1745-6606.2001.tb00102.x

Mumtaz, M., & Pirzada, S. S. (2014). Impact of corporate social responsibility on corporate financial performance. *Research on Humanities and Social Sciences*, 4(14), 7–15.

Naumann, E. (1995). *Customer satisfaction measurement and management: Using the voice of the customer*. Thomson Executive Press.

Nelson, E. C., Rust, R. T., Zahorik, A., Rose, R. L., Batalden, P., & Siemanski, B. A. (1992). Do Patient Perceptions of Quality Relate to Hospital Financial Performance? [December.]. *Journal of Health Care Marketing*, •••, 6–13.

Öberseder, M., Schlegelmilch, B. B., Murphy, P. E., & Gruber, V. (2014). Consumers' perceptions of corporate social responsibility: Scale development and validation. *Journal of Business Ethics*, 124(1), 101–115. DOI: 10.1007/s10551-013-1787-y

Orlitzky, M. (2013). Corporate social responsibility, noise, and stock market volatility. *The Academy of Management Perspectives*, 27(3), 238–254. DOI: 10.5465/amp.2012.0097

Özdamar, K. (2017). *Olcek ve test gelistirme yapisal esitlik modellemesi IBM SPSS, IBM SPSS AMOS ve MINTAB uygulamali* [Scale and test development Structural equation modeling IBM SPSS, IBM SPSS AMOS and MINTAB applied]. Nisan Kitabevi.

Pakseresht, A. (2010). Brand equity and corporate responsibility: A review of brand valuation methods. https://www.essays.se/essay/9e20739689/ (accessed 23 January 2011).

Pérez, A., Salmones, M. M. G., & Bosque, I. R. (2013a). The effect of corporate associations on consumer behaviour. *European Journal of Marketing*, 47(1/2), 218–238. DOI: 10.1108/03090561311285529

Piercy, N. F., & Lane, N. (2009). Corporate social responsibility: Impacts on strategic marketing and customer value. *The Marketing Review*, 9(4), 335–360. DOI: 10.1362/146934709X479917

Pokorny, G. (1995) Building brand equity and customer loyalty. Retrieved January 23, 2019, from http://findarticles.com/p/articles/mi_qa3650/is_199505/ai_n8728762/pg_3/?tag=content;col1

Post, C., Rahman, N., & Rubow, E. (2011). Green governance: Boards of directors' composition and environmental corporate social responsibility‖. *Business & Society*, 50(1), 189–223. DOI: 10.1177/0007650310394642

Raman, M., Lim, W., & Nair, S. (2012). The impact of corporate social responsibility on consumer loyalty. *Kajian Malaysia: Journal of Malaysian Studies, 30*(2).

Ringle, C. M, Wende, S., & Becker, J., M., (Producer) (2015). SmartPLS 3. Retrieved from http://www.smartpls.com

Salmones, M. M. G., Crespo, A. H., & del Bosque, I. R. (2005). Influence of corporate social Responsibility on loyalty and valuation of services. *Journal of Business Ethics*, 61(4), 369–385. DOI: 10.1007/s10551-005-5841-2

Sambala, G. L. (2015). *The role of company's corporate social responsibility in community development: The case of Morogoro Municipality* (Doctoral dissertation, Mzumbe University).

Solomon, R., & Hansen, K. (1985). *It's good business*. Atheneum.

Srivastava, R. K., Shervani, T. A., & Fahey, L. (1998). Market-based assets and shareholder value: A framework for analysis. *Journal of Marketing*, 62(1), 2–18. DOI: 10.1177/002224299806200102

Stanaland, A. J. S., Lwin, M. O., & Murphy, P. E. (2011). Consumer perceptions of the antecedents and consequences of corporate social responsibility. *Journal of Business Ethics*, 102(1), 47–55. DOI: 10.1007/s10551-011-0904-z

Stanwick, P. A., & Stanwick, S. D. (1998). The relationship between corporate social performance and organizational size, financial performance, and environmental performance: An empirical examination. *Journal of Business Ethics*, 17(2), 195–204. DOI: 10.1023/A:1005784421547

Story, J., & Neves, P. (2015). When corporate social responsibility (CSR) increases performance: Exploring the role of intrinsic and extrinsic CSR attribution. *Business Ethics (Oxford, England)*, 24(2), 111–124. DOI: 10.1111/beer.12084

Sureshchandar, G. S., Rajendran, C., & Anantharaman, R. N. (2002). The relationship between service quality and customer satisfaction—A factor specific approach. *Journal of Services Marketing*, 16(4), 363–379. DOI: 10.1108/08876040210433248

Swaen, V., & Chumpitaz, R. C. (2008). Impact of Corporate social responsibility on consumer trust. *Recherche et Applications en Marketing*, 23(4), 7–33. DOI: 10.1177/076737010802300401

Usakli, A., & Baloglu, S. (2011). Brand personality of tourist destinations: An application of self-congruity theory. *Tourism Management*, 32(1), 114–127. DOI: 10.1016/j.tourman.2010.06.006

Valentine, S., & Godkin, L. (2016). Ethics policies, perceived social responsibility, and positive work attitude. *Irish Journal of Management*, 35(2), 114–128. DOI: 10.1515/ijm-2016-0013

(●●●). variables and measurement error. *JMR, Journal of Marketing Research*, 18(1), 39–50.

Vlachos, P. A. (2012). Corporate social performance and consumer- retailer emotional attachment: The moderating role of individual traits. *European Journal of Marketing*, 46(11/12), 1559–1580. DOI: 10.1108/03090561211259989

Wagner-Tsukamoto, S. (2019). In search of ethics: From Carroll to integrative CSR economics. *Social Responsibility Journal*, 15(4), 469–491. DOI: 10.1108/SRJ-09-2017-0188

Welford, R. (Ed.). (2005). *Corporate environmental reporting and disclosure in China*. CSR Asia.

Westin, L., & Parmler, J. (2020). Inclusion of CSR in the extended performance satisfaction index–new development. *Total Quality Management & Business Excellence*, ●●●, 1–12. DOI: 10.1080/14783363.2020.1856651

Xuezhou, W., Hussain, R. Y., Hussain, H., Saad, M., & Qalati, S. A. (2022). Analyzing the impact of board vigilance on financial distress through the intervention of leverage structure and interaction of asset tangibility in the non-financial sector of Pakistan. *International Journal of Financial Engineering*, 9(02), 2150004. DOI: 10.1142/S2424786321500043

Yang, A. S., & Baasandorj, S. (2017). Exploring CSR and financial performance of full-service and low-cost air carriers. *Finance Research Letters*, 23, 291–299. DOI: 10.1016/j.frl.2017.05.005

Chapter 3
Effect of Informal and Out-of-Court Resolutions on the Post-Bankruptcy Performance of Companies:
Empirical Evidence From India

Santosh Kumar
Christ University, India

S. Parameswaran
Christ University, India

ABSTRACT

The need for seeking a timely & cheaper resolution of distressed companies has always been the top priority for creditors & corporate debtors alike. In this regard the current study analyses the role of informal & out of court settlement on the Post-Bankruptcy financial performance of Companies. This is a sample study of insolvent companies approved for out of court settlement under section 12 A of IBC in India. In this study the effect of financial, operational & portfolio restructuring actions under out of court settlement are analysed during pre & post bankruptcy period.The outcome of this research provides strong evidence of changes due to restructuring actions.

DOI: 10.4018/979-8-3693-5733-0.ch003

INTRODUCTION

Out-of-court settlement involves debt restructuring which essentially means changing the composition and/or structure of assets and liabilities of debtors in financial difficulty, with limited judicial intervention along with the objective of promoting efficiency, restoring growth, and minimizing the costs associated with the debtor's financial difficulties. An out-of-court restructuring of debt is free from judicial obligation, control or monitoring and, hence does not permanently alter, change, impair, or prejudice the legal rights of (and continuing obligations owed to) holders of debt. Restructuring activities can include measures that restructure the debtor's day to day business (operational restructuring), or efficient asset utilization (Portfolio restructuring) and measures that restructure the debtor's finances (financial restructuring). In situations of financial difficulty, the debtor and the creditors can protect their respective interests more effectively if an informal solution is implemented. An out-of-court restructuring of company avoids bankruptcy consequences for all creditors and other stakeholders, under section 362 of US Bankruptcy Code (section 14 of IBC) which provides automatic stay of payments to creditors, and possible material damage to a company's business operations and going concern value that might be caused by the stigma of Insolvency Process. An out-of-court restructuring avoids the high costs of traditional court monitored resolution including professional fees incurred by the company and creditor representatives, costs of bankruptcy-related litigation, distractions to management, the attendant costs of complying with bankruptcy reporting requirements, and judicial oversight. Insolvency Resolution Process costs can be enormous, especially if the process is contentious and litigated. Another fundamental benefit of an out-of-court restructuring is that its consensual nature reduces restructuring uncertainties and closing risks. On the other hand, a traditional (i.e., non-prepackaged, non-prearranged) bankruptcy resolution poses outcome uncertainties because these court driven cases are inherently litigious. An announced out-of-court financial restructuring that improves the company's balance sheet and liquidity leads to reduced stress or uncertainties among employees, suppliers, other trade creditors, and customers. In an out-of-court process, incumbent management continues to manage and control the company as well as the restructuring process, unless creditors demand new or replacement management as a condition of out-of-court debtholder concessions. There are various methods of informal restructuring ranging from purely contractual agreements that are enhanced by the existence of norms or other types of contractual or statutory arrangements to "hybrid procedures" where the involvement of the judiciary or other authorities is an integral part of the procedure, but is less intensive than in formal insolvency proceedings.

Theoretical Background

Empirical studies indicate that a large number of companies do not reorganize out of court settlement as a credible or legitimate method of bankruptcy resolution process and rather decided to seek court driven formal bankruptcy resolution (CIRP or Chapter 11). An analysis of 169 financially distressed public companies was performed by Gilson et al. (1990). They find that 47% of the firms restructured their debt out of court, while 53% of the firms had no success with this restructuring strategy and subsequently filed for Chapter 11. Moreover, they show that private workouts are more common when firms have fewer distinct classes of debt.

In terms of out-of-court restructuring, Betker (1997) and Gilson, John, and Lang (1990) report an average cost of 0.6% and 2.5%, respectively, of the book value of assets from analyzing exchange offers. In addition, Chatterjee, Dhillon, and Ramirez (1995) capture the stock market reaction and show fewer negative abnormal returns related to private restructuring in comparison with Chapter 11 filings. Because of the high cost of reorganization in court, firms favor private restructuring. Gilson et al. (1990) and Gilson, Hotchkiss, and Ruback (2000) distinguish the characteristics of the firms that solve financial distress through private workouts from those of firms that use traditional court procedures. Chatterjee, Dhillon, and Ramírez (1996) indicate that options for court or out-of-court restructuring depend on firms' liquidity, leverage, level of economic distress, and creditor coordination problems. Gilson, John & Lang (1990), show that negotiations in informal workouts are more likely to succeed when firms have closer relationships with their bank and deal with a smaller pool of banks. Gilson & al. (1990) also find that the firms with a larger proportion of intangible assets in their asset structure prefer informal workouts to a formal restructuring procedure in which they have a higher chance of losing firm value through fire sales or loss of customers. Finally, Chatterjee, Dhillon, and Ramirez (1995) show that the choice of out-of-court restructuring depends on the firm's debt level, its short-term liquidity and probability of occurrence of coordination problems among creditors.

Context of This Study

Insolvency & bankruptcy code (IBC) – the landmark legislation for insolvency & bankruptcy law in India has been seeking to facilitate corporate distress resolution through both traditional and out of court settlement process. The Insolvency and Bankruptcy Board of India (IBBI), the Insolvency regulator, through its multiple directions under CIRP regulations 2016 has effected changes through operational, financial & portfolio restructuring of Insolvent companies to ensure a positive and meaningful outcome from resolution. These restructuring are initiated either under formal (CIRP) resolution or Out of court settlement u/s 12 A of IBC. The initiation into CIRP (bankruptcy process) leads to only two possible revival option for the distressed company. Either, the Company gets sold to new buyer/ resolution applicant as per the competitive bidding process, or alternatively the Creditor and Debtors reach informal settlement leading to closure or withdrawal of CIRP under section 12A of IBC. This study seeks to analyze the post-bankruptcy financial performance of companies, withdrawn from CIRP under section 12 A of IBC. In this empirical study we seek to test, whether the restructuring action initiated under the control of original promoter or existing management results in better or worse financial performance of company, Secondly, we analyze the individual effects of operational, financial & portfolio restructuring actions and compare their direct effects on Profitability / Post-Bankruptcy performance, Third we find the effect of Liquidity on the post-bankruptcy performance.

Statement of Problem

Empirical data as well as views from creditors & debtors alike suggests that there are numerous advantages associated with out-of-court settlements of corporate bankruptcy resolution in India. Yet a significant number of creditors rely mostly on court-driven procedures like CIRP to seek corporate distress resolution. This raises critical questions on the possible benefits to creditors or the reason for seeking court-based resolution over a much cheaper & less complicated resolution through out-of-court settlements. While existing literature highlights lack of legal obligation under informal resolutions, complex nature of credit contracts, large credit exposure, future legal complications & overall trust deficit on the informal mode of resolution etc as the reason behind a large number of creditors seeking court driven resolution. On the other hands those opting for informal or out of court resolution points to benefits such as reduced litigation, preservation of existing management, continuity of business, cost saving, positive effects on existing & new customers, new credit opportunity etc. More so, as the IBC law is new to India, while the out of court settlement u/s 12 A as a tool for resolution was introduced from Oct, 2018 only, hence there has been limited empirical study to find out any potential financial benefit, implication or consequences of choosing informal resolution. In this study we analyze the financial performance of companies during the post-bankruptcy period. Through a holistic understanding of the implications of out-of-court resolution on firm-level performance, it becomes easier to enforce effective bankruptcy resolution strategies and promote sustainable corporate recovery. These resolutions are enforced through the Corporate restructuring actions on the distressed companies. Therefore, the problem statement revolves around the need for comprehensive analysis of the determinants influencing out-of-court settlements on the financial distress resolution of companies. This study has a limited objective in finding out the implication of various restructuring actions on the post- bankruptcy performance of companies in India.

Motivation For This Study

As per the recent data released by IBBI, as on 31st March 2022, the National Company Law tribunal (NCLT) 3406 application have been settled/ closed. Out of these a total of 586 application has been withdrawn under 12 A of IBC basis out of court settlement with debtors, while 480 cases have got resolution through court driven CIRP process . (Refer to Table 1). This means that in almost 14% of total closed cases the creditors preferred court driven resolution while in almost 17% cases informal / out of court settlement under 12 A of IBC. Here it is to be noted that, while the court driven CIRP process has been available since 28th May, 2016, while the option of withdrawal through section 12 A was made available only from IBC on 6th June, 2018 onward. Yet total no of bankruptcy settlement under 12 A route is much higher as compared to court based resolution. Hence in this study we explore the evidence behind the higher preference for out of court settlement . The study also explores the reasons & overall effects of out of court resolution / settlement on the profitability of company.

Out Of Court Resolution Of Companies in India (u/s 12 A of IBC 2016)

In India, Insolvency & Bankruptcy Code (IBC) 2016, provides options for corporate debtors to pursue informal & out of court resolution of distressed companies admitted for Insolvency Resolution Process (CIRP) under section 7,9 or 10 of IBC. This provision of IBC empowers the Adjudicatory Authority (NCLT) to allow the withdrawal of CIRP application with approval of 90% voting shares of the Committee of Creditors (COC). This special feature of law under 12 A was inserted in IBC on June, 2018 on the recommendations of the Insolvency Law Committee (March, 2018). This study is based on the companies admitted for insolvency resolution under CIRP and subsequently allowed for withdrawal under section 12 A of IBC.

Significance of This Study

The current study seeks to analyze the post-bankruptcy financial performance of companies, withdrawn from CIRP under 12 A of IBC on account of out of court settlement between debtor and creditor. The resolution of insolvent company depends on the outcome of negotiation between debtor and creditor. In this case, while CIRP is a court monitored process, yet if the creditor and debtor agree to informally settle their dispute, the NCLT (IBC) can allow withdrawal from CIRP and hence facilitate out of court settlement. Today there are multiple tools available for companies to initiate distress resolution, like CIRP, voluntary insolvency, liquidation, Pre-Pack or Out of court settlement u/s 12A etc., yet as per available data there are overwhelming preference for a debtor driven out of court settlement under 12 A of IBC. The current study aims to examine the effects of restructuring of companies as per out of court settlement between debtor and creditor, after withdrawal from CIRP. The proposed restructuring proposal includes but not limited to financial, Operational & Portfolio restructuring of companies. The current study is based on companies which were initiated to Insolevncy resolution process (CIRP) by creditors, but later sought pre-mature closure / withdrawal from CIRP on account of out of court settlement with corporate debtor. In this empirical study we seek to test, whether the restructuring action initiated under the control of original promoter or management results in better or worse financial performance of company, Secondly, we analyze the individual effects of operational, financial & portfolio restructuring actions and compare their direct effects on Profitability / Post-Bankruptcy performance, thirdly, we find the effect of Liquidity on the post-bankruptcy performance.

Relevant Studies in India

While corporate restructuring has been used as a tool for corporate distress resolution in India, especially under the RBI mandated CDR which was initiated in 2001, now it is also used as an integral and dedicated tool under IBC for insolvency resolution. Since, the IBC as the legal framework for insolvency resolution, came in operation only from April, 2016, hence limited studies are available on the overall effect of resolution / restructuring. Most of these studies have been carried under severe limitation of data, time period, research model & scope of study. In this reference, Gupta, S K (2021) carried out a detailed analysis of the operational & financial performance of Electro steel Steel Limited over the five-year period i.e 2015 till 2019. He evaluated the performance of company across multiple performance metrics, namely current ratio, ROCE, ROA, EBITM, DuPont ratio to compare the performance of these companies across 4-year period. The current study while in continuation of earlier studies, seeks a much detailed and wider analysis of a group of companies across pre and post- bankruptcy period. Here we take help of Multiple regression analysis to validate the significance of changes in the financial performance of companies during post-bankruptcy period.

Objectives of Study

1.8.1 To find the effects of Informal Resolution / Out of Court Settlement on the post-bankruptcy performance of companies.

1.8.2 To find the strength & direction of Corporate Restructuring actions on the Post-Bankruptcy Performance of Companies.

1.8.3 To find the individual effect of Financial, Operational & Portfolio restructuring actions on the Post-Bankruptcy Performance of company.

REVIEW OF LITERATURE

There are multiple studies alluding to the role of private negotiation & out of court settlement of debt contract in reducing financial distress. Following are the some of the other important contributions in regards to the effect of out of court settlement on post-bankruptcy performance. Chatterjee, Dhillon, and Ramírez (1996) indicate that options for court or out-of-court restructuring depend on firms' liquidity, leverage, level of economic distress, and creditor coordination problems. Gilson & al. (1990) also find that the firms with a larger proportion of intangible assets in their asset structure prefer informal workouts to a formal restructuring procedure in which they have a higher chance of losing firm value through fire sales or loss of customers. Chatterjee, Dhillon, and Ramirez (1995) show that the choice of out-of-court restructuring depends on the firm's debt level, its short-term liquidity and probability of occurrence of coordination problems among creditors. Bharath, S., & Shumway, C. (2008) suggests that loan re-negotiations, which is quite common under out-of-court financial restructuring method, can be effective in improving the financial health of distressed firms. It was found that firms that negotiate their debt with lenders under private or informal terms often experience less stringent leverage condition and improved profitability post-restructuring as compared to seeking resolution under formal court driven resolution. In another study, Cai, Y., & Chen, X. (2017) compares the success rates of out-of-court restructurings across different industries and countries. His study finds that firms with strong pre-restructuring financial performance, good relationships with lenders, and clear turnaround plans are more likely to succeed in out-of-court settlements. John, G., & O'Donnell, S. (2010) research paper examines the use of operational restructuring strategies, such as cost-cutting and process improvements, in out-of-court restructuring. The study finds that firms that implement comprehensive operational restructuring plans during out-of-court settlements tend to show greater improvements in efficiency and profitability post-restructuring. Study by Li, J., & Tang, Y. (2019) suggests that a key driver of success in out-of-court restructurings is the ability to improve operational efficiency through initiatives such as lean manufacturing, supply chain optimization, and workforce management. Firms that focus on operational excellence tend to see greater improvements in profitability and long-term sustainability post-restructuring. Another study by Almeida, P., & Ferreira, M. (2012) examines the use of portfolio restructuring, such as asset divestitures and acquisitions, in out-of-court restructurings from a value creation perspective. Their study suggests that divestitures of non-core assets can unlock hidden value and improve focus, while acquisitions should be carefully evaluated to ensure strategic alignment and synergy. Similarly, the research by Chung, Y., & Lee, D. (2014) suggests that well-executed asset sales can be an effective way for distressed firms to improve their financial position and create value for stakeholders during out-of-court settlements. They emphasize the importance of careful planning, market timing, and finding the right buyers to maximize the benefits of asset sales. Li, Z., & Wang, F. (2020) uses panel data analysis to examine the relationship between portfolio restructuring and the success of out-of-court restructurings. The study finds that the effectiveness of portfolio restructuring depends on factors such as the type of assets restructured, the firm's industry, and the economic environment. Research work from Gilson, S., & Schwartz, A. (2009) highlights the challenges of maintaining adequate liquidity during out-of-court restructurings. Firms need to balance short-term cash flow needs with long-term investment requirements to ensure they can sustain operations and execute their restructuring. restructuring by comparing the performance of firms that restructure out-of-court to those that file for court driven bankruptcy. Bharath, Sreedhar T., and David I. Denis. (2010) examines the role of secured creditors in the choice between out-of-court restructuring and formal bankruptcy. They find that secured creditors are more likely to push for out-of-court restructuring when they have a large stake in the firm. This suggests that secured creditors may use their bargaining power to extract concessions from debtors in exchange for avoiding bankruptcy. Kalay, Singhal, and Tashjian (2007) indicate a high likelihood of efficiency gains for companies in reorganization. However, firms with more classes of debt show less improvement in performance. Hotchkiss (1995) argues that firm size is the main determinant of a successful reorganization. The availability of divestment proposals to fund operations and pay creditors is crucial for a firm to overcome a reorganization period.

Lomuscio, Alberto, et al, compares the outcomes of out-of-court and in-court methods, highlighting the role of factors like legal frameworks, creditor coordination, and information asymmetry in determining success. Hotchkiss (1995) finds that more than 40% of companies continued to have operating losses in the three years after reorganization. Compared to other firms in the same industry, more than 70% of the firms in reorganization showed lower performance.

Research Gap

It's evident that while most studies have focused on individual factors effecting the outcome of out of court settlement on bankrupt companies, till date there has been no study to explore a comprehensive impact / effects of restructuring action namely operational, financial and portfolio restructuring actions on the financial performance of companies. The current study for the first time attempts an integrated and comprehensive study of restructuring actions on the post- bankruptcy performance of companies.in India. This study is primarily based on empirical data of performance of companies under IBC in India. These sample companies have already been approved for out of court settlement under section 12 A of IBC. More specifically this study analyses the post-bankruptcy performance of companies seeking out of court settlement under section 12 A of IBC in India. The outcome of this study though has important lessons for companies pursuing informal resolution across different geographies.

METHODOLOGY FOR EMPIRICAL RESEARCH

Research Method

The research study is operationalized through two distinct stages i.e (i) Pre bankruptcy phase, beginning when the firm fails or become insolvent and hence forced in to bankruptcy proceeding (CIRP) u/s 7, 9 or 10 of IBC by Financial and/or Operational Creditor(s) or the corporate debtor itself. This Insolvency Resolution process (CIRP) is finally completed during the period from April, 2018 till March, 2019. In this study pre-bankruptcy period & Post-Bankruptcy period is identified as below,

Table 1. Timeline of Study

Pre-Bankruptcy Phase	1st April, 2015 till 31st March, 2018
Bankruptcy Phase	1st April, 2018 till 31st March, 2019
Post- Bankruptcy Phase	1st April, 2019 till 31st March, 2022

Research Hypothesis

3.2.1 Null Hypothesis {H(0)}- Out of Court corporate Restructuring doesn't result in any significant effect on the Post-Bankruptcy Performance of Company.

3.2.2 Alternative Hypothesis {H(a)} – Out of court Financial restructuring results in significant effect on the Post-Bankruptcy Performance of company.

3.2.3 Alternative Hypothesis ({H(b)} – Out of court Operational restructuring results in significant effect on Post-Bankruptcy financial performance of company.

3.2.4 Alternative Hypothesis {H(c)} – Out of court Portfolio Restructuring results in significant effect on Post-Bankruptcy financial performance of company.

3.2.5 Alternative Hypothesis {H(d)} – Liquidity under out of court restructuring has significant effect on Post-Bankruptcy financial performance of company.

The above hypothesis is tested through comparative analysis of Pre & Post-Bankruptcy financial performance of companies along with use of multiple regression analysis on the Post-bankruptcy performance of companies. While we analyse the pre & post-Bankruptcy financial performance data of companies to measure the actual effect of restructuring action, the Regression analysis is used to find the individual role of restructuring actions on the post-bankruptcy performance of companies. We find the effect of individual restructuring action (Independent variable) on outcome variable (Profitability) of the company.

Year Selected For Out of Court Restructuring

We have chosen FY 2018-19 (April, 2018 till March, 2019) as the Year when the company is approved for Out of Court Restructuring. Since it was only in June, 2018 that the govt of India, introduced section 12 A of IBC, allowing for out of court settlement and subsequent withdrawal of CIRP cases before completion. Further, the year has been chosen to facilitate performance data of companies for six years, providing three year each for pre & Post Bankruptcy performance analysis of data, from March, 2016 till March 2022

Dependent, Independent and Controlled Variable

To carry out multiple regression analysis we consider Profitability Ratio represented by Return On Profit (RoA) as dependent variable also known as Post-bankruptcy performance in this research study. Corporate restructuring Actions i.e Financial, Operational & Portfolio Restructuring actions are represented by Debt to Equity ratio, Return on Sales and Gross Fixed Asset Utilisation ratio (GFAUR) respectively. These are the independent also known as explanatory or predictor variable. Controlled variables are represented by excess liquidity i.e Current Ratio during the time of out of court settlement.

Data Source

We have relied upon CMIE-Prowess database for sourcing the financial / accounting performance data of companies chosen in the sample. Under this research study we analyse performance ratios of a select 7 companies which have been approved for Out Of Court Settlement u/s 12 A of IBC.

Sample Size & Sampling method

The current study considers only those companies approved for out of court settlement during the year 2018-19 . Hence out of total 586 active companies approved for withdrawal/ Closure of CIRP under 12 A of IBC, from 1st April, 2016 till 31st, march 2022, only 97 companies were approved for 12 A settlement (out of court settlement) by NCLT (bankruptcy court) during period April, 2018 and March, 2019. Of these 97 companies, 40 had very small claim amount i.e less than INR 10 Million. Post-exclusion of these 40 companies, we are left with 57 companies. Out of the 57 companies, we make a convenient sample of 7 companies representing seven unique industries. Hence the current study is conducted on 7 companies approved for out of court settlement u/s 12 A of IBC.

Sample Representation:

The sample consist of name of 7 Companies representing 7 unique industries & business segment in India. These are into Real Estate, Agri-Product, Mineral & Mining, Printing, Pharma, Engineering Goods. We have shortlisted these companies to analyse their comparative pre & post -bankruptcy financial condition as per profitability, liquidity, leverage and efficiency ratios. All these are active companies not listed on stock exchange.

RESULT & ANALYSIS

Table 2. Comparative Analysis of Pre & Post Bankruptcy Performance

Notation	Parameter	Pre-Bankruptcy	Post-Bankruptcy	Absolute Change	Percentage Change
	Profitability Ratios				
P1	ROA (%)	-14.2	8.93	22.13	143.0
P2	Return on Sales (%)	-49.39	-1.3	48.09	97.4
	Liquidity Ratios				
P3	Current Ratio (Times)	1.01	2.31	1.3	128.7
	Solvency / Leverage Ratios				
P4	Debt To Equity Ratio (Times)	4.16	4.05	-0.11	-2.6
	Turnover / Efficiency Ratios				
P5	Gross Fixed Asset Turnover (Times)	2.9	4.52	1.62	55.9
	Insolvency Predictor				
P6	Altman Z-Score (Pvt Manufacturing)	0.695	0.67	-0.025	3.60%

Where, Altman Z- Score (Insolvency Predictor Ratio) (P5) for Private Manufacturing / Non-Financial company =

Altman Z Score (Z) = $0.717X_1 + 0.847X_2 + 3.107X_3 + 0.420X_4 + 0.998X_5$

X_1 = Working Capital / Total Assets (%), X_2 = Retained earnings / Total assets (%), X_3 = EBIT/Total Assets (%), X_4 = Book value of equity/total liabilities (%), X_5 = sales/total assets (times).

The firm is classified as financially sound if Z>2.99 and financially distressed (bankrupt) if Z<1.81

Result:

Table 3. Pre & Post Bankruptcy Performance

Post- Restructuring P1 > Pre-Bankruptcy P1
Post-Restructuring P2 > Pre-Restructuring P2
Post-Restructuring P3 > Pre -Restructuring P3
Post-Restructuring P4 < Pre-Restructuring P4
Post-Restructuring P5 > Pre-Restructuring P5

Analysis & Interpretation:

As per the outcome, it is evident that across all financial performance ratio there is an improvement from pre-bankruptcy period. In this case, Profitability ratio, Leverage / solvency ratio, Operating Profit Margin, Gross Fixed asset utilisation ratio, Liquidity ratio of the company has improved from Pre- Bankruptcy to Post-Bankruptcy period. Hence the result clearly proves that corporate restructuring actions initiated on the distressed companies as under Out of court settlement u/s 12 A, has resulted in significant improvement in Post-bankruptcy financial performance of company.

Altman Z Score

– Evaluation of Insolvency Predictor During Pre & Post restructuring Period for companies under out of court settlement u/s 12 A of IBC

Altman-Z score - Comparative analysis

Post -Restructuring P6 < Pre-Restructuring P6

Analysis & Interpretation:

Altman Z-Score (Pvt Manufacturing Companies): The Altman Z-Score remained relatively stable, showing a slight decrease from 0.695 to 0.670. The outcome clearly proves that Restructuring actions under out of court settlement has resulted in a stable financial condition for the company. Clearly after restructuring action there are lessor chance of companies getting into bankruptcy condition as they have improved their performance across sales, profitability, leverage ratio even as the Altman Z-Score in this case has neither reduced nor improved during post-bankruptcy period.

Multiple Regression Analysis

Diagnostic Tests

Test of Normality

Shapiro Wilk Test
Null Hypothesis:
H0 (Null) – Residual of variable in panel regression is normally distributed
H_0 hypothesis Since p-value > α, we accept the H_0. Where, p-value equals 0.7685, Test statistic W equals 0.9433, Effect size KS - D is very small, 0.1641

In view of the above, it is assumed that the data is normally distributed.

Test of Heteroscedasticity

White Test
Null Hypothesis (H0): There is no heteroscedasticity present in the regression model.

To conduct the White test in Python, we can use the following code:
Output Code: 0.7593 0.525366

Here The F-statistic for the White test is 0.7593, and the p-value is 0.525366. The p-value is greater than 0.05, so we cannot reject the null hypothesis that there is no heteroskedasticity in the model. This is consistent with the p-value of 0.525366.

Hence it is established that there is no heteroskedasticity in the regression model.

Test of Multicollinearity - VIF Test

To find any evidence of multicollinearity in the residual data, we conduct VIF test for multicollinearity. Hence will need to calculate the VIF values for each independent variable. Table 4. **The VIF (Variance Inflation Factor) for each predictor variable**

Table 4

Independent / Predictor Variable	VIF
Constant (B0)	
Financial Restructuring (X1)	1.7797
Operational Restructuring (X2)	1.7103

continued on following page

Table 4. Continued

Independent / Predictor Variable	VIF
Portfolio Restructuring (X3)	1.1573
Liquidity Ratio (X4)	1.1894

In the above table VIF value of less than < 4- 10 indicates that there is no evidence of multicollinearity. **Therefore, we can conclude that there is no evidence of multicollinearity in the independent variables.**

Test of Autocorrelation - Durbin Watson Statistics

To perform the Durbin-Watson test for autocorrelation, we will need to calculate the Durbin-

Here is the Python code for calculating the Durbin-Watson statistic:
Output code is: 1.695565 = d

The Durbin-Watson statistic (d) is 1.69. The critical values for the Durbin-Watson test are:

- d < 1: positive autocorrelation
- d > 4: negative autocorrelation
- 2 < d < 3: no autocorrelation

The Durbin-Watson statistic of 1.69 is more than 1 and less than 2, which indicates that **there is not very strong evidence of autocorrelation in the residuals**.

Panel Regression analysis of companies under 12 A Settlement

Panel Regression Analysis

$\hat{Y} = 4.971434 - 0.333276 X_1 - 0.429332 X_2 + 1.913019 X_3 - 1.685914 X_4$

Where, $Y^\wedge$ = Profitability, X1= Financial Restructuring, X2 = Operational Restructuring, X3= Portfolio Restructuring, X4 = Liquidity Ratio (Controlled Variable)

Results of the multiple linear regression indicated that there was a very strong collective non-significant effect between the X1, X2, X3, X4, and Y. These variable have statistically Non-Significant effect on the dependent variable.

Table 5. **Summary of outcome under Panel Regression Test – 12A Settlement**

Predictor		Co-efficient Estimate	Standard Error	t-Statistic	P-value	VIF
Constant	β0	4.9714	6.3003	0.7891	0.5128	
Financial Restructuring (X1)	β1	-0.3333	1.1614	-0.287	0.8011	1.7707
Operational Restructuring (X2)	β2	-0.4293	0.1004	-4.2778	0.0505	1.7103
Portfolio Restructuring (X3)	β3	1.913	0.4078	4.6913	0.0426	1.1573
Liquidity Ratio (X4)	β4	-1.6859	1.0000	-1.6859	0.2339	1.18938
Summary of Overall Fit						
R-Squared:		\multicolumn{5}{c	}{r2=0.9599}	
Adjusted R-Squared:		\multicolumn{5}{c	}{r2adj=0.8797}	
Residual Standard Error:		\multicolumn{5}{c	}{6.9 on 2 degrees of freedom.}	
Overall F-statistic:		\multicolumn{5}{c	}{11.965 on 4 and 2 degrees of freedom.}	
Overall p-value:		\multicolumn{5}{c	}{0.0786}	

Analysis of Variance Table					
Source	Df	SS	MS	F-statistic	p-value
Regression	4	2279	569.7	11.965	0.0786
Residual Error	2	95.2	47.61		
Total	6	2374	395.6		

The panel regression analysis results suggest that the model explains 95.99% of the variance in the dependent variable. After adjusting for the number of predictors in the model, the adjusted R-squared is 87.97%. This indicates that the model has a good fit to the data. The F-statistic is 11.965 and the p-value is 0.0786. The p-value is greater than 0.05, so we fail to reject the null hypothesis that the coefficients of all the predictors are zero. This suggests that the overall model is statistically significant, but we need to further investigate the individual coefficients to determine which predictors are significant. The panel regression analysis suggests that Operational Restructuring and Portfolio Restructuring are statistically significant predictors of the dependent variable. Financial Restructuring and Liquidity Ratio are not statistically significant predictors of the dependent variable. The model has a good fit to the results.

Test of Hypothesis

Basis comparative analysis of performance during three year post-Bankruptcy period, it is evident that almost across every financial performance parameter the distressed companies have performed positively. There have been significant positive improvement in the Profitability, Operating Profit margin, Fixed Asset utilisation, Liquidity & Solvency Ratio of the companies during post -bankruptcy period. Similarly the analysis of Altman-Z score of companies reflecting the potential distress condition of companies have significantly improved due to corporate restructuring actions. The significant improvement across solvency and other condition proves less chance of companies going into default. In view of the above, the **NULL Hypothesis (H0) is rejected.**

On the basis of the outcome from regression analysis, it is proved that out of court restructuring leads to significant effect on the post-bankruptcy profitability of company.

As per the result of regression analysis, there is a significant effect of Operational and Portfolio Restructuring on the post-bankruptcy financial performance of company. In view of the same we **reject** the **NULL Hypothesis (H0)**

For, Alternative Hypothesis (Ha), (Hb), (Hc), (Hd), we take reference from regression analysis. while Operational restructuring has significant but negative effect on the profitability of company, Portfolio restructuring has a significant but positive effect on the profitability. The regression analysis also proves that Financial Restructuring has a non-significant and negative effect on the profitability. The Liquidity, a controlled variable has a negative effect on Profitability of the company. Hence in of the same, we accept alternative Hypothesis II and III i.e (Hb) and (Hc) but only partly accept Alternative Hypothesis I and IV i.e (Ha) and (Hd).

In view of the above it is proved that Corporate restructuring action esp Operational and Portfolio restructuring has a significant effect on post-bankruptcy performance while Financial restructuring action has a non-significant effect on Post-Bankruptcy performance of company. It is also prove that liquidity as a controlled variable has non-significant effect on Post-Bankruptcy performance. In terms of correlation between profitability and restructuring action, it is proved that while Operational changes in company esp. cost rationalisation, employee retrenchment, technological innovation results in negative effect on the profitability, Portfolio restructuring which results in higher asset utilisation, Merger & Acquisition, Asset sales etc. results in positive effect on profitability. Similarly, financial restructuring i.e change in debt structure, leverage or solvency of the company leads to negative impact of profitability .

DISCUSSIONS

It is clear from the analysis of empirical data that, the comparative analysis of the actual performance or the Altman-Z-score of companies proves significant positive changes in performance of companies. The regression model shows that the effect of out of court restructuring on distressed companies, while significant yet do not provide a comprehensive result. While every company chosen for restructuring actions do experience changes across different financial parameters these are not necessarily significant or positive during post-bankruptcy period. The 7 insolvent companies chosen for out of court restructuring represent seven unique industries in India. Accordingly, based on the nature of industries represented by respective insolvent companies the outcome or effect of restructuring actions seems either significant, Non-significant, Positive or negative etc. Our study clearly shows that there is no sweeping effect of restructuring actions on Post-bankruptcy performance. While companies representing a particular industry may be significantly impacted by restructuring actions, but each companies are not necessarily impacted by changes in operational, financial or portfolio performance.

Effect Of Financial Restructuring on Profitability / Post-Bankruptcy Performance

If we look at the data of companies from March, 2016 till March 2022, it can been clearly observed that the leverage ratio has been more or less similar i.e not much changes in solvency or liability of companies during six year period of pre & post-bankruptcy period. Even during post restructuring period there is not much change in debt to equity ratio from pre-bankruptcy conditions. This outcome is very much in line with theoretical submissions made by Hotchkiss, (1995), Gilson, John & Lang (1990). Peek and Rosengren (2005), Inoue et al. (2008). In their study they found that out-of-court restructurings of troubled firms in Japan were less effective in improving profitability than restructurings under Chapter 11 in the United States. However, we find that restructurings associated with new capital injections and new outside management are more likely to lead to genuine improvement in financial performance. In case of out of court restructuring since the final deal or negotiation between debtor and creditor is based on mutual comfort, convenience and compromise hence no drastic reduction in liabilities or expense s cut down on liabilities or expenses are initiated in companies. Hence as applicable in case of typical debtor in possession model the inefficiency in the company continues. It is also important to note that as per regression analysis, the financial restructuring i.e change in Debt to equity ratio does not have any positive effect on profitability. The outcome of this result proves that unless the debt restructuring leads to drastic reduction in liabilities or financial debt of companies it would not have any positive effect on profitability.

Effect of Operational Restructuring on Profitability

In this study change in return on sale or operating profit margin represent the operational restructuring action. If we analyse the data from march, 2016 till March 2022, it is crystal clear that on an average the operating profit margin of the company has been increasing on year to year basis. During the post -bankruptcy period the operating profit margin has been continuously showing upward trend across march, 20, March 21, March 22. This means that the insolvent companies as part of operational restructuring process has been continuously focussing on improved operating profit margin by way cut down in unnecessary operating expenses & optimising productivity through introduction of new efficient technology, cut down in manpower expenses, cut down in capital expense, cheaper logistic expenses, new market opportunities etc. A change in Return on Sales (RoS) i.e operating profit margin would most definitely have positive impact on profitability. It is clearly observed through regression analysis that Operational restructuring has significant and positive effect on post- bankruptcy performance. In fact as per this study the operational restructuring action brings the most critical structural change having potential to positively impact the profitability of insolvent companies. Under out of court settlement, operational restructuring is the most easily implementable action by existing debtor which does not require too much compromise or any drastic changes in company. Hence in view of the same it can be implemented & acted upon without much objection or difficulty.

Effect of Portfolio Restructuring Action on Post-Bankruptcy Performance / Profitability.

In this study we represent the portfolio restructuring by way of changes in Gross Fixed Asset Utilisation ratio (GFAUR). This means effect of changes in fixed asset usage on post-bankruptcy performance. A close analysis of Fixed Asset Utilisation ratio during march 2016 till March 2022, proves that over the years there has been decrease in fixed asset utilisation. This means that the company has not been able to fully utilise the fixed asset available with the company. This means productivity of company has been negatively impacted due to less usage of fixed asset. The company has been working inefficiently and not able to utilise its full potential. As per regression analysis, any change in Fixed asset utilisation ratio has a significant and positive effect on post-bankruptcy performance. In this analysis the under-utilisation of fixed asset as reflected through decrease in gross fixed asset utilisation ratio clearly has direct relation to decrease in profitability of the company. The result clearly shows that Portfolio restructuring has significant and positive effect on Post Bankruptcy performance, meaning if the change in fixed asset utilisation would have been increased on year to year basis it would have positively impact the Profitability of the company (ROA). In this case it is opposite hence the decrease in ROA. This outcome is very much in sync with theoretical studies by Li, Z., & Wang, F. (2020) who finds that the effectiveness of portfolio restructuring depends on factors such as the type of assets restructured, the firm's industry, and the economic environment.

Effect of Liquidity as Controlled Variable on Post-Bankruptcy Performance

In this case it was found that change in liquidity or current ratio has a negative but insignificant effect on post-bankruptcy performance. This means that if liquidity is controlled for regression analysis, any change in liquidity would have negative nit non-significant effect on post-bankruptcy performance. In case of out of court resolution the more liquid a company it have positive effect on profitability. Studies conducted by Vintila & Nenu (2016) and Bellouma (2011) found that negative correlation existed between profitability and liquidity.

CONCLUSION

The culmination of this study offers profound insights into the efficacy of out-of-court restructuring mechanisms in shaping the post-bankruptcy financial performance of distressed companies. The result from this study proves that out of court restructuring does result in significant changes in the post-bankruptcy financial performance of a company. The study makes an important contribution in establishing Private & Informal resolution mechanism as a credible tool of bankruptcy reslution in India. The study also provides an empirical evidence of the effectiveness of individual restructuring actions undertaken during post-bankruptcy period. The following three key conclusions can be drawn from the study,

Out of court settlement or Debtor in Possession (DIP) resolution model has significant positive impact on profitability or going concern value of company. The study provides evidence through statistical and regression analysis towards a much more positive and effective impact of debtor friendly resolution process on profitability. More importantly, the outcome of this study makes a strong case for exploring resolution / restructuring of company as against liquidation to facilitate debt recovery. The study also proves that corporate restructuring drastically improves the financial distress / bankruptcy condition (or the Altman Z score) of the company during post-bankruptcy period.

The study proves that among all other forms of restructuring, the Operational Restructuring has the most significant effect on the post-bankruptcy performance of company. The operational restructuring refers to cost reduction, technological improvement, employee retrenchment, change in Operational profit margin, reduction in Operational cost etc. resulting in operational efficiency in the company. These operational changes directly or indirectly effects the profitability of the company. While operational restructuring in some case may lead to negative impact on profitability in the short term, but in the longer run it would have a positive impact on profitability.

The study further proves that financial restructuring under out of court settlement, has a non-significant and negative effect on the profitability. Most evidence suggests de-leveraging or reduction of debt or enhancing the solvency position of the company through debt restructuring, debt transfer, distress sale or pay out etc. is the single most important priority for restructuring. Hence if there is no drastic changes in liability or debt condition it wold have negative impact on profitability. There are multiple studies which proves that a drastic reduction in debt would have positive impact on the profitability of the company.

Similarly, the study proves that Portfolio restructuring has a significant and positive effect on the post-bankruptcy financial performance of company. This means that any positive change in the usage of fixed asset or increase in efficient use of resources would have significant and positive effect on the profitability / post-bankruptcy financial performance of company. This outcome is in sync with studies that an efficient use of fixed asset would leads to higher productivity and increase in profitability for the company. But in certain cases if the increase in asset utilisation is not backed up by operational restructuring i.e cost reduction, technological changes, operating margin etc in the company, then it would have negative or no effect on profitability.

It is further concluded that in order to have an effective and meaningful effect of Out of court corporate restructuring on the company, there is a need to get the company subjected to a much longer term restructuring process. As per multiple studies, it takes a minimum of 6-10 years to show any significant effect of restructuring action on the long term financial health, profitability, going concern value and future business potential for the company. Accordingly any proposed resolution plan must be planned for a much longer years of resolution post- approval of resolution plan for the company.

The outcome from this study provides positive encouragement for Banks, NBFCs & other institutional creditors to seriously pursue / explore Corporate restructuring through out of court or informal resolution as the most preferred and primary method for corporate distress resolution. In this the key focus should be on Operational & Portfolio Restructuring along with Debt Restructuring for resolution. This would ensure a successful and value maximizing outcome for the company.

The findings underscore several critical conclusions:

Effect on Companies

Significant Positive Impact on Profitability: Out-of-court restructuring, facilitated through mechanisms like debtor-in-possession (DIP), demonstrates a significant positive impact on the profitability and financial health of companies post-bankruptcy. This highlights the effectiveness of private and informal resolution processes in revitalizing distressed businesses.

Significant Role Of Operational Restructuring: Operational restructuring emerges as a linchpin in the post-bankruptcy recovery process. Actions such as cost reduction, technological enhancement, and operational efficiency improvements play a pivotal role in driving sustained profitability and long-term viability.

Marginal Effects of Financial Restructuring: While financial restructuring is essential, its impact is nuanced. While a reduction in debt and enhancement of solvency are crucial, the study reveals that merely restructuring financial obligations may not suffice to drive substantial improvements in profitability. Drastic reductions in liabilities are necessary to yield positive outcomes.

Positive Effects of Portfolio restructuring: This is particularly in terms of optimizing fixed asset utilization, demonstrates a significant positive influence on post-bankruptcy performance. Efficient use of resources and strategic asset management contribute to enhanced productivity and profitability.

Long Term Perspective Of Study: The study underscores the importance of adopting a long-term perspective in corporate distress resolution. While immediate improvements may be observed, sustainable recovery and value maximization often require persistent efforts and continued restructuring initiatives over an extended period.

Business Implications

The findings of this study hold several implications for businesses, financial institutions, and policymakers:

Strategic Focus on Operational Efficiency: Companies facing financial distress should prioritize operational efficiency enhancements through cost optimization, technological innovation, and productivity improvements to drive post-bankruptcy recovery effectively.

Holistic Approach to Restructuring: Businesses and restructuring professionals should adopt a holistic approach to restructuring, encompassing operational, financial, and portfolio aspects to maximize the efficacy of recovery efforts.

Debt Reduction as a Priority: Financial institutions and creditors should recognize the importance of debt reduction in facilitating post-bankruptcy recovery. Negotiating substantial reductions in liabilities is crucial for restoring financial health and profitability.

Asset Optimization Strategies: Companies should focus on optimizing asset utilization and portfolio management strategies to enhance productivity and profitability post-bankruptcy. Strategic asset divestitures, mergers, and acquisitions can unlock value and drive sustainable growth.

Limitations Of Study

The study suffers from limitations of data, small sample size and limited evaluation period, which may constrain the generalizability of the findings. Despite these constraints, this research offers valuable contributions to understanding the dynamics of corporate distress resolution within the Indian context, providing actionable insights for stakeholders navigating these challenges. It provides important value addition to discussion on the effectiveness of corporate distress resolution more so in the context of out of court settlement. Even as the outcome of the study does not provide any definitive answers to our research questions yet it certainly points to positive directions.

REFERENCES

Acharya, V. V., & Agrawal, A. (2013). "Is Out-of-Court Restructuring Really Efficient? An Empirical Examination." *Journal of Financial Economics* 110 (2): 205-230. [Aghion, P., Hart, O., & Moore, J. (1992). The economics of bankruptcy reform. *Journal of Law Economics and Organization*, 8(3), 523–546.

Agrawal, A., González-Uribe, J. A., & Martínez-Correa, J. (2020). Measuring the Ex-Ante Incentive Effects of Bankruptcy Reorganization Procedures. *The Journal of Finance*, 75(1), 233–271.

Almeida, H., Campello, M., Cunha, I., & Weisbach, M. S. (2014). Corporate liquidity management: A conceptual framework and Survey. *Annual Review of Financial Economics*, 6(1), 132–145. DOI: 10.1146/annurev-financial-110613-034502

Altman, E. I. (1983). Measuring the ex-ante incentive effects of bankruptcy reorganization procedures. *The Journal of Finance*, 39(4), 1067–1089. DOI: 10.1111/j.1540-6261.1984.tb03893.x

Altman, E. I. (1983). A Further Empirical Investigation of the Bankruptcy Cost Question. *The Journal of Finance*, 38(2), 203–218.

Altman, E. I., & Hotchkiss, E. (2006). *Corporate financial distress and bankruptcy* (3rd ed.). John Wiley & Sons.

J. S. Ang, J. H. Chua and J. Mconnel, (1982). *The Administrative Costs Of Corporate Bankruptcy- A Note,* Journal Of Finance, vol. XXXVii, no.1

Annabi, A., Breton, M., & François, P. (2012). Resolution of financial distress under chapter 11. *Journal of Economic Dynamics & Control*, 36(12), 1867–1887. DOI: 10.1016/j.jedc.2012.06.004

Aslan, H., & Öztekin, Ö. (2019). The Effect of Out-of-Court Restructuring on Post-Restructuring Financial Performance: Evidence from Emerging Markets. *Emerging Markets Review*, 38, 100618.

Barnett, E. A., & Clark, R. C. (1996). The Determinants of Successful Turnarounds During Bankruptcies and Out-of-Court Workouts. *Journal of Economic Behavior & Organization*, 29(3), 459–489.

Bebchuk, L. A., & Fried, J. (2004). Executive Compensation and the Choice Between Bankruptcy and Out-of-Court Debt Restructuring. *The Journal of Finance*, 59(5), 2049–2082.

Berkovitch, E., & Israel, R. (1999). Optimal bankruptcy laws across different economic systems. *Review of Financial Studies*, 12(2), 347–377. DOI: 10.1093/rfs/12.2.347

Bernstein, S., Colonnelli, E., Giroud, X., & Iverson, B. (2019). Bankruptcy spillovers. *Journal of Financial Economics*, 133(3), 608–633. DOI: 10.1016/j.jfineco.2018.09.010

Betker, B. L. (1997). The administrative cost of debt restructurings: Some recent evidence. *Financial Management*, 26(4), 56–68. DOI: 10.2307/3666127

Bharath, S. T., & Denis, D. I. (2010). Do Secured Debtholders Dictate the Choice of Bankruptcy Procedures? An Empirical Investigation. *Journal of Financial Economics*, 95(1), 103–120.

Bharath, S. T., & Hertzel, M. G. (2005). The Choice Between Out-of-Court Debt Restructurings and Chapter 11 Bankruptcy: A Test of Competing Theories. *The Journal of Finance*, 60(2), 639–668.

Bolton, P., & Scharfstein, D. S. (1996). Optimal debt structure with multiple creditors. *Journal of Political Economy*, 104(1), 1–25. DOI: 10.1086/262015

Bris, A., Deroose, C., & De Schutter, O. (2004). The Impact of Out-of-Court Restructurings on Post-Bankruptcy Performance: Evidence from France. *Journal of Business Finance & Accounting*, 31(5-6), 875–912.

Bris, A., Welch, I., & Zhu, N. (2006). The costs of bankruptcy: Chapter 7 liquidation versus chapter 11 reorganization. *The Journal of Finance*, 61(3), 1253–1303. DOI: 10.1111/j.1540-6261.2006.00872.x

Broadie, M., Chernov, M., & Sundaresan, S. (2007). Optimal debt and equity values in the presence of chapter 7 and chapter 11. *The Journal of Finance*, 62(3), 1341–1377. DOI: 10.1111/j.1540-6261.2007.01238.x

Brown, D. T., James, C. M., & Mooradian, R. M. (1993). The information content of distressed restructurings involving public and private debt claims. *Journal of Financial Economics*, 33(1), 93–118. DOI: 10.1016/0304-405X(93)90026-8

Butler, H. N., & Mahoney, M. J. (1997). The Effect of Pre-Bankruptcy Restructuring on Debt Renegotiations. *The Journal of Finance*, 52(4), 1541–1570.

Cai, H. (2000). Delay in multilateral bargaining under complete information. *Journal of Economic Theory*, 93(2), 260–276. DOI: 10.1006/jeth.2000.2658

Campello, M., Gao, J., Qiu, J., & Zhang, Y. (2018). Bankruptcy and the cost of organized labor: Evidence from union elections. *Review of Financial Studies*, 31(3), 980–1013. DOI: 10.1093/rfs/hhx117

Carapeto, M. (1999). Does debtor-in-possession add value? (IFA Working Paper No. 294-1999). Retrievefrom https://papers.ssrn.com/sol3/papers.cfm?abstract_id=161428

Chatterjee, S., Dhillon, U. S., & Ramirez, G. G. (1995). Coercive tender and exchange offers in distressed high-yield debt restructurings: An empirical analysis. *Journal of Financial Economics*, 38(3), 333–360. DOI: 10.1016/0304-405X(94)00815-I

Chatterjee, S., Dhillon, U. S., & Ramírez, G. G. (1996). Resolution of financial distress: Debt restructurings via chapter 11, pre-packaged bankruptcies, and workouts. *Financial Management Association*, 25(1), 5-18.

Chung, K. N.. (2021). Debt Restructuring, Operating Efficiency, and Long-Term Growth: Evidence from Distressed Firms. *Strategic Management Journal*, 42(1), 159–189.

Dahiya, S., John, K., Puri, M., & Ramirez, G. (2003). The dynamics of debtor-in-possession financing: Bankruptcy resolution and the role of prior lenders. *Journal of Financial Economics*, 69, 259–280. DOI: 10.1016/S0304-405X(03)00113-2

DeAngelo, H., & Stark, R. W. (1986). Bankruptcy Reorganization and Stockholder-Bondholder Conflicts. *The Journal of Finance*, 41(2), 347–364.

DeStefano, A., & Gottlieb, D. (1997). Out-of-Court Workouts vs. Formal Bankruptcy: An Empirical Investigation of Distressed Real Estate Ventures. *Real Estate Economics*, 25(2), 297–330.

Ducháček, M., & Schőnlaub, M. (2015). Restructuring and Resolution of Distressed Banks: Lessons from the Great Financial Crisis. *Journal of Banking & Finance*, 57, 30–41.

Eberhart, A. C., Altman, E. I., & Aggarwal, R. (1999). The equity performance of firms emerging from bankruptcy. *The Journal of Finance*, 54(5), 1855–1868. DOI: 10.1111/0022-1082.00169

Froot, K. A., & Shleifer, A. Y. (2000). Financial Crises and Restructuring: Some Lessons from East Asia. *The Journal of Law & Economics*, 43(2), 249–294.

Garrido, J. M. Out-Of-Court Debt Restructuring, World Bank Study, World Bank (2012)

Gertner, R., & Scharfstein, D. (1991). A theory of workouts and the effects of reorganization law. *The Journal of Finance*, 46, 1189–1222.

Gertner, R., Scharfstein, D., & Stein, J. (2013). Internal and External Governance and the Choice Between Out-of-Court Restructuring and Bankruptcy. *The Journal of Finance*, 68(5), 1911–1944.

Gertner, R., & Skeel, D. (1999). The Dynamics of Out-of-Court Workouts. *The Journal of Finance*, 54(6), 1559–1579.

Giammarino, R. M. (1989). The resolution of financial distress. *Review of Financial Studies*, 2(1), 25–47. DOI: 10.1093/rfs/2.1.25

Gilson, R. J. (2003). A Model of Out-of-Court Debt Restructuring. *The Journal of Finance*, 58(3), 1145–1162.

Gilson, S., John, K., & Lang, L. (1990). Troubled Debt Restructurings - An Emperical Study Of Private Reorgination Of Firms In Default. *Journal of Financial Economics*, 27(2), 315–353. DOI: 10.1016/0304-405X(90)90059-9

Gilson, S. C., John, K., & Lang, L. H. P. (1990). Troubled debt restructurings: An empirical study of private reorganization of firms in default. *Journal of Financial Economics*, 27(2), 315–353. DOI: 10.1016/0304-405X(90)90059-9

Gilson, S. C., & Murphy, K. J. (1998). Troubled debt restructurings: An efficient approach to corporate workouts. *Journal of Applied Corporate Finance*, 10(3), 84–97.

Gupta, S. K. (2020). Performance Analysis of Electrosteel Steels Ltd. Pre, During and Post CIRP: A Case Study. *The Management Accountant Journal*, 55(2), 91–95. DOI: 10.33516/maj.v55i2.91-95p

Holder-Webb, L., Lopez, T., & Regier, P. (2005). The Performance Consequences of Operational Restructurings. *Review of Quantitative Finance and Accounting*, 25(4), 319–339. DOI: 10.1007/s11156-005-5458-7

Hotchkiss, E., John, K., Thornbern, K., & Mooradian, R. (2008). *Bankruptcy and The resolution of Financial Distress* (Vol. 2). Handbook Of Emperical Corporate Finance.

Hotchkiss, E. S. (1995). Post-bankruptcy performance and management turnover. *The Journal of Finance*, 50(1), 3–21. DOI: 10.1111/j.1540-6261.1995.tb05165.x

Hotchkiss, E. S., John, K., Mooradian, R. M., & Thorburn, K. S. (2008). Bankruptcy and the resolution of financial distress. In Eckbo, B. E. (Ed.), *Handbook of Empirical Corporate Finance* (Vol. 2, pp. 235–287). North Holland: Elsevier. DOI: 10.1016/B978-0-444-53265-7.50006-8

Jensen, M. C. (1989). Active investors, LBOs, and the privatization of bankruptcy. *The Bank of America Journal of Applied Corporate Finance*, 2(1), 35–44. DOI: 10.1111/j.1745-6622.1989.tb00551.x

Kalay, A., Sighal, R., & Tashjian, E. (2007). Is Chapter 11 costly? *Journal of Financial Economics*, 84(3), 772–796. DOI: 10.1016/j.jfineco.2006.04.001

Kovak, D., & Srhoj, S. (2022). The Impact of Bargaining Failures in Out-of-Court Restructuring: Evidence from a Novel Dataset. *Journal of Corporate Finance*, 78, 102664.

Lomuscio, A.. (2015). Debt Restructuring in Distress: Out-of-Court vs. In-Court Workouts. *Journal of Financial Transformation*, 34(3), 207–242.

Mateti, J. K. (2013). R.S and G. Vaudevan, *Resolution of financial distress: A theory of the choice between Chapter 11 and workout. Journal of Financial Stability*, 9(2), 196–209. DOI: 10.1016/j.jfs.2013.03.004

Modigliani, F., & Miller, M. H. (1958). The cost of capital, corporation finance, and the theory of investment. *The American Economic Review*, 48(3), 261–275.

Mooradian, R. M. (1994). The effect of bankruptcy protection on investment: Chapter 11 as a screening device. *The Journal of Finance*, 49(4), 1403–1430. DOI: 10.1111/j.1540-6261.1994.tb02459.x

Ram Singh and Hitesh kumar Thakkar (2021). Settlements and Resolutions Under the Insolvency and Bankruptcy Code: Assessing the Impact of Covid-19. Journal of Business Ethics, 197(3), 607-626.

Shevlin, P., & Skeel, D. (2005). Out-of-Court Workouts, Formal Bankruptcy, and Value Maximization. *The American Bankruptcy Law Journal*, 79(3), 489–545.

Shleifer, A., & Vishny, R. W. (1992). Liquidation values and debt capacity: A market equilibrium approach. *The Journal of Finance*, 47(4), 1343–1366. DOI: 10.1111/j.1540-6261.1992.tb04661.x

Srhoj, S., Kovač, D., Shapiro, J. N., & Filer, R. K. (2023). The Impact of Delay: Evidence from Formal Out-of-Court Restructuring. *Journal of Corporate Finance*, 78, 102626. DOI: 10.1016/j.jcorpfin.2022.102319

Tashjian, E., Lease, R. C., & McConnell, J. J. (1996). Prepacks: An empirical analysis of Pre-packaged bankruptcies. *Journal of Financial Economics*, 40(1), 135–162. DOI: 10.1016/0304-405X(95)00837-5

Vintilă Georgeta and Elena Alexandra Nenu (2016) " Liquidity and Profitability Analysis on the Romanian Listed Companies", *Journal of Eastern Europe Research in Business & Economics*, Vol. 2016 (2016).

Wang, J.. (2016). Financial Restructuring, Operational Turnaround, and Firm Performance: Evidence from China. *Strategic Management Journal*, 37(12), 2507–2532.

Warner, J. B. (1977). Bankruptcy costs: Some evidence. *The Journal of Finance*, 32(2), 337–347. DOI: 10.2307/2326766

Warner, J. T., & Tortellini, R. E. (1997). Financial reconstructing under different legal systems: Evidence from out-of-court restructures. *The Review of Economics and Statistics*, 79(4), 612–625.

White, M. J. (1994). Corporate bankruptcy as a filtering device: Chapter 11 reorganizations and out-of-court debt restructurings. *Journal of Law Economics and Organization*, 10(2), 268–295.

APPENDIX

Status of CIRPs as on March 31, 2022. Table 1

Status of CIRPs	No. of CIRPs
Admitted	**5258**
Closed	**3406**
Closed on Appeal / Review / Settled	731
Closed by Withdrawal under Section 12A	586
Closed by Resolution	480
Commencement of Liquidation	1609
Pending outcome	**1852**

(sourc: IBBI Newsletter January -March, 2022, Volume 33)

Chapter 4
Corporate Disclosure and Transparency as a Tool of Socially Responsible Risk Management

Hammad Hassan Mirza
University of Sargodha, Pakistan

Haroon Hussain
https://orcid.org/0000-0002-6499-2227
University of Sargodha, Pakistan

Rana Yassir Hussain
https://orcid.org/0000-0002-6951-1322
University of Education, Lahore, Pakistan

Muhammad Waqar Ahmed
University of Sargodha, Pakistan

Muhammad Adil
University of Education, Lahore, Pakistan

ABSTRACT

The issue of access to information becomes more critical when it comes to the modern corporate world. The importance of easily accessible information, as and when needed, in corporate governance has been widely recognized in the literature. Transparency in corporate practices can help in attracting capital and maintaining confidence in the capital markets. The demand for transparency and disclosure is driven by investors who continuously demand better reporting and greater access

DOI: 10.4018/979-8-3693-5733-0.ch004

to information because such information is material to their investment decisions. Disclosure facilitates corporate governance by enabling shareholders to monitor the actions of management and hold them accountable. However, the relationship between disclosure and corporate governance practices especially when it comes to risk management is complex. Increase in disclosure without assurances that the information can be effectively used by shareholders may not necessarily result in improved governance practices.

INTRODUCTION

In this era of digitalization and technology not only individuals but also organizations need access to free and authentic information to make prompt decisions. The access to information helps and promote effective decision making and reduces chances of error. The issue of access to information becomes more critical when it comes to the modern corporate world. The importance of easily accessible information, as and when needed, in corporate governance has been widely recognized in the literature. Transparency in corporate practices can help in attracting capital and maintaining confidence in the capital markets, while weak disclosure and non-transparent practices can contribute to unethical behavior and a loss of market integrity. The demand for transparency and disclosure is driven by investors who continuously demand better reporting and greater access to information because such information is material to their investment decisions. Disclosure facilitates corporate governance by enabling shareholders to monitor the actions of management and hold them accountable. However, the relationship between disclosure and corporate governance practices especially when it comes to risk management is complex. Increase in disclosure without assurances that the information can be effectively used by shareholders may not necessarily result in improved governance practices. To be effective, disclosure must be accessible and reliable in the sight to investors. Disclosure of material information contributes to liquid and efficient markets by empowering investors to make informed decisions. Corporate governance framework should ensure that disclosure requirements should not place redundant administrative expenditure on companies. But still transparency and disclosure are the critical tools for influencing corporate behavior and protecting investor interests.

Organizational Risk Management Framework (ORMF)

The importance of risk management framework for a modern day corporation is vital. According to Investopedia "An effective risk management framework seeks to protect an organization's capital base and earnings without hindering growth.

Furthermore, investors are more willing to invest in companies with good risk management practices. This generally results in lower borrowing costs, easier access to capital for the firm, and improved long-term performance". Such frameworks not only help corporation in sustainable growth of its capital base but also ensure long run profitability and solvency of the organization. Therefore risk management framework is considered to be the most critical factor of a business success. Risk management framework can be defined in number of ways and its components may also vary from organization to organization. Generally, risk management framework is defined as a

"Systematic process designed by the organization to identify, assess, mitigate and monitor the risk associated with its business operations with an ultimate goal of protecting organizational objectives from external and internal uncertainties either financial or administrative"

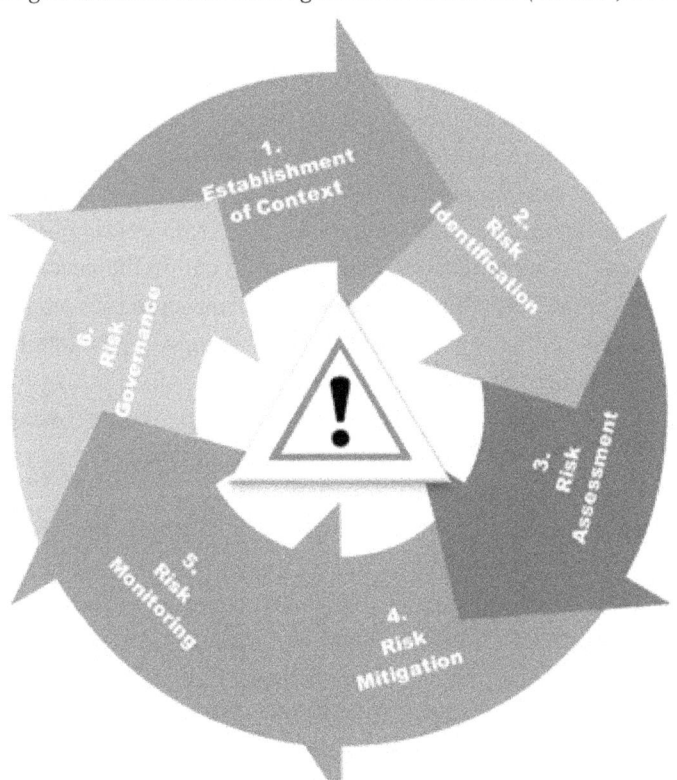

Figure 1. Organizational Risk Management Framework (ORMF) Flow

A typical corporate risk management framework consists of six key stages. The first stage is establishment of context of risk management. Organization faces multidimensional risk which can be related to its financial relationships with customers and fund providers e.g. banks and sometimes such risks are critical but non-financial in nature e.g. human resource risk or operational risks. An ideal ORMF should be cable of distinguishing different types of risk based on their nature and put them in their right context. The second important stage is identification of potential or severity of risk for the organization. Once organization successfully put risk into its right context it is equally important to priorities these risks in terms of their severity. The risk which can be highly damaging for the organization are those which leaves long lasting impact on the organization and are costly to recover. Such high potential risk whether financial in nature or otherwise must be addressed on priority basis. The third stage is risk assessment which meant to calculate the likelihood of occurrence of respective risky event. Not all risk events occur at the same time therefore, organization should know the likelihood of occurrence. This will further help organization to allocate funds in an appropriate manner to make risk mitigation strategies which is the fourth stage of ORMF. Risk mitigation is all about making decision to control the impact of risk on organizational goals and objectives. These strategies can include both vanilla and exotic strategies. Vanilla strategies include the common risk management techniques which are mostly used by other participants of the same industry e.g. making portfolios or using derivative instruments in case of financially risky event while exotic strategies may include more complicated methods of risk management e.g hedging using exotic options etc. In the next stage it is also important to monitor the outcomes of the risk mitigation strategies on organizations objectives. If the risk mitigation strategy is not giving desired results then organization should quickly take the counter strategy to overcome the loss occurred due the previous strategy. Finally, risk governance is a broader context which includes training of organizational machinery and ensure compliance of safety procedures so that organization can be proactive in managing risk.

The ORMF helps an organization to prioritize its strategies for efficient control of future risks. Every organization has limited supply of resources in terms of money and human resource therefore, it cannot afford to waste its resources on all types of risks all the times. An effective organizational management demands efficiency use of resources while managing risk. This calls for classification of risk in terms of urgency and severity. Following it the ORMF matrix which arises as result of discrete classification of risk types in terms of urgency and severity. In this chapter we name them as Fire Snake Risk, Calendar Risk, Crank Risk and Future Risk. The most crucial and damaging event which is both urgent in nature and also severe can be called Fire-Snake Risk. These risk are the result of a paper agreement with a creditor organization from whom organization has made any loan arrangement and whose dead line is approaching at a predetermined point of time in near future. Any change in interest rates may cause real damage to the financial health of the organization therefore, such risks should be identified as most crucial and organization should make effective strategies to manage these risks. On the other hand calendar risks are the routine short term risks and less damaging for an organization. Theses risk are mostly related with the learning curves of the organizational system. As people get trained these risk automatically starts disappearing with the time because these risks emerge as result of wrong decision of management in day to day business. Risk can be further categories into Crank risk which is not severe in nature but must be addressed on urgent basis because it can have damaging impact on corporate social repute. Environmental hazard are crank risk which an organization can delay without impacting its profitability but they are often urgent in nature due to the fact that environmental protection agencies may put ban of operations of the organization. That is why most organizations tries to address such risk on urgent basis. Finally there are risk which an organization cannot address at present time but they can be extremely damaging for the organization in future. In case of business dependent upon import of raw materials or exports of finish good, exchange rate risk is a future potential risk. To manage such risk organization may apply hedging strategies so protect its operations form exchange rate exposure.

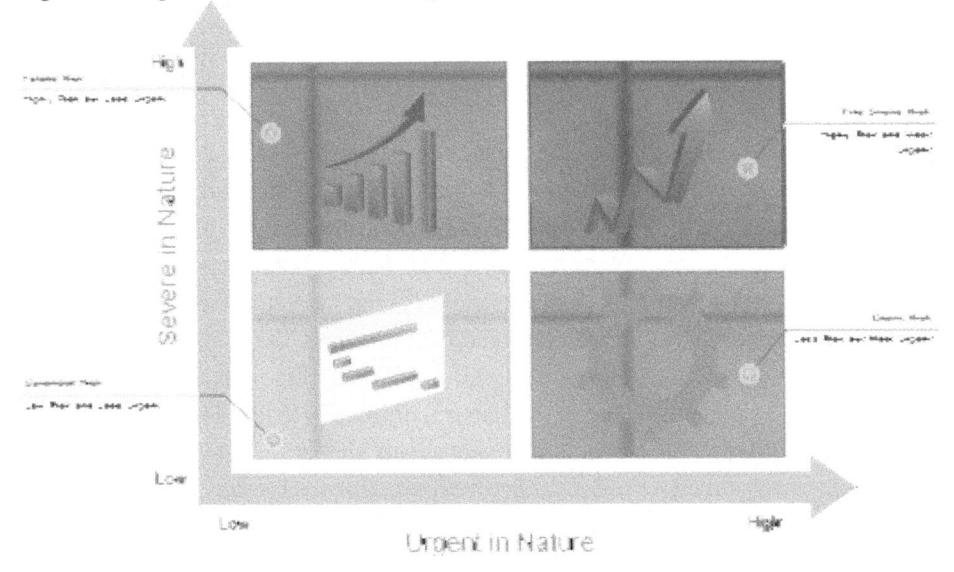

Figure 2. Organizational Risk Management Framework Matrix

Information Asymmetry Problem

The seminal work of George Ackerlof in the year 1970, laid the foundation of theory of information asymmetry. Akerlof's analysis begins with a fundamental concept: information asymmetry. In many markets, sellers possess more information about the quality of goods or services than buyers. This information asymmetry can lead to adverse selection, where the presence of low-quality products drives out high-quality ones, resulting in market failure. Akerlof uses the market for used cars as a paradigmatic example of the "Market for Lemons." In this market, sellers possess superior information about the quality of their vehicles compared to potential buyers.

Figure 3. Balancing of Information availability between Buyer and seller

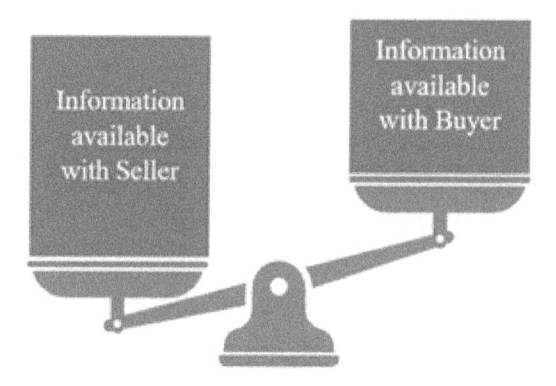

While some used cars are of high quality ("peaches"), others may suffer from hidden defects or problems ("lemons"). Buyers face uncertainty about the true condition of the cars they consider purchasing. In the presence of information asymmetry, **adverse selection and moral hazard** occur as buyers adjust their expectations based on the average quality of goods available in the market. As a result, sellers of high-quality products may be discouraged from entering the market, leading to a disproportionate presence of low-quality goods. This adverse selection process can undermine trust and confidence in the market, ultimately leading to its unraveling. Akerlof highlights the role of signaling mechanisms in mitigating the adverse effects of information asymmetry. Signaling involves the use of observable characteristics or signals to convey information about the quality of goods or services. In the context of the used car market, sellers may employ signaling strategies such as warranties, vehicle inspections, or maintenance records to signal the quality of their cars and distinguish them from lemons.

Figure 4. Thin line between moral hazard and adverse selection

Adverse Selection
- Occurs before the transaction
- Has a chance to get into the trasaction when it was not eligible

Moral Hazard
- Occurs after the transaction
- Has incentive to engage in risk activities

Role of Disclosure Regulations

The essence of the above discussion is that business needs to reduce information asymmetry to get better reward in terms of investors and creditors confidence. The "Market for Lemons" has profound implications for market efficiency and the role of regulation. Inefficient outcomes, such as reduced trade volume and diminished consumer welfare, can result from information asymmetry and adverse selection. Policymakers may intervene through regulatory measures, such as disclosure requirements, quality standards, or certification programs, to improve market transparency and mitigate adverse selection. While Akerlof (1978) analysis focuses on the used car market, the concept of the "Market for Lemons" has broader applications across various industries and markets characterized by information asymmetry. The insights gleaned from Akerlof's research extend to sectors such as insurance, financial services, healthcare, and online marketplaces, where information disparities influence consumer decision-making and market outcomes. In conclusion, George Akerlof's research on the "Market for Lemons" offers invaluable insights into the dynamics of information asymmetry and adverse selection in markets. By recognizing the challenges posed by asymmetric information, we gain a deeper understanding of the mechanisms driving market outcomes and the potential for market failure. As we contemplate the implications of Akerlof's findings, it becomes evident that signaling mechanisms and regulatory interventions play crucial roles in addressing information asymmetry and enhancing market efficiency. Moving forward, policymakers and market participants must remain vigilant in addressing the adverse effects of information asymmetry to foster more transparent, efficient, and equitable markets.

Corporate Disclosure and Agency Problem

In the light of Akerlof's theory of information asymmetry it is understandable that lack of information can have fatal financial consequences for any organization and calls for disclosure and transparency in organizational operations. It is therefore, in the best interest of the organization to disclose its information to their stakeholders and make their operations transparent. However, there is a dark side of disclosure and transparency and that is rival's reaction. The corporate world is prone to a high level of competition and undue disclosure of internal business information, business secrets, can make an organization liable to face rival's reaction. Therefore, there is a tradeoff between disclosure and completion. More disclosure can put the organization into a more competitive environment and low disclosure can cause problems associated with information asymmetry, as discussed in previous section.

In summary, risk disclosure involves communicating relevant information. Companies disclose information for several reasons, such as reducing agency costs, lowering information asymmetry among market participants, decreasing shareholder uncertainty, reducing the cost of capital, and improving the market price of securities. Several studies have been conducted to explain the phenomenon of disclosure and the variation in disclosure practices among companies and its impact on corporate governance practices. The theoretical domain of these studies include agency theory, signaling theory, stakeholder theory, political cost theory, and benefit-cost theory. These theories help us understanding the effects of various factors, such as corporate governance and disclosure practices on corporate decision making. We suggest that some of these theories are relevant for discussing the motivations behind risk disclosure.

Agency theory, introduced by Jensen and Meckling (1976) has been particularly influential in accounting over the past three decades. The theory explains how information asymmetry between shareholders, managers, and creditors can be mitigated by monitoring the opportunistic behaviors of managers. The theory highlights the inherent moral hazard between shareholders (principals) and managers (agents), which leads to agency costs. It is important to note that firm and its related parties is the unit of analysis in agency theory and it advocates relationship which links various partners of the firm. The theory addresses issues that arise when the goals of the principal and agent conflict and when they have different attitudes toward risk.

In recent years, corporate risk reporting has gained significant attention among academicians and practitioners (See for instance Liu et al., 2024; He et al. 2024; Hummel & Jobst, 2024 etc). Agency theory views disclosure as a mechanism to reduce cost of conflict among parties. For instance, by publishing annual report a particular corporation tries to reduce information asymmetry and let their stakeholders aware about their state of affairs. Disclosure thus serves to assure shareholders and other stakeholders that the company is well-managed and accountable, thereby enhancing shareholder confidence and reducing information asymmetry, agency costs, and investor uncertainty.

Corporate risk related disclosure involves communicating information about how various risks are identified, managed, analyzed, and evaluated (Amran et al., 2008). According to previous studies this information includes a firm's strategies, characteristics, operations, and external factors. Jensen and Meckling emphasized that a firm's motivations, objectives, and policies are crucial for effective disclosure. Financial reports should therefore serve as valuable assets that enable users to assess the firm's financial position and performance. Disclosure is influenced by a variety of supply and demand forces, creating an information lag between managers, who prepare financial reports, and investors, who use the reports. It is unanimously agreed among researchers that disclosure is essential for mitigating agency problems. From an agency perspective, increased transparency through disclosure reduces information asymmetries and the cost of capital. Managers must present relevant information to demonstrate they are acting in the best interests of shareholders and debtholders.

A pertinent question to ask is that why investor needs information? Investors demand information from companies because organization has more knowledge about the true and fair state of current and future performance of organization than outside investors. Financial reports provide investors with an opportunity to evaluate disclosed information and assess the various risks a firm may face in the future. These reports are designed to meet the needs of different user groups, enabling them to make accurate investment decisions. This also allows investors to make decisions based on expected returns and risk considerations of the respective organization.

Every company faces a unique type of risk due its unique organizational setup and operations it is involved in. Investors therefore, need to understand the nature and exposure of these risks and the strategies which the company is expected to employ to control of mitigate them. The role of information become crucial because information helps investors identify the types of risks a company might encounter and assess its value through stock price forecasts. The Institute of Chartered Accountants in England and Wales (ICAEW) has published multiple studies on financial risk reporting and prospective financial information. According to the ICAEW, corporate risk disclosure enhances risk management, boosts accountability for investor protection, and improves the usefulness of financial reporting. Lins, Servaes and Tamayo (2017) found that during the 2008-2009 financial crisis, high corporate socially responsibility firms earned higher stock returns than did low corporate social responsibility firms.

Several studies reveal a significant market reaction as a result of company's disclosure about its investment in a resource planning system which acmes the importance of including future non-financial information in financial reports. Risk disclosures offer several benefits to companies, including change management, reducing capital costs, increasing shareholder wealth, lowering the likelihood of financial failure, determining the company's risk profile, and estimating the market value of securities. This underscores the critical role of risk disclosure for companies.

One important critical point to be considered at this point is the reliability of informational disclose by the organization. If information is fabricated or is not accurate, it can have severe consequences for both the organization and the economy. The 2008 global financial crisis, which impacted several companies, drew significant attention from investors. Additionally, the 2017 fraud cases involving British Telecom shook investor confidence in the financial information provided by companies. These events have prompted companies to be more transparent with investors. Besides financial information, companies must also disclose non-financial information, which includes details about the risks they face. The quality of risk information is reflected in corporate risk disclosures.

Contributing Towards Socially Responsible Governance

Corporate Finance Institute (https://corporatefinanceinstitute.com/) defines corporate social responsibility (CSR) as follows. "CSR refers to strategies that companies put into action as part of corporate governance that are designed to ensure the company's operations are ethical and beneficial for society". Socially Responsible Governance (SRG) aims to develop corporate strategies which in the best interest of the society in general. It calls for commitment to openness and honesty in financial dealings, attract investor through transparent financial reporting and access to financial information. Investopedia explains CSR as:

- Corporate social responsibility is a business model by which companies make a concerted effort to operate in ways that enhance rather than degrade society and the environment.
- CSR can help improve society and promote a positive brand image for companies.
- CSR includes four categories: environmental impacts, ethical responsibility, philanthropic endeavors, and financial responsibilities.

In the context of risk management strategies following are some important points an organizational manager should consider before making risk mitigating strategy so the organization may achieve it goal in accordance with the dynamics of socially responsible governance.

Figure 5. Risk management strategies

Factors Influencing Organizational Risk Taking
- *Internal factors*: organizational culture, leadership style, and risk tolerance,
- *External factors:* industry competition, regulatory environment, and market dynamics.

Risk Management Practices
- Risk assessment, risk monitoring, and risk mitigation methods e.g insurance, hedging, and diversification.

Organizational Culture and Risk-taking
- Cultural norms, values, and beliefs shape organizational risk perceptions, influencing decision-making and risk tolerance. Leaders can foster a risk-aware culture by promoting transparency, education, and inclusive risk management practices.

Leadership and Decision Making
- Transformational leadership encourages risk-taking by inspiring innovation and trust, while transactional leadership may discourage it by emphasizing routine and adherence to established procedures, potentially stifling creativity and initiative.

Risk Appetite and Risk Tolerance
- Risk appetite is the level of risk an organization is willing to pursue for potential rewards, while risk tolerance is the acceptable variation from set objectives. Organizations measure risk tolerance through risk assessments, setting thresholds, and monitoring key performance indicators.

Behavioral Aspects of Risk-taking
- Behavioral economics principles like loss aversion and overconfidence, along with psychological factors such as groupthink and confirmation bias, significantly shape organizational risk-taking by affecting decision-making processes.

Summary and Conclusion

Organizations can integrate social responsibility principles into their risk management frameworks by incorporating ethical considerations, environmental concerns, and social impacts into their risk assessment and mitigation strategies in the following ways:

Ethical Considerations

a) *Code of Conduct*: Establishing a code of conduct that aligns risk management practices with ethical standards.
b) *Stakeholder Engagement*: Engaging stakeholders to understand their ethical concerns and expectations.
c) *Transparent Reporting*: Ensuring transparency in decision-making processes and reporting on ethical considerations.

Environmental Concerns

a) *Sustainability Assessments*: Conducting environmental impact assessments to evaluate the potential effects of organizational activities on the environment.
b) *Green Initiatives*: Implementing strategies to reduce carbon footprints, such as energy-efficient processes and waste reduction.
c) **Compliance**: Adhering to environmental regulations and standards to mitigate legal and reputational risks.

Social Impacts

a) *Community Engagement*: Engaging with local communities to understand their needs and address potential social impacts.
b) *Social Investment*: Investing in community development projects and social programs that align with organizational goals.
c) *Human Rights*: Ensuring that business practices do not violate human rights and are aligned with social responsibility standards.

By incorporating these principles into their risk management frameworks, organizations can enhance their reputation, build stakeholder trust, and achieve long-term sustainable success. This integration can be achieved through dedicated corporate social responsibility (CSR) policies, regular training for employees, and embedding these principles into the strategic planning and decision-making processes.

REFERENCES

Akerlof, G. A. (1978). The market for "lemons": Quality uncertainty and the market mechanism. In *Uncertainty in economics* (pp. 235–251). Academic Press. DOI: 10.1016/B978-0-12-214850-7.50022-X

Amran, A., Manaf Rosli Bin, A., & Che Haat Mohd Hassan, B. (2008). Risk reporting: An exploratory study on risk management disclosure in Malaysian annual reports. *Managerial Auditing Journal*, 24(1), 39–57. DOI: 10.1108/02686900910919893

He, F., Chen, L., Hao, J., & Wu, J. (2024). Financial market development and corporate risk management: Evidence from Shanghai crude oil futures launched in China. *Energy Economics*, 129, 107250. DOI: 10.1016/j.eneco.2023.107250

Hummel, K., & Jobst, D. (2024). An overview of corporate sustainability reporting legislation in the European Union. *Accounting in Europe*, 1-36.

Lins, K. V., Servaes, H., & Tamayo, A. (2017). Social capital, trust, and firm performance: The value of corporate social responsibility during the financial crisis. *the Journal of Finance*, 72(4), 1785-1824.

Liu, W., Lin, G., & He, Q. (2024). Enhanced management information disclosure responsibilities and corporate risk-taking: Evidence from the accountability system for errors in China. *International Review of Economics & Finance*, 89, 511–531. DOI: 10.1016/j.iref.2023.10.028

Meckling, W. H., & Jensen, M. C. (1976). *Theory of the Firm.* Managerial Behavior, Agency Costs and Ownership Structure.

Chapter 5
The Auditor's Guide to Corporate Social Responsibility:
Enhancing Ethical Practices

Shujah ur Rahman
https://orcid.org/0000-0002-7794-9279
University of Education, Lahore, Pakistan

Nyla Saleem
School of Humanities and Social Sciences, Pakistan

Yasir Habib
Institute of Energy Policy and Research, Malaysia

Saba Sattar
Government Technical Training Institute for Women, Pakistan

ABSTRACT

Auditors are essential in guiding companies toward responsible and sustainable business practices. Their expertise in assessing and verifying CSR initiatives is crucial for ensuring that organizations meet the expectations of stakeholders, comply with regulatory standards, and contribute positively to society and the environment. As CSR continues to gain prominence in corporate strategy, the role of auditors will remain integral to fostering ethical business practices and driving meaningful change. To ensure accountability and transparency, auditors must verify that CSR disclosures are accurate and comply with frameworks set by organizations such as the Global Reporting Initiative (GRI) and the Sustainability Accounting Standards Board (SASB). The importance of technology and innovation in the auditing process

DOI: 10.4018/979-8-3693-5733-0.ch005

cannot be overstated. Auditors can boost stakeholders' trust and confidence in the company's ethical and sustainable operations by employing advance technology to ensure the quality of CSR reports.

INTRODUCTION

Corporate Social Responsibility (CSR) has become an essential component of modern business practices, impacting how corporations operate and interact with stakeholders. This chapter investigates the interactions of auditing, marketing, and accounting with CSR. CSR contributes significantly to auditing by increasing transparency, accountability, and stakeholder trust in a company's ethical, social, and environmental activities. Auditors are responsible for checking the quality and completeness of CSR disclosures and ensuring that they adhere to relevant standards such as the Sustainability Accounting Standards Board (SASB) and the Global Reporting Initiative (GRI). This verification process entails analysing the methodology used to measure and report CSR operations, examining the efficacy of CSR-related risk management strategies, and incorporating CSR concerns into overall financial audits (Christensen et al., 2021). Auditors assist organisations in demonstrating their commitment to sustainable and responsible business practices by ensuring the trustworthiness of CSR information, creating more confidence among investors, regulators, and the general public. Regardless of troubles such as a lack of standardised criteria and the ever-changing nature of CSR requirements, auditors play an important role in promoting long-term company sustainability and ethical leadership (Albuquerque et al., 2019; Becchetti et al., 2015).

1. The Importance of CSR for Auditors

Auditors play a vital role in assuring the correctness, transparency, and dependability of CSR-related disclosures. As firms increasingly integrate CSR into their core operations, auditors are responsible with ensuring that these activities are appropriately documented and in compliance with set standards (Boubaker et al., 2020). Auditors analyse the effectiveness of CSR policies, assess associated risks, and ensure that CSR activities are accurately recorded in financial statements. This supervision is critical for preserving stakeholder trust and corporate integrity since it validates that a company's CSR claims are true and supported by verifiable facts. Auditors contribute to accountability, ethical corporate practices, and the legitimacy of CSR activities in the eyes of investors, regulators, and the general public by providing this assurance (Cai et al., 2016).

CSR efforts cover a wide range of activities aimed at encouraging ethical behaviour, environmental sustainability, and social welfare. Understanding CSR is critical for auditors for a number of reasons:

Reporting and Regulatory Compliance: Auditors play an important role in ensuring that corporations follow an ever-increasing number of CSR-related legislation and reporting requirements, including those described by the Global Reporting Initiative (GRI) and the Sustainability Accounting Standards Board (SASB). This includes carefully reviewing CSR disclosures to ensure that they accurately reflect the company's actions and impacts, as well as that they meet regulatory requirements. Effective auditing in this context aids in the prevention of discrepancies, reduces the risk of noncompliance, and improves the credibility of corporate social responsibility reports. Auditors contribute to the overall goal of ethical and responsible business operations by verifying that CSR disclosures match regulatory standards (Du et al., 2020).

Risk Management: Auditors place a high value on CSR in risk management since it aids in the identification, evaluation, and mitigation of potential risks related with a company's social, environmental, and governance activities. CSR activities can have an impact on a company's risk profile by addressing issues like environmental sustainability, labour standards, and ethical governance, all of which can have significant legal, financial, and reputational ramifications. Auditors evaluate how well a firm manages these CSR-related risks and if enough controls are in place to reduce them. This includes assessing the strength of the company's CSR strategies and how they fit into the overall risk management framework. Auditors assist in ensuring that potential risks are proactively managed and disclosed, so protecting the organisation from unexpected liabilities and improving overall business resilience. This proactive strategy not only promotes good risk management, but it also reaffirms the company's commitment to ethical and sustainable practices, ultimately contributing to long-term organisational stability and stakeholder trust (Godfrey, 2005).

Financial Management: Auditors place a high value on Corporate Social Responsibility (CSR) since it influences and reflects a company's overall financial health and stability. Auditors examine how CSR initiatives impact financial performance by analysing associated costs, benefits, and potential returns on investment (Cheng et al., 2014).

2. CSR Evaluation and Auditors' Role

Auditors play an important role in evaluating Corporate Social Responsibility (CSR) by ensuring that CSR-related actions and disclosures are accurate, transparent, and accountable. Their major role is to ensure that a company's CSR claims are supported by accurate data and follow specified reporting guidelines. This entails a thorough evaluation of the methodology used to measure and report on CSR initiatives, ensuring that they accurately reflect real performance and effect. Auditors evaluate the performance of CSR initiatives, finding potential areas for improvement and ensuring that all CSR-related risks are properly addressed. They also assess whether CSR initiatives are integrated into the company's overall risk management and governance structures.

Verification of CSR Disclosures: Auditors examine and validate the accuracy and completeness of CSR disclosures. The verification process entails reviewing the methodology and data sources utilised by the organisation to report on its CSR initiatives, such as environmental impact, social contributions, and governance standards. They undertake rigorous audits to uncover any discrepancies or inconsistencies in the reporting, protecting the company's reputation and stakeholder trust from misleading or false information. The verification method used by auditors helps organisations maintain responsibility while also demonstrating their commitment to ethical and sustainable practices.

Assessment of CSR Risks: Auditors assess how well a firm identifies, manages, and mitigates potential risks from its social, environmental, and governance operations. This is a thorough examination of the company's CSR plans to assess whether they appropriately handle risks such as regulatory noncompliance, environmental liabilities, social conflicts, and reputational harm. Auditors examine the company's risk management frameworks to ensure that CSR considerations are incorporated and evaluate the effectiveness of internal controls designed to mitigate these risks. Furthermore, by identifying potential vulnerabilities and gaps in CSR procedures, auditors assist organisations in proactively addressing issues that may have an impact on financial performance and stakeholder trust.

Integrating CSR into Financial Audits: In order to make sure that the financial effects of a company's CSR programs are fairly reflected in its financial statements, auditors are essential in including Corporate Social Responsibility (CSR) issues into financial audits. Auditors check for accurate accounting and disclosure of CSR-related expenses and potential liabilities, such as environmental remediation costs or regulatory compliance. They also consider the financial implications of CSR activities, such as cost savings from increased energy efficiency or revenue growth from improved brand recognition. By adding CSR into the financial audit process, auditors present a more complete picture of the company's financial health, emphasising the relationship between ethical activities and financial results. This technique assists stakeholders in understanding the financial impact of CSR projects and enables informed decision-making. As firms prioritise sustainability and corporate responsibility, the auditor's role in integrating CSR into financial audits becomes increasingly important for assuring transparency, accountability, and long-term value generation.

3. CSR, Auditing, and Challenges

Auditing Corporate Social Responsibility (CSR) presents various issues, including a lack of standardised reporting measures, the subjective nature of qualitative assessments, and the need to stay current on changing rules and stakeholder expectations (Gunn et al., 2024).

Lack of Standardization: The absence of standardisation in CSR reporting and measurement techniques is a substantial auditing challenge. Unlike financial reporting, which adheres to well-established frameworks and accounting rules, CSR reporting frequently lacks consistent requirements, resulting in inconsistency in how businesses disclose their social and environmental activities. Due to this variability, auditors find it difficult to accurately assess and verify CSR statements. Each organisation may use multiple measures and procedures to assess their CSR impact, complicating the audit process and reducing comparability between firms and industries (Hamed et al., 2022).

Subjectivity in CSR Reporting: Auditing Corporate Social Responsibility (CSR) requires negotiating the issues of subjectivity in CSR reporting, which can complicate the evaluation process for auditors. CSR reports frequently include qualitative assessments and narratives that are difficult to quantify, making it challenging for auditors to objectively verify the information. Companies may employ various frameworks and procedures to measure and report their CSR operations, resulting in discrepancies and a lack of comparability between reports. This subjectivity can lead to differing judgements of what constitutes success or compliance in CSR operations. Furthermore, firms may highlight certain accomplishments while downplaying or ignoring fewer positive aspects of their CSR performance. Auditors must develop robust techniques and standards to examine these subjective factors, ensuring that the reported material is credible and accurately represents the company's CSR efforts.

Expectations and Regulations Evolving: Auditing Corporate Social Responsibility (CSR) presents considerable issues due to changing rules and stakeholder expectations. As worldwide standards and frameworks for CSR reporting, auditors must be knowledgeable about the most recent modifications to assure compliance. This continual change creates a complex landscape in which auditors must react swiftly to new needs, often with little direction or precedent. Furthermore, the subjective character of some CSR activities, such as community engagement and ethical practices, complicates the auditing process because they lack clear, quantitative metrics. These issues entail auditors not just having a thorough awareness of growing standards, but also developing creative methodologies for properly evaluating

CSR activities, ensuring that organisations fulfil both regulatory and stakeholder expectations (Farber, 2005).

4. CSR and Auditor's Evolving Role

Auditors' evolving position in Corporate Social Responsibility (CSR) reflects the increasing complexity and importance of sustainability and ethical business practices. Traditionally focused on financial correctness and compliance, auditors are now increasingly entrusted with assessing a company's CSR activities and ensuring they conform with recognised frameworks. This transition necessitates auditors broadening their knowledge to encompass environmental, social, and governance (ESG) elements and understanding how they affect a company's overall performance and risk profile. Traditionally focused on financial correctness and compliance, auditors are now increasingly entrusted with assessing a company's CSR activities and ensuring they conform with recognised frameworks.

Advisory Services: The developing role of auditors in Corporate Social Responsibility (CSR) increasingly involves offering consulting services, indicating a transition from traditional assurance functions to more proactive, consultative engagements. As businesses attempt to improve their CSR efforts, auditors provide vital insights and advice on creating, implementing, and enhancing these activities. They help companies pinpoint their main areas of influence, match corporate social responsibility initiatives to their overarching goals, and incorporate sustainable practices into all aspects of their business operations. Auditors, as trusted consultants, play an important role in establishing a culture of sustainability and ethical responsibility within organisations, emphasising the value of CSR as a strategic asset rather than a compliance duty (El Ghoul et al., 2011).

Engagement of Stakeholders: Auditors serve as a bridge between businesses and their various stakeholders. More openness and accountability in corporate reporting are demanded by stakeholders including investors, customers, regulators, and communities as companies incorporate CSR into their fundamental operations. Because they make sure that CSR disclosures are accurate, dependable, and in line with stakeholder expectations, auditors are essential in fostering this conversation. They appraise the efficacy of an organization's tactics for engaging stakeholders, focussing on how successfully the corporation conveys its corporate social responsibility initiatives and addresses stakeholder issues. Auditors contribute to the development of confidence and credibility by offering assurance on CSR reports, confirming the company's genuine commitment to sustainable and ethical activities. With the ever-changing expectations, auditors need to modify their strategies to help businesses successfully navigate the complicated world of stakeholder engagement, which will ultimately boost the long-term success and reputation of their organisations (Rahman et al., 2023).

Innovations and Technological Changing: Innovation and technological breakthroughs have an immense impact on how auditors' position in Corporate Social Responsibility (CSR) is evolving. Auditors are using technology to increase the accuracy, efficiency, and scope of their evaluations as businesses increasingly use digital tools to boost their CSR operations. Auditors can evaluate vast amounts of CSR-related data, spot trends, and spot anomalies that could point to possible compliance problems or areas for improvement thanks to data analytics and artificial intelligence. These technologies enable more thorough assessments of an organization's environmental, social, and governance (ESG) performance, offering more profound understanding of the efficacy and significance of corporate social responsibility (CSR) initiatives. Additionally, blockchain technology is being investigated for its ability to improve CSR reporting traceability and transparency by guaranteeing that information revealed is true and unchangeable. The use of technology into the auditing process not only improves operational efficiency but also increases the credibility of CSR assessments, allowing auditors to provide more rigorous assurance to stakeholders. In order for auditors to stay at the forefront of CSR evaluation and contribute to the continuous evolution of moral and sustainable business practices, they will need to acquire new skills and methodologies in tandem with the rapid advancement of technology.

Discussion

Modern corporate practices now place a greater emphasis on Corporate Social Responsibility (CSR), particularly when it comes to marketing, accounting, and auditing. As organisations integrate CSR into their operations, auditors confront both possibilities and obstacles when evaluating these initiatives. Due to various obstacles in CSR auditing, including the absence of standardised reporting measures, the subjectivity of qualitative evaluations, and the ever-changing legal landscape, auditors must constantly innovate and adapt. A proactive strategy to evaluate CSR operations and a deep awareness of new standards are necessary due to the constantly changing rules and stakeholder expectations. In order to preserve accountability and openness, auditors must make sure that CSR disclosures are true and compliant with guidelines set out by organisations like the Global Reporting Initiative (GRI) and the Sustainability Accounting Standards Board (SASB).

It is impossible to exaggerate the value of innovation and technology in the auditing process. Technological innovations like blockchain, artificial intelligence, and data analytics have improved auditors' capacity to assess CSR-related data more effectively and precisely. These tools provide insights into the efficacy and impact of corporate social responsibility (CSR) programs and enable a more thorough knowledge of a company's environmental, social, and governance (ESG) performance. Using technology, auditors can give stakeholders with greater certainty regarding the integrity of CSR reports, increasing trust and confidence in the company's ethical and sustainable operations.

CONCLUSION

The incorporation of CSR into auditing processes is critical for encouraging ethical leadership and long-term sustainability in firms. Auditors have an important role in validating CSR disclosures, identifying CSR risks, and incorporating CSR into financial audits. Notwithstanding obstacles including changing laws and a lack of uniformity, auditors are adjusting by implementing new technology into their assessments. This evolution not only improves the credibility of CSR assessments, but also helps organisations demonstrate their commitment to responsible business practices. The growing importance of corporate social responsibility (CSR) will mean that auditors' responsibilities will also grow, with new methods and continual professional growth becoming crucial. A company's reputation, stakeholder trust, and overall success can all be positively impacted by CSR initiatives, and auditors can make sure of this by using technical improvements and properly resolving the issues.

References

Albuquerque, R., Koskinen, Y., & Zhang, C. (2019). Corporate social responsibility and firm risk: Theory and empirical evidence. *Management Science*, 65(10), 4451–4469. DOI: 10.1287/mnsc.2018.3043

Becchetti, L., Ciciretti, R., & Hasan, I. (2015). Corporate social responsibility, stakeholder risk, and idiosyncratic volatility. *Journal of Corporate Finance*, 35, 297–309. DOI: 10.1016/j.jcorpfin.2015.09.007

Boubaker, S., Cellier, A., Manita, R., & Saeed, A. (2020). Does corporate social responsibility reduce financial distress risk? *Economic Modelling*, 91, 835–851. DOI: 10.1016/j.econmod.2020.05.012

Cai, L., Cui, J., & Jo, H. (2016). Corporate environmental responsibility and firm risk. *Journal of Business Ethics*, 139(3), 563–594. DOI: 10.1007/s10551-015-2630-4

Cheng, B., Ioannou, I., & Serafeim, G. (2014). Corporate social responsibility and access to finance. *Strategic Management Journal*, 35(1), 1–23. DOI: 10.1002/smj.2131

Christensen, H. B., Hail, L., & Leuz, C. (2021). Mandatory CSR and sustainability reporting: Economic analysis and literature review. *Review of Accounting Studies*, 26(3), 1176–1248. DOI: 10.1007/s11142-021-09609-5

Du, S., Xu, X., & Yu, K. (2020). Does corporate social responsibility affect auditor-client contracting? Evidence from auditor selection and audit fees. *Advances in Accounting*, 51, 100499. DOI: 10.1016/j.adiac.2020.100499

El Ghoul, S., Guedhami, O., Kwok, C. C. Y., & Mishra, D. R. (2011). Does corporate social responsibility affect the cost of capital? *Journal of Banking \& Finance*, 35(9), 2388–2406.

Farber, D. B. (2005). Restoring trust after fraud: Does corporate governance matter? *The Accounting Review*, 80(2), 539–561. DOI: 10.2308/accr.2005.80.2.539

Godfrey, P. C. (2005). The relationship between corporate philanthropy and shareholder wealth: A risk management perspective. *Academy of Management Review*, 30(4), 777–798. DOI: 10.5465/amr.2005.18378878

Gunn, J. L., Li, C., Liao, L., Yang, J., & Zhou, S. (2024). Audit firms' corporate social responsibility activities and auditor reputation. *Accounting, Organizations and Society*, 113, 101569. DOI: 10.1016/j.aos.2024.101569

Hamed, R. S., Al-Shattarat, B. K., Al-Shattarat, W. K., & Hussainey, K. (2022). The impact of introducing new regulations on the quality of CSR reporting: Evidence from the UK. *Journal of International Accounting, Auditing & Taxation*, 46, 100444. DOI: 10.1016/j.intaccaudtax.2021.100444

Rahman, M. J., Zhu, H., & Chen, S. (2023). Does CSR reduce financial distress? Moderating effect of firm characteristics, auditor characteristics, and covid-19. *International Journal of Accounting \&. Information & Management*, 31(5), 756–784.

Chapter 6
The Impact of Artificial Intelligence on Achieving Corporate Social Responsibility

Yasir Aleem
The University of Sargodha, Pakistan

Saifullah Hassan
https://orcid.org/0009-0002-2046-9730
The University of Sargodha, Pakistan

ABSTRACT

The emergence of the concept of social responsibility in the early decades of 20th centuries, the businesses or companies started to strengthen the relationship with stakeholders including employees, customers, and communities. The Artificial Intelligence can help the corporations to measure the demanding CSR's initiatives, related to the specific population, community, or a country, including but not limited to the community engagement, employee well-being, human rights, education and skills development, promotion of health, climate change and advancement to the access of technology and literacy in remote and deserving communities. This chapter will address the role of Artificial Intelligence in addressing the CSR's followed by the corporations. Further, the chapter will discuss the gap analysis between the risk attached to the ethical use of AI in data analysis. Lastly, the chapter will scrutinize the impact of AI to provide robust backing to the corporations.

INTRODUCTION

The emergence of the concept of social responsibility in the early decades of 20th centuries, the businesses or companies started to strengthen the relationship with stakeholders including employees, customers, and communities. CSR is bonded with the concept of "Corporate Citizenship" and vastly acknowledged in this postmodern era of industrialization to the big data, meaning thereby, the emergence of the promising role of Artificial Intelligence has already revolutionized the different sectors of industries and businesses. The Artificial Intelligence can help the corporations to measure the demanding CSR's initiatives, related to the specific population, community, or a country, including but not limited to the community engagement, employee well-being, human rights, education and skills development, aid during natural or humanized disasters, promotion of health, climate change and advancement to the access of technology and literacy in remote and deserving communities. This chapter will address the role of Artificial Intelligence in addressing the CSR's followed by the corporations. Further, the chapter will discuss the gap analysis between the risk attached to the ethical use of AI in data analysis and the regulations attached to the unethical or unacceptable high risks during the use of AI's data analysis and decision-making techniques. Lastly, the chapter will scrutinize the existing trends in achieving the CSR's and the impact of AI to provide robust backing to the corporations.

An Overview of AI and Method of its Working

Innovatively, in 1950, a mathematician Alen Turning raised a question concerning "whether machines can think?" (OECD, 2019). However, the first time AI term was used in 1955 by different computer scientists like John McCarthy, Nathaniel Rochester and others. John McCarthy was a cognitive scientist and a computer scientist who technically posed the AI term and also founded the discipline of AI (Biresaw, 2022). As far as AI research is concerned, the patent families of about 340,000, as well as more than million and a half scientific papers regarding the different aspects of AI remained published from the early 1960's until 2018. The submission of AI related patent applications increased by 6.5% on an annual basis from 2011 to 2017 (WIPO, 2018).

The large accessibility of data. computational power and connectedness breakthroughs the opportunities for machine learning including deep learning and neural networks along with increased funding herald the new era of creativeness and innovation in the IT sector of AI. (Ben-Ari, et al, 2017).

Figure 1. AI System (Developed by Authors)

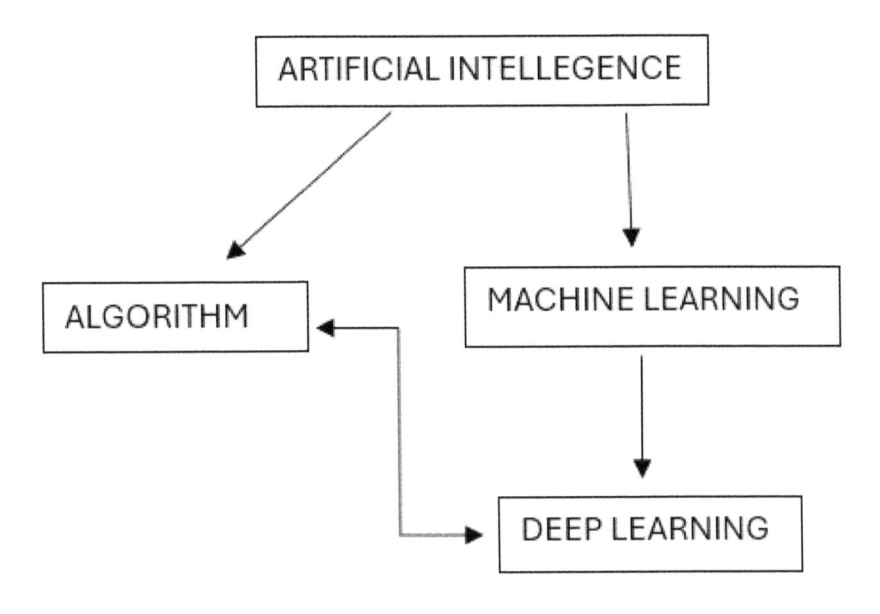

```
        ARTIFICIAL INTELLEGENCE
         /              \
        /                \
   ALGORITHM  ←——  MACHINE LEARNING
        ↑                  |
        |                  ↓
        └————————→  DEEP LEARNING
```

Definition of Artificial Intelligence.

An Artificial Intelligence is based on a system that works by following certain algorithmic patterns including self-learning driven through deep learning and machine learning, meaning thereby, it performs certain cognitive capabilities of humans by execution through processing the provided data, information, adopting decisions, sensors and captivating actions in an autonomous manner (Biresaw, 2022; OECD, 2019).

i) Algorithm

The 'algorithm' term, in context of computer science and mathematics, can be defined as "an unambiguous procedure for solving a given class of problems and the 'algorithm' means something closer to 'automated algorithm': a procedure used to automate reasoning or decision-making processes" (Whittlestone J, & et al., 2019). A system that is driven by the algorithm resolves the pursuing problems through a constituted structured process. Although, execution of algorithmic system creates possibility for making various automated decisions, searching, tasks, scoring, ranking, data classification, selecting, ordering and filtering (Ballel, 2019).

ii) Machine Learning

Machine learning is another major component of AI, and it describes the parsing of data, learn and adopt the variable based decision (Ghahramani Z, 2015). Machine learning based programs complete the tasks correctly and effectively by following provided instructions or even without provided instructions about the method of accomplishing the specific task. As revolutionary component of AI, these programs can judge and learn from the data of previously accomplished tasks that were similar but not of identical nature (Biresaw, 2022).

iii) Deep Learning.

Deep learning enables autonomous systems and machines to work under example-based mechanisms and is basically a technique used within the algorithmic components of machine learning. In deep learning predetermined instructions does not provide to the system but a model, that based on patterns and examples, provides to the machine to resolve future problems, meaning thereby, AI can harmoniously apply the provided components or patterns and process them to give required outcomes (Yeoh P, 2019).

AN OVERVIEW OF CORPORATE SOCIAL RESPONSIBILITY

A company's voluntarily contributions and efforts to enhance the environmental, economic and social impacts that goes beyond its financial benefits and performances categorically fall under the impression of Corporate Social Responsibility (CSR). Therefore, the company is owning the responsibility intended for its actions and decides to make positive impact on society and world. It is an important corporate duty which has significant effect in corporate relationship amongst ethical policies, its actions including financial performance and decision-making (Arlow & Gannon, 1982). The corporate actions related to CSR are for the benefit of society but go beyond the financial interests of company, meaning thereby, the CSR actions are not legally compulsory but demanding in nature that goes beyond obligations under the law. So, a company that avoids and prevents the commission of certain actions against the minorities and women, within their business premises, does not consider as 'socially responsible act'; it has merely abided the legal obligations under the law (McWilliams A, & Siegal D, 2001).

In a broader context, the company's approach to CSR depends on certain factors including its size, level of development, diversification and research, consumer income, advertising, labor market conditions and the scale of industry and its life cycle (McWilliams A, & Siegal D, 2001). These factors influence the scope of socially responsible acts of company and the demands for CSR from the stakeholders to the managers of corporate.

CSR in Theoretical Perspective

There are several theories of CSR that discuss the role and impact of corporate sustainability in society but in this chapter, we will discuss the most relevant CSR theories that directly relates to the impact of AI on CSR i.e stakeholder theory, corporate accountability theory, legitimacy theory, and corporate sustainability theory. These theories provide guidelines about why and how companies should have to conduct and follow corporate social responsibility.

i) Corporate Accountability Theory

The theory imposes the additional responsibility on a company for the consequences of its actions, either intentional or unintentional, towards stakeholders. The theory further prescribes that the CSR is not only giving generous charities or the stewardship activities and these are voluntary actions that are obviously grasped by the businessmen, therefore, the CSR involves the inherent fundamental obligations and seemingly becoming the "spirit of life" within business practices and systems. It also implies that the CSR approach is the logical consequence that underlines the human rights provided to the company by the state in order to thrive and live in a particular environment (Putra Y. H. S., Yati S, & Wahyuni N, 2015). However, if in case of disharmony amongst that factors of human rights in CSR and the company's obligations in such environment then there would be a gainer and loser, obviously, the company will be gainer and society will be the loser (Dellaportas S, & et al, 2005). The balance between the above discussed factors are compulsory according to the accountability theory.

ii) Stakeholder Theory.

This theory prescribes the correlation involving corporation and its stakeholders. The stakeholder can be defined as "any group or individual who can affect or is affected by the achievement of the firm's objectives" (Fernando, & et al, 2014). The theory identifies that the sustainability and success of a company integrated with the numerous interests of its stakeholders. If a company successfully balances the stakeholders' interests, then the it will attain their support and will enjoy growth in its market share, profits and sales. This theory identifies that the company's existence needs the stakeholders' support and approval for the various activities of a company (Putra Y. H. S., Yati S, & Wahyuni N, 2015). Stakeholder theory implies that the company, as entity, should not only operates for its own interests and profits but should have to provide certain benefits to the stakeholders including creditors, suppliers, shareholders, customers, public and the government. (Garriga E, & Mele D, 2004; Freeman R. E, 1984)

iii) Corporate Legitimacy Theory

The theory perceives that the surrounding community and the company create a close relationship because of their linkage through *social contract*. In fact, the legitimacy theory can be defined as "a generalized perception or assumption that the actions of an entity are desirable, proper, or appropriate within some socially constructed system of norms, values, beliefs, and definitions" (Suchman M. C, 1995). The establishment of a company in an area has based on the regulations and laws made by government and the people representatives in parliament, hence, it amounts to an indirect social contract between the company and the surrounding community in context of benefits and costs including corporate sustainability. Although, the CSR as a company's fundamental obligations should be executed in a manner that those actions and activities can be agreed and accept by the community (Putra Y. H. S., Yati S, & Wahyuni N, 2015).

iv) Corporate Sustainability Theory

This is the most compelling theory that describes the coherence between the economic factors and growth both for the company and society. According to 'corporate sustainability theory' there are three major pillars for business development a) economist b) social, and c) environment that perceive with integrated manner. However, the theory prescribes that for the growth of sustainability the corporations shall have to adopt those business goals that align with the environmental and social objectives. The theory advocates the profitability and growth of corporations as essential factors, meaning thereby, corporations should also have to follow societal goals, mostly, related to the 'sustainable development' including social justice, economic development, equity and the environmental protection (Putra Y. H. S., Yati S, & Wahyuni N, 2015).

Types of Corporate Social Responsibility.

According to Online Harvard Business School (2021) the CSRs are traditionally divided into four main categories including philanthropic, economic, environmental and ethical responsibility.

i) Environmental Responsibility.

Environmental responsibility is considered as the most common category of CSR in which organizations belief that their behavior should be environmentally friendly as far as it is possible for them. The initiatives taken under the category of environmental responsibility, in some cases, are considered as "environmental stewardship" by some companies. Companies can take several forms of initiatives while seeking to embrace CSR (Stobierski T, 2021). These "environmental stewardship" includes, a) by reduction industrial harmful practices, in furtherance to, the decrease the emission of greenhouse gas, reduction of pollution, water consumption, and decreasing general waste, b) by counteracting the negative impact on environment, meaning thereby, support the projects for planting trees, donations and funding research for this purpose, and c) by adapting energy consumptions related to the renewable energy and increase reliance on it, further to support sustainable resources, and the use of recycled material.

ii) Philanthropic Responsibility

In furtherance of achieving the environmental responsibility under CSR, the corporations determined for philanthropic responsibility invest, a portion of their earnings, on charitable purposes and nonprofits that associate with their organizational mission. For making the society and the world 'a better place', these organizations donate to these worthy causes and somehow to make the greater positive impact build the charitable organizations or trusts by supervising and potentially contributing to philanthropic responsibility.

iii) Ethical Responsibility.

In addition to 'environmental responsibility' and 'philanthropic responsibility', the organizations concerned, as ethical responsibility, to operate their businesses in a fair and ethical manner. The companies which are committed to embrace the 'ethical responsibility' follow the best business practices including the corporate ethical behavior while treating with all company's stakeholders including investors, employees, customers, and the suppliers. The response towards 'ethical responsibility' may embrace in various manners, for instance, if the government of a state mandated the minimum wage for any employee; but it does not amount to "livable wage" and the organization might set the 'higher minimum wage' for its employee. Further, the organizations adopt a policy and make it compulsory to acquire products, materials, ingredients or related components by following the standards of free trade and prevent or reject to purchase products that made and resulting from child labor or slavery (Stobierski T, 2021).

Economic Responsibility.

One of the main purposes of incorporation of a company is to earn profits, meanwhile, the company practices and backs all its major financial decisions in commitment to embrace positive impact and to do good for society in following its 'economic responsibility'. The ultimate goal of company is not only to maximize its profits but to ensure that the business operations of company should have positive impact on people, society, and the environment.

iv) Other Social Initiatives under CSR.

The companies demonstrating their commitments while embracing CSR can strengthen their long-term objectives of business. Further, the contribution towards equitable trade, safe and secure laboring conditions, education, activism, volunteerism, and human rights related to CSR's success can be extracted quantitively and the quantitative achievement is so desirous for parties willingly engaging in CSR. The safe working environment for women at workplace is an essential part in CSR objectives, "the heart and soul of effective CSR is essentially about relationship building that fuels opportunities for workers, in particular for women and girls in the workplace and in their communities" (Chin M, 2019).

AI Governance and CSR.

The term 'AI governance' incorporates with the perception of 'AI and corporate governance'. It based on the legislative acts, AI regulations and formal rules including voluntary governance principles that provide guidelines to AI practitioners during the development, research and maintenance of AI based systems (Butcher J, Beridze I, 2019). The rationale for following the responsible 'AI governance' is to ensure the directional limitations for automated systems based on AI algorithms, deep learnings and 'machine learning' to support the organizations and professionals to attain their objectives and long-term goals; and to protect the interests of organizations stakeholders during the process to achieve their long-term objectives.

For maximizing the CSR impact on society and other organizational goals, the responsible 'AI governance' requires from the leaders of organizations to comply with AI regulations and follow relevant legislations. These organizational leaders are also expected, in addition to AI regulations, to comply with standards and ethical norms (Koniakou V, 2023; Corea F, & et al, 2022).

Implementing CSR through AI

Many companies have increased their reliance on the AI algorithms before deciding on any strategic decisions (Janiesch C & et al, 2021). These automated technologies that work independently and based on algorithms are helping companies in improving their organizational performance. Online users can be interacted by AI innovations by two-way communications. Their AI's algorithmic dialogue methods assist while responding to certain questions (Camilleri M A, 2023), by admitting or rejection of requests, if the questions are not recognized to be appropriate.

Now, there are many companies using algorithms based on 'machine learning' or 'deep leaning' mechanisms for fraud prevention, detection of malware, filtering the spam, 'business process automation' (BPA) and further, not limited to the maintenance of the recommender system etc. Further, these AI based technologies have the ability to scrutinize the contents of email and enable the business practitioners to effectively and urgently respond to the extremely important massages, therefore, it is useful for the enhancement of 'customer relationship management' (CRM) system (Camilleri M A, 2023; Engel C, & et al., 2022). These AI based advanced systems are enabled to provide responses, in the most effective and fast way, to the customers. In furtherance, there are other applications, based on algorithms of 'machine learning and deep learning', can be applied to identify different trends, essential information within datasets, point out certain cycles, patterns, and anomalies from the information of big data and reveal information from the small data (Carvalho C, & et al., 2019). These technological applications can be used by the companies for the recruitment process and for identification of potential candidates, by scrutinizing the information databases related to human resources, for open positions in a company, however, it can also be used in other business-related purposes.

The corporate practitioners can enable to avail the AI based modules to track activities during processing and data collection, in order to protect the customer's interests like call centers or the service businesses and can also include, in AI modules, the preventative corporate practices and security policies. The AI and the associated technologies with it like internet of things and robotics will enable to enhance the capability of corporations in societies for the detection of environment and climate change. There are numerous scientific reports that has identified the applicability of AI and field of automation to address the biodiversity loss, effective monitoring, climate change and natural resources usages, and further, to increase progress for the achievements of 'sustainable development goals' (SGD's) (Galaz V, & et al., 2021).

The organizations should enable their AI efforts and tie them responsibly with the strategies of CSR's and imply that central ideas into responsible AI like fairness, bias prevention and transparency as are aligned with the CSR's fundamental principles. As per the 'socially responsibility standards' of 'international standards organizations' the organizations and corporations ought to have been transparent and accountable to their stakeholders (Renieris E M, & et al, 2022). However, these principles are non-binding but encourage the corporations to uphold the ethical behavior, regard the international norms as to corporate behavior, value 'the rule of law', and to uphold the human rights (Camilleri M A, 2019). The CSR's decisions made, and behavior adopted by these corporations are projected to be justified before the corporate stakeholders and concerned policymakers.

Use of AI and Ethics in Data Analysis for CSR

The AI deep learning modules or algorithms build the ability of computers and AI neural networks to collect, assemble and further process big data, just like the working of a human brain. These AI tools are enabled to provide insights on processed data, including texts, audio, images and video, in a reliable manner and can make predictions regarding the future. (Buhmann A, & Fieseler C, 2023). There several networks which are based on architecture of deep-learning including, deep neural network, convolutional neural network, network of deep belief, deep reinforcement learning, neural network of recurrent and transformers are vastly applicable in diverse form of fields, for data collection, scrutiny and process, including computer vision, processing of natural language, recognition of speech, machine translation and other related areas, meaning thereby, AI Algorithms are resilient and providing significant results as output that are comparable and to some extent surpassing the performance of human experts (LeCun Y, & et al., 2015).

While using AI, the corporate practitioners encounter with several challenges as to the latest developments in the world and un-ability of huge data that, for any reason whatsoever, are not uploaded to the system based on AI; so, all the previous learnings of AI will become outdated and quickly obsolete for that specific purpose and no longer be able to apply for the problems of near future. For instance, if a question of reliability regarding the responses is ask to the ChatGPT then it point out the existing data available to it and mention the following factors.

"AI language model, ChatGPT strives to provide accurate and helpful responses based on the input it received. However, it's important to note that my responses are generated algorithmically, and therefore, there may be instances where my responses are not completely accurate or may not fully address the question being asked. Additionally, my responses are based on the data available to me at the time of my training and knowledge cutoff date, so any new developments or information that have emerged since then, may not be reflected in my responses. It's always a good idea to verify information obtained from any source, including AI language models like ChatGPT, with other credible sources to ensure its accuracy and reliability" (Camilleri M A, 2023). Therefore, the corporations, while applying AI tools for CSR, should have to scrutinize the reliability on data analysis by AI both in terms of up-to-date data learnings by AI language modules and the correctness of data provided by the corporation regarding the impact of CSR on society.

i) Allocative Harms and Algorithmic Biases

In few years, the impact and risks that attached to the possibility of allocative harms and algorithmic biasedness has attracted the considerable attention, meaning thereby, the use in the domains of policing and health sector. Therefore, the biasedness and inconsistencies during data training, including security breaches that may cause to distorted data capture and corrupt data, systems of decision-making and as consequence, the flawed models of AI can lead to the detrimental effect of AI systems (Galaz V, & et al., 2021). These types of algorithmic biases have different sources and may emerge in sustainability corelated domain in the following mode:

ii) Biases in Training Data.

The biases, based on the training data, can occur when there are flaws in training the AI-systems and poorly designed with biased or limited data sets. For instance, a developed AI-system for the precision agriculture based on the poor or limited data contexts can, if such data is not properly scrutinized or validated with the opinion of a local expert and by local knowledge, cause harm and may lead to incorrect results and recommendations to farmers, despite their demanding efforts for their high and stable agricultural yields (Jimenez D, & et al, 2019).

iii) Transfer Context Biases.

The biases, based on the context of transfer data, can occur when the AI-system's algorithms are designed for one particular climate and ecological or in context of social-ecological purpose but incorrectly applied or transfer to another situation.

Although, the above-described training data and related resulting modules may have more effective and suitable impact on initially described social-ecological situation but on the other hand, using the same data in a completely different situation may have ineffective impact and can lead to the damaging and flawed results. The emergence of aforementioned biases are possible if companies or individuals use the AI-software's that are off-the-shelf for such purposes (Galaz V, & et al., 2021).

iv) Interpretation Biases.

Regardless of the appropriateness and correctness of 'training data' and the data context in which the AI algorithms were designed; the application of these algorithms can still enable to the interpretation bias because it depends on the ability of its user. In this category of biasedness, the appropriateness and working of AI system might have sustainability as per the intention of AI designer, but to the contrary, the first-hand user does not have the ability to understand or properly familiar to its utility and tries to make different inferences that the AI system might not support.

The biases of AI algorithms are common, whether it based on the inappropriate or limited training data, unsuitable or unsupportive data context, or the errors made by AI user, therefore, it must be thoroughly and accurately considered for sustainability domains (Galaz V, & et al., 2021).

CONCLUSION

The actions of corporations related to CSR are for the vast interests of stakeholders and the greater good of society. However, the corporations are not legally bound to practice it but due to the changing trends of CSR, nowadays beyond the financial interests of corporations, it is becoming the part of core-values of corporations. Further, 'Artificial Intelligence' has revolutionized every field of life, so far, AI has aiding companies in achievement of their long-term CSR objectives. Notably, the use of AI based data analysis in implementing CSR for environmental protection, education in a particular area etc., helping the corporations to identify the different areas of CSR that need more attention than its other social responsibilities.

However, there are also risks attached to the AI based system; both during process of AI analysis and the outdated data or improper data available for AI training. The leaders of corporations should cautiously have to apply the AI based suggestions and need to re-investigate them through local expert. When the corporations enable responsible AI with their strategies of CSR then it will imply fairness, effective monitoring, detection of environment and climate change; and ultimately improve the impact of CSR and will make good impact on society and the world.

References:

Arlow, P., & Gannon, M. (1982). Social responsiveness, corporate structure, and economic performance. *Academy of Management Review*, 7(2), 235–241. DOI: 10.2307/257302

Ben-Ari, D., Frish, Y., Lazovski, A., & Eldan, U.. (2017). "Artificial Intelligence in the Practice of Law: An Analysis and Proof of Concept Experiment" 23 (2). *Rich. J. L. & Tech*, 3, 53.

Biresaw, S. (2022). "The Impacts of Artificial Intelligence on Research in the Legal Profession". SSRN *Electronic Journal*. 1-29.

Buhmann, A., & Fieseler, C. (2023). Deep learning meets deep democracy: Deliberative governance and responsible innovation in artificial intelligence. *Business Ethics Quarterly*, 33(1), 146–179. DOI: 10.1017/beq.2021.42

Butcher, J., & Beridze, I. (2019). What is the state of artificial intelligence governance globally? *RUSI Journal*, 164(5–6), 88–96. DOI: 10.1080/03071847.2019.1694260

Camilleri, M. A. (2019). Measuring the corporate managers' attitudes towards ISO's social responsibility standard. *Total Quality Management & Business Excellence*, 30(13–14), 1549–1561. DOI: 10.1080/14783363.2017.1413344

Camilleri, M. A. (2023). *Artificial intelligence governance: Ethical considerations and implications for social responsibility.* John Wiley & Sons Ltd., DOI: 10.1111/exsy.13406

Carvalho, A., Levitt, A., Levitt, S., Khaddam, E., & Benamati, J. (2019). Off-the-shelf artificial intelligence technologies for sentiment and emotion analysis: A tutorial on using IBM natural language processing. *Communications of the Association for Information Systems*, 44, 918–943. DOI: 10.17705/1CAIS.04443

Chin, M. (2019). Be the opportunity: The heart and soul of corporate social responsibility. *Journal of Fair Trade*, 1(1), 27–35. DOI: 10.13169/jfairtrade.1.1.0027

Corea, F., Fossa, F., Loreggia, A., Quintarelli, S., & Sapienza, S. (2022). A principle-based approach to AI: The case for European Union and Italy. *AI & Society*, 38(2), 521–535. DOI: 10.1007/s00146-022-01453-8

Dellaportas, S., Gibson, K., Alagiah, R., Hutchinson, M., Leung, P., & Homing, D. V. (2005). *Ethics Governance and Accountability* (1st ed.).

Engel, C., Ebel, P., & Leimeister, J. M. (2022). Cognitive automation. *Electronic Markets*, 32(1), 339–350. DOI: 10.1007/s12525-021-00519-7

Fernando, S. (2014, Fall). Lawrence & Stewart, (2014), "A Theoretical Framework for CSR Practices: Integrating Legitimacy Theory, Stakeholder Theory And Institutional Theory. *The Journal of Theoretical Accounting*, 10(1), 149–178. https://www.researchgate.net/profile/Susith-Fernando/publication/290485216_A_theoretical_framework_for_CSR_practices_Integrating_legitimacy_theory_stakeholder_theory_and_institutional_theory/links/5a8629ee458515b8af890861/A-theoretical-framework-for-CSR-practices-Integrating-legitimacy-theory-stakeholder-theory-and-institutional-theory.pdf

Freeman, R. E. (1984). *Strategic Management: A Stakeholder Approach*. Pitman.

Galaz, V., Centeno, M. A., Callahan, P. W., Causevic, A., Patterson, T., Brass, I., Baum, S., Farber, D., Fischer, J., Garcia, D., McPhearson, T., Jimenez, D., King, B., Larcey, P., & Levy, K. (2021). Artificial intelligence, systemic risks, and sustainability. *Technology in Society*, 67, 101741. DOI: 10.1016/j.techsoc.2021.101741

Garriga, E., & Mele´, D. (2004). Corporate Social Responsibility Theories: Mapping the Territory. *Journal of Business Ethics*, 53(1/2), 51–71. DOI: 10.1023/B:BUSI.0000039399.90587.34

Ghahramani, Z. (2015). "Probabilistic Machine Learning and Artificial Intelligence" 521. *Nature*, 452, 459.

Janiesch, C., Zschech, P., & Heinrich, K. (2021). Machine learning and deep learning. *Electronic Markets*, 31(3), 685–695. DOI: 10.1007/s12525-021-00475-2

Jiménez, D., Delerce, S., Dorado, H., Cock, J., Muñoz, L. A., Agamez, A., & Jarvis, A. (2019). A scalable scheme to implement data-driven agriculture for small-scale farmers. *Global Food Security*, 23, 256–266. DOI: 10.1016/j.gfs.2019.08.004

Koniakou, V. (2023). From the "rush to ethics" to the "race for governance" in artificial intelligence. *Information Systems Frontiers*, 25(1), 71–102. DOI: 10.1007/s10796-022-10300-6

LeCun, Y., Bengio, Y., & Hinton, G. (2015). Deep learning. *Nature*, 521(7553), 436–444. DOI: 10.1038/nature14539

McWilliams, A., & Siegel, D. (2001). Corporate Social Responsibility: A Theory of the Firm Perspective. *Academy of Management Review*, 26(1), 117–127. https://www.jstor.org/stable/259398. DOI: 10.2307/259398

OECD. (2019), "Artificial Intelligence in Society". *OECD Publishing*, Paris, 20. https://www.oecd-ilibrary.org/science-and-technology/artificial-intelligence-in-society_eedfee77-en

Renieris, E. M., Kiron, D., & Mills, S. (2022). "Should organizations link responsible AI and corporate social responsibility? It's Complicated". *MIT Sloan*https://sloanreview.mit.edu/article/should-organizations-link-responsible-ai-and-corporate-social-responsibility-its-complicated/

Rodrıguez de las Heras Ballell, T. (2019). "Legal Challenges of Artificial Intelligence: Modeling the Disruptive Features of Emerging Technologies and Assessing their possible Legal Impact" 24. *University of Florida Law Review*, 302, 314.

Stobierski, T. (2021), *Online Harvard Business School*, https://online.hbs.edu/blog/post/types-of-corporate-social-responsibility

Suchman, M. C. (1995). Managing Legitimacy: Strategic and Institutional Approaches. *Academy of Management Journal*, 20(3), 571–610.

Whittlestone, J., Nyrup, R., Alexandrova, A., Alexandrova, A., Dihal, K., & Cave, S. (2019). "Ethical and societal implications of algorithms, data, and artificial intelligence: A roadmap for research" *London* [Ethical-and-Societal-Implications-of-Data-and-AI-report-Nuffield-Foundat.pdf] [nuffieldfoundation.org]. *Nuffield Foundation*, 1, 59.

WIPO "Technology Trends 2019 Artificial Intelligence", 39.

Yeoh, P. (2019). "Artificial Intelligence: Accelerator or Panacea for Financial Crime?" 26 (2). *Journal of Financial Crime*, 634(2), 646. DOI: 10.1108/JFC-08-2018-0077

Yuniarti Hidayah Suyoso Putra, Sri Yati, Nanik Wahyuni, (2015) "Acting Green: Theoretical Framework on Corporate Social Responsibility". *Australian Journal of Basic and Applied Sciences*, 9(7) A, pp. 248-250.

Chapter 7
Theoretical and Conceptual Approach of Corporate Governance and CSR Activities in Financial Decision Making

Rabia Arshad
The University of Faisalabad, Pakistan

Faiq Mahmood
Government College University, Faisalabad, Pakistan

Maryam Saleem
The University of Faisalabad, Pakistan

ABSTRACT

In today's business world, corporate social responsibility (CSR) and corporate governance have become essential components. They have a big impact on financial decision-making processes in addition to organizational behavior. The objective of this chapter is to offer a thorough theoretical and conceptual framework for comprehending how financial decision-making, CSR initiatives, and corporate governance interact inside businesses. Foundations of Corporate Governance Theoretically explain about how agency theory clarifies how shareholders and management interact as principals and agents, highlighting how important it is to have aligned interests to reduce agency conflicts. Examine how this theory emphasizes the wider societal impact of company actions by promoting the consideration of multiple stakeholder interests beyond shareholders and Analyze how this theory

DOI: 10.4018/979-8-3693-5733-0.ch007

affects governance frameworks and decision-making procedures by emphasizing how dependent organizations are on outside resources.

OBJECTIVES:

The purpose of this chapter is to examine the complex interplay that exists between financial decision-making, corporate social responsibility (CSR), and corporate governance in organizations. The following goals will be accomplished by the chapter through the use of a theoretical and conceptual framework:

- Establish clear definitions of corporate governance and CSR, highlighting their significance in the modern business landscape.
- Examine the theoretical foundations of corporate governance and corporate social responsibility (CSR), such as institutional theory, agency theory, and stakeholder theory, to comprehend the ways in which they affect financial decision-making.
- Examine how governance structures and CSR commitments influence the financial decision-making processes of organizations.

INTRODUCTION

This chapter aims to provide a comprehensive understanding of the theoretical and conceptual approaches to corporate governance and CSR, highlighting their critical roles in shaping financial decisions within organizations. Corporate governance and corporate social responsibility (CSR) have emerged as pivotal concepts in the realm of modern business management. Their significance extends beyond ethical imperatives to encompass strategic and financial decision-making. It explores their implications for financial decision-making, illustrating how these concepts can drive sustainable growth and ethical business practices. Through a review of key theories, governance mechanisms, CSR activities, and case studies, the chapter seeks to elucidate the critical role of corporate governance and CSR in contemporary business management.

Definition of Corporate Governance

The term "Corporate Governance" is defined in many different ways as:
"The structure that defines the business relations between management teams, shareholders, the board of directors, and all other significant stakeholders is known as corporate governance"

"The Financial Times (6 April 1992) suggested that "Corporate governance is all about identifying techniques to make companies run more effectively"

"In other words, if management is concerned with operating the business, corporate governance is concerned with ensuring that the business is run effectively, according to (Tricker, Tricker 2015).

(Keasey and Wright 1993) distinguished accountability a subset of corporate governance that deals with the observation, assessment, and management of organizational agents to guarantee that they act in the best interests of shareholders and other stakeholders from corporate governance, which is concerned with the structures and procedures related to production, decision-making, control, and other activities within an organization (Governance 2015).

A key component of sustainable performance, corporate governance (CG) is a mechanism that encompasses the set of policies, procedures, and practices that guide and manage an organization. More precisely, empirical studies showed that CG characteristics have a significant impact on a firm's ability to function well in terms of its economic, social, and environmental aspects, Rashid, M. M., & Kabir, M. R. (2024).

Definitions of "corporate governance" can be both wide and narrow. Fundamentally, it's about the interactions amongst directors, shareholders, and business managers. It may also include the way a company interacts with its stakeholders and the community. In a wider sense, "corporate governance" can refer to the set of rules, laws, listing requirements, and optional private sector activities that allow the company to raise money, run profitably, attract investors, and satisfy legal requirements as well as societal norms (Gregory and Simms 1999).

Importance of Corporate Governance

Globally, society are depending increasingly on the private sector to drive economic growth as markets grow more global and open and as business gets more complicated. A greater share of economic activity in both developed and developing countries is conducted by companies. Laws create corporations, and societies permit the creation of corporations because they understand that incorporation offers an effective organizational structure that helps society overall.

To create goods and services that benefit society, corporations mobilize and combine capital, labor, raw materials, management skills, and intellectual property from a range of sources. By doing this, businesses buy products and services, create jobs and revenue, divide profits, pay taxes, and contribute to foreign exchange earnings. All things considered, businesses support economic expansion and progress, which raise living standards and reduce poverty, both of which should result in more stable political regimes. The significance of corporate governance stems from the fact that it affects a company's ability to: (1) use resources efficiently; (2) recruit low-cost capital; (3) fulfill societal expectations; and (4) perform altogether (Gregory and Simms, 1999).

Corporate governance refers to the mechanisms, processes, and relations by which corporations are controlled and directed. It encompasses the practices and procedures that ensure a company is managed in the best interests of its shareholders and other stakeholders, thereby promoting transparency, accountability, and fairness in corporate conduct. Effective corporate governance is instrumental in mitigating risks, enhancing corporate performance, and fostering investor confidence (Shleifer and Vishny 1997, Oecd 2004).

An analysis of the notable expansion of the empirical literature on corporate governance in the fields of accounting, economics, finance, management, and corporate strategy reveals the significance of this subject. Conventional research studies look at how various corporate governance frameworks affect CEO behavior and/or restrain it, as well as how they affect organizational performance (Larcker & Richardson et al., 2005)

Theoretical Foundations

The theoretical foundations of corporate governance are rooted in several key theories:

Agency Theory:

Adam Smith examined this notion and discovered the agency issue in the joint-stock business. The basic idea behind agency theory is that corporate management should behave in the stakeholders' best interests. According to the principle, business leaders have a financial and moral obligation to work in the parties' best interests. This theory addresses the conflicts of interest between principals (shareholders) and agents (managers). It underscores the need for mechanisms to align the interests of management with those of the shareholders and to minimize agency costs (Meckling and Jensen 1976).

Most large companies, particularly those quoted on stock exchanges, are not managed by the shareholders (the principals); rather they are run on behalf of the principals by a board of directors (the agents). Although directors are employed to act in the best interests of the owners whose interests they represent, in reality directors are typically rational individuals who maximize their own returns – it is after all human nature to act in one's own self-interest.

Types of agency theory:

There are various kinds of relationships that are intricately linked and encounter conflict when it comes to business and the idea of agency theory, (Panda and Leepsa, 2017).

1. Principal & Agent Problem
2. Principal & Principal Problem
3. Principal & Creditor Problem

1. Principal & Agent Problem

Since the beginning of major corporations, there has been an agency issue between owners and managers in these organizations as a result of the separation of ownership and control. In the hopes that the managers will act in the owners' best interests, the owners give the managers the responsibility of running the company. Managers, meanwhile, are more concerned about maximizing their pay. Human behavior is logical and driven to maximize one's own goals, according to the rationality of human behavior theory, which forms the basis of the argument on the agent's self-satisfying behavior. The conflict is known as principal-agent conflict and is caused by the misalignment of interests between the principal and the agent as well as the inadequate supervision brought on by the scattered ownership structure (Panda and Leepsa 2017).

2. Principal & Principal Problem

The conflict of interest between the major and minor owners is the fundamental premise of this kind of agency dilemma. Major owners are defined as an individual or group of individuals who possess the majority of a company's shares, whereas minor owners are those who control a very small percentage of the company's shares. Minor shareholders' interests are harmed by the majority owners' or blockholders' ability to make decisions that benefit them and have greater voting power. When ownership is concentrated in the hands of a small number of people or family owners, as is the case in a nation or business, minority shareholders find it challenging to safeguard their interests or wealth (Panda and Leepsa 2017).

3. Principal & Creditor Problem

The initiatives that are undertaken and the financing decisions made by the shareholders give birth to the dispute between the owners and creditors. Since they anticipate a larger return, the stockholders attempt to invest in riskier enterprises. The risk associated with the projects affects the creditors by driving up the cost of financing and lowering the value of the underlying loan. In the event that the project is successful, the owners will reap enormous profits, but the creditors' interest will be restricted because they will only be paid a set interest rate. However, in the event that the project fails, the creditors will be required to bear a portion of the losses, and this issue typically arises in these kinds of situations (Panda and Leepsa 2017).

Stewardship Theory:

Contrasting agency theory, stewardship theory posits that managers, as stewards, are inherently motivated to act in the best interests of the shareholders. This theory emphasizes the role of trust and intrinsic motivation in management practices (Davis, Schoorman et al. 1997). Stewardship theory was developed so that researchers may look at circumstances in which CEOs, acting as stewards, are driven to behave in the best interests of their principals. It has roots in psychology and sociology (Donaldson, Brown et al. 1989). Stewardship theory states that because a steward works to achieve the organization's goals (such as increased sales or profitability), their behavior is collective. Because the steward is advancing the goals of the outside owners and managerial subordinates, this action will also benefit those principals. Outside owners will gain from the favorable effects of profits on dividends and share prices. Theorists of stewardship believe that there is a direct correlation between the organization's success and the principal's happiness. By maximizing corporate performance, a steward safeguards and optimizes shareholders' money, as doing so maximizes the steward's utility functions. Stewardship theory is opposite to agency theory as there are some factors that differentiate these two theories (Davis, Schoorman et al. 1997).

Psychological Factor:

1. Motivation

The first major distinction between stewardship and agency theory is motivation. Extrinsic incentives, or tangible, exchangeable commodities with quantifiable "market" worth, are the main emphasis of agency theory. The compensation schemes that stand in for the agency theory's control mechanisms are based on these extrinsic incentives. Stewardship theory, on the other hand, is concerned with inherent benefits that are difficult to measure. These benefits include chances for development, accomplishment, connection, and self-actualization. These intrinsic rewards strengthen subordinates in a stewardship relationship and encourage them to put in more effort on behalf of the company. Stewardship is "the way in which someone organizes and looks after something," according to the MacMillan dictionary (Contrafatto 2014).

2. Identification

Identification is the third way that agency and stewardship theories diverge. When managers adopt the mission, vision, and goals of a certain organization, they describe themselves as members of that organization. This process is known as identification (Contrafatto 2014). Agency theory focuses on managing and mitigating potential conflicts between principals and agents, stewardship theory assumes a more collaborative and aligned relationship where managers naturally act in the best interest of the organization.

3. Use of power

The definition of influence according to research is "a change in a person's belief, attitude, or behavior—the target of influence—that arises from the action, or presence, of another person or group of people—the influencing agent." "Potential for such influence" is his definition of social power. Unlike (Weber 1947), this notion of power is objective (Saam 2007). Several studies have discovered that the use of power both satisfies and motivates managers. Principal-agent connections and principal-steward relationships can be distinguished from one another by the forms of power that are employed in the relationship. Agency theory uses power to control and align interests through monitoring and incentives due to concerns about potential conflicts, whereas stewardship theory uses power to empower and trust managers, assuming that they are naturally motivated to act in the best interest of the organization.

Stakeholder Theory: This theory expands the focus from shareholders to include all stakeholders—employees, customers, suppliers, and the broader community. It argues that companies should create value for all stakeholders to ensure long-term sustainability and ethical conduct (Freeman and Medoff 1984). Stakeholder theory is an organizational management and ethics theory. Indeed, all theories of strategic management have some moral content, though it is often implicit. This is not to say that all such theories are moral, as opposed to immoral. Instead, moral content in this case means that the subject matter of the theories are inherently moral topics. The term "stakeholder" is powerful because, to a significant degree, it is conceptually broad. The term means many different things to many different people and hence evokes praise or scorn from a wide variety of scholars and practitioners of myriad academic disciplines and backgrounds (Friedman and Miles 2002).

Resource Dependence Theory: This theory highlights the importance of external resources and the necessity for organizations to manage dependencies on external entities. Effective corporate governance can help companies secure critical resources and navigate complex external environments (Pfeffer and Salancik 2015). According to the resource dependency theory, businesses are open systems that rely on the whims of their surroundings. There are a number of strategies to reduce ambiguity and reliance on external factors, including executive succession, political action, board of commissioners, and vertical merger of company integration. Companies require the function of a board of commissioners, one of which is resource access, in order to lessen reliance on the outside world and the requirement for vital resources. In addition to offering resources and assistance, the board of commissioners is responsible for initiating initiatives, actively participating in decision-making, and implementing chosen courses of action (Mentari, Zahroh et al. 2019).

Definition of Corporate Social Responsibility (CSR)

Corporate Social Responsibility (CSR) is a process that aims to accept accountability for a company's actions and promote beneficial effects on the environment, customers, workers, communities, stakeholders, and any other members of the public that may also be regarded as stakeholders through its operations Yusif, S., & Hafeez-Baig, A. (2024).

"Corporate social responsibility (CSR) is defined as "a commitment to improve [societal] well-being through discretionary business practices and contributions of corporate resources." In today's socially conscious market climate, CSR is a key topic on the global corporate agenda" (Du, Bhattacharya et al. 2010).

Using the notion of "social responsibility" found in ISO 26000, the International Standards Organisation (ISO) offers one method of defining CSR. The following can be used to summarise their dimensions: transparency, human rights, law-abiding behaviour, ethical behaviour, social responsibility, environment, and stakeholder, Paul, K. (2024).

A self-monitoring business concept known as "corporate social responsibility" (CSR) assists an organization in being held socially responsible by the public, its stakeholders, and itself. Businesses may help society while enhancing their brands by participating in CSR initiatives, giving to charities, and volunteering. Both the corporation and its shareholders hold socially responsible companies accountable. Large firms frequently use CSR as a strategy. A firm has an increased need to set an example of moral behavior for its competitors, peers, and industry as a whole, in proportion to its success and visibility.

CSR represents a company's commitment to operating in an economically, socially, and environmentally sustainable manner. It extends beyond compliance with legal requirements to voluntarily adopting practices that benefit society and the environment. CSR initiatives can include activities such as reducing carbon footprints, improving labor policies, engaging in fair trade, and contributing to community development (Carroll 1991, Kramer and Porter 2006). In the domains of corporate governance and CSR, a number of noteworthy and significant studies have found a positive relationship between the financial and non-financial aspects of businesses Pagkalou, F. I., Galanos, C. L., & Thalassinos, E. I. (2024).

There are four different types of CSR which is mentioned below:

Environmental Responsibility:

Protecting the environment is at the core of corporate social responsibility. A business can practice environmental stewardship by cutting manufacturing pollution and emissions, recycling waste, restocking natural resources like trees, or developing CSR-compliant product lines.

Ethical Accountability:

Fair and ethical behavior is a part of corporate social responsibility. Fair treatment of all consumers, regardless of their age, race, culture, or sexual orientation, competitive pay and benefits for staff, vendor utilization across demographics, complete disclosures, and investor openness are a few examples of ethical responsibility in action.

Philanthropic Responsibility:

Corporate Social Responsibility (CSR) mandates that businesses give back to the community. This can take many forms, such as profit donations to charitable organizations, limiting business dealings to suppliers or vendors who share the company's values, supporting employee-led charitable endeavors, or supporting fundraising events.

Financial Responsibility:

A company may have plans to become more socially, ethically, and environmentally conscious, but these plans must be supported by financial investments in programs, grants, or product development, including the creation of sustainable products, the hiring of a diverse workforce, or the implementation of DEI, social awareness, or environmental initiatives.

CSR is underpinned by various theoretical perspectives:

Carroll's Pyramid of CSR:

(Carroll 2016) proposed a hierarchical model of CSR, encompassing economic, legal, ethical, and philanthropic responsibilities. This model suggests that companies must be profitable, comply with the law, operate ethically, and contribute to societal welfare. Corporate social responsibility (CSR) has been interpreted as the rules and practices that businesspeople use to ensure that stakeholders—those other than business owners—are taken into account and safeguarded in their operations and strategies. Virtually all definitions include business giving or corporate philanthropy as part of CSR, and many observers equate CSR with philanthropy only, ignoring these other categories of responsibility. Some definitions of CSR argue that an action must be purely voluntary to be considered socially responsible; others argue that it embraces legal compliance as well; still others argue that ethics is a part of CSR. The conversation that follows provides a brief explanation of each of the four categories that make up Carroll's four-part definitional framework, which serves as the foundation for the pyramidal model. "Corporate social responsibility encompasses the economic, legal, ethical, and discretionary (philanthropic) expectations that society has of organizations at a given point in time," according to Carroll's initial four-part definition of CSR. This list of four responsibilities establishes a framework or foundation that aids in defining and characterizing the specific obligations that businesses have to the society in which they operate (Carroll 2016).

Economic Responsibilities:

The primary responsibility of a business is to be profitable. This involves producing goods and services that society needs and desires, at a price that they are willing to pay, thereby generating profits for the owners and shareholders. This profitability ensures that the business can continue to operate and provide jobs, products, and services.

Legal Responsibilities:

Businesses are expected to comply with the laws and regulations established by governments. This means adhering to local, state, federal, and international laws and ensuring that their operations do not violate any legal standards. Compliance with laws ensures that businesses contribute to the legal framework of the society in which they operate.

Ethical Responsibilities:

Beyond economic and legal requirements, businesses have ethical responsibilities that encompass doing what is right, just, and fair. This includes operating in a manner that is consistent with the expectations of societal norms and values, even when not mandated by law. Ethical responsibilities involve considering the broader impact of business decisions on stakeholders, including employees, customers, suppliers, and the community.

Philanthropic Responsibilities:

Philanthropic responsibilities refer to the voluntary activities that businesses undertake to improve the quality of life for employees, the community, and society as a whole. This can include charitable donations, community engagement, and other forms of social contribution. These actions are not required by law or business ethics but are driven by the business's desire to make a positive impact on society.

Triple Bottom Line: (Elkington 1997) introduced the concept of the triple bottom line, emphasizing that companies should focus on three dimensions of performance: economic, social, and environmental. This framework advocates for balancing profit with social and environmental considerations. Most theories of corporate social responsibility acknowledge that the Triple Bottom Line (TBL) concept, first presented during the Brundtland Commission in 1987, is the cornerstone of the theory. John Elikngton gave it its official name in 1994. The three pillars or 3Ps theory is another name for this one. According to this statement, a business has three responsibilities: profit, people, and planet, or social, environmental, and economic responsibility. A company may only be considered sustainable if it attends to all three Triple Bottom Line characteristics, as they are intricately linked. It is just and equitable when profit and people are taken care of, but the planet is doomed when environmental protection is neglected. Nonetheless, CSR policies become intolerable if one ignores profit in favor of the planet and people, even if businesses depend on profits to stay in operation. Once more, (Cane 2013) asserts that it is feasible and beneficial for a corporation to prioritize Profit and Planet before People, but doing so may eventually lower employee morale and violate the social compact.

Profit

Profit is a mandatory requirement, thanks to which a company has a possibility to develop. Hopefully profit leads also to certain measures committed to responsible behaviour. However, the economic part of CSR is not only about making profit, the most important task is to use it well. The profit part of TBL has not been discussed often in the last years, as there is a common view that it is well-tended, as most of managers do not need a reminder to provide value for their shareholders. CSR is primarily concerned with the direct and indirect financial effects that a company's operations have on the surrounding community and other stakeholders. Over time, socially conscious businesses can turn a profit and reduce expenses. Consequently, a business that respects that has a higher chance of avoiding any negative social repercussions and maximizing positive social benefits. Furthermore, completing that assignment might inspire the business to grow even more (KsiężaK and Fischbach 2017).

People

Employees are an organization's lifeblood. Raising living standards is essential to the social component (KsiężaK and Fischbach 2017). CSR is a tool that helps an organization and society build and maintain positive relationships. In the interactions between small and medium-sized businesses and local communities, this is crucial. SMEs typically hire people from the local community, which means that employees also bear a twofold responsibility to the community (Gołaszewska-Kaczan 2009).

Because of this, those businesses are typically more affluent and aware of the most pressing issues in society. However, the people who live in the region are not the sole members of the local community. It also includes every organization and group operating in the neighborhood. A company's social duty encompasses all of the individuals it touches or is impacted by. In this way, businesses assume responsibility for ensuring employees' well-being and invest in the skills necessary for the hiring process. Businesses cannot function without their employees, clients, or supply chain partners.

Planet

Planet serves as both a business and a people's home. Big businesses will be just as impacted as anything else on Earth if their actions cause environmental pollution and bring the planet to ruin.

Everyone bears responsibility for the natural environment, but companies bear the brunt of this duty since they are frequently the initial cause of harm to it. The main detrimental effects of businesses on the environment include trash production, the release of polluting byproducts, and the careless use of natural resources. Consequently, the least those businesses can do is lessen or completely eradicate their negative environmental effects.

The company can be environmentally sustainable in a lot of ways. It may, first and foremost, ensure that the products it produces do not negatively impact the environment in any manner. This isn't yet feasible for all industries, though. For example, a lot of CO_2 is released by items in the automotive industry. As more environmentally friendly vehicles are developed, environmental harm is still done, albeit to a smaller degree. Waste reduction is an activity that can be carried out by all businesses. Any firm can reduce its use without even thinking about it; for example, it can stop printing emails that don't need to be printed or just recycle. Businesses that generate extremely toxic waste have to be concerned and take all necessary steps to reduce the amount of toxicity (KsiężaK and Fischbach 2017)

Institutional Theory: This theory examines how institutional pressures, such as regulations, norms, and cultural expectations, influence CSR practices. It posits that companies adopt CSR initiatives to gain legitimacy and align with societal values (DiMaggio and Powell 1983). Stakeholder theory (Donaldson and Preston 1995), agency theory (McWilliams and Siegel 2001), legitimacy theory (Guthrie and Parker 1989), and signaling theory have all been major sources of information for CSR research. These studies have also brought attention to the institutional environment's tacit influence on the adoption of CSR practices and transparency. For example, (Scholtens 2009) reports that in the countries that make up the Organization for Economic Co-operation and Development (OECD), savings accounts are made available to the general public by specialized banks, who guarantee to use the funds deposited in the accounts to finance environmentally friendly projects or to assist new business owners who are unable to obtain financing from traditional financial institutions. It is acknowledged that, in contrast to Greece and Hungary, the majority of the government-imposed constraints on the banks in Denmark are applied by the government. However, the government of Hungary is involved in enforcing the application of specific laws, such those pertaining to environmental preservation or equal opportunities (Metaxas and Tsavdaridou 2010). Similarly, (Soh, Kim et al. 2014) offer other explanations for understanding the differences in

CSR reporting standards between Asian-Pacific nations and Western nations, which are represented by the United States and the United Kingdom. First, a sophisticated system of governance may be established in Western nations thanks to the strength of the law (Mohamed and Salah 2016).

INTEGRATION IN FINANCIAL DECISION MAKING

Integrating corporate governance and CSR into financial decision-making involves aligning business objectives with ethical and sustainable practices. This strategic alignment requires setting clear goals, developing policies, and implementing frameworks that promote responsible behavior. Financial decisions should prioritize investments that foster long-term sustainability, manage risks proactively, and engage stakeholders effectively. Integrating corporate governance and corporate social responsibility (CSR) into financial decision-making is becoming increasingly essential for businesses aiming for sustainable growth and long-term value creation. Several studies discovered a positive relationship between corporate social responsibilities and corporate governance, Ben Fatma, H., & Chouaibi, J. (2024).

The results of the research showed that corporate social responsibility and strong corporate governance may reduce financial statement fraud. Additionally, ethical principles and a business culture that discourages the use of misleading financial statements must support efforts at prevention and detection. While some areas have demonstrated the ability to establish a strong governance structure that makes it efficient in managing fraud incidents by taking accurate financial decision, others have not been able to do so. Empirical evidence indicates that the components of governance subjected to quantitative investigation still provide diverse outcomes. Positive outcomes are not consistently obtained from the system for the category of excellent corporate governance. Moreover, good governance and CSR are essential in financial decision-making to reduce fraud and makes profitable or sustainable investments, Andayani, W., & Wuryantoro, M. (2023).

Corporate governance involves the systems, principles, and processes by which companies are directed and controlled, ensuring accountability, fairness, and transparency in a company's relationship with its stakeholders (Cadbury 1992). Incorporating CSR into this framework means that financial decisions are not only driven by profit motives but also consider the environmental, social, and governance (ESG) impacts of business activities. This integration helps manage risks, enhance corporate reputation, and comply with regulatory requirements (Eccles, Ioannou et al. 2014). Companies that effectively integrate CSR into their corporate governance structures are better positioned to address stakeholder concerns, foster investor confidence, and achieve competitive advantages. For instance, research has shown that firms with strong CSR practices often experience lower capital constraints and improved financial performance (Cheng, Ioannou et al. 2014). Thus, the synergy between corporate governance and CSR is crucial for ensuring that financial decision-making supports sustainable and ethical business practices, ultimately contributing to the overall resilience and success of the organization.

CONCLUSION:

The theoretical and conceptual framework for corporate governance and CSR initiatives in financial decision-making, emphasizes the significance of moral leadership, openness, and stakeholder involvement. Financial decisions are made within the framework of corporate governance, which guarantees responsibility and alignment with long-term organizational objectives. By taking into account the interests of a wider range of stakeholders, such as consumers, employees, and the community, incorporating CSR into this framework improves the sustainability of financial processes. In addition to reducing risks, this connection of governance and social responsibility improves the financial performance and reputation of the company. In the end, the partnership between CSR and corporate governance encourages ethical decision-making, building confidence and generating long-term benefits for all parties involved.

LIMITATIONS AND FUTURE DIRECTION:

The difficulty of integrating a variety of, diverse, and often conflicting objectives is one drawback of the theoretical and conceptual approach to corporate governance and CSR (Corporate Social Responsibility) activities in financial decision-making. Stakeholder value maximization has always been the primary goal of corporate governance, but CSR places more emphasis on social, environmental, and ethical duties. These competing agendas may make it challenging to create coherent, broadly applicable frameworks that strike a compromise between short-term financial objectives and long-term social objectives. Furthermore, because theoretical models are sometimes predicated on assumptions that fail to take into account regional regulatory variances or industry-specific complexities, they may be devoid of empirical support. Furthermore, the dynamic nature of corporate governance laws and CSR standards implies that anything applicable now might quickly become out of date, which restricts the frameworks' long-term usefulness in decision-making processes. Their inability to be consistent and flexible can make it difficult to apply them in real-world financial strategy. More empirical research may be done to investigate how CSR and CG practices affect financial performance in the long run. This entails investigating the effects of incorporating ESG criteria on the cost of capital, shareholder value, and risk management. Refinement of decision-making models that take into consideration financial and non-financial performance indicators will be aided by an understanding of this association. The development of AI and big data analytics opens up new possibilities for evaluating the effects of CG and CSR on financial choices in real-time. Future studies could focus on how technology might improve CSR performance assessment, accountability, and transparency, which would improve governance procedures and guide investment choices.

IMPLICATIONS:

1. Alignment of Ethical Values with Financial Goals: Ethical factors are integrated into financial decision-making through a theoretical and conceptual approach to corporate governance and corporate social responsibility (CSR). This encourages a company's financial objectives to be in line with more general society principles. Businesses that embrace corporate social responsibility (CSR) are likely to take into account not only financial gain but also how their activities affect stakeholders like consumers, workers, and the environment, which results in longer-term financial plans that are more sustainable.
2. Financial Stability and Risk Management: When associated with CSR initiatives, sound company governance helps lower financial risks. Similar to accountability and openness, ethical governance measures reduce the likelihood of fraud, legal problems, and adverse effects on reputation. Strong CSR initiatives help a company be viewed as a more reliable investment since they are thought to handle risks better, which improves financial stability and decision-making.
3. Improved Investor Confidence and Corporate Reputation: A company's reputation is improved when it implements CSR through sound corporate governance. Strong CSR practices are becoming increasingly preferred by investors since they are linked to better management and fewer risks. This may result in easier access to financing, cheaper borrowing costs, and higher stock prices, all favorably influencing financial decisions.
4. Long-Term vs. Short-Term Financial Focus: Long-term financial decision-making is supported by a robust governance structure. When sustainable and ethical practices are prioritized over short-term profits, operational efficiency, increased stakeholder loyalty, and lower environmental and regulatory expenses result in long-term financial rewards.

5. Increased Compliance and Regulatory Alignment: Adhering to changing regulatory frameworks that support sustainability and moral behavior has an influence on financial decision-making. Firms with strong corporate social responsibility (CSR) frameworks integrated into their governance are better positioned to achieve these obligations without facing financial penalties as governments and international agencies impose stronger laws on environmental impact, diversity, and social responsibility.
6. Stakeholder-Driven Decision-Making: Integrating CSR with corporate governance modifies the process of decision-making. This strategy takes into account a wider variety of stakeholders (workers, community, consumers) rather than just shareholders. This might lead to more inclusive financial decisions that better balance social impact and profitability.
7. Improved Operational Efficiency: CSR projects frequently concentrate on boosting social welfare, cutting waste, and strengthening environmental sustainability. These can result in operational gains like lower resource usage and higher worker productivity, which can save money and have an impact on decisions about whether to invest in new technology or procedures.
8. Financial Analysis: Social and Environmental Metrics: Non-financial measures including environmental, social, and governance (ESG) performance are becoming more and more integrated into financial decision-making. Theoretical approaches to corporate governance place a strong emphasis on how these indicators are integrated, which has an impact on risk assessments, valuations, and financial analysis, ultimately altering how financial success is assessed.
9. Incentivizing Responsible Leadership: CSR-focused corporate governance may influence leadership style and motivate CEOs to make prudent financial choices. This can encourage financial strategies that put sustainability and stakeholder value first by creating incentive structures that reward long-term value creation rather than short-term profit maximization.
10. Global Competitiveness and Market Access: Adopting CSR principles and incorporating them into governance frameworks is crucial for multinational corporations to get access to international markets. Higher CSR standards are required by many worldwide marketplaces, and businesses who don't meet them may find it harder to compete. This might have an influence on strategic financial choices about product development or market growth.

References

Andayani, W., & Wuryantoro, M. (2023). Good Corporate Governance, Corporate Social Responsibility and Fraud Detection of Financial Statements. *International Journal of Professional Business Review: Int.J. Prof. Bus. Rev.*, 8(5), 9.

Ben Fatma, H., & Chouaibi, J. (2024). The mediating role of corporate social responsibility in good corporate governance and firm value relationship: Evidence from European financial institutions. *Meditari Accountancy Research*, 32(4), 1084–1105. DOI: 10.1108/MEDAR-08-2022-1762

Cadbury, A. (1992). Report of the committee on the financial aspects of corporate governance, Gee.

Cane, P. (2013). *Atiyah's accidents, compensation and the law*. Cambridge university press. DOI: 10.1017/CBO9781139548885

Carroll, A. B. (1991). The pyramid of corporate social responsibility: Toward the moral management of organizational stakeholders. *Business Horizons*, 34(4), 39–48. DOI: 10.1016/0007-6813(91)90005-G

Carroll, A. B. (2016). "Carroll's pyramid of CSR: taking another look." International journal of corporate social responsibility **1**: 1-8.

Cheng, B., Ioannou, I., & Serafeim, G. (2014). Corporate social responsibility and access to finance. *Strategic Management Journal*, 35(1), 1–23. DOI: 10.1002/smj.2131

Contrafatto, M. (2014). Stewardship theory: Approaches and perspectives. Accountability and social accounting for social and non-profit organizations, Emerald Group Publishing Limited: 177-196.

Davis, J. H., Schoorman, F. D., & Donaldson, L. (1997). Toward a stewardship theory of management. *Academy of Management Review*, 22(1), 20–47. DOI: 10.2307/259223

DiMaggio, P. J., & Powell, W. W. (1983). The iron cage revisited: Institutional isomorphism and collective rationality in organizational fields. *American Sociological Review*, 48(2), 147–160. DOI: 10.2307/2095101

Donaldson, K., Brown, G. M., Brown, D. M., Bolton, R. E., & Davis, J. M. (1989). Inflammation generating potential of long and short fibre amosite asbestos samples. *Occupational and Environmental Medicine*, 46(4), 271–276. DOI: 10.1136/oem.46.4.271

Donaldson, T., & Preston, L. E. (1995). The stakeholder theory of the corporation: Concepts, evidence, and implications. *Academy of Management Review*, 20(1), 65–91. DOI: 10.2307/258887

Du, S., Bhattacharya, C. B., & Sen, S. (2010). Maximizing business returns to corporate social responsibility (CSR): The role of CSR communication. *International Journal of Management Reviews*, 12(1), 8–19. DOI: 10.1111/j.1468-2370.2009.00276.x

Eccles, R. G., Ioannou, I., & Serafeim, G. (2014). The impact of corporate sustainability on organizational processes and performance. *Management Science*, 60(11), 2835–2857. DOI: 10.1287/mnsc.2014.1984

Elkington, J. (1997). "The triple bottom line." Environmental management: Readings and cases 2: 49-66.

Freeman, R. B., & Medoff, J. L. (1984). What do unions do. *Indus. & Lab. Rel. Rev.*, 38, 244.

Friedman, A. L., & Miles, S. (2002). Developing stakeholder theory. *Journal of Management Studies*, 39(1), 1–21. DOI: 10.1111/1467-6486.00280

Gołaszewska-Kaczan, U. (2009). *Corporate social commitment*. Publishing House of the Bialystok University of Technology.

Governance, C. (2015). What is corporate governance.

Gregory, H. J., & Simms, M. E. (1999). Corporate governance: what it is and why it matters. *9th International Anti-Corruption Conference*, Kuala Lumpur.

Guthrie, J., & Parker, L. D. (1989). Corporate social reporting: A rebuttal of legitimacy theory. *Accounting and Business Research*, 19(76), 343–352. DOI: 10.1080/00014788.1989.9728863

Keasey, K. and M. Wright (1993). "Issues in corporate accountability and governance: An editorial." Accounting and business research 23(sup1): 291-303.

Kramer, M. R., & Porter, M. E. (2006). Strategy and society: The link between competitive advantage and corporate social responsibility. *Harvard Business Review*, 84(12), 78–92.

KsiężaK, P. and B. Fischbach (2017). "Triple bottom line: The pillars of CSR." Journal of corporate responsibility and leadership 4(3): 95-110.

Larcker, D. F.. (2005). "How important is corporate governance?" Available at SSRN 595821.

McWilliams, A., & Siegel, D. (2001). Corporate social responsibility: A theory of the firm perspective. *Academy of Management Review*, 26(1), 117–127. DOI: 10.2307/259398

Meckling, W. H., & Jensen, M. C. (1976). *Theory of the Firm.* Managerial Behavior, Agency Costs and Ownership Structure.

Mentari, S., ... (2019). Effectiveness of the Board of Commissioners Role: Review of Resources Dependence Theory. 3rd International Conference on Accounting, Management and Economics 2018 (ICAME 2018), Atlantis Press.

Metaxas, T., & Tsavdaridou, M. (2010). Corporate social responsibility in europe: Denmark, Hungary and Greece. *Journal of Contemporary European Studies*, 18(1), 25–46. DOI: 10.1080/14782801003638679

Mohamed, I. M. A., & Salah, W. (2016). Investigating corporate social responsibility disclosure by banks from institutional theory perspective. *Journal of Administrative and Business Studies*, 2(6), 280–293.

Oecd, O. (2004). The OECD principles of corporate governance. *Contaduría y Administración*, •••, 216.

Pagkalou, F. I., Galanos, C. L., & Thalassinos, E. I. (2024). Exploring the Relationship between Corporate Governance, Corporate Social Responsibility and Financial and Non-Financial Reporting: A Study of Large Companies in Greece. *Journal of Risk and Financial Management*, 17(3), 97. DOI: 10.3390/jrfm17030097

Panda, B. and N. M. Leepsa (2017). "Agency theory: Review of theory and evidence on problems and perspectives." Indian journal of corporate governance 10(1): 74-95.

Paul, K. (2024). Why corporate social responsibility should be recognized as an integral stream of international corporate governance. *Green Finance*, 6(2), 348–362. DOI: 10.3934/GF.2024013

Pfeffer, J., & Salancik, G. (2015). External control of organizations—Resource dependence perspective. Organizational behavior 2, Routledge: 355-370.

Rashid, M. M., & Kabir, M. R. (2024). Corporate governance and corporate sustainability performance: The mediating role of CSR expenditure. *Asian Review of Accounting*. Advance online publication. DOI: 10.1108/ARA-12-2023-0350

Saam, N. J. (2007). Asymmetry in information versus asymmetry in power: Implicit assumptions of agency theory? *Journal of Socio-Economics*, 36(6), 825–840. DOI: 10.1016/j.socec.2007.01.018

Scholtens, B. (2009). Corporate social responsibility in the international banking industry. *Journal of Business Ethics*, 86(2), 159–175. DOI: 10.1007/s10551-008-9841-x

Shleifer, A., & Vishny, R. W. (1997). A survey of corporate governance. *The Journal of Finance*, 52(2), 737–783. DOI: 10.1111/j.1540-6261.1997.tb04820.x

Soh, C.. (2014). Corporate social responsibility (CSR) implementation in South Korea: Lessons from American and British CSR policies. *Journal of International and Area Studies*, ●●●, 99–118.

Tricker, R. I. (2015). *Corporate governance: Principles, policies, and practices.* Oxford University Press.

Tricker, R. L. "Part 1—The Concept of Corporate Governance."

Weber, M. (1947). The theory of economic and social organization. In *Trans. AM Henderson and Talcott Parsons*. Oxford University Press.

Yusif, S., & Hafeez-Baig, A. (2024). Impact of stakeholder engagement strategies on managerial cognitive decision-making: The context of CSP and CSR. *Social Responsibility Journal*, 20(6), 1101–1121. DOI: 10.1108/SRJ-05-2023-0295

Chapter 8
Risk and Uncertainty Factors in Managerial Economics

Saqib Muneer
https://orcid.org/0000-0003-4575-9566
University of Ha'il, Saudi Arabia

ABSTRACT

The concept of risk in managerial economics encompasses various unexpected events such as natural disasters, risk, economic challenges, uncertainty or product failures that lead to undesirable outcomes. Risk arises from incomplete information about future events, which makes the results unpredictable. The inherent uncertainty of the future because of the unpredictable nature of the universe, further complicates the understanding and management of risk. Scientific uncertainty, defined as any deviation from complete determinism, illustrates the difficulty in clearly defining risk. Sometimes managerial economics explores risk through its two primary dimensions, highlighting its complexity and the challenges it presents to decision-makers.

INTRODUCTION

The probability and result of unreliable future events can be measured with the help of a Risk. Risk can be defined as undesirable consequences (Yoe, 2019). Fire, flood, virus, death, economic obstacle, or some types of danger, or unexpected results are not realized because of some unmatched product features with our expectations, your investment failed to achieve desirable beneficial outcomes, the disturbed ecosystem or any other failures are causes of Risk. Incomplete information about future events helps to create a chance for risk factors. The future is profoundly

DOI: 10.4018/979-8-3693-5733-0.ch008

unexpected therefore we don't know about the results because the universe is characteristically inconstant. These all factors cause uncertainty in results. According to, scientific uncertainty and this phenomenon can be defined as "any departure from the unachievable ideal of complete determinism". The following explanation of risk suggests that risk can't be defined clearly. Basically, two dimensions of risk have been explained in different textbooks.

Some basic concepts of risk describe it as uncertainty. Some consequences, that is, harms, may be uncertain and the sequence of events that leads to them may, likewise, be uncertain. There can be uncertainty about their amount, occurrence, duration, and the like even when consequences and their contributing events are acknowledged. ItIt's the researcher's duty to identify the major uncertainties that may cause expected risks and may help in calculations and management of managerial activities (Roger Strand, 2009). The risk of concerns can be estimated clearly with the help of this identification process. The risk of dam failure, the risk of bankruptcy, risk of acrylamide are common examples to understand risk practices. Significant confusion about the exact nature of a risk can be produced by this shorthand communication. Before they return to shorthand explanations of risks risk administrators, inspectors, and correspondents must identify the the risk of concerns clearly and recognizably with the process (Roger Strand, 2009). It is discussed that the valuation process can be divided into two parts because the velour is "unable to specify and price accurately all current and future influences on the value of the asset" (Adhair & Hutchison, 2005).

According to Kinzer (1982)"decision making would call purely for competent calculation" but on the other hand with the deficiency of uncertainty "decision making would no longer encountered as imaginative, creative determination''. Before configuring a problem a manager must create the specific strategy predict desired outcomes assign probabilities to possible outcomes and choose an "ends-means framework" that describes what is relevant to him. Kirzner (1982) stated that "acting man must choose a framework that confirms what entrepreneurial gifts he can display because cannot be supposed to be sure of the framework relevant for calculative activity' 'The model of market uncertainty has not been directly recommended in the studies of fields of the consumer but Ram and Sheth (1989) have been presented some similar concepts to market uncertainty. They recognized that innovation can be restricted by risk barriers one of the resistance-inducing factors and they defined risk associated with the production stage (Ram & Sheth, 1989). Sheth

Arrow, (1971) described risk and uncertainty as most people list down all the possibilities and outcomes of a state of nature but they doubt what state is suitable for them and don't know about the results of their activities, and also difficult to respond effectively and efficiently to make obvious organizational changes (Tripsas & Gavetti, 2000). Companies are facing a turbulent, complex, and uncertain business environment that causes demands for the companies that are frequently changing. In other words, they consider sustained prosperity and growth as their ultimate goals to achieve, and increasing dynamism and discontinuous change are major challenges for them (Brown & Eisenhardt, 1997). Routine decision-making is easy and simple because all relevant data is available but under uncertainty and risk decision-making is a greater cognitive challenge (Bedenk & Mieg, 2018). According to Demir (2009), the profitability of a firm can be affected negatively due to increasing uncertainty. Moreover, Ahmad and Qayyum (2008, 2009) argued that private investments can be challenged and crushed by macroeconomic uncertainty.

Risk and Uncertainty:

When two conditions overlap risk is classified as the sum of threats and vulnerabilities (Birch & McEvoy, 1992) .In the activities of an organization, the thing that has a conflicting effect is a threat. Any independent specific threat allows a threat to create a venture and vulnerability is due to the physical system. The clarity of risks is defined as how many times risk occurs from vulnerability and threat catalog risk effect. William, (1994) Determines risk and analyzes it for project management risk by process of project risk register and classifies each risk factor into event contractual. Peer group information availability and intellectual properties of individual education carriers are factors that have an impact on the development of Rick these factors are determined by (Choffray & and Johnson, 1977) and (Ritchie & Marshall, 1993). To describe and explain the types of enterprise and organizational risk various studies were made before half-century (Hoskisson & Chirico, 2017) At the unit level the properties of the manager and risk objectives have an impact on the decision-making process less information is about these factors (Cain and McKeon, 2016; Hoskisson et al., 2017). For making the managerial decision-making framework the study relates two questions to define risk and uncertainty (Knight, 1921). First, in the manager risk-taking process how ideas and variables are linked to defined, and second, in the corporate setting manager-level decision-making is affected by relationships between ideas. Significant risk-taking properties study proposed by MacCrimmon et al. (1986). Personal business and financial risk are determined by interviews and surveys of 500 executives working in Canada and the USA. They describe almost all managers and policymakers have "stereotyped views about who does and who does not take risks" (MacCrimmon & Wehgur, 1990) Risk-taking behavior model given by (Sitkin & Wiengart, 1995).

At Risk, individual organizational and contextual properties of behavior have a direct relationship and this view is raised from industry-wide use of simplified models this is according to Sitkin and Pablo. Surrounding risk terms have less definitional clarity due to model development. To understand risk determinants common definitional framework is significant MacCrimmon and Wehrung (1990) and Sitkin and Pablo (1992). According to Le Roy and Singell (1987) objective probabilities make the difference between risk and uncertainty. Knight's (1921) view about uncertainty is more controversial than Keness's (1937). .The Keyness assumption of uncertainty is not based on the quantifiable probability distribution but is based on the knowledge level of future events (Andrade, 2011).When we have temporary knowledge about present than decision made on the basis of that knowledge is not factual based and improper future results so uncertainty is not the property of reality it is the property of knowledge .Cognitively unreachable nature events affected by time gap between decision and decision outcome because it is a key factor Keynes highlights it.

Assigning probability to outcomes not required so much distinction more distinction is required with the first stage of regrouping random outcomes (Langlois & Cosgel, 1993) .Estimated possible results are required to decision maker to predict occurrence under uncertainty. Uncertainty reduce in to risk is the risk estimation defined by (Rowe, 1977) and he shared the of understanding of Knights (1921). In the classical perspective of finance risk means to logic and instrumental rationality that associated with risk management. Social norms associated with risk are a risk policy. To shape anyone risk profile seven factors combine and work together that work is done (Carr, 2014).The difference in the way of people decision making that have risk that all is in the risk profile .Risk prefer (Knight, 1921)ence and perception and need to take risk and risk knowledge risk composure risk capacity and risk tolerance are factors include in Carr's model. Financial Risk profile elements clarified by Carrs original work done by him.

Bank lending strategies greatly affected by macroeconomics uncertainty For instance, Baum et al.(2009) ; Company profitability have inverse relationship with uncertainty (Demir, 2009).The relationship between expectation and risk premium concluded (Bernanke, 2004). The significant factors to control the inflation are controlling the inflation expectation this relationship is proposed by Bernanke (2004). The inflation is reflected by predicted inflation expectation this idea is according to Bernank.

1. Perception:

Business manager can analyze the risk associated with the decision and has awareness that each decision is little bit similar with other decision although it is somehow different from other decisions and manager think risk is mostly in defining the problem (Knight, 1921). Both the micro and macro level the perception created about problem will be different (Walker, 2003).The four factors on the basis of which risk is perceived are cultural background social political institution affective cognitive and heuristics (Renn & Benighaus, C, 2013) . Miller (2007) stated, "The freedom of others to act creatively is a source of irreducible uncertainty" (p. 66).

2. Risk Capacity:

In risk assessment process the risk ability is a different term, due to risky decision the loss which have to bear a person or an organization is known as risk capacity or risk ability (Cordell, 2001). Framework of risk capacity is developed that describe how much resources lost is bearable for a decision maker and having idea of finance for future aims (Kitces, 2006). To develop anyone risk profile risk capacity is important factor (Nobre & Grable, 20155). To determine income stability and presence of insurance properties idea of risk capacity is important that is actually given by Carr (2014). Bearing the loss of business depends upon the type of business Shackle's (1966) and risk capacity is a property of firm in the business management.

3. Risk Need:

To reach the target that developed before the intensity of risk taken to reach that target is known as risk need (Grable & Lytton, 1999).To make objectives real and when the individual have cleared goals than they are more involved in risky attitude that is shown by the results (Jeffery, 2009).In financial and business domain the risk need is as like a moving force under the risky attitude. Organization goals with respect to time shown by present risk model are risk need. Risky decision is required to achieve main objective in very short time duration.

4. Risk Composure:

Individual try to take or keep away from risk that is the property of individual personality which is risk composure. Risk competence is described in literature by same concept (Carr, 2014). To take or keep away from risk is risk competence (Sitkin & Wiengart, 1995). Although competence is not a stable property but it's a continual property. The Continual behavior about risk somehow relates but it's a meaningless. Explained in prospect theory that Competence to take risk is not continual property. When a person investing in business where no security valued here he takes risk but when the business is at peak level he tried not to take risk this concept is according to prospect theory. Every individual has different expectations and needs so that is the reason of existing difference between them. According to some other risk competence is stable. When decision maker interested in risk decision and skills risk competence is similar to across domains (Nicholson, 2005).

5. Risk Preference:

Involving of person in risky attitude is a risk priority (Kitces, 2006). Risk priority deal with initial intuitions (Roeser, 2010) or (Nobre & Grable, 2015) one decision is better than other this is a perception it is also possible the experience cal also affect the individual preority (Slovic et al., 2004) risk is feelings, the significant dimension and approaches indicate risk priority. Conformity is plural according to condition and energetic this concept is when risk priority is as a whole is considered. Priority help to rank alternatives according to attraction this concept is helpful in decision making (Miller, 2007).

6. Risk Perception:

Personal Subconscious assessment of attitude and condition is related with risk observation. Abilities of personal to process information received from environment are on the basis of risk observation. In a given condition risk involved in personal assessment on the basis of this concept considered as this definition is true (Cooper & Faseruk, 2011); intellectual activities that comprise accurate assessment of external condition and personal abilities at these base opinions are developed. Perception include (Ji & You, 2011); "processing of physical signals and/or information and the formation of a judgement about seriousness, likelihood, and acceptability" of a condition (Renn & Benighaus, C, 2013).Risk perception include risk knowledge and risk bareness in existing model.

7. Risk knowledge:

Risk in decision is also affected by another term which is risk knowledge. When we have all information about the factors that have linkage with the risky decision it means we know all about that factors and tradeoffs is a risk knowledge (Cordell, 2001). To have an idea of possible results and outcomes and to understand the effect direct judgment enable to classify observations and this term risk knowledge initiate from early decision frame work research (Knight, 1921). To reduce the uncertainty it is significant to understand the kind of risk (Walker, 2003) .They can accept risk because they have information about risk so it is hard to measure that context (Ahmad & Safwan, 2011). Over confidence ambiguity and disliking cal divert data these are the main factors when the risk knowledge measured comprehensively (Gilovich, 2002) . In addition, when there is lot of question and they are not process oriented or not relate with the context of risky decision (Fitzpatrick, 1983).

8. Risk Bearing:

Wealth threat for a manager is a risk bearing. Managers tried to increase the money and the decisions are made according to principles there is very little control of property (Wiseman & Gomez-Mejia, 1998). The wealth threat enables a manager to avoid risky attitude he do not take risky decision if the goals do not match.

9. Risk Tolerance:

When a person taking a decision the uncertainty in results of that taken decision and decision maker ability to bears that uncertainty is risk tolerance (Grable, J.E, 2000). The ability to bear risk is almost related with therisk tolerance (Carr, 2014). The decision maker can divide the two different things risk disliking and risk tolerance on the division scale according to the definition. (Fehrand Hari, 2014) .Risk tolerance is similar to risk behavior (Fehr & Hari, 2014). Personality components also include risk (Weber, 2002). (VanDe Venteretal., 2012) individual's property is risk bareness. For every decision maker the risk tolerance is different with respect to different goals. The each individual have different properties so due to their own different properties they have different effects on risk tolerance (Hunter, 2002) Risk tolerance also depends upon which kind of decision is taken by the person (Hunter, 2002).When there is little quantity of financial value in risky decision normally decision is taken no matter if some people are not ready to accept a risk (Hanna, 2013).

10. Credit Risk:

Credit risk is the default risk which is the likelihood of a borrower or counterparty not repaying an obligation as and when agreed. In layman's terms, it is the possibility that a debtor will default on a payment that he owes. This risk is always present in any credit or lending business, be it in a bank, a corporate bond or even a credit card purchase.

Credit risk management is an important component of most organisations especially those in the financial industry. For purposes of evaluating and managing credit risks, there are several methods that are employed by lenders, such as credit rating, analysis of financial statements and security accepted. While assessing creditworthiness of a borrower, the lenders try to measure risks of default and the probable loss in case of such an eventuality. Credit risk management therefore requires striking a fine balance between the number of credit origination and the credit losses.

Uncertainty, Capital Investment, and Risk Management:

Different survey of financial managers shows that during financial and capital investment decisions making firms major hurdles like uncertainty (Graham & Harvey, 2001). Definitely, organizations face long-lasting financial and economic issues due to negative effects of uncertainty on investment and financing policies (Myers, 1984). The literature shows that managers try to avoid or manage financial risk on different times because of dependable and important role of uncertainty in decision making at organizational level (Campello, 2011).Firstly, due to our research about crude oil future possibilities we are able to establish progressive and longstanding methods for our output price uncertainty.

Continuously growing and progressive price uncertainty of the unrelated agents that trade in expected marketplaces can be predicted through uncertainty measures being resulting from the marketing clearance possibility prices over time (Singleton, 2013). The present works indicates that financial frictions influence real investment decisions at organizational level (Almaida & Campello, 2007). External financing costs could be control by soften costs of financial sufferings, organizations can start risk management or prevarication by getting benefits from financial frictional incentives (Froot, 1993).Conceptual and empirical researches on uncertainty indicates that uncertainty exaggerates the finance related restrictions by increasing liability costs which cause decrease in investment (Kumar & Yerramilli, 2017). Financially constrained organization must be effected negatively due to the negative effect of uncertainty on capital investment (Kumar & Yerramilli, 2017),which decrease their capability in competition to reduce former post cost of financial suffering.

Though, Role of real options effect may decreases in financially constrained firms to accelerate investment that emerges due to the threat of future financing limitations (Boyle & Guthrie, 2003).Adam et al. (2007) claim that in the case of hedging and uncertainty an organization must which has valued real options should focus to sustain the scope of price uncertainty and may restricted the price uncertainty at minimum level. Collateral restrictions effects the tradeoff between the investment and risk management and predict that it's not necessary for restricted organization to reduce their investment but should hedge less (Rampini & Sufi, 2014).

Supply Chain Risks:

A streamlined process transforms raw materials into end products, which are then distributed to customers through retailers (Cohen & Moon, 1990). For purchasing firms, supply chain risk refers to the potential disruptions in planning, executing, monitoring, and controlling supply chain operations, which could result in financial losses (Zsidisin, 2003). In modern business, an increasing number of managers and globalized enterprises leverage innovative technologies to gain competitive advantages (Chan & Qi, 2003). The supply chain encompasses all activities associated with the movement and transformation of goods from the raw material stage to the end user, requiring coordination and collaboration among partners (Handfield & Nichols, 1999). The success of a supply chain partner is crucial for ensuring profitability and continuity (Tang, 2006).

Although there is limited literature on this subject (Kleindorfer & Saad, 2005), two key organizational factors—perceived operational similarity and market leadership—significantly influence a risk manager's ability to learn from other firms' operational losses (Hora & Klassen, 2013). Another finding indicates that improved internal integration of core business functions enhances demand visibility and reduces demand risk (Kache & Seuring, 2014). While the importance of supply chain risks to firm performance is widely recognized (Cao & Zhang, 2011), the impact of these risks on financial performance has been analyzed. Numerous scholars and practitioners have conducted extensive research to develop Supply Chain Risk Management (SCRM) models by identifying and examining the factors that determine risk performance in supply chains (Cucchiella & Gastaldi, 2006). For instance, purchasing organizations have developed contingency plans and implemented process improvements and buffer strategies to mitigate supply risks, based on an analysis of in-depth interviews with purchasing professionals from nine manufacturing companies (Zsidisin, 2000).

Procurement Decisions Making Under Uncertainty:

Today, the manufacturing industry is marked by intense competition, with companies vying on the basis of price, quality, and logistics (Roberta & Christopher, 2014). To stay competitive, many manufacturers have begun outsourcing non-core business activities (Kremic, 2006). However, this trend has made supply chains more complex and difficult to manage. A survey by Computer Science Corporation revealed that approximately 43 percent of firms report facing disruption risks (Tang, 2006). In the financial industry, risk is well-defined as the variability in returns, which can significantly impact expected yields (Markowitz, 1952).

Risk management has become an increasingly critical concern in supply chain management, as uncertainty in one part of the supply chain can trigger a cascade of undesirable effects throughout the network (Finch, 2004). For example, material costs account for 45 percent of expenses in the German automobile industry, and price fluctuations can be difficult to predict. To achieve optimal procurement under uncertain market conditions, combining contracts with open market purchases is recommended to reduce risk (Mahapatra, 2017). Optimal decision-making in Procurement Risk Management (PRM) under uncertainty should consider various potential risks, such as demand fluctuations, price volatility, and supply yield. Scholars have conducted extensive research in this area, with Martel (1995) examining the challenges of procurement planning over rolling horizons amid uncertain demand.

Procurement involves coordinating processes to acquire resources—including materials, skills, capabilities, and facilities—necessary for executing core business activities (Turban, 2008). Jessop (1994) defines procurement as the acquisition of external management resources to maintain and manage a company's activities under the most favorable conditions. While there is no universally accepted definition of procurement risk, supply risk is broadly defined by Zsidisin (2003) as "the probability of an incident associated with inbound supply from individual supplier failures or the supply market, which results in the purchasing firm's inability to meet customer demand or threatens customer life and safety." Kraljic's (1983) supply matrix categorizes different types of purchased items based on their supply impact, guiding the selection of appropriate procurement strategies. Extensive research has been conducted to optimize supply control by considering factors such as operational costs, product availability, and demand information (Agrawal & Nahmias, 1997). However, there remains no clear definition of Procurement Risk Management (PRM) according to the existing literature.

a. Unreliable Yield:

Several sources of supply have uncertain yields, often failing to deliver all products on time due to limited production capabilities (Erdem & Özekici, 2002). Additionally, not all products from suppliers meet the required standards, meaning only a portion can be used further (Bollapragada & Morton, 1999). Suppliers generally fall into two categories: Type A, which offers perfect quality at a high cost, and Type B, which offers imperfect quality at a lower cost. For a comprehensive review of yield uncertainty, Yano and Lee (1995) provide an extensive literature survey on lot sizing under uncertainty. The directory model illustrates that ordering policies remain relatively stable when there is only one Type A supplier, while the rest are Type B. To reduce yield uncertainty, collaboration with suppliers is key, such as through capital investments to enhance production lines or establish inspection centers (Talluri, 2010).

b. Disruption Risks:

Even with provider interruption chance, purchaser may design the stockpile base with reinforcement providers. Utilized choice tree to decide the quantity of providers (Ruiz-Torres & Mahmoodi, 2007). Truth be told, the model researched two circumstances: same disappointment likelihood of every provider or diverse disappointment likelihood of every provider. Yet, as the provider turns out to be less solid, extra providers might be expected to acquire the most minimal expense. Meena, (2011) built up a calculation to acquire the quantity of providers under cataclysmic occasions disturbance through considering the mix of disappointment rate, wasteful limit and it is critical to locate the ideal answer for limiting the all out expenses. Wagner, (2009) utilized copula capacities to catch the default reliance between providers. Copula work is away to speak to joint dissemination. An exact information fromaut to rationale providers assisted with showing the significance to examine provider default reliance in a provider portfolio. Both single and different sourcing when there is provider default hazard (Costantino & Pellegrino, 2010). Silbermayr and Minner (2014) contemplated a purchaser obtains from different provider who are having the danger of supply interference, the creator mode leda Semi-Markov choice procedure to show the advantage of numerous sourcing over single sourcing.

c. Multiple Uncertainties:

Because of the present complex business condition, the previously mentioned dangers would be interrelated, which cause an increasingly damaging financial outcome. Moreover, erroneously distinguishing the hazard causes the under-use of the normal provider and over-use of the reinforcement provider (Guo, 2016). So as to more readily address the inventory network dangers, considering various unsure components would be progressively significant. Li, (2017) considers an organization secures from two providers that are exposed to "win big or bust" disturbance hazard and irregular yield chance individually, to satisfy its deterministic interest. The scientist conducts three models for the above situations including no asset and requesting asset from one provider. Subsequently, the creator can figure out which procedures including single sourcing and double sourcing ought to be received for every situation to get the ideal request amount. Guo,(2016) considered the unforeseen limit system while sourcing from a normal provider having the above vulnerabilities with a questionable interest, the creator called attention to that the possibility arranging of requesting amount from ordinary provider ought to be more than reinforcement provider if the general stock hazard stays unaltered. Aside from considering interruption and yield chance, Shi (2011) examined the uncertainty of demand and costs in the Chinese market. The authors developed a portfolio procurement approach to mitigate procurement risk by utilizing various strategies, including long-term contracts, spot purchases, and option-based inventory contracts. They created a multi-stage stochastic programming model to assess the effectiveness of this portfolio approach over a specified time horizon. The results indicate that the proposed portfolio approach performs well in terms of profitability and reducing procurement risk exposure.

Managerial Decision Making Under Risk and Uncertainty:

Key basic leadership under vulnerability has consumed specialists for a considerable length of time and has been investigated from alternate points of view, for example, prospect hypothesis (Kahneman & Tversky, 1979), exchange cost hypothesis and, all the more as of late, genuine choices hypothesis (Krychowski & Quélin, 2010). Right now, choices rationale is embraced to investigate the powers that impact chiefs' vital choices to put and strip even with vulnerability. Since the time the expression "genuine choices" was presented (Myers, S. C, 1984) and applied in the administration writing (Kogut, 1991), analysts have considered its significance to settling on vital choices under vulnerability and to deciding how to assemble advancement portfolios to meet an unusual future (McGrath & MacMillan, 2009).A reason of genuine alternatives rationale is that vulnerability is of focal significance to whether a venture merits making (Dixit & Pindyck, 1995).In a circumstance without vulnerability, where tomorrow is relied upon to be equivalent to today, the present estimation of a business movement is a decent indicator for tomorrow's worth.

Be that as it may, if vulnerability is high, the present estimation of any business movement might be a terrible indicator of tomorrow's worth. Be that as it may, past genuine alternatives inquire about is regularly single-sided; it either centers on speculation choices (Wooster, 2016), that is practicing a call choice, or on divestment choices (O'Brien, 2009), that is, practicing a put alternative. Ostensibly, this center leaves an inadequate image of how venture and divestment choices are practiced to construct an all-out portfolio. This investigation tries to address this hole by breaking down both venture and divestment choices. In any event, when the requirement for authoritative change is self-evident, reacting productively and successfully is troublesome (Tripsas & Gavetti, 2000). The present business situations are tempestuous, complex, and questionable, and organizations face requests that are continually evolving. Accepting that a definitive objectives of the present organizations are continued success and development, they face the difficulties of expanding dynamism and spasmodic change (Darker and Eisenhardt, 1997).Sustained thriving and development require advancement and key reestablishment, which "incorporates the procedure, substance, and result of the refreshment or substitution of characteristics of an association that can possibly significantly influence its long haul possibilities" (Agarwal & Helfat, 2009). At the end of the day, vital recharging expects organizations to experiment or extraordinary.

Settling on choices under vulnerability is a greater psychological test than routine basic leadership in view of predispositions toward the known and existing (Bedenk & Mieg, 2018). Organizations will in general raise pledge to a current strategy instead of leave when confronted with negative outcomes, with the danger of the "sunk cost paradox" or "incurring further loss" (Staw, 1981). Genuine alternatives hypothesis, notwithstanding, challenges the view that sunk expense is constantly a misrepresentation, as industriousness and the choice to "keep a watch out" are viewed as genuine choices (Xie, 2009). Real choices inquire about regularly centers around speculation choices, for example, joint endeavors or Research and development, yet choices to strip are a piece of the rationale also (O'Brien, 2009). For instance, vulnerability makes organizations progressively hesitant to practice their put choices (Damaraju, 2015). Therefore, it may be normal that organizations would settle on more speculation choices than divestment choices (for example practicing more call choices than put choices). Then again, inquire about likewise proposes that organizations have reasons not to act by any means: way reliance (Sydow, 2009), hierarchical characters (Albert, 1985), and inheritances (Morais-Storz, 2018). At the end of the day, not settling on a decision is additionally settling on a decision.

The elucidating hypothesis gives us a few clarifications why individuals settle on choices the manner in which they really do and why the proposed standardizing rules for basic leadership under hazard and vulnerability are not followed (Simon, 1955). For example individuals settle on choices by following notable ways and by following entrenched and worked in standards, see e.g (Schein, 1992)and the conversation concerning Essential Basic Suppositions. We have, in the ongoing past, seen an expanding enthusiasm for the communication between regularizing, spellbinding and prescriptive hypotheses of basic leadership (Keeney, 1992).In request to create choice guides it is critical to realize the similitudes just as the contrasts between the three speculations see (Brown & A. Vari, 1992), and (.Moreover, basic leadership and hazard taking is setting subordinate (Walk & Z. Shapira, 1987) which settles on it essential to examine the basic leadership setting. The setting influences the type of choice investigation from multiple points of view and the manner in which choices are made (Walk & Z. Shapira, 1987)"No choice happens in vacuo: there is constantly a unique circumstance" (French, 2000), Risks: The Administration of Vulnerability. New York: Free Press.. At the end of the day, the structure just as the way of life of associations should likewise be inspected, since the two of them impact the basic leadership procedures as it were. Except for an investigation by (MacCrimmon K. R., 1986) and, observational research has not for the most part centered around the originations of hazard and hazard taking held by directors (Shapira, 1995). Since nobody, up until this point, has contemplated chiefs' hazard dispositions in corresponding with their genuine conduct when taking care of hazardous possibilities, the region despite everything remains moderately dim.(Shapira, 1995)

CONCLUSION:

Due to less information managers did not do the right things and they take wrong decisions, they are not able to handle the risky conditions because they do not follow the rules of organization. There are also many unwritten rules in the organization that developed in to the culture of organization and help managers in decision making and it is also a fact that manager feels stress of these unwritten rules. To avoid the traditional methods that already developed for the purpose of decision making the best way or method for decision making is computer based support system.

For both approach and practice this analysis is applicable. If the tasks and responsibilities not enforce carefully on the power companies of Norwegian by the local and regional government the results could be ineffective and it will become difficult to gain competitive advantage. To operate the things freely in the uncertain conditions the managers need flexibility and it is good to operate the things in right way. It is also not good to invest very much amount because the flexibility decreases by investing such great amount. The proper analysis of problems that are related with the manager's decisions is beneficial for the organization it is reveal from the analysis of attitude of the managers. Computer based tools are helpful for analyzing the conditions of decision making, especially when you are estimating the results and risk of different things. Managers do not use computer tools for decision making and there are very small numbers of managers that use computers for decision making.

References

A, A., & N, H. (2005). The reporting of risk in real estate appraisal property risk scoring. *Journal of property investment and finance, 23*(3), 254-68.

Adam, T., Dasgupta, S., & Titman, S. (2007). Financial constraints, competition, and hedging inIndustry equilibrium. *The Journal of Finance*, 62(5), 2445–2473. DOI: 10.1111/j.1540-6261.2007.01280.x

Adhair, N., & Hutchison, N. (2005). The reporting of risk in real estate appraisal property risk scoring. *Journal of Property Investment & Finance*, 23(3), 254–268. DOI: 10.1108/14635780510599467

Agarwal, R., & Helfat, C. (2009). Strategic renewal of organizations. *Organization Science*, 20(2), 281–293. DOI: 10.1287/orsc.1090.0423

Agrawal, N., & Nahmias, S. (1997). Rationalization of the supplier base in the presence of Yield Uncertainty. *Production and Operations Management*, 6(3), 291–308. DOI: 10.1111/j.1937-5956.1997.tb00432.x

Ahmad, A., & Safwan, N. (2011). How demographic characteristics affect the perception of investors about financial risk tolerance. *Interdisciplinary Journal of Contemporary Research in Business*, 3(2), 412–417.

Ahmad, I., & Qayyum, A. (2008). Effect of Goverment spending and macro economic uncertainty on private investment on services sector:evidence from Pakistan. *European Journal of Economics*, 11, 84–96.

Albert, S. (1985). Research in organizational behavior. *Organizational identity, 7*, 263–295.

Almaida, H., & Campello, M. (2007). Financial constraints, asset tangibility, and corporate investment. *Review of Financial Studies*, 20(2), 1429–1460. DOI: 10.1093/rfs/hhm019

Andrade, R. (2011). A construção do conceito de incerteza: Uma comparação das contribuições de Knight, Keynes, Shackle e Davidson. *Nova Economia*, 21(2), 171–195. DOI: 10.1590/S0103-63512011000200001

Arrow. (1971). *Essays on Theory of Risk-Bearing Chicago,* . Illusions: Markham Publishing Company.

Baum, C., Canglayan, N., Ozkan, N., & Talavera, O. (2006, January). The impact of macroeconomic uncertaintyonnon-financial firms 'demandforliquidity. *Review of Financial Economics*, 15(4), 289–304. DOI: 10.1016/j.rfe.2006.01.002

Bedenk, S., & Mieg, A. (2018). Failure in innovation decission making. *Strategies in failure mangement: Scintific insight, case stuudies and tools*, 95-106.

Bernanke, B. (2004). Speech at the Bond Market Association Annual Meeting. *the Economic Outlook and Monetary Policy*.

Birch, D. G., & McEvoy, M. (1992). 'Risk analysis for information systems. *Journal of Information Technology*, 7(1), 44–53. DOI: 10.1177/026839629200700107

Bollapragada, S., & Morton, T. (1999). Myopic heuristics for the random yield problem. *Operations Research*, 47(5), 713–722. DOI: 10.1287/opre.47.5.713

Boyle, G., & Guthrie, G. (2003). Investment,uncertainty,andliquidity. *The Journal of Finance*, 58(5), 2143–2166. DOI: 10.1111/1540-6261.00600

Brown, R. V., & Vari, A. (1992). Towards a research agenda for prescriptive decision science: The normative tempered by the descriptive. *Acta Psychologica*, 80(1-3), 33–47. DOI: 10.1016/0001-6918(92)90039-G

Brown, S., & Eisenhardt, B. (1997). The art of continous change:Linking complexity theory and time paced evaluation in relentlessly shifting organnization. *Administrative science Quaterly, 42*(1), 1-34. DOI: 10.2307/2393807

Cain, M., & McKeon, S. (2016). CEO personal risk-taking and corporate policies. *Journal of Financial and Quantitative Analysis*, 51(1), 139–164. DOI: 10.1017/S0022109016000041

Campello, M., Lin, C., Ma, Y., & Zou, H. (2011). The real and financial implications of corporate hedging. *The Journal of Finance*, 66(5), 1615–1647. DOI: 10.1111/j.1540-6261.2011.01683.x

Cao, M., & Zhang, Q. (2011). Supply chain collaboration: Impact on collaborative advantage and firm performance. *Journal of Operations Management*, 29(3), 163–180. DOI: 10.1016/j.jom.2010.12.008

Carr, N. (2014). Reassessing the assessment: exploring the factors that contribute to comprehensive financial risk evaluation.

Chan, F., & Qi, H. (2003). An innovative performance measurement method for supply chain management. *Supply Chain Management*, 8(3), 209–223. DOI: 10.1108/13598540310484618

Choffray, J. M., & Johnson, P. (1977). 8). Measuring perceived pre-purchase risk for a new industrial product'. *Industrial Marketing Management*, ●●●, 333–334.

Cohen, M., & Moon, S. (1990). Measuring supply chain performance. *International Journal of Operations & Production Management*, 19(3), 275–292.

Cooper, T., & Faseruk, A. (2011). Strategic risk, risk perception and risk behavior: Meta-analysis. *Journal of Financial Management and Analysis*, 2, 20–29.

Cordell, D. (2001). Risk PACK: How to evaluate risk tolerance. *Journal of Financial Planning*, 14(6), 36–40.

Costantino, N., & Pellegrino, R. (2010). Choosing between single and multiple sourcing based on supplier default risk: A real options approach. *Journal of Purchasing and Supply Management*, 16(1), 27–40. DOI: 10.1016/j.pursup.2009.08.001

Cucchiella, F., & Gastaldi, M. (2006). Risk management in supply chain: A real option approach. *Journal of Manufacturing Technology Management*, 17(6), 700–720. DOI: 10.1108/17410380610678756

Damaraju, N. L., Barney, J. B., & Makhija, A. K. (2015). Real options in divestment alternatives. *Strategic Management Journal*, 36(5), 728–744. DOI: 10.1002/smj.2243

Demir, F. (2009). Financializatiion and manufacturing firm profitability under uncertainty and macroeconomics volatility:ecidence from emerging market. *Review of Devellopment Economics, 13*(9), 592-609. doi:org/DOI: 10.1111/j.1467

Dixit, A. K., & Pindyck, R. (1995). The options approach to capital investment. *Harvard Business Review*, 73(3), 105–115.

Erdem, A., & Özekici, A. (2002). Inventory models with random yield in a random environment. *International Journal of Production Economics*, 78(3), 239–253. DOI: 10.1016/S0925-5273(01)00165-7

Fehr, R., & Hari, J. (2014). Assessing the risk attitudes of private investors using the implicit association test. *Journal of Financial Service Professionals*, 68(6), 50–62.

Finch, P. (2004). Supply chain risk management. *Supply Chain Management*, 9(2), 183–196. DOI: 10.1108/13598540410527079

Fitzpatrick, M. (1983). The definition and assessment of political risk in international business: A review of the literature. *Academy of Management Review*, 8(2), 249–254. DOI: 10.2307/257752

French, S. (2000). Statistical Decision Theory.

Froot, K., Scharfstein, D. S., & Stein, J. C. (1993). Risk management: Coordinating corporate investment and financing policies. *The Journal of Finance*, 48(5), 1629–1658. DOI: 10.1111/j.1540-6261.1993.tb05123.x

Gilovich, T. (2002). *Heuristics and Biases: The Psychology of Intuitive Judgement*.

Grable, J., & Lytton, J. (1999). Financial risk tolerance revisited: The development of a risk assessment instrument. *Financial Services Review*, 8(3), 163–181. DOI: 10.1016/S1057-0810(99)00041-4

Grable, J. E. (2000). Financial risk tolerance and additional factors that affect risk taking in everyday money matters. *Journal of Business and Psychology*, 14(4), 625–630. DOI: 10.1023/A:1022994314982

Graham, J., & Harvey, C. (2001). the theory and practice of corporate finance: Evidence from the field. *Financial Econom*, 187–243.

Guo, S., Zhao, L., & Xu, X. (2016). Impact of supply risks on procurement decisions. *Annals of Operations Research*, 241(1-2), 411–430. DOI: 10.1007/s10479-013-1422-4

Handfield, R., & Nichols, E. (1999). (P.-H. upply Chain Management, Ed.)

Hanna, S. (2013). Assessing risk tolerance. *Theory and Management*, 99-120.

Hora, M., & Klassen, R. (2013). Learning from others' misfortune: Factors influencing knowledge acquisition to reduce operational risk. *Journal of Operations Management*, 31(1-2), 52–61. DOI: 10.1016/j.jom.2012.06.004

Hoskisson, R., & Chirico, F. (2017). Managerial risk taking: a multitheoretical review and future research agenda. *43*(1), 137-169.

Hunter, D. (2002, Septembe). Risk perception and risk tolerance in aircraft pilots. *Risk_Perception_and_Risk_Tolerance_in_ Aircraft Pilots*. Retrieved from www.researchgate.net

Jeffery, S. (2009). Goal attainment as a resource: The cushion effect in risky choice above a goal. *Journal of Behavioral Decision Making*, 23(2), 191–202. DOI: 10.1002/bdm.645

Jessop, D. (1994). Purchasing management, analysis, planning and practice: AJ van Weele Chapman & Hall London (1994). *European Journal of Purchasing & Supply Management*, 3(1), 194–195. DOI: 10.1016/0969-7012(94)90010-8

Ji, M., You, X., Lan, J., & Yang, S. (2011). The impact of risk tolerance, risk perception and hazardous attitude on safety operation among airline pilots in China. *Safety Science*, 49(10), 1412–1420. DOI: 10.1016/j.ssci.2011.06.007

Kache, F., & Seuring, S. (2014). Linking collaboration and integration to risk and performance in supply chains via a review of literature reviews. *Supply Chain Management*, 19(5/6), 664–682. DOI: 10.1108/SCM-12-2013-0478

Kahneman, D., & Tversky, A. (1979). Prospect theory: An analysis of decision under risk. *Econometrica*, 47(2), 263–292. DOI: 10.2307/1914185

Keeney, R. L. (1992). On the foundations of prescriptive decision analysis. *Utility theories: Measurement and applications.*

Keynes, J. (1936). the General Theory of Employment. *Interest, and Money.*

Kinzer, I. (1982). Uncertainty, Discovery and human action: A study of enterprenurial Profile in the Misesian System. *Method, Process and Austrian Economics:Eassays in Honor of Ludwing Von Mises.*

Kitces, M. (2006, March). Rethinking risk tolerance. *Financial Planning*, 51-59.

Kleindorfer, P.R, & Saad, G. (2005). Production and Operations Management. *Managing disruption risks in supply chains, 14*(1), 53-58.

Knight, F. (1921). (B. M. Houghton Mifflin Company, Ed.) *Risk, Uncertainty, and Profit.*

Kogut, B. (1991). Joint ventures and the option to expand and acquire. *Management Science*, 37(1), 19–33. DOI: 10.1287/mnsc.37.1.19

Kraljic, P. (1983). Purchasing must become supply management. *Harvard Business Review*, 61(5), 109–117.

Kremic, T., Icmeli Tukel, O., & Rom, W. O. (2006). Out sourcing decision support: A survey of benefits, risks, and decision factors. *Supply Chain Management*, 11(6), 467–482. DOI: 10.1108/13598540610703864

Krychowski, C., & Quélin, B. (2010). Real options and strategic investment decisions: Can they be of use to scholars? *The Academy of Management Perspectives*, 24(2), 65–78. DOI: 10.5465/AMP.2010.51827776

Kumar, P., & Yerramilli, V. (2017). Optimal capital structure and investment with real options and end ogenous debt costs. *Review of Financial Studies*, 31(9), 3452–3490. DOI: 10.1093/rfs/hhx093

Langlois, R., & Cosgel, M. (1993). Frank knight on risk, uncertainty, and the firm: A new interpretation. *Economic Inquiry*, 31(3), 456–465. DOI: 10.1111/j.1465-7295.1993.tb01305.x

Leroy, S., & Singel, L. (1987). Knight on risk and uncertainty. *Journal of Political Economy*, 95(2), 394–406. DOI: 10.1086/261461

Li, X. (2017). Optimal procurement strategies from suppliers with random yield and all-or-nothing risks. *Annals of Operations Research*, 257(1-2), 167–181. DOI: 10.1007/s10479-015-1923-4

MacCrimmon, K., & Wehgur, D. (1990). Characteristics of Risk Taking Executives. *Management Science*, 36(4), 422–435. DOI: 10.1287/mnsc.36.4.422

MacCrimmon, K., Wehgur, D., & Stanbury, W. (1986). *Taking Risks: The Management of Uncertainty.*

MacCrimmon, K. R. (1986). Taking Risks. *The Management of Uncertainty.*

Mahapatra, S., Levental, S., & Narasimhan, R. (2017). Market price uncertainty, risk aversion and procurement's combining contracts and open market sourcing alternatives. *International Journal of Production Economics*, 185(3), 34–51. DOI: 10.1016/j.ijpe.2016.12.023

Markowitz, H. (1952). Portfolio selection. *The Journal of Finance*, 7(1), 77–91.

Martel, A., Diaby, M., & Boctor, F. (1995). Multiple items procurement under stochastic nonstationary demands. *European Journal of Operational Research*, 87(1), 74–92. DOI: 10.1016/0377-2217(94)00019-9

McGrath, R., & MacMillan, I. (2009). *Discovery driven growth. A break through process to reduce risk and seize opportunity.*

McGrath, R. G., & Nerkar, A. (2004). Real options reasoning and a new look at the R&D investment strategies of pharmaceutical firms. *Strategic Management Journal*, 25(1), 1–21. DOI: 10.1002/smj.358

Meena, P., Sarmah, S. P., & Sarkar, A. (2011). Sourcing decisions under risks of catastrophic event disruptions. *Transportation Research Part E, Logistics and Transportation Review*, 47(6), 1058–1074. DOI: 10.1016/j.tre.2011.03.003

Miller, K. (2007). Risk and rationality in entrepreneurial processes. *Strategic Entrepreneurship Journal*, 1(1-2), 57–74. DOI: 10.1002/sej.2

Morais-Storz, M., Stoud Platou, R., & Berild Norheim, K. (2018). Innovation and metamorphosis towards strategic resilience. *International Journal of Entrepreneurial Behaviour & Research*, 27(7), 1181–1199. DOI: 10.1108/IJEBR-11-2016-0369

Myers, S. C. (1984). Finance theory and financial strategy. *Interfaces*, 14(1), 126–137. DOI: 10.1287/inte.14.1.126

Myers, S. C. (1984). Finance theory and financial strategy. *Interfaces*, 14(1), 126–137. DOI: 10.1287/inte.14.1.126

Nicholson, N. (2005). Personality and domain-specific risk taking. *Journal of Risk Research*, 157-176. Nobre, L., & Grable, J. (20155). The role of risk profiles and risk tolerance in shaping client investment decisions. *Journal of Financial Service Professionals*, 69(3), 18–21.

O'Brien, J., & Folta, T. (2009). Sunk costs, uncertainty and market exit: A real options perspective. *Industrial and Corporate Change*, 18(5), 807–833. DOI: 10.1093/icc/dtp014

Ram, S., & Sheth, J. (1989). Consumer resistance to innovations: The Market problem and its solutions. *Journal of Consumer Marketing*, 6(2), 5–14. DOI: 10.1108/EUM0000000002542

Rampini, A., Sufi, A., & Viswanathan, S. (2014). Dynamic risk managemen. *Journal of Financial Economics*, 111(2), 271–296. DOI: 10.1016/j.jfineco.2013.10.003

Renn, O., & Benighaus, C. (2013). Perception of technological risk: Insights from research and lessons for risk communication and management. *Journal of Risk Research*, 16(3-4), 293–313. DOI: 10.1080/13669877.2012.729522

Ritchie, B., & Marshall, D. (1993). Business. *Risk Management*.

Roberta, C., & Christopher, P. (2014). Achieving supply chain resilience: The role of procurement. *Supply Chain Management*, 19(5/6), 19. DOI: 10.1108/SCM-09-2013-0346

Roeser, S. (2010). Intuitions, emotions and gut reactions in decisions about risks: Towards a different interpretation of "neuroethics. *Journal of Risk Research*, 13(2), 175–190. DOI: 10.1080/13669870903126275

Roger Strand, D. O. (2009). Risk and Uncertainty as a Research Ethics Challenge. Norway: The National Committee for Research Ethics in Science and Technology (NENT).

Rowe, W. (1977). *Anatomy of Risk*.

Ruiz-Torres, A., & Mahmoodi, F. (2007). The optimal number of suppliers considering the costs of individual supplier failures. *Omega*, 35(1), 104–115. DOI: 10.1016/j.omega.2005.04.005

Schein, E. (1992). *Organizational Culture and Leadership*.

Shackle, G. (1966). Policy, poetry and success. *Economic Journal (London)*, 76(304), 755–767. DOI: 10.2307/2229081

Shapira, Z. (1995). Risk taking:a managerial perspective.

Shi, Y., Wu, F., Chu, L. K., Sculli, D., & Xu, Y. H. (2011). A portfolio approach to managing procurement risk using multi-stage stochastic programming. *The Journal of the Operational Research Society*, 62(11), 1958–1970. DOI: 10.1057/jors.2010.149

Silbermayr, L., & Minner, S. (2014). A multiple sourcing inventory model under disruption risk. *International Journal of Production Economics*, 149(3), 37–46. DOI: 10.1016/j.ijpe.2013.03.025

Simon, H. (1955). A behavioral model of rational choice. *The Quarterly Journal of Economics*, 69(1), 99–118. DOI: 10.2307/1884852

Singleton, K. (2013). Investor flows and the 2008 boom/bust in oil prices. *Management Science*, 60(2), 300–318. DOI: 10.1287/mnsc.2013.1756

Sitkin, S., & Wiengart, L. (1995). Determinants of risky decision-making behavior: A test of the mediating role of risk perceptions and propensity. *Academy of Management Journal*, 38(6), 1573–1592. DOI: 10.2307/256844

Slovic, P., Finucane, M., Peters, E., & Mecregor, D. (2004). Risk as analysis and risk as feelings: Somethoughtsaboutaffect,reason,risk,andrationality. *Risk Analysis*, 24(2), 311–322. DOI: 10.1111/j.0272-4332.2004.00433.x

Staw, B. M. (1981). The escalation of commitment to a course of action. *Academy of Management Review*, 6(4), 577–587. DOI: 10.2307/257636

Sydow, J. (2009). Academy of Management Review. *Organizational path dependence: Opening the black box, 34*(4), 689–709.

Talluri, S., Narasimhan, R., & Chung, W. (2010). Manufacturer cooperation in supplier development under risk. *European Journal of Operational Research*, 207(1), 165–173. DOI: 10.1016/j.ejor.2010.03.041

Tang, C. (2006). Perspectives in supply chain risk managemen. *International Journal of Production Economics*, 103(2), 451–488. DOI: 10.1016/j.ijpe.2005.12.006

Tripsas, B., & Gavetti, G. (2000). Capabilities, condition and inertia: Evidence from digital imaging. *Strategic Management Journal*, 21(10/11), 1147–1161. DOI: 10.1002/1097-0266(200010/11)21:10/11<1147::AID-SMJ128>3.0.CO;2-R

Turban, E. (2008). A Managerial Perspective. *Electronic Commerece 2008.*

Wagner, S., Bode, C., & Koziol, P. (2009). Supplier default dependencies: Empirical evidence from theautomotiveindustry. *European Journal of Operational Research*, 199(1), 150–161. DOI: 10.1016/j.ejor.2008.11.012

Walk, J. G., & Shapira, Z. (1987). Managerial perspectives on risk and risk taking. *Management Science*, 33(11), 1404–1418. DOI: 10.1287/mnsc.33.11.1404

Walker, W., Harremoës, P., Rotmans, J., van der Sluijs, J. P., van Asselt, M. B. A., Janssen, P., & Krayer von Krauss, M. P. (2003). Defining Uncertainty: A Conceptual Basis for Uncertainty Management Model base Decision Support. *Integrated Assessment*, 4(1), 5–17. DOI: 10.1076/iaij.4.1.5.16466

Weber, E., Blais, A.-R., & Betz, N. E. (2002). A domain-specific risk-attitude scale: Measuring risk perceptions and risk behaviors. *Journal of Behavioral Decision Making*, 15(4), 263–290. DOI: 10.1002/bdm.414

William, T. M. (1994). Using a risk register to integrate risk management in project definition. *International Journal of Project Management*, 12(1), 17–22. DOI: 10.1016/0263-7863(94)90005-1

Wiseman, R., & Gomez-Mejia, L. R. (1998). A behavioral agency model of managerial risk taking. *Academy of Management Review*, 23(1), 133–153. DOI: 10.2307/259103

Wooster, R. B., Blanco, L., & Sawyer, W. C. (2016). Equity commitment under uncertainty: A hierarchical model of real option entry mode choices. *International Business Review*, 25(1), 382–394. DOI: 10.1016/j.ibusrev.2015.07.006

Xie, F. (2009). Managerial flexibility, uncertainty, and corporate investment. *The real options effect.International Review of Economics & Finance*, 18(4), 643–655. DOI: 10.1016/j.iref.2008.11.001

Yano, C., & Lee, H. (1995). Lot sizing with random yields: A review. *Operations Research*, 43(2), 311–334. DOI: 10.1287/opre.43.2.311

Yoe, C. E. (2019). *Principles of risk analysis: decision making under uncertainty*. Taylor & Francis Group, LLC. DOI: 10.1201/9780429021121

Zsidisin, G. (2003). Managerial perceptions of supply risk. *The Journal of Supply Chain Management*, 39(4), 14–26. DOI: 10.1111/j.1745-493X.2003.tb00146.x

Zsidisin, G. A., Panelli, A., & Upton, R. (2000). Purchasing organization involvement in risk assessments, contingency plans, and risk management: An exploratory study. *Supply Chain Management*, 5(4), 187–198. DOI: 10.1108/13598540010347307

Chapter 9
The Roll Of Managerial Economics In Business Development

Saqib Muneer
https://orcid.org/0000-0003-4575-9566
University of Ha'il, Saudi Arabia

ABSTRACT

This study aims to explore the relationship between family involvement in a business and the managerial factors that influence the success of recent business developments. The research is guided by three key questions focusing on the connection between family involvement and managerial factors, how these factors are managed in family firms, and the differences in management approaches between family and non-family firms. Utilizing the Johansen-Juselius cointegration method, the study examines the end-of-day relationship between financial development and economic strategies in Chinese firms. Findings suggest that managerial quality, as signaled through reputation and past performance, plays a critical role in securing government support and resource allocation, ultimately influencing the economic strategy in China.

INTRODUCTION:

Managerial economics is an exciting area of study that seeks to satisfy the demand of integrating theory and application in the management of the business. It enables the managers to possess a good number of tools and ideas to take effective decisions in the present day more challenging and competitive business world. Thereby, applying rationality of economics to business issues enables organizations

DOI: 10.4018/979-8-3693-5733-0.ch009

to run efficiently, become profitable and make decisions in the face of risks (Huang et al., 2022).

As a sub-discipline of economics, managerial economics is mainly centered on the general problems that organizations encounter in their operations. This includes the processes of analyzing factors that determine the performance of a business such as the price models, cost of production, market demand and competition. Analyzing these economic factors as well as their interactions, the managers will be able to make more efficient decisions concerning the distribution of resources, the creation of new products, market penetration or leaving the particular market, and other key strategies of the companies (Lestari et al., 2023; Zhang & Kajikawa, 2021).

The strength of place of managerial economics is that it is all encompassing. It can be used in any field and in different aspects of a business ranging from a small-scale business to international business. Whether identifying the right level of production, estimating the probable payback for a new venture or measuring the effect of changes in government policies, managerial economics offers a systematic approach to decision making that helps organizations to succeed in a rapidly changing business environment (Zarghami, 2024).

Importance of Strategic Decision-Making in today's Business Environment.

In the current world, business environment is changing dynamically due to globalization, advancement in technology and increased competition hence, strategic decision making is more critical now than before. It is no longer an option that only big firms have to consider it as a necessity in the current world of business for any firm that is alive to the challenges of the business world today. It is a long-term decision, affecting a company's future course, results and destiny, as opposed to tactical decision that have short-term implications on its operations (Feng et al., 2022; Rinta-Kahila et al., 2022).

This is because the strategic decision-making process plays a significant role in charting the direction to follow especially when dealing with the issues of complexity and uncertainty. It is thus important for businesses to critically assess their strengths, weaknesses, opportunities, and threats with the view of effectively being able to forecast the future trends and make sound decisions that would be inline with it's overall business strategy. This way allows the companies to act effectively in changing conditions, take opportunities and avoid potential threats that can hamper the process.

Finally, it allows strategic management to define goals and provide rational decision-making for companies that helps to avoid reacting to circumstances. It is the process of decision-making that is in line with the vision, mission, and the overall values of the company so that all the steps taken will lead to its success. With the strategic management approach, organizations are well placed for long term revenue generation, enhanced profitability and a long-term niche in the market (Abu Rumman & Al-Abbadi, 2023; Larsen & Stanley, 2021).

The Need for Risk Mitigation in Uncertain Market Conditions.

It is widely stated that the contemporary business environment is a stormy ocean where it is difficult to keep one's balance. Fluctuations in the economic environment, shifts in geopolitics, emergence of innovative technologies, and changes in customers' preferences contribute to the existence of this environment that is characterized by change and risk. To not only sustain but to fructify during such an environment of volatility, it is no more an imperative but an absolute necessity for firms to have a strong risk management strategy in place (Hortovanyi et al., 2024; Medina-Serrano et al., 2022).

This means that, failure to consider risk is similar to going to sea without considering the conditions of the day or the stability of the boat. The outcomes can be in the form of small glitches to full-fledged disasters. Disruptions involving supplies, customers, profit margins and even the survival of the business may be occasioned by the occurrence of events which were not anticipated. Risk management thus plays the role of a hedge against these contingencies by preparing organizations to identify possible threats, evaluate their effects, and come up with ways of preventing the adverse effects from occurring (Abu Rumman & Al-Abbadi, 2023).

It is possible to incorporate risk management approaches that enable organizations turn uncertainty into an opportunity and a strength. This entail encouraging organizational culture where risk management identification and evaluation becomes part of the organizational culture at all levels. In the long run, the best approach to risk management is to embrace a proactive and systematic approach that enables companies to cope with acts of God, harness new opportunities and set the course for a successful and sustainable business model.

Chapter Objectives and Outline.

In this chapter, the author explores one of the most important areas of business management, namely, decision-making and business risk management in the context of managerial economics and business development. It offers a clear approach on how these aspects are connected to determine organizational outcomes in today's complex business world. To this end, readers will be able to learn from various concepts and tools, and a variety of case studies to make the right decisions in the face of risk and uncertainty.

The chapter starts with a clear introduction to the topic of managerial economics and stresses on the fact that it is an applied branch of economics. In this case it leads to the fundamental concepts of strategic management focusing on the value of strategic decision making in managing complex environments, managing for and avoiding risks and looking for opportunities. The next sections discuss some of the other analytical tools and techniques that have their origin in the field of managerial economics, including cost-benefit analysis, decision tree analysis, and sensitivity analysis, all of which are illustrated by examples designed to illustrate their use in assessing strategic choices and making optimal decisions.

Moreover, risk management is a subject of interest in the chapter as well as the authors explore the significance of risk management in the contemporary conditions characterized by high levels of risk. It exposes various forms of risks that are associated with business ventures ranging from financial and operations risks to strategic and reputational risks. Therefore, the knowledge of these risks and the right measures to take in order to minimize them enables organizations to improve on their robustness and flexibility. Last but not the least, the chapter is concluded with the understanding of the linkage between strategic management, economics, risk management, and business development so that the readers can get the overall view of achieving sustainable competitive advantage in the new age global environment.

UNDERSTANDING MANAGERIAL ECONOMICS

Definition and Scope of Managerial Economics.

Managerial economics is an interesting subject that helps to combine the knowledge of theories and their practical application in the economy of the enterprise. It is a branch of management that offers the managers an array of theories, models, and tools they can apply to make appropriate decisions to improve their organization's profitability, productivity and competitiveness. Unlike other branches of economics that are more of the theoretical form, managerial economics focus on the practical use of economic models in explaining different occurrences in the economy and as such it is a very useful tool for managers at all levels in different industries (Huang et al., 2022; Lestari et al., 2023).

More specifically, managerial economics is primarily concerned with the efficient utilization of resources in an organization to realize intended goals. This entails the systematic consideration of a number of elements that characterise a firm's operations including production costs, market demand, prices, competitive forces and the legal structure. Knowledge of these economic factors and their interaction will help the managers to make better decisions on product offering, resources, investment, pricing policies, markets entry or exit, and organizational strategies.

The field of study covered in managerial economics is vast and the information useful to businesses of the current generation is enormous. These are demand analysis and forecast, production and cost analysis, understanding market structure and pricing policies, analysis of risks and their control, capital budgeting, and economic predictions. Thus, through the application of principles and tools of managerial economics, managers are able to make sense of the data; to weigh the options available to them; and, therefore, to make decisions that will best support their organization's strategic objectives and promote its sustainable success (Abu Rumman & Al-Abbadi, 2023).

Key Concepts: Demand Analysis, Cost-Benefit Analysis, Pricing Strategies, and Market Structures.

Demand analysis may be described as the process of going beneath the surface of the consumer's psyche. It's simply about knowing how they behave – their needs, their budget, and their possible evolution. Concerning the factors such as consumer income, taste, availability of substitute products, firms are able to make estimates on future demand, hence adjust their production and marketing strategies. Demand analysis is therefore a critical component of pricing, production and even new product development strategies.

Cost-benefit analysis brings realism into decision-making process. Technique used to assess the tradeoffs of a particular course of action in relation to the probable expenses and gains. It is not solely based on quantitative factors, but qualitative factors are also incorporated in this analysis. Through the use of quantitative analysis in compare and contrast of the impact several business decisions can have regarding investments, expansion and changes in operations, better decisions are made as to where to best utilize resources.

Pricing strategies are all about the identification of the perfect middle ground where a business could be as profitable as possible while at the same time being able to lure customers with their prices. In fact, there are no universal rules in pricing as the right pricing strategy is going to depend on the specificities of the product such as perceived value, competition, and cost. The strategies can be as basic as the cost-plus pricing system where a markup is put on the cost of production and on the other extreme, the value system where the price is determined according to the perceived value by the customer. It is therefore very important to select the right pricing strategy to be able to attract customers, make sales and revenues, and in the long run make profits.

Market structures give a structure of the competition that is faced by a business organization. From perfect competition with many small firms right to the monopolies that are dominated by a single firm, each of these structures has it own special features. This is because the industry structure such as the number of rivals, the level of product differentiation, and entry barriers provide the condition that has to be worked within by business entities. Market structures involve recognizing the environment in which firms operate with a specific focus on setting the appropriate price, producing the right products and the right position in the market.

How Managerial Economics Informs Strategic Decisions.

In particular, managerial economics is instrumental in presenting a systematically constructed theoretical system for solving a wide range of business issues and assessing various management options. It helps managers to stop relying on instincts and hunches while making decisions for their organizations; it helps them make decisions that are informed by data and facts that are likely to support the achievement of the organization's strategic vision (Feng, Pan, et al., 2022; Hortovanyi et al., 2024)

In as much as managerial economics is used in the formulation of strategies, it offers an understanding of the market. Through such concepts as demand analysis, market players are able to understand consumers' behavior, the market, and forces that may be present in it. Such information is vital for product development strategies, pricing, entry and exit strategies in the market and competition strategy development. In addition, managerial economics assists firms to evaluate organizational strengths and weaknesses and hence, where they could obtain competitive advantages (Feng, Han, et al., 2022; Zhang & Kajikawa, 2021).

Furthermore, managerial economics provides the managers with a number of analytical techniques that they can use in order to analyse strategic options and their likely impacts. Analyzing costs and benefits of different decisions, finding the break even point, and sensitivity analysis help business organizations to measure the financial consequences of various decisions, evaluate the risks and uncertainties of the business environment and make decisions that are most profitable and adds value to shareholders. It assists managers in decision making process by offering a sound structure within which to manage the uncertainties of the modern business world (Feng, Han, et al., 2022).

STRATEGIC DECISION-MAKING IN BUSINESS

The Process of Strategic Decision-Making.

Strategic decision making is not one time process but a continuous and a cyclic process that determines the course of an organization for many years. It is a process of decision making that creates a preferred future today, despite conditions characterized by ambiguity and feasibility. This process is a sequence of related activities, every one of which is important for making the decision proper, coordinated with overall strategies and capable of providing the firm with a competitive advantage (Rinta-Kahila et al., 2022).

The process starts with the identification of the current status of the organization and its position down the road map. This entails a process of scanning the internal and external environments, of resources, capabilities, and competencies on one hand and of the market forces, trends, competitors, economy, and politics on the other hand. The analysis of opportunities and threats allows setting attainable and challenging objectives that will determine the organizational strategies (Feng, Pan, et al., 2022; Rinta-Kahila et al., 2022).

The second process, which follows the identification of the destination, is the development and assessment of possible strategies for achieving the destination. This entails creativity, innovation, and, a readiness to take risks and unbend set practices. All the possible strategies have to be evaluated in terms of their practicality, functionality, and permissiveness in terms of the company's values, costs, and benefits, and others. It then provides the framework for defining concrete operational plans, resource allocation, and performance measurement and control of progress towards targets and objectives set (Feng, Han, et al., 2022; Larsen & Stanley, 2021).

The Role of Data and Economic Analysis in Business Strategy.

We are living in the age of data, so the synergy of analytical approaches and economics has emerged as the key to developing an efficient business strategy. It is no longer possible to rely solely on the experience, hunches and personal insights for the management of an organization. When analyzed from an economics perspective, data plays a crucial role in marketing since it gives valuable information on the market and its trends, demand and supply, competitors' activities, and other factors that determine economic conditions and which help to make the right decisions to achieve growth, profitability, and stability (Zhang & Kajikawa, 2021).

Data analysis enables business organizations to eliminate guess work and gain insight of the target market. Analyzing the customers' characteristics, their buying habits and their behavior on the internet helps the companies to properly position their products, services and advertising messages. In addition, data analysis can identify trends and relationships that are not easily identifiable manually helping to identify new opportunities, threats and improvement possibilities in the market. These data-driven insights are explained using economic theories giving business organizations the ability to determine the feasibility of strategic choices, the likely demand in the future, and whether to set high or low price, where to invest, and when to enter or exit a particular market (Klatt et al., 2021).

These two data and economic analysis tools are most helpful in today's unpredictable and complex business setting. Economic factors include inflation rates, interest rates, and consumer confidence indices which are very important when assessing and evaluating the general economic environment and its possible effects on business activities. With the help of incorporating these macroeconomic factors with microeconomic factors such as sales, costs and customers' behavior business can create better forecasts, predict the market changes and make some preventive adjustments to avoid the potential threats and take the advantage of the new opportunities. In other words, the deliberate operationalization of data and economic analysis enables organizations to overcome the uncertainty and achieve success (Klatt et al., 2021; Zhang & Kajikawa, 2021).

RISK MITIGATION THROUGH MANAGERIAL ECONOMICS

Identifying Types of Business Risks

The first important step towards risk management is therefore to identify all possible business risks that may be faced. It is true that no enterprise, be it big or small and be it from which sector it originates, does not have numerous internal and external threats that can affect the enterprise in terms of its revenues and even its existence. As a result, understanding the nature of these risks and how they can manifest themselves within a business, organisations are able to put in place measures that would help to alleviate the impact of such risks and thus increase their resilience in times of uncertainty (Hortovanyi et al., 2024),

Business risks can also be classified based with regard to the origin of the risks. Internal risks result from within the organization and include factors such as internal control weaknesses, internal processes inefficiency, poor strategic decisions and lack of competent personnel. External risks can be defined as those that are beyond the reach of the company's control such as a downturn in the economy, changes in legislation, natural disasters or disruption to the supply chain. The most well-known strategy is risk categorization according to the risks' characteristics or potential consequences. Strategic risks, for example, are those risks that are likely to compromise the future existence of the business while operational risks are the ones that interfere with business operations. Financial risks affect the company's financial status while compliance risks stem from noncompliance to legal requirements (Abu Rumman & Al-Abbadi, 2023; Medina-Serrano et al., 2022).

When businesses map out their operating environment carefully, they are able to rate the various risks that are inherent in their operation across the different categories of risks and thus be in a position to develop a well-firms risk profile that will help them in risk management. This entails evaluating the possibility of risk occurrence, the consequences that this might have on the business, and the measures that are used in controlling the risk. It helps the businesses to decide where to focus their efforts, in terms of risk management, to ensure that they are protecting themselves from the largest dangers out there. Please bear in mind that risk identification is not a standalone activity and a manager has to be on the lookout for new risks, modify the existing risk assessment and mitigation strategies, and adapt to new conditions as they emerge (Abu Rumman & Al-Abbadi, 2023; Medina-Serrano et al., 2022).

The Use of Economic Models and Forecasting to Predict Risks.

Economic models and forecasting techniques are imperative when it comes to a business trying to avoid possible risks that would come their way. As a result, these tools help gain better insight into what might happen in the future, any changes that may occur in the market, and the results of implementing various risks for business activity.

Economic theories are formulated in the form of equations and /or model which seeks to explain the interrelation between and among the various economic factors like interest rate, inflation, expenditure, investment etc. With the help of such models, businesses can enter historical data and make certain assumptions about future conditions in order to obtain forecast of key economic indicators, such as GDP growth, industry performance, or commodity prices. These forecast assist in strategic planning for businesses by identifying possible threats and opportunities which may be present in the future, changing the investment plans, and preparing for different economic conditions (Feng, Pan, et al., 2022; Phillips et al., 2023).

But it is worth emphasizing that economical forecasts are not magic crystals. They are derived from past records and factors that may not be true in the future. That is why, it is necessary to apply more than one model, have several scenarios in mind and update forecasts every time new information appears. Thus, using the principles of economic modeling along with common sense, the businesses can make the right decisions, avoid possible pitfalls and achieve success in a constantly evolving economic environment.

Techniques for Mitigating Risks:

As the theoretical approach to analysing business risks and their solutions, managerial economics boasts a powerful set of weapons for combating threats in general, and non-core business risks in particular; diversification, flexible and strategic pricing, and market research are amongst the torchstones of any viable business strategy. These techniques, when applied properly, can minimize the organization's exposure to various kinds of uncertainties and thereby improve its capacity to manage dynamic business environments (Zhang & Kajikawa, 2021).

Risk diversification normally referred to as 'do not put all your eggs in one basket' means there is an expansion of risk through investment in many securities or areas of operation. This approach lowers the effect of any one adverse occurrence on the general well-being of business. For instance, a company that has a varied product range has more chances of coping with changes in people's preferences for a particular product. Likewise, the risks due to specific geographic conditions such as a decline in the economy or political issues in a region can be moderated through geographic diversification (Huang et al., 2022).

On the same note, it can be seen that pricing strategies help in minimising risk since they guarantee that a business will be in a position to generate its revenue and turn a profit regardless of the prevailing economic conditions. This is true of cost-plus pricing where all costs are recovered alongside the addition of a profit margin which helps to cover for any additional costs. Compared to this, the concept of value based pricing takes into account the perceived value of a product or service by the customer and enables companies to charge more for the same and possibly earn more profits in the process. This type of pricing is popular in the online industry and involves changing the price frequently in response to the market forces, competitors, and stock availability so as to maximize on sales and reduce on opportunities of having unsold stocks.

Last but not the least, adequate market research is crucial in reducing risk by getting the necessary information which can be used in decision making. Thereby, consumers' needs and wants, market and competitors' dynamics help business to evaluate the threats and opportunities that may appear and adjust strategies in due time. Market research as an aspect of market analysis offers an opportunity for business organizations to determine the feasibility of new products or services, the appropriate price to charge, and marketing strategies, all of which reduce risks and increase the probability of success in the long run (Medina-Serrano et al., 2022).

INTEGRATING MANAGERIAL ECONOMICS WITH RISK MANAGEMENT

How Economic Theories Guide Risk Management Decisions.

The study of managerial economics, which is centered on the rationality of decisions in situations of scarcity and risk, offers a useful theoretical foundation for the management of risks. Thus, the theoretical background found in economical literature is highly beneficial for understanding decision-making processes of individuals and organisations concerning potential losses, which in turn assists risk managers in the process of identification, evaluation and management of risks.

There are several economic theories when it comes to risk management but one of them is expected value theory. This theory postulates that, in exercising their choices, people's aim is to avoid negative consequences or, at least, minimize them and, at the same time, achieve positive consequences as often as possible. In the context of risk management this means that potential risks need to be assessed based on their probability and likely consequences and then ranked for management based on the expected value. For instance, a company may wish to allocate a disproportionately large amount of resources to managing a high consequence, low likelihood risk such as a hurricane rather than a low consequence, high likelihood risk such as a small tool breakdown (Hortovanyi et al., 2024; Jackson et al., 2024).

The other key cost concept is risk aversion. People and companies are usually bearish the majority of the time since it is natural for them to be more inclined towards certain outcomes rather than taking a chance on an uncertain outcome which may be more profitable. This principle can be used to explain why companies will spend their money in managing risks in cases that they do not even get to experience a loss through insurance or hedging. Because these measures decrease the level of risk and possibility of huge losses, the feeling of safety and stability in the process of its implementation overcomes the expenses. With the knowledge of these and other economic theories, risk managers can make better decisions concerning use of resources, protection and allocation of resources and in general improve the operational performance of their organizations in the face of risk (Klatt et al., 2021; Larsen & Stanley, 2021).

Case Studies Where Managerial Economics was Used to Mitigate Business Risks.

The practical use of managerial economics in avoiding or reducing risks in business activities is well illustrated across various industries. One such example is related to a large airline facing volatility of fuel prices as one of the critical operational threats. Indeed, through econometric modeling and forecasting the airline was in a position to forecast the future prices of fuel with a reasonable level of certainty. This enabled them to deploy a hedging technique where they were able to fix fuel prices in advance thus reducing risks of high costs. Therefore, the airline was able to remain profitable since fare levels could be kept constant despite fluctuations in fuel costs, which goes to prove that economic prediction is critical in managing risks (Hortovanyi et al., 2024; Medina-Serrano et al., 2022).

In another case a large retail chain that was experiencing increased competition decided to improve on the pricing as well as inventory of its products. The retailer then analysed various factors that affected customer's purchase behaviour as well as price elasticity for various products. This helped them in achieving the kind of pricing strategy where prices are changed frequently as a response to demand, stock availability, and competitor's prices. At the same time, they also streamlined the inventory management process, hence cutting on the storage expenses and avoiding situations whereby they ordered too many stocks or none at all. These decisions based on economic theories helped the retailer to generate higher sales, lower the costs, and enhance the company's profitability (Abu Rumman & Al-Abbadi, 2023).

These cases demonstrate the relevance of the topic as they show how managerial economics can be used as a tool to manage risks. By making the use of economic theories, forecasting procedures, and data analysis, it is possible to provide the essential information concerning resource allocation, prices, investment options, and operational activities, which will help improve the stability and competitiveness of the business in the given conditions of the uncertain environment (Abu Rumman & Al-Abbadi, 2023).

The Role of Cost-Benefit Analysis in Evaluating Risk.

It is an important concept in the management of risk since it involves the identification of risks, comparison of costs and benefits of risk taking and formulation of appropriate strategies to take. In its simplest form, CBA entails a systematic evaluation of the likely cost and benefit of undertaking a specific action, say, to put in place a safety program or to acquire new technology or to diversify into a new market. It enables one to estimate these factors in monetary terms and then compare them and decide on which options are more desirable by having the advantages exceeding the disadvantages (Medina-Serrano et al., 2022).

In a risk management setting, CBA is especially useful in comparing the costs and expenses of mitigating a certain risk as well as the benefits that come with it. For instance, a business planning to install a new cybersecurity system will compare the cost of the system installation and its maintenance, the cost of training employees how to use it with the benefits that the business will accrue such as the likelihood of experiencing a data breach, insurance costs and customer confidence. By placing a dollar sign to these factors it will be easier for the company to justify the investment based on the amount of risk exposure that is expected to be reduced.

However, it is also to be noted that CBA has some drawbacks or limitations with it. Some costs and benefits are difficult to measure especially those which relate to intangible aspects such as reputation or morale of the employees. Furthermore, CBA generally involves predicting future events, and, as we know, predictions are not always accurate. Nonetheless, CBA can still be considered as a practical model for risk management as it offers a logical and clear approach to decision making in conditions of risk that enables businesses to allocate their resources more effectively and choose the right investment projects that will help them to improve their position in case of risk occurrence (Abu Rumman & Al-Abbadi, 2023; Feng, Han, et al., 2022; Medina-Serrano et al., 2022).

MANAGERIAL ECONOMICS AND BUSINESS DEVELOPMENT

The Impact of Informed Decision-Making on Business Growth and Development.

Thus, managerial economics is a critical tool in the growth and development of businesses through offering a tool for decision making. Through the use of economics and economic models, business organizations are in a better position to make the right decisions regarding resource use, find opportunities for exploitation and deal with competition. Using such approaches, organizations are in a position to make coherent decisions for the achievement of their strategic goals and objectives hence leading to growth and expansion (Abu Rumman & Al-Abbadi, 2023; Feng, Han, et al., 2022).

Another area, where managerial economics plays an important role is the assessment of the market opportunities for development. Such tools as market researches, demand forecasts, competitors analysis, and others, help to obtain comprehensive insights into the markets, clients, and competitors. They are useful in identifying market opportunities that have not been explored, creating new products or services that cater for customers needs that may not have been met before, as well as formulating efficient marketing and prices that will appeal to the target market. Therefore, by having sound and accurate information on markets to venture into, the product lines to invest on and how to effectively position themselves in order to beat the competition, businesses can reach their full growth potential and gain a competitive edge.

In addition, it offers a conceptual tool that enables the management to better arrange its internal affairs and resources that are vital to the growth of the firm. Using cost analysis, manufacturing, and capacity management, organizations and companies can improve the way they work and reduce the amount of wasted resources. It enables the businesses to earn more profits, which they can reinvest in growth strategies and expansion and thus expand their operations. By making rational choices in relation to the pricing policy, production intensity, stock and capital investments, companies can establish a positive spiral of the company's growth, profitability and sustainability (Hortovanyi et al., 2024; Jackson et al., 2024).

Long-term vs. Short-term Strategies in Business Development.

This paper posits that in the ever-evolving environment of business development, establishing sustainable strategic balance and tactical flexibility is critical. Tactical planning is planning with a time horizon of less than a year and the key to tactical planning is to focus on specific and specific initiatives to increase revenue, reduce costs, or respond to current issues. Such might range from marketing promotions, stock movements, or organization's internal process optimization. Besides being crucial for sustaining the momentum, short-term focus may become a major problem which leads to short-sighted decisions that undermine long-term growth (Klatt et al., 2021).

On the other hand, long term strategies go beyond the current issues affecting the organization and contain a vision of the firm's future usually up to several years or even a couple of decades at most. The implementation of these strategies requires heavy investments in areas such as research and development, new market entry and brand development or acquisitions. In the long-term strategies, there is more likely to be larger returns but this comes with the disadvantage of having to wait longer, to plan and to deny short term gains.

The results obtained suggest that there is a significant relationship between the two perspectives of business development; however, the question of how to strike the right balance between the two remains the question of interest. It is clearly understood that a business should have both short-term and long-term objectives that would define how the firm should be run in the short run while achieving the long-term vision. This needs analysis of the industry and competitors and an evaluation of the organisation's resources and capabilities. Since short-run and long-run goals are often inconsistent, it is possible to achieve short-run objectives while keeping an eye on long-run goals and maneuvering between short-run pressures and long-run strategic positioning (Medina-Serrano et al., 2022; Rinta-Kahila et al., 2022).

Managerial Economics as a Tool for Innovation and Competitive Advantage.

Innovation and achieving a sustainable competitive advantage is possible through the use of Managerial economics toolkit in the business world today. Through the use of economic concepts and theories, firms can make appropriate choices in their investment on research and development, new product development, and processes improvement that would allow them to adapt to changes and even surpass competitors. This approach to innovation assists the businesses in the creation of exclusive value propositions that help the firms to stand out in the marketplace and capture a greater share of the market (Zhang & Kajikawa, 2021).

In one aspect, managerial economics contributes to innovation by offering a structure for analysing ROI for various innovation strategies. It is the nature of business to evaluate the Pros and Cons of the new technologies, product and service attributes or process changes where the cost-benefit analysis should help the business in ranking the opportunities that offer the most potential for revenue growth, cost reduction or both. This way of managing innovation makes it possible to direct efforts and money to those innovations which will generate more value and improve the competitive advantage of the firm.

Furthermore, it assists the managerial in comprehending the forces at play in the competition and coming up with ways to disrupt the market. Market trends, competitors' actions, and customer needs help to discover new market opportunities and to invent new products or services that radically differ from the well-established business models and generate new sources of value. Such an approach to innovation management helps organizations to be ready for changes in consumers' preferences and, thus, gain a sustainable competitive advantage and recognition within the markets in which they operate (Medina-Serrano et al., 2022; Zarghami, 2024).

MANAGERIAL IMPLICATIONS

Practical Application of Managerial Economics:

Managerial economics is a branch of economics that prepares the managers with a broad range of economic tools and methods that can help them to avoid reliance purely on their instinct while making business decisions and come up with rational business decisions that are in sync with the organizational objectives. By recognizing supply and demand, elasticity, cost, and forecast, managers will be in a position to make better estimates of the conditions in the market, consumers' behavior, and possible consequences of various business strategies. This enables them to make the right pricing strategies, right production and inventory, right resource allocation, and right strategies in view of the changes in the competition environment.

In particular, one highly useful application of managerial economics concerns the management of prices. Price elasticity of demand, cost of production and competitors' prices are some of the factors that managers can use in order to set the right price level at which maximum profits can be made without reducing the sales. Likewise cost functions and techniques of production help the managers to plan the resources in a better way and reduce the wastage in operations. This means that decisions made in the firm are based on facts, costs are regulated so that the company can remain competitive in the current market.

Moreover, it offers the means of evaluating risk as well as making strategic decisions concerning investments, entry into a new market, and expansion. Some of the tools which are used by the managers to measure the cost or the benefit of undertaking certain course of action includes cost benefit analysis, break- even analysis and forecasting. This enables them to avoid pitfalls that may be associated with such investments or new products, markets and other business development plans, while at the same time increasing the chances of success. Applying the principle of economics in managerial decision making enables the managers to lead his/her organization towards economic prosperity in the current volatile business environment.

Risk Management in Practice:

Risk management is one of the essential strategies that determine the success of any business; economic forecasting and analysis are central to the identification of risks and the most appropriate measures to be taken to minimize the risks. Using market and economic intelligence and forecasting, organisations can predict, evaluate and mitigate risks so as to reduce their effects and improve organisational readiness for risks that arise in unpredictable environments. It makes risk management proactive instead of reactive – it helps to prevent problems, create plans to tackle them, and make correct decisions to protect company's assets, reputation, and future (Hortovanyi et al., 2024; Medina-Serrano et al., 2022).

The following economic forecasting is a useful instrument helping to evaluate possible threats and benefits to be expected in the future. Through historical data analysis, economic indicators' tracking and statistical modeling the businesses are able to forecast the future market conditions, possible shifts in supply and demand and the possible effects of various factors such as regulatory changes or political instabilities. It helps businesses to prepare for any risks that may be likely to affect their operations, their supply chain, or their financial status hence comes up with preventive measures. For instance, the management of a firm expecting a downturn in the economy might have to stock up their inventories, cut on their expenses or look for new products or markets to venture into.

In addition, economic analysis offer roadmap to assess the efficiency of various risk control measures and guide on the right resource allocation. Cost benefit analysis help in determining the relative pros and cons of formulating strategies to minimize risks for instance insurance, changing a supplier, or creating new safety measures. Such an approach guarantees that only the most efficient risk management measures are and only those costs should be incurred in order to achieve the maximum benefit/loss ratio in the case of risk materialization. Economic forecasting and analysis should therefore form part of risk management framework in business organizations in order to enable them make proper decisions which would act as a hedge against risks and thus improve the performance of the business in the face of rising risks in future (Abu Rumman & Al-Abbadi, 2023; Medina-Serrano et al., 2022).

Optimizing Business Resources:

The use of managerial economics is essential in the management of business resources since it offers a guide in decision making processes on how best to allocate resources, on the right pricing strategies and even on market positioning. It also enables the usage of resources in the most efficient manner possible, the determination of the best price levels that would help in achieving the right balance between price and quantity, and the strategic positioning of products in the market, thereby ensuring the achievement of sustainable competitive advantage. This strategic approach to resource management helps businesses to optimize their utilization of resources, reduce wastage and provide value for money in achievement of organizational financial and operational objectives (Feng, Han, et al., 2022).

Resource allocation is another area that is informed by managerial economics in a bid to enhance the usage of resources within organization. Therefore, through the analysis of things such as cost of production, opportunity cost and profitability of various products or services, business people are able to determine how to best utilize the resources including capital, labor and raw materials in order to ensure that they get the highest possible returns on their investment. This could entail focusing on those products that offer high margins, acquiring better technologies to lower costs, or moving certain operations to outsourcing to generate less overhead. The efficient allocation of resources can be facilitated by using data to make resource allocation decisions as this will help in maximizing the value of resources used.

In addition, managerial economics offer the tools for the evaluation of the pricing policies and positioning on the markets. As such, factors such as price elasticity of demand, consumer preferences, competitor's price, and cost of production are some of the factors that business organizations use to set the appropriate price to capture the market and at the same time ensure that they achieve their objectives of making profits. Besides, through market, competitor and consumer analysis, it is possible to optimize the allocation of resources and select the right strategies to conquer the most lucrative niches, introduce distinctions into the services provided, and build up a powerful brand image. This strategic move in pricing and positioning makes it possible for organizations to earn maximum value from its products or services while at the same time maintaining the competitive advantage (Jackson et al., 2024; Larsen & Stanley, 2021).

Decision-Making Framework:

It is possible to agree with the opinion that the construction of an efficient decision-making framework which will allow to balance the risks and the opportunities of the contemporary business environment is an urgent task. This framework developed here can be anchored in economic theory to take the manager above the level of mere guessing and bring his decision making process in conformity with the goals set out by the organization, the potential benefits and the potential costs. This analytical approach to decision-making helps the businesses to establish the probabilities of risks that are likely to occur, and the chances of taking opportunities that can help it to grow and become more sustainable (Rinta-Kahila et al., 2022).

One of the important concepts in constructing such a framework is the concept of risk analysis that should be applied at every level of decision making. It entails the identification of risks that may occur and the likelihood of their occurrence and the effects that may be expected if they occur and how they can be controlled. Economic tools that are useful for this purpose are for instance the sensitivity analysis through which a manager can determine how changes in certain variables might affect the decision, and the scenario planning which involves preparing for different possibilities that may exist in the future. When risks and opportunities are measured in economistic terms, managers are in a better position to weigh the costs and benefits and to choose the best courses of action that have better risk-reward ratios (Feng, Pan, et al., 2022).

Moreover, a strong decision-making process should also have the provision of ongoing monitoring and evaluation as well as flexibility. This involves monitoring the organization's performance by using benchmark indicators, evaluating the impact of prior decisions and modifying the decision-making process in accordance with the findings. When management encourages learning and improvement in organizations, it becomes easier for them to make better decisions over time and therefore, be in a better position to identify opportunities for the business while avoiding or minimizing risks. This is because this approach to decision-making, contingent upon models of economic rationality, allows businesses to respond more effectively to shifts in the conditions of their environment and to exploit such changes where these are advantageous (Abu Rumman & Al-Abbadi, 2023).

Enhancing Competitive Advantage:

Concisely, managerial economics is a powerful tool in the hands of business managers who wish to gain competitive advantage by using economic knowledge to make sound decisions about production, pricing, distribution and positioning of products in the market. Applying economic theories and quantitative methods, it allows the participants in the business process to understand the nature of changes in consumer demand and determine potential strategies to overtake the competitors and ensure long-term success. Such a strategic approach to attaining competitive edge effectively keeps the businesses on their toes, ever ready to act in response to new trends that emerge in the market and seize any opportunity that might be presented to the business (Abu Rumman & Al-Abbadi, 2023).

In one way, managerial economics contributes to improving competitive advantage by availing instruments that can be used to assess and leverage on trends. Through the data analysis of markets, the observation of the competitors' actions, and the assessment of the market trends and indicators, companies can identify the changes in consumers' behavior or the appearance of new technologies and disruptions that may redefine industries. Such a concept enables organizations to foresee shifts in the competitive environment, discover new opportunities for growth, and design new goods or solutions that would address consumers' emerging needs. It is thus possible for the business to position itself as an industry pioneer by the early adoption of these innovations hence grabbing market share from the competitors who are still lagging behind.

In addition, the use of managerial economics enhances the internal performance by offering a blueprint for its improvement, which would enable the organization to achieve a sustainable competitive advantage. The use of production cost analysis enables businesses to assess their operations' performance, establish inefficiencies, and then seek to optimize those operations. This leads to the ability of the businesses to offer attractive price points, reasonable profit levels, and the capability to invest in innovation and business development. In this way, businesses can also find the ways to improve their competitiveness, to increase the indicator of their profitability and to provide themselves with the long term prospects for development (Feng, Pan, et al., 2022; Zarghami, 2024; Zhang & Kajikawa, 2021).

CHALLENGES AND OPPORTUNITIES

Nevertheless, there are some problems which businesses encounter in applying managerial economics in managing risks and making strategic decisions. A major challenge lies with data: access and quality. Economic models rely on quality and timely information to be able to make sensible recommendations in given business environments but this often presents a challenge since data has to be collected, cleaned and integrated. Besides, the economic factors are volatile and this means that the information collected in the past may not be very useful and the process of forecasting is never easy. Further, the communication of economics analysis to decision-makers who may have less or no understanding of economics can be challenging, thus, constraining the ability to translate the insights into implemented strategies. To overcome these challenges, organizations need to ensure that they devise great ways of storing data and also encourage the cooperation between the data analysts and the management teams as well as ensure that data is used as a critical tool by everyone in the organization.

It is important to note that there are numerous opportunities that are available for businesses to use economic analysis to its advantage and minimize the risks involved in its integration in the business world. Through the use of data analytics and predictive modeling, business organisations are in a position to be in a position to view potential changes in the market, adjust price levels and view other possibilities in the market. In addition, economic analysis can used in decision making regarding investment since it will assist the firms in identifying which project will yield the highest return given the risk involved. Furthermore, with the increased adoption of data-driven approaches in business, economic insights can be used in improving organisational processes, supply chain management and customer experience. The capability to utilise the impact of economic analysis would be even more important for firms to grow in a more competitive and integrated global setting.

Several trends are clearly discernible as the field of managerial economics and strategic decision-making moves forward into the future. The increased usage of big data and artificial intelligence is also allowing the business to have more insight into information and analytical tools such as forecasting, risk management and decision making. Also, the amplified consciousness of environmental and social impacts in the world has made business organizations to introduce the incorporation of environment and social factors into their economic theories. Additionally, the increasing trend of the Academia and business entities to address behavioral economics is bringing psychological factors into the economic decision-making process, thus making firms to take account of cognitive effects and heuristics when formulating their operational strategies. As these trends progress, those companies that continue to employ the use of analytics in decision making, respond to change appropriately, and who act in an ethical and sustainable manner, will be the ones that shall be well placed to deal with any future changes or take advantage of any future opportunities as they emerge.

CONCLUSION

Thus, this discussion of the topic of managerial economics has revealed its importance to strategic management decisions especially in situations where there is risk and uncertainty. Through economics, the tools and principles taught, companies can reduce the amount of guess work in decision-making and instead make decisions based on facts and critical evaluation. In terms of the allocation and pricing of resources, in the choice of the right market trends and in the management of possible risks, managerial economics offers a sound theoretical foundation for successful management and sustainable growth in today's world.

One of the main conclusions is the necessity of inclusion of risk assessment in to each phase of the decision making. By measuring risks and opportunities in monetary terms, organizations can make better decisions based on relative value, invest in the areas that will yield the most significant value and have a plan for how to deal with the potential negative aspects of a certain opportunity. Moreover, the use of data analytics and predictive modeling helps businesses to be ready for the new shifts in the market, set the right price levels, and define new markets for their products or services, which in turn increases business flexibility and its competitive advantage when operating in the environment characterized by high volatility.

Thus, the inclusion of managerial economics in strategic management is not just an exercise in theory but a reality that has to be embraced by companies which want to succeed in the contemporary and increasingly complex global environment. To avoid falling into the trap of uncertainty and not being able to identify emerging opportunities that have the potential to drive sustainable growth while at the same time avoiding potential risks, businesses need to be able to integrate data into the decision-making process, create and uphold a culture of learning and adapt to the ever-changing markets. With the ever-changing business environment, the knowledge of economic factors will play a critical role of sustaining and advancing business objectives and growth.

References:

Abu Rumman, A., & Al-Abbadi, L. (2023). Structural equation modeling for impact of Data Fabric Framework on business decision-making and risk management. *Cogent Business and Management*, 10(2), 2215060. Advance online publication. DOI: 10.1080/23311975.2023.2215060

Feng, J., Han, P., Zheng, W., & Kamran, A. (2022). Identifying the factors affecting strategic decision-making ability to boost the entrepreneurial performance: A hybrid structural equation modeling – artificial neural network approach. *Frontiers in Psychology*, 13, 1038604. Advance online publication. DOI: 10.3389/fpsyg.2022.1038604

Feng, J., Pan, Y., & Zhuang, W. (2022). Measuring the Enterprise Green Innovation Strategy Decision-Making Quality: A Moderating—Mediating Model. *Frontiers in Psychology*, 13, 915624. Advance online publication. DOI: 10.3389/fpsyg.2022.915624

Hortovanyi, L., Szepesi, B., & Pogacsas, P. (2024). Navigating crisis: SME strategies for risk mitigation through strategic upgrading. *Cogent Business and Management*, 11(1), 2392043. Advance online publication. DOI: 10.1080/23311975.2024.2392043

Huang, Q., Xiong, M., & Xiao, M. (2022). Does managerial ability affect corporate financial constraints? Evidence from China. *Ekonomska Istrazivanja*, 35(1), 3731–3753. DOI: 10.1080/1331677X.2021.2004186

Jackson, I., Ivanov, D., Dolgui, A., & Namdar, J. (2024). Generative artificial intelligence in supply chain and operations management: A capability-based framework for analysis and implementation. *International Journal of Production Research*, 62(17), 6120–6145. Advance online publication. DOI: 10.1080/00207543.2024.2309309

Klatt, S., Noël, B., Schwarting, A., Heckmann, L., & Fasold, F. (2021). Adaptive Gaze Behavior and Decision Making of Penalty Corner Strikers in Field Hockey. *Frontiers in Psychology*, 12, 674511. Advance online publication. DOI: 10.3389/fpsyg.2021.674511

Larsen, K. L., & Stanley, E. A. (2021). Leaders' Windows of Tolerance for Affect Arousal—And Their Effects on Political Decision-making During COVID-19. *Frontiers in Psychology*, 12, 749715. Advance online publication. DOI: 10.3389/fpsyg.2021.749715

Lestari, P., Pratiwi, U., & Irianto, B. S. (2023). The moderating effects of gender on managerial performance assessment and dysfunctional behaviour: Evidence from Indonesia. *Cogent Business and Management*, 10(1), 2193207. Advance online publication. DOI: 10.1080/23311975.2023.2193207

Medina-Serrano, R., González, R., Gasco, J., & Llopis, J. (2022). Do risk events increase supply chain uncertainty? A case study. *Ekonomska Istrazivanja*, 35(1), 4658–4676. DOI: 10.1080/1331677X.2021.2016462

Phillips, W., Roehrich, J. K., & Kapletia, D. (2023). Responding to information asymmetry in crisis situations: Innovation in the time of the COVID-19 pandemic. *Public Management Review*, 25(1), 175–198. DOI: 10.1080/14719037.2021.1960737

Rinta-Kahila, T., Someh, I., Gillespie, N., Indulska, M., & Gregor, S. (2022). Algorithmic decision-making and system destructiveness: A case of automatic debt recovery. *European Journal of Information Systems*, 31(3), 313–338. DOI: 10.1080/0960085X.2021.1960905

Zarghami, S. A. (2024). 'There are also unknown unknowns': A resilience-informed approach for forecasting and monitoring management reserve in projects. *International Journal of Production Research*, 1–21. Advance online publication. DOI: 10.1080/00207543.2024.2359044

Zhang, Y., & Kajikawa, Y. (2021). Editorial: Advanced Analytics and Decision Making for Research Policy and Strategic Management. In *Frontiers in Research Metrics and Analytics* (Vol. 6). Frontiers Media SA. DOI: 10.3389/frma.2021.778622

Chapter 10
The Impact of Financial Policies and COVID-19 on Sustainable Performance

Rashid Mehmood
University of Education, Lahore, Pakistan

Ilyas Ahmad
University of Education, Lahore, Pakistan

Shujah Ur Rahman
University of Education, Lahore, Pakistan

Sohail Rizwan
Fatima Jinnah Women University, Rawalpindi, Pakistan

Saba Sattar
Government Technical Training Institute for Women, Pakistan

ABSTRACT

This study is basically the impact of corporate finance on the firm performance. Two major pillars of the corporate finance are capital structure and dividend policy which play vital role for long term financial success of a firm. We investigate the influence of financial policies such as capital structure and dividend policy on firm sustainable performance. The study also captures the role of COVID-19 as control variable in influencing the sustainable performance. The analysis is done on panel data of 150 non-financial firms listed on Pakistan Stock Exchange from 2010 to

DOI: 10.4018/979-8-3693-5733-0.ch010

2023. Our findings show that capital structure has significant and negative effect on sustainable performance, while there is positive correlation between dividend policy and firm sustainable performance.

INTRODUCTION

The COVID-19 pandemic has caused financial instability among firms across the world since its start in China during January 2020 (Ali et al., 2022). In response to this pandemic, firms significantly changed their daily business activities which considerably declined their sustainable performance. Additionally, firms have also change their financial policies such as dividend policy and capital structure (Meyer et al., 2022). Finance is the backbone of every business, individual and every business entity. Business aim to control risk that ultimately results in insolvency (Hussain et al., 2022), therefore, firms need strong financial policies to be successful. For this, an optimal cash level is required to meet such crisis (Hunjra et al., 2022). Finances and the financial decisions always play a pivotal role for the better performance and profit maximization of a firm. It is important for governance to implement strong policies with improved monitoring the acts of management (Abbassi et al., 2021). Major corporate finance decisions include capital structure mix and dividend policy. However, COVID-19 resulted in social distance policy which ultimately negatively influenced the economic activities and financial outcomes of the business. Therefore, corporate finance decisions of the firms also adversely affected by the happening of COVID-19.

For example, many firms stopped paying dividend or decreased the amount of dividend paid during this pandemic period (Krieger et al., 2021). This pandemic severely affected Pakistani financial markets mainly non-financial firms. The selection of non-financial sector of Pakistan is based on the fact that the pandemic has significantly influenced those industries such as non-financial sector that are more sensitive to the COVID-19 and change in government policies (Ngo & Duong, 2024). Considering the importance of financial outcomes of non-financial sector of Pakistan during this pandemic, the current study aims to analyse how financial policies such as dividend policy, and capital structure along with COVID-19 pandemic influence sustainable performance of the firms. Therefore, the study will focus to answer the following research questions:

1. What is the impact of capital structure on sustainable performance of non-financial sector of Pakistan?
2. How the sustainable performance of non-financial sector of Pakistan is affected by dividend policy?

Problem Identification

This study scrutinizes the sway of two main corporate finance mainstay's capital structure, its' design and the policy of profit disbursement in form of dividend. This study investigates the impact of both of these mainstream financial decisions on the value of firm especially the manufacturing sector. The pooled impact of both of these strategies has not been discussed before especially in Pakistan collectively. The manufacturing and food sectors are considered as the backbone for a country as almost 65% of their population is earning their livelihood directly or indirectly from manufacturing, agriculture and food sector. This also caters more variables and a wider sample size covering the recent decade.

Pakistan Stock exchange non-financial listed firm can be taken into consideration categorically as dummy variable and find their impact on firm value. Our study is helpful for shareholders to adopt new trends by which they can achieve their ultimate goal which profit intensification. This goal can be only achieved by constructing optimal capital structure and also by announcing solicited dividend policy. Corporate decision makers also reap the benefits of this research for a longer period of time.

Research Objectives

The core objective of this study is to judge the collective impact of two corporate finance variables on the firm performance. This kind of holistic study is not executed before. The primary objectives can be defined as under.

1: To analyze the impact of capital structure on the sustainable firm performance.
2: To estimate the effect of dividend policy on the sustainable firm performance.

Above mentioned objectives are assessed during this study. The in depth impact of these variables is observed while employing fixed effect and system GMM regression techniques.

Review of Literature and Hypotheses Formulation

Capital structure and profit arrangement are the most predominant choices taken by the firm. It enables firms to limit the weighted normal cost of capital and hold a particular total of cash for specific purposes. The association between capital structure and estimation of the firm is a far from being obviously true issue both observationally and hypothetically. Writing with respect to capital structure designing and profit strategy proposes that it has noteworthy effect on company's worth.

Capital Structure and Firm Sustainable Performance

Capital structure as part of a firm's performance is determined by a number of factors, within the business environment. In fact, Modigliani and Miller (1958) came up with theory of capital structure which postulated that under ideal conditions that include no taxes and bankruptcy costs, firm value is not influenced by capital structure. But, in real life, they admitted that tax advantages of debt may also increase the firm value. In the same way, trade off theory postulates that firms balance the tax advantages of debt against the costs of financial distress (Kraus & Litzenberger, 1973). This supposes that although low level of debt may boost performance through tax shields, high level of it is more likely to negative impact because of the high risks of bankruptcy. There is considerable empirical research analyzing the link between capital structure and firm performance, the nature of which has been identified as positive and negative. The research results obtained from these investigations are mixed.

The study conducted by Gleason et al. (2000) also shows that capital structure of firms in European countries have a negative and significant correlation with the performance of the firms using ROA as well as profit margin as performance indicators. This is however contrary to findings from several studies conducted in other parts of the world. n this study, Abor (2005) investigate the nexus between the capital structure and profitability among the firms listed on the Ghana stock exchange. The study found a positive relationship between short-term debt as a proportion of total assets and return on equity. Further, author stated that, indeed short-term financing is quite popular in Ghanaian firms as it constitutes 85% of their total debt indicating it an important mode of financing. On the same note, Holz (2002) also established a positive correlation between capital structure and firm performance.

Ebaid (2009) discovered that Egypt firms' capital structure has a very poor negative correlation with firm performance. Using statistical analysis, he found that short term, long term as well as total debt to total assets had insignificant negative relationship with the performance of the firm as measured by return on equity. As for the gross profit margin, he also found out that there is an insignificantly positive correlation between capital structure and gross profit margin. Weill (2008) examine the impact of financial leverage on firm performance using data from seven European countries. He discovered that financial leverage has a significant and positive relationship with the performance of the firm in Spain and Italy. However, the result was significantly negative in France, Norway, Germany, and Belgium, and insignificant positive relationship in Portugal. In the same way, Li Meng et al. (2008) also explored the effect of financial leverage on performance and discovered that there is inverse link between them when tested by the return on asset but, positive influence in case of return on equity. After reviewing above literature, we formulate the following hypothesis.

Hypothesis 1: Capital structure has a significant impact on sustainable performance.

Dividend Policy and Firm Sustainable Performance

The topic of dividend policy is vital in today's business environment. Dividend policy is therefore a set of standards adopted by a firm to guide the determination of the amount of dividend to be paid at a particular time to its shareholder (Nissim & Ziv, 2001). This decision has a direct impact on firms' financial status, Investors relationship and its performance. According to Gordan (1963), bird-in-hand theory, states that investors prefer to receive cash dividends than waiting for potential capital gains. Jensen and Meckling (1976) outlined agency theory, which suggests that there are always conflicts between managers and shareholders, and these conflicts affect the dividend policy of a firm. Additionally, Easterbrook (1984) mentioned more details on the cost implications of agency theory, categorizing them into two types: the costs incurred in monitoring the actions of managers and the risk that emanates from agency costs between managers and shareholders. Agyei and Yiadom (2011) sought to examine the association between dividend policy and bank performance in Ghana which was done with cross-sectional survey data from 16 banks spanning 5 years. They discovered that these banks paid a dividend of 24.65% on average. Likewise, Amidu (2007) studied GSE-listed firms and observed that dividend payment has a positive increased influence on return on assets, further emphasizing the significance of dividend policy on firms' performance.

Ali et al. (2015) sought to establish the effects of dividend policy on the firm performance based on high and low levels of debt for non-financial firms listed in KSE. Utilizing secondary data from the State Bank of Pakistan, covering balance sheet analyses from 2006 to 2011 with a sample of 122 companies, the researchers focused on two performance measures: Tobin's Q and Return on Equity, while controlling for firm size and growth, with debt as a moderating variable. They identified a positive significant association between the DPR and both Tobin's Q and return on assets for the various groups irrespective of the debt levels. They found no moderating effect of debt on the relationship between dividend pay out ratio and firm performance among these non-financial firms.

Hypothesis 2: Dividend policy has a significant impact on sustainable performance.

METHODOLOGY

We evaluate the influence of capital structure, and dividend policy on firm sustainable performance. We take panel data of 150 non-financial firms of Pakistan. We select non-financial firms as they are not protected by different guarantees and provisions (Xuezhou et al., 2022). We use annual reports, and Pakistan Stock Exchange (PSX) as sources to gather data. The sample time frame ranges from 2010 to 2023. As our sample time covers the years of COVID-19 pandemic, therefore, our analysis considers the influence of this pandemic on firm sustainable performance. The measurement and description of the variables are provided in Table 1 below.

Table 1. Description and measurement of variables

Variables	Proxies	Symbols	Measurements	Reference
Dependent Variables	Return on Assets	ROA	Net income / Total assets	Mehmood et al. (2019)
Independent Variables	Capital Structure	CS	Total debts / Total assets	Tayachi et al. (2023), Hussain et al. (2021)
	Dividend Policy	DPO	Dividend paid / Net income	Wahjudi (2020)
Control Variables	COVID-19	COVD-19	Dummy variable 1 in the years when firms are affected by COVID-19, otherwise 0	Ngo and Duong (2024)
	Firm size	FSZ	Natural log of total assets	Hussain et al. (2020), Hunjra et al. (2022)
	Firm age	AGE	Number of years of incorporation	Aiello et al. (2024)
	Growth	GRT	Percentage growth in sales	Nguyen et al. (2021)

Statistics

Following is the statistical model that is employed in this study for evaluating the results.

$$(FSP)_{i,t} = \alpha + \beta_1(CS)_{i,t} + \beta_2(DIVP)_{i,t} + \beta_3(COVID\text{-}19)_{i,t} + \beta_4(SZ)_{i,t} + \beta_5(AGE)_{i,t} + \beta_6(GRT)_{i,t} + \mu_{i,t} \quad \ldots (1)$$

Where, FSP is firm sustainable performance, CS represents capital structure, DIVP shows dividend policy, COVID-19 is taken as control variable with binary number, SZ is size, AGE describes age of the firms, GRTH is the sales growth, α is alpha, whereas μ show error term.

RESULTS

We provide descriptive statistics, correlation analysis, and variance inflation factor in Table 2. Descriptive statistics shows the summary of the overall variables data with no outliers. Correlation result also indicates no sign of multicollinearity as the highest value of correlation does not exceed limit. In addition, outcomes of the VIF test indicate that our data does not have multicollinearity problem as the values are within the limit. Regression model shows the degree of variation of one variable into another variable. In regression test on the basis of Hausman test, we select the fixed effect model and random effect model. The value of Hausman test of the variable is or less (Prob>chi2 = 0.05), then we select fixed effect model for the variable otherwise random effect.

Regression results indicate that capital structure has significant and negative impact on sustainable performance, while dividend policy encourages sustainable performance. These results suggest that when firms have more debt finding in their capital structure, they are keen to pay fixed charges to fund providers, therefore, they have to manage fixed interest charges which ultimately reduces financial performance. This further increases financial risk for a firm due to mandatory interest payments. Therefore, firms must keep cash to meet such necessary requirements. Negative impact of debt financing source on sustainable firm performance is in line with study of Vătavu (2015). In addition, positive impact of dividend policy on firm sustainable performance indicates that when firms pay more dividends, they are in a position to generate more equity financing. Due to increase in investment, firms operating activities are improved which increases financial performance. Positive effect of dividend policy on firm sustainable performance supports the results of the study investigated by Nguyen et al. (2021).

ROBUSTNESS CHECK

As our primary regression technique is fixed effect, while we employ a two step system GMM regression estimation for testing robustness of the main findings. This technique is helpful to overcome the issue of endogeneity in the data. Interestingly, we conclude the same outcomes as are generated from fixed effect regression.

Table 2. Descriptive statistics and correlation analysis

Variables	Mean	SD	VIF	1/VIF	ROA	CS	DIVP	FSZ	AGE	GRT
ROA	0.176	0.836	___	___	1					
CS	0.492	0.773	1.895	0.528	-0.098	1				
DIVP	0.328	0.637	2.477	0.404	0.183		1			
FSZ	15.263	0.984	1.761	0.568	-0.132	0.063	0.114	1		
AGE	29.635	0.993	1.635	0.612	0.265	-1.195	0.084	-0.076	1	
GRT	0.098	0.276	2.132	0.469	0.145	0.274	0.225	0.157	0.177	1

Table 3. Regression estimates

Variables	Fixed effect		One step system GMM	
	Coef.	T-values	Coef.	T-values
L1.	0.053**	(2.136)	0.081**	(2.083)
CS	-0.004***	(-5.936)	-0.002***	(-7.193)
DIVP	0.037*	(1.815)	0.134**	(2.083)
COVID-19 Dummy	Yes		Yes	
SZ	-0.175**	(2.293)	(-0.245)	(-0.896)
AGE	0.759	(0.935)	0.463	(1.082)
GRT	0.028*	(1.795)	0.271*	(1.831)
C	0.048***	(8.263)	0.274***	(6.139)
Sargan P-values			0.541	
R1 P-values			0.073	
R2 P-values			0.734	
R Square	0.296		0.341	
F Stats (P-values)	0.000		0.000	

CONCLUSION

The objective of our study is to investigate the effects of important financial policies such as capital structure and dividend policy on firm sustainable performance of the non-financial firms listed on PSX. For analysis purpose, we employ both fixed effect and GMM techniques. Findings suggest that when firms have more debt financing in their overall financing, their financial performance is decreased. This shows that with more long term debt financing, firms have to pay fixed interest which may cause financial risk. Therefore, overall sustainable performance is reduced. Furthermore, when firms pay more dividend to shareholders, their performance is improved. This is due to the fact that with more dividend payments, firm image is improved in front of investors and therefore they are more encouraged to invest in the firms which is beneficial for long term financial success. These positive signs of the firms due to payment of dividend enhance sustainable firm performance. The findings indicate that firms should encourage equity financing in order to avoid financial distress. Furthermore, firms may pay regular dividends to the shareholders increase dividend payments to the shareholders for sustainable success.

REFERENCES

Abbassi, W., Hunjra, A. I., Alawi, S. M., & Mehmood, R. (2021). The role of ownership structure and board characteristics in stock market liquidity. *International Journal of Financial Studies*, 9(4), 74. DOI: 10.3390/ijfs9040074

Abor, J. (2005). The effect of capital structure on profitability: An empirical analysis of listed firms in Ghana. *The Journal of Risk Finance*, 6(5), 438–445. DOI: 10.1108/15265940510633505

Agyei, S. K., & Marfo-Yiadom, E. (2011). Dividend policy and bank performance in Ghana. *International Journal of Economics and Finance*, 3(4), 202–207. DOI: 10.5539/ijef.v3n4p202

Aiello, F., Cardamone, P., Mannarino, L., & Pupo, V. (2024). Networks, ownership and productivity does firm age play a moderating role? *Journal of Economic Studies (Glasgow, Scotland)*, 51(9), 212–231. DOI: 10.1108/JES-10-2023-0547

Ali, A., Jan, F. A., & Atta, M. (2015). The impact of dividend policy on firm performance under high or low leverage; evidence from Pakistan. *Journal of Management*, 2(4), 16–25.

Ali, N., Rehman, M. Z. U., Ashraf, B. N., & Shear, F. (2022). Corporate dividend policies during the COVID-19 pandemic. *Economies*, 10(11), 263. DOI: 10.3390/economies10110263

Amidu, M. (2007). How does dividend policy affect performance of the firm on Ghana stock Exchange. Investment management and financial innovations, 4(2), 103-112.

Easterbrook, F. H. (1984). Two agency-cost explanations of dividends. *The American Economic Review*, 74(4), 650–659.

El-Sayed Ebaid, I. (2009). The impact of capital-structure choice on firm performance: Empirical evidence from Egypt. *The Journal of Risk Finance*, 10(5), 477–487. DOI: 10.1108/15265940911001385

Gleason, K. C., Mathur, L. K., & Mathur, I. (2000). The interrelationship between culture, capital structure, and performance: Evidence from European retailers. *Journal of Business Research*, 50(2), 185–191. DOI: 10.1016/S0148-2963(99)00031-4

Gordon, M. J. (1963). Optimal investment and financing policy. *The Journal of Finance*, 18(2), 264–272.

Holz, C. A. (2002). The impact of the liability–asset ratio on profitability in China's industrial state-owned enterprises. *China Economic Review*, 13(1), 1–26. DOI: 10.1016/S1043-951X(01)00054-2

Hunjra, A. I., Tayachi, T., Mehmood, R., & Hussain, A. (2022). Does economic risk affect corporate cash holdings? *Journal of Economic and Administrative Sciences*, 38(3), 471–484. DOI: 10.1108/JEAS-05-2020-0069

Hunjra, A. I., Tayachi, T., Mehmood, R., & Hussain, A. (2022). Does economic risk affect corporate cash holdings? *Journal of Economic and Administrative Sciences*, 38(3), 471–484. DOI: 10.1108/JEAS-05-2020-0069

Hussain, R. Y., Wen, X., Butt, R. S., Hussain, H., Ali Qalati, S., & Abbas, I. (2020). Are growth led financing decisions causing insolvency in listed firms of Pakistan? *Zagreb International Review of Economics & Business*, 23(2), 89–115. DOI: 10.2478/zireb-2020-0015

Hussain, R. Y., Wen, X., Hussain, H., Saad, M., & Zafar, Z. (2022). Do leverage decisions mediate the relationship between board structure and insolvency risk? A comparative mediating role of capital structure and debt maturity. *South Asian Journal of Business Studies*, 11(1), 104–125. DOI: 10.1108/SAJBS-05-2020-0150

Hussain, R. Y., Xuezhou, W., Hussain, H., Saad, M., & Qalati, S. A. (2021). Corporate board vigilance and insolvency risk: A mediated moderation model of debt maturity and fixed collaterals. *International Journal of Management and Economics*, 57(1), 14–33. DOI: 10.2478/ijme-2020-0032

Jensen, M. C., & Meckling, W. H. (2019). Theory of the firm: Managerial behavior, agency costs and ownership structure. In *Corporate governance* (pp. 77–132). Gower.

Kraus, A., & Litzenberger, R. H. (1973). A state-preference model of optimal financial leverage. *The Journal of Finance*, 28(4), 911–922.

Krieger, K., Mauck, N., & Pruitt, S. W. (2021). The impact of the COVID-19 pandemic on dividends. *Finance Research Letters*, 42, 101910. DOI: 10.1016/j.frl.2020.101910

Li, H., Meng, L., Wang, Q., & Zhou, L. A. (2008). Political connections, financing and firm performance: Evidence from Chinese private firms. *Journal of Development Economics*, 87(2), 283–299. DOI: 10.1016/j.jdeveco.2007.03.001

Mehmood, R., Hunjra, A. I., & Chani, M. I. (2019). The impact of corporate diversification and financial structure on firm performance: Evidence from South Asian countries. *Journal of Risk and Financial Management*, 12(1), 49. DOI: 10.3390/jrfm12010049

Meyer, B. H., Prescott, B., & Sheng, X. S. (2022). The impact of the COVID-19 pandemic on business expectations. *International Journal of Forecasting*, 38(2), 529–544. DOI: 10.1016/j.ijforecast.2021.02.009

Modigliani, F., & Miller, M. H. (1958). The cost of capital, corporation finance and the theory of investment. *The American Economic Review*, 48(3), 261–297.

Ngo, H. T., & Duong, H. N. (2024). Covid-19 pandemic and firm performance: Evidence on industry differentials and impacting channels. *International Journal of Social Economics*, 51(4), 569–583. DOI: 10.1108/IJSE-02-2023-0072

Ngo, H. T., & Duong, H. N. (2024). Covid-19 pandemic and firm performance: Evidence on industry differentials and impacting channels. *International Journal of Social Economics*, 51(4), 569–583. DOI: 10.1108/IJSE-02-2023-0072

Nguyen, A. H., Pham, C. D., Doan, N. T., Ta, T. T., Nguyen, H. T., & Truong, T. V. (2021). The effect of dividend payment on firm's financial performance: An empirical study of Vietnam. *Journal of Risk and Financial Management*, 14(8), 353. DOI: 10.3390/jrfm14080353

Nguyen, A. H., Pham, C. D., Doan, N. T., Ta, T. T., Nguyen, H. T., & Truong, T. V. (2021). The effect of dividend payment on firm's financial performance: An empirical study of Vietnam. *Journal of Risk and Financial Management*, 14(8), 353. DOI: 10.3390/jrfm14080353

Nissim, D., & Ziv, A. (2001). Dividend changes and future profitability. *The Journal of Finance*, 56(6), 2111–2133. DOI: 10.1111/0022-1082.00400

Tayachi, T., Hunjra, A. I., Jones, K., Mehmood, R., & Al-Faryan, M. A. S. (2023). How does ownership structure affect the financing and dividend decisions of firm? *Journal of Financial Reporting and Accounting*, 21(3), 729–746. DOI: 10.1108/JFRA-09-2021-0291

Vătavu, S. (2015). The impact of capital structure on financial performance in Romanian listed companies. *Procedia Economics and Finance*, 32, 1314–1322. DOI: 10.1016/S2212-5671(15)01508-7

Wahjudi, E. (2020). Factors affecting dividend policy in manufacturing companies in Indonesia Stock Exchange. *Journal of Management Development*, 39(1), 4–17. DOI: 10.1108/JMD-07-2018-0211

Weill, L. (2008). Leverage and corporate performance: Does institutional environment matter? *Small Business Economics*, 30(3), 251–265. DOI: 10.1007/s11187-006-9045-7

Xuezhou, W., Hussain, R. Y., Salameh, A. A., Hussain, H., Khan, A. B., & Fareed, M. (2022). Does firm growth impede or expedite insolvency risk? A mediated moderation model of leverage maturity and potential fixed collaterals. *Frontiers in Environmental Science*, 10, 841380. DOI: 10.3389/fenvs.2022.841380

Chapter 11
The Role of Corporate Governance in Bank Risk-Taking

Rashid Mehmood
University of Education, Lahore, Pakistan

Ilyas Ahmad
University of Education, Lahore, Pakistan

Shujah Ur Rahman
University of Education, Lahore, Pakistan

Saba Sattar
Government Technical Training Institute for Women, Pakistan

ABSTRACT

Bank credit risk is the significant factor that needs to be managed effectively. For better management of credit risk in banks, an effective corporate governance is an important factor. We examine the effect of corporate governance on bank risk taking. We use the data of 85 banks of South Asian countries while taking data from time period of 2010-2023. We apply the generalized method of moments (GMM) to analyze the results. We find that the corporate governance such as gender diversity, CEO duality and board meetings have significant negative effect on bank credit risk.

INTRODUCTION

Corporate governance has become a significant key topic in international business practices. Corporate governance is certainly not just corporate law. The definitions of corporate governance vary. Corporate governance is the combination of rules, process, law by which business are operated, regulated or controlled. Risk taking behavior of firms or financial institution become a major research issue after 2008 financial crisis of certain extent credit to excessive risk-taking behavior by financial institution as well as banks (Moussa, 2019). Several studies have been conducted to understand those factors that influence risk taking behavior in banks or other financial institutions to make right policies from policy makers to further avoid financial crisis as a result of excessive risk taking. In addition, better corporate governance practices promoted more effective bank operating outcomes after the period of financial crisis (Calomiris & Carlson, 2016). The banking sector is mainly important in economies where banks play a primary role in the financial system. Furthermore, the corporate governance is an additional element that assign to risk exposure toward the banks. Banking sector is backbone of emerging economies (Hunjra et al., 2021) producing major part of revenues for the economies. Better corporate governance practices results in reducing the likelihood of default risk of banks. The present study aims to investigate the influence of corporate governance practices on risk-taking of banks in developing countries which will enable management of banks to employ better governance policies to handle the potential losses.

When evaluating the corporate governance, ownership structure may be particularly crucial to corporate governance in the banking sector (Barry et al., 2011). This is due to the fact that regulations frequently oblige banks to maintaining a specific level of capital, which can be altered by bank ownership. Perhaps based on how much ownership is concentrated. In recent years, the academic community has paid close attention to corporate governance and bank credit risk. Similarly, there is a chance that a consumer won't pay their invoices if a business extends credit to them. In order to better understand the connection between corporate governance and risk behavior in the banking industry of MENA nations, Oteros et al. (2019) carried out a study. Indeed, financial practices like credit pay or return back are related with corporate governance.

The effectiveness of risk management and good corporate governance implementation is needed to enable banks to identify problems early. Bank failures can stem from manager behavior or compensation contracts. Agency problems may arise from excessive salaries, inadequate risk management efforts or risk shifts from creditors to shareholders. For the banking sector, Fu et al. (2014) indicate that commercials bank can improve their public accountability, minimize risk exposure, create value and enhance operational efficiency if they have effective corporate governance.

About risk management, Chen and Ling (2016) found that various risks faced by banks, such as interest liquidity risk, rate risk and credit risk, are related to each other, but these interactions can be moderated through corporate administration and administrative instruments. Credit risk is the chance of suffering a loss as a result of a borrower's failure to make loan payments or fulfil contractual commitments. Financial institutions are subject to a variety of credit risks, including institutional risk, downgrade risk, nation risk, concentration risk, and default risk. Credit risk is the possibility that a borrower will not fulfil their contractual responsibilities, such as making payments or adhering to deadlines. An effective board structure with strong monitoring acts can reduce the likelihood of occurrence of credit risk (Hussain et al., 2022). Recent times have seen concerted attempts by various economists and policy makers to identify the factors that contribute to bank credit risk due to the detrimental effects of banking distress on numerous economies as a result of the financial crisis of 2008/2009.

Importance of Banking Sector

Economists, decision-makers, and financial specialists have all universally understood the importance of the banking industry. The events underline the importance of the banking industry: By stating that a well-functioning banking sector is crucial for economic development, since it provides the financial resources that are needed to invest in new technologies and expand productive capacity, the World Bank has highlighted the significance of the banking sector in fostering economic growth (World Bank, 2016). The role of the banking industry in promoting financial growth and economic stability has been recognized by the International Monetary Fund (IMF). The existence of a well-supervised banking sector is essential for the financial system's smooth operation and for growth in the economy, according to the IMF (IMF, 2017). According to the European Central Bank (ECB), banks play a critical role in intermediating financial resources, allocating credit, and managing financial risks, thereby promoting economic growth and social welfare. The banking industry is vital for the supply of effective financial services to individuals and businesses (ECB, 2019). In conclusion, top international organizations, central banks, and academic scholars have all highlighted the importance of the banking industry and its critical role in improving the economy, financial stability, and social welfare.

The objective of our study is to examine the effects of corporate governance on bank risk taking in South Asia. The motive behind the study is essence of effective corporate governance policies to mitigate risk taking of banks. Developing countries have not yet formulated a well-structured business environment which leaves a literature gap relating to corporate governance and its potential impact on risk taking of banks (Tayachi et al., 2023). In South Asian region, banks promote economic activities of other sectors through providing loans for the purpose of investment projects and other business activities (Hunjra et al., 2021). Throughout their operating procedures, banks consistently face different forms of risks that may have negative influence on their business activities. Therefore, it is pertinent to evaluate the role of corporate governance in managing the activities that may lead to risk and ultimately financial distress.

LITERATURE REVIEW

Corporate management operates as an operator for shareholders and will be fully aware of its interface rather than as an intelligent and sensible shareholder as would be expected under good stewardship (Xuezhou et al., 2022). Office hypotheses holds that management cannot be relied upon to act in the best interests of shareholders or the general public at large. Caprio et al. (2007) point out that lack of transparency and monitoring in corporate governance structure of the banks leads bank management to manipulate earnings and valuation which may cause risk. Board of directors are more important in banking sector as compared to any other sector (Felicio et al., 2018). With agency theory, several ideas about corporate governance develop. According to this theory, management of a corporation must be overseen and managed to ensure that all relevant regulations and directives are followed. On the other hand, several research found less evidence of a significant and direct impact of corporate governance structure and attributes on the performance of the banking industry during the pandemic era (Akhtar et al., 2021). In the first quarter of 2020, Demir and Danisman (2021) examined 1927 banks from 110 different nations. They found that during the Covid-19 epidemic, governance scores had no appreciable impact on bank returns. During Covid-19, banks faced challenges implement effective governance structure to overcome credit risk (Khaskheli et al., 2023).

Mutamimah et al. (2020) suggested that Small Medium Enterprise (SMEs') credit risk was unaffected by the corporate governance demonstrated by accountability, independence, and fairness. In other words, accountability and openness are useful in lowering the credit risk for SMEs. Moreover, financial literacy can increase the effectiveness of accountability, responsibility, and transparency in lowering loan risk for SMEs in Indonesia. According to Gulzar et al. (2021), to intensify the impact of corporate governance on banking risk inside Pakistan's banking sector, the board has to be strengthened. Large board has ability and strength to reduce credit risk of banks in developing countries (Cheng, 2008).

This makes it possible for management to safeguard the interests of all parties involved, not just its own. The findings unambiguously show that bigger boards in Pakistani banks lead to inefficient governance through increasing loan loss provisions, but independent directors and director attendance at meetings do not appear to matter (Moussa, 2019). Results show that the higher the number of board members, the lower the quality of credit is and, consequently, the credit risk increases. Furthermore, an effective corporate governance has the ability to control credit risk (Hussain et al., 2021). Djebali and Zaghdoudi (2019) finds that that credit risk and liquidity risk are directly related to bank governance mechanisms. Lower credit risk levels are correlated with a larger supervisory board and shorter term debt (Hussain et al., 2022). Based on the above literature review, we propose the study hypothesis as follow.

H1: Corporate governance mechanisms have significant influence on bank credit risk.

METHODOLOGY

Our study is based on secondary study. This study is an applied study on the banks operating in South Asia. To achieve the study's goal, the content analysis of financial and corporate governance reports published by the study sample banks which have relied on. The current study aims to test the corporate governance effect on reducing banking risks over the period (2010-2023). We collect data from 2010 to 2023 from financial statements of respective listed banks of South Asia. Bank risk taking is level of risk which a bank is willing to take in order to achieve its objective. In which bank is will to take credit risk by lending to borrowers with high level of chance of the default. As the same measurement is used by Hunjra et al. (2023).

NPLs = NPL / TL Where NPL is non-performing loan and TL is total loan   (1)

Corporate governance is the framework of policies, customs, and procedures that businesses propose to govern and monitor their operations (Abbassi et al., 2021). Financial reporting, CEO compensation, shareholder rights, and board composition are only a few of the many aspects discussed by corporate governance. Corporate governance contains following variables in it: Gender diversity is equitable or fair representation of people of different genders. It most commonly refers to an equitable ratio of men and women, but also includes people of non-binary genders (Mehmood et al., 2023). CEO duality occurs when the CEO also serves as the chairman of the board of directors (Mehmood et al., 2019). A board meeting is a meeting of the board of directors that sets the policy and strategic direction for a corporation, publicly-traded company, government body, or non-profit. Bank age is total time period from when the bank is established till yet.

Bank age = current year – year of establishment (Mehmood et al., 2019) (2)

Liquidity play a vital role for the management of short term debt obligation and give opportunity to further invest in different classes where companies get more profit. Tangibility (TANG) is defined as the ratio of tangible assets (net fixed assets) to total assets.

Statistics

We apply following static panel technique for investigation purpose.

$$BCR_{i,t} = \alpha + \beta_1 GD_{i,t} + \beta_2 CEOD_{i,t} + \beta_3 BMBR_{i,t} + \beta_4 BM_{i,t} + \beta_5 LIQ_{i,t} + \beta_6 AGE_{i,t} + \beta_7 TAN_{I,t} + \varepsilon \quad (3)$$

Where BCR is bank credit risk, GDIV stands for gender diversity, CEOD is CEO duality, BMEM are board members and board of directors, BMTG stands for board meetings, LIQ stands for liquidity ratio, AGE mean the age of bank, TAN means tangibility and α is the constant, β is the coefficient, and ε is error term.

RESULTS

We display descriptive statistics in Table 1 which is used to show the summary of data.

Table 1. Descriptive statistics

Variable	Obs	Mean	Std dev.	Min	Max
BCR	648	0.096	0.220	0.000	2.537
GDIV	648	0.067	0.069	0.000	0.333
CEOD	648	0.195	0.396	0.000	1.000
BMEM	648	10.557	3.1140	4.000	24.000
BMTG	648	10.859	6.1108	2.000	30.000
LIQ	648	0.898	1.0589	0.001	16.557
TAN	648	0.027	0.0954	0.001	2.254
Age	648	36.929	29.612	1.000	158.000

We ensure from the outcomes that our data does not have any outlier which means normality of the data exists.

Table 2. Correlation analysis

Variables	BCR	GDIV	CEOD	BMEM	BMTG	LIQ	TAN	AGE
BCR	1.000							
GDIV	-0.036	1.000						
CEOD	-0.120	0.192	1.000					
BMEM	-0.140	0.214	0.180	1.000				
BMTG	-0.080	0.233	0.040	0.433	1.000			
LIQ	-0.016	0.005	-0.009	-0.028	-0.074	1.000		
TAN	0.060	-0.060	-0.075	-0.087	-0.093	0.011	1.000	
AGE	0.280	0.050	0.321	0.047	0.080	-0.009	-0.033	1.000

Further, in Table 2, we report correlation analysis to check the strength of relationships among variables. However, our findings signify that there is no high correlation among our explanatory variables which means multicollinearity issue does not prevail in our data.

Table 3. Regression estimates (GMM)

Variables	Coefficient	S.D	t-value	p-value
L1	0.155	0.006	256.20	0.000
L2	-0.055	0.003	-147.98	0.000
GDIV	-0.484	0.001	-257.26	0.000
CEOD	-0.421	0.002	-17.40	0.001
BMEM	-0.026	0.002	-178.20	0.000
BMTG	-0.009	0.004	-104.65	0.000
LIQ	0.023	0.001	20.24	0.001
TAN	2.690	0.003	775.36	0.000
AGE	0.001	0.005	77.39	0.000
C	0.378	0.002	217.16	0.000
Sargan (p-value)	0.251			
AR1 (p-value)	0.035			
AR2 (p-value)	0.769			

For analyzing the effects of corporate governance variables on bank credit risk, in Table 3, we apply GMM regression technique which is helpful to control endogeneity problem in the data. This technique also covers unobserved heterogeneity in the data. We use lagged values which are helpful in dynamic panel data. Our findings reveal that all the corporate governance variables have significant and negative impact on bank credit risk. These results indicate that with inclusion of female members on boards, bank credit risk is reduced because female members are not risk taker. Further, when there is increase in board meetings, it is less likely for the board to take more risk as they share their knowledge and experience. More board members also take less risk in order to avoid any financial distress. When CEO holds two positions at a time, risk taking activities are reduced as CEO might hesitate to take risky actions with performing more responsibilities. Among control variables, tangibility, liquidity, and age have significant and inverse influence on bank risk in South Asia.

CONCLUSION

The objective of our study is to investigate the potential effects of corporate governance on credit risk of the banks operating in South Asia. Findings of the study reveal that corporate governance mechanisms such as board gender diversity, CEO duality, board members, and board meetings significantly reduce credit risk of the banks. These findings provide policy implications for the management of the banks that they should formulate an effective corporate governance policy in order to enhance financial outcomes and reduce credit risk. Further, banks should keep optimal level of board members so that they may share the knowledge and experience which ultimately provide financial benefits and reduce bank risk. Dual role of CEO is beneficial for banks as with dual responsibilities, CEOs do not take risky decisions. Firms should encourage female directors on the board for smooth and effective outcomes. More board meetings enhance firms' strategic decisions and ensure that risk management of the banks align with strategic decision making. Therefore, banks should encourage more board meetings to identify the potential credit risk through regular discussion and sharing knowledge.

REFERENCES

Abbassi, W., Hunjra, A. I., Alawi, S. M., & Mehmood, R. (2021). The role of ownership structure and board characteristics in stock market liquidity. *International Journal of Financial Studies*, 9(4), 74. DOI: 10.3390/ijfs9040074

Akhtar, S., Hussain, H., & Hussain, R. Y. (2021). Contributing role of regulatory compliance and Islamic operations in bank risk: Evidence from Pakistan. *Nankai Business Review International*, 12(4), 618–635. DOI: 10.1108/NBRI-07-2020-0037

Barry, T., Lepetit, L., & Tarazi, A. (2011). Ownership structure and risk in publicly held a privately owned banks. *Journal of Banking & Finance*, 35(5), 1327–1340. DOI: 10.1016/j.jbankfin.2010.10.004

Calomiris, C. W., & Carlson, M. (2016). Corporate governance and risk management at unprotected banks: National banks in the 1890s. *Journal of Financial Economics*, 119(3), 512–532. DOI: 10.1016/j.jfineco.2016.01.025

Caprio, G., Laeven, L., & Levine, R. (2007). Governance and bank valuation. *Journal of Financial Intermediation*, 16(4), 584–617. DOI: 10.1016/j.jfi.2006.10.003

Chen, H. J., & Lin, K. T. (2016). How do banks make the trade-offs among risks? The role of corporate governance. *Journal of Banking & Finance*, 72, S39–S69. DOI: 10.1016/j.jbankfin.2016.05.010

Cheng, S. (2008). Board size and the variability of corporate performance. *Journal of Financial Economics*, 87(1), 157–176. DOI: 10.1016/j.jfineco.2006.10.006

Demir, E., & Danisman, G. O. (2021). Banking sector reactions to COVID-19: The role of bank-specific factors and government policy responses. *Research in International Business and Finance*, 58, 101508. DOI: 10.1016/j.ribaf.2021.101508

Djebali, N., & Zaghdoudi, K. (2020). Testing the governance-performance relationship for the Tunisian banks: A GMM in system analysis. *Financial Innovation*, 6(1), 1–24. DOI: 10.1186/s40854-020-00182-5

Felicio, J. A., Rodrigues, R., Grove, H., & Greiner, A. (2018). The influence of corporate governance on bank risk during a financial crisis. *Ekonomska Istrazivanja*, 31(1), 1078–1090. DOI: 10.1080/1331677X.2018.1436457

Fu, X. M., Lin, Y. R., & Molyneux, P. (2014). Bank efficiency and shareholder value in Asia Pacific. *Journal of International Financial Markets, Institutions and Money*, 33, 200–222. DOI: 10.1016/j.intfin.2014.08.004

Gulzar, U., Khan, S. N., Baig, F. J., Ansari, M. A. A., Akram, R., & Kamran, M. (2021). The Impact Of Corporate Governance On Risk Management: Evidence From The Banking Sector Of Pakistan. [BBE]. *Bulletin of Business and Economics*, 10(3), 196–207.

Hunjra, A. I., Hanif, M., Mehmood, R., & Nguyen, L. V. (2021). Diversification, corporate governance, regulation and bank risk-taking. *Journal of Financial Reporting and Accounting*, 19(1), 92–108. DOI: 10.1108/JFRA-03-2020-0071

Hunjra, A. I., Hanif, M., Mehmood, R., & Nguyen, L. V. (2021). Diversification, corporate governance, regulation and bank risk-taking. *Journal of Financial Reporting and Accounting*, 19(1), 92–108. DOI: 10.1108/JFRA-03-2020-0071

Hunjra, A. I., Jebabli, I., Thrikawala, S. S., Alawi, S. M., & Mehmood, R. (2024). How do corporate governance and corporate social responsibility affect credit risk? *Research in International Business and Finance*, 67, 102139. DOI: 10.1016/j.ribaf.2023.102139

Hunjra, A. I., Zureigat, Q., Tayachi, T., & Mehmood, R. (2020). Impact of non-interest income and revenue concentration on bank risk in South Asia. *Banks and Bank Systems*, 15(4), 15–25. DOI: 10.21511/bbs.15(4).2020.02

Hussain, R. Y., Wen, X., Hussain, H., Saad, M., & Zafar, Z. (2022). Do leverage decisions mediate the relationship between board structure and insolvency risk? A comparative mediating role of capital structure and debt maturity. *South Asian Journal of Business Studies*, 11(1), 104–125. DOI: 10.1108/SAJBS-05-2020-0150

Hussain, R. Y., Xuezhou, W., Hussain, H., Saad, M., & Qalati, S. A. (2021). Corporate board vigilance and insolvency risk: A mediated moderation model of debt maturity and fixed collaterals. *International Journal of Management and Economics*, 57(1), 14–33. DOI: 10.2478/ijme-2020-0032

Khaskheli, M. B., Wang, S., Hussain, R. Y., Jahanzeb Butt, M., Yan, X., & Majid, S. (2023). Global law, policy, and governance for effective prevention and control of COVID-19: A comparative analysis of the law and policy of Pakistan, China, and Russia. *Frontiers in Public Health*, 10, 1035536. DOI: 10.3389/fpubh.2022.1035536

Mehmood, R., Hunjra, A. I., & Chani, M. I. (2019). The impact of corporate diversification and financial structure on firm performance: Evidence from South Asian countries. *Journal of Risk and Financial Management*, 12(1), 49. DOI: 10.3390/jrfm12010049

Mehmood, R., Khan, M. A., Khan, M. M., & Javed, N. (2023). The influence of board attributes and gender diversity on risk-taking in banking sector. *Journal of Namibian Studies: History Politics Culture*, 35, 4565–4585.

Moussa, F. B. (2019). The influence of internal corporate governance on bank credit risk: An empirical analysis for Tunisia. *Global Business Review*, 20(3), 640–667. DOI: 10.1177/0972150919837078

Mutamimah, M., Tholib, M., & Robiyanto, R. (2021). Corporate governance, credit risk, and financial literacy for small medium enterprise in Indonesia. *Business: Theory and Practice*, 22(2), 406–413. DOI: 10.3846/btp.2021.13063

Otero, L., Alaraj, R., & Lado-Sestayo, R. (2020). How corporate governance and ownership affect banks' risk-taking in the MENA countries? *European Journal of Management and Business Economics*, 29(2), 182–198. DOI: 10.1108/EJMBE-01-2019-0010

Tayachi, T., Hunjra, A. I., Jones, K., Mehmood, R., & Al-Faryan, M. A. S. (2023). How does ownership structure affect the financing and dividend decisions of firm? *Journal of Financial Reporting and Accounting*, 21(3), 729–746. DOI: 10.1108/JFRA-09-2021-0291

Xuezhou, W., Hussain, R. Y., Hussain, H., Saad, M., & Qalati, S. A. (2022). Analyzing the impact of board vigilance on financial distress through the intervention of leverage structure and interaction of asset tangibility in the non-financial sector of Pakistan. *International Journal of Financial Engineering*, 9(02), 2150004. DOI: 10.1142/S2424786321500043

Chapter 12
An Exploratory Study of the Complex Interplay Between Society and Finance:
Ways of Empowerment and Elements of Precarity

Muhammad Sohail Ahmad
University of Education, Pakistan, Pakistan

Taskeen Fatima
University of Education, Pakistan, Pakistan

ABSTRACT

This study aims to evaluate the relationship between society and finance using Butler's theory of precarity. People are the workforce of society and they are divided into multiple institutions like family, education, religion, healthcare finance etc. The study addresses how these institutions especially that of finance work to empower society and vice versa. The study uses Butler's theory of precarity to highlight the elements that lead to social and financial precarity. Moreover, how precarity in one of the two factors i-e; finance and society leads to the same in the other. The study concludes that not only are the marginalized or differentiated groups precarious, but when financial or social precarity prevails, every single life becomes a victim.

DOI: 10.4018/979-8-3693-5733-0.ch012

INTRODUCTION

Society and finance have a direct relationship with each other. Both these factors have a great potential impact on each other. Society is defined as a group of individuals living together in the same place over the same time and sharing commonalities. People living in a society share common values and interests and have respect for each other. They share a common culture, norms, traditions and institutions. Societies operate over a particular geographical boundary and timeframe. People living in a society interact with one another and cooperate to maintain a sense of sustainability, belonging and order in the society. They get their needs fulfilled by working together. A single person cannot be a society but the representative of the whole society. Society is made up of people and these people are the controllers of them. Society is made up of multiple institutions that serve for the betterment of people of a society. These institutions play a very vital role in the development of society, the promotion of societal values and norms, and the performance of sustainability practices along with the overall well-being of people and communities living in the society.

Some of the institutions include family, education, finance, government, religion, law and the healthcare system. Family is the building unit of society where people are brought up and nurtured. The education sector serves to promote literacy and develop knowledge and skills among the people. It teaches good values and ethics to the society. The government is the controlling body of society that maintains and ensures well-being and order in society. The institute of law seeks to establish the rules and regulations, the performance of lawful activities and punishment for those who try to spoil the society. The institute of religion seeks to provide the religious teachings and religious grounds of a society. The healthcare institutions are based on the aim of developing means and resources to ensure good physical health and stability of the people. Finally, the most important institution that serves the base of all the institutions operating in society is the institution of finance and economy. This is the most crucial sector of society because all the other sectors are directly or indirectly dependent on this sector.

The institution of finance provides resources to others for their proper work. The finance sector deals with the identification of financial resources, their management and how and where to make financial investments. The good and effective utilization of the available financial resources leads to a good, effective and sustained economy of a society. The economic well-being of the society depends largely on its financial well-being (Rinaldi, 2016). If a society has a good, progressive and healthy finance sector the economic aspects of the society will be very much strong. But if the finance sector is weak, society has to struggle a lot to meet the economic expenses. There are a lot of components upon which the finance of a society is based.

Some of the key elements include industries, businesses, firms, banks, insurance companies, mortgages and loans, consumer finance companies, real estate brokers and real estate investment trusts. All these components serve to develop a society's finances. The financial services sector is the most potential segment of finance. It ensures the good availability of financial services between people, government and financial firms. It can be regarded as a monitoring or controlling body of finance (Rinaldi, 2016). Offices involved in the financial services department manage and control the flow of money between finance and other institutions of the society. They monitor the availability, provision, use and profit of the financial resources.

There are a lot of things from society that contribute to the development of finance. Finance gets a lot of money from loans and mortgages. The money collected as interest with the loans provides sustainability to the finance. Investments in terms of insurance and banking profit also serve to strengthen the field of finance. Taxation is one of the best practices performed by governments to invest more and more in their finance. The money collected as tax from the people of the society serves as a crucial element in building up the finances. The export sector and business also aid in vitalizing the finance of society. People in society are the most crucial elements who play their direct roles in maintaining and progressing the finances.

How do Society and Finance Empower Each Other?

Empowerment means to enhance the potential of something. It is the act of upholding the strengths of any segment, department, institution or phenomenon. To empower means to build up something more strongly and firmly. Both society and finance serve to empower each other. As stated by Christine Lagarde (2014) there is a need for inclusion in the finance sector to empower it. People from multiple fragments of society must be included to empower the finances of their society. By empowering the individuals and families living in the society we can lead the finance of our society to great progressive outcomes. All the people must cooperate and collaborate to create financial stability and empowerment in society. All the institutions working in the society have to engage according to the principles of inclusion so that the finance may flourish. For a lot of years in history, Mexico has stood as a role model of financial inclusion for other countries. For Mexico, financial inclusion is the key element of their agenda. Financial inclusion can serve as a great tool for empowering the society. If the finances of the society are stringer and inclusive, the whole society progresses (Vaia et al., 2017). Because every other sector of society requires resources and budgets, finance is the one that provides these things. If the finances are healthy and strong, the society is considered to be very wealthy and stable. Similarly, the people of the society according to the inclusion principle serve to make the finances healthy and strong. The hardworking people with the help of their skills, knowledge and hard work lead to great financial outcomes for the society. For example, if people work hard in industries, banks, companies, agriculture and other areas, the finance of the society will be increased tremendously. In this way, we can say that both finance and society depend upon each other for their development and progress and both support each other. Finance provides resources to the people and they strive to return them by doubling them.

Ways of empowerment:

The following measures can relatively empower society and finance:

1. Education:

Education is the key to development. By investing in the field of education, the quality of education is enhanced and improved. Consequently, the quality of the skills and knowledge of the people living in the society also improves. It improves their personalities and empowers them. Educated people use their expertise in the workplace and work very hard for the betterment of their people. The educated people invest their learnings and education in various sectors of society. This investment will bring a lot of profit to society.

2. Resource management:

Society is rich with the resources that aid in financial development. These resources include manpower, technology, electricity, income, and natural and environmental resources. These resources need to be effectively managed. There should be no exploitation of any of these resources. These resources should be used according to the needs. In this way, the resources are used as well as protected.

3. Sustainable principles:

Sustainable development refers to the process of meeting the needs of the current generation without overlooking the capacities and abilities of future generations to meet their needs. It means the available resources should be used in such a way that meets the needs of the present generation but not ignores the future generations. It means the present society and finance need nit to be selfish.

4. Skill development:

The people of society must be empowered by skills. Those who have skills have a good earning hand. Skill learning gives the people of society an earning hand for their livelihood. If people in a society are self-sufficient, they are not a burden on the economy of the society. But they support the economy by earning a good income. But if people do not work hard and instead depend on others for their needs to be fulfilled. Such people become a burden for the finances of the society.

5. Infrastructure:

A society must prepare an effective infrastructure with the help of other institutions for the effective and long-term development of finance and society. Through the financial profit obtained from multiple institutions and public-private sectors in a society, a great infrastructure can be developed. A sustained infrastructure is the key towards effective sustainability practices leading to the advancement of society and finance.

In short, we can state that both society and finance have empowering impacts on each other. Sustainability in one leads to the same in the other.

What Creates Precarity?

Certain factors prevail in society and can be potential elements to create an atmosphere of precarity in society. The term precarity is synonymous with "uncertainty", "vulnerability" and "unpredictability". Judith Butler stated precarity and precariousness as two different terminologies and concepts, precariousness is a concept that revolves around all people in the world who are vulnerable or marginalized either in their sufferings and injuries while precarity particularly relates to those people who are poor, impotent, deeply affected by traumatic events or natural diseases and disasters, feel discrimination and get marginalized by social networks. Certain populations are vulnerable towards violence, death, injury, disease, starvation, inflation and many other situations resulting in political and economic failure (Butler Judith, 2015, p33). It is not about the fact that living off a certain group or population becomes vulnerable, rather every living being is naturally born with precariousness and their lives rely upon multiple social factors whether they are going to live or die, it is essential to protect living being so it may enjoy the survival (Butler, 2009).

On the other hand, Lorey (Berlant et al., 2013) remarked that precarity is not associated with labourers only. The terms in the concept of precarity and its conditions also apply to affluent people related to different social classes like bourgeois and elite white populations likewise Simon During suggested that precarious societies are associated and linked with many cultures and religions, the people who have inadequate income are more exposed to restless and unsafe environment, insecure access to institutions and communities that can give them recognition (During, 2015, p37). In the eyes of Wacquant, precarity is a state of marginalization and susceptibility and he gave the concept of "advanced marginality" and "postindustrial precariat" (Wacquant, 1999, p.254).

If precarity prevails in this manner in the society, not only the people become precarious but all the pillar institutions of the society also suffer from the same disorder. A precarious society cannot entertain sustainable finance in any way to its people.

Precarity is prominently integrated with "gender norms" that the law, government, police and other authorities fail to protect in any case (Butler Judith, 2015, p34). She further points out that the opposite precarious society is not a safe and secure society but the establishment of an "egalitarian", social and political order to promote the condition of "livable interdependency" (p69). No one can escape this aspect of precarity. Standing talked about the three fractions of precarious people, first who belong to the old working class and look backwards, second are migrants and minorities who face pressure and third are progressives who lose their future and have plenty of debt, these people reject old conservative thoughts (Standing, 2019). In a society in which there is no political or economic stability, the finances of the society can never be developed. In this way, society as a whole, faces difficulties to survive.

This condition of precarity is faced globally in the form of identity crisis, economic crisis, exploitation of basic human rights and immigrants' oppression. Here are some examples of societies that face precarity, like Jerusalem, Syria, Iraq, India, Europe, Indonesia, America and also in Pakistan. Jerusalem is an extremely precarious state where insecurity is obvious and lives are vulnerable. In line with Foucault and Agamben, an Italian philosopher, there is a "biopolitical" conflict between the life that is "included" (that must live) and the life that is "excluded" (that must die), leading to the concept of "inclusive exclusion". Precariousness in Jerusalem has become evident since the Al-Aqsa intifada at the hands of Israelites and their conspiracy from "temporariness to permanence". Palestinians are precarious within their homes, mosques and streets, especially at the checkpoints where they are being stripped, living the life of "other".

Israel by taking advantage of the war on terror claimed its brutal actions on Palestinians as a war against Islamism. Palestine at the mercy of Israel faces precariousness in the world as they are unable to live their lives and enjoy social status in the world. Israeli politics use different metaphors (cancer, mosquitoes, cockroaches) to depict Palestinians as contagion agents. Israel in 1948 passed legislation that all Palestinians who were under Israeli control were denationalized, they became stateless and helpless (Penny, 2010). It is estimated that out of 70.8 million people 25.8 million are refugees, refugees face marginalization all around the world. In Syria, about 6.4 million people are displaced internally and 3.7 million have moved to neighbouring countries. By December 2016 the number of registered Syrians in

Turkey reached 2,783,617 according to the Ministry of Interior Directorate General of Migration Management. Of these, 1,301,026 were Syrian women. Syrian refugees face educational, economic, social, political and gender issues in Turkey. Around 83% of Syrian children are getting education from homes and unofficial Syrian schools that are not funded and recognized by the government. The lowest uneducated Turkish workers are replaced by Syrians. The host country considers Syrians as guests, not refugees. Syrians have no right to legal status, unable to register themselves as natives or make their identity cards. The gender-related problems, severe labour and precarious livelihood are more faced by Syrian women than men.

Due to their precarious immigration status, and not being legally registered, they are subjected to insecurity, exploitation and trafficking at the hands of employers and traffickers (Ertorer, 2021; Vallejo-Martín et al., 2020; Wall et al., 2017). An anthropologist, Muhammad Al-Hyder writes about the precarity faced by Iraqis at the time of invasion. He writes about the kidnapping of Jaber, an event that throws light on the precariousness of life, that one precarious event when happens in the lives of people and further uncovers other such events with which Iraqi people have to struggle with their living, hence living the life of "others". (Al-Mohammad, 2012). For such societies, it becomes extremely challenging to maintain a healthy survival.

In South Asia, the precarity comes to encompass Pakistani people in terms of social, economic, political and gender. The Naya Pakistan Housing Scheme (2020) and Ashiana Housing Projects (2010) introduced by the Pakistan Government are unable to provide houses to low-income groups. The inadequate coordination among government agencies, stakeholders, builders, contractors and suppliers with the public, poor financial opportunities provided to low-income groups and the absence of an economic housing policy are notable for the inability of people to buy houses for their families. The distrust in the credibility of the poor and insufficient databases of borrowers are the main barriers to providing approval for the poor. Low-income groups have become precarious in their land where they are incapable of building their houses even from government projects (Malik et al., 2020). Moreover, health conditions in the country are also precarious, health benefits are not equally enjoyed by all the citizens leading to the poor health state in the country(Abbas et al., 2020).

By examining a complex relationship between society, financial elements and precarity-inducing conditions, we can state that a society that is facing the challenges of survival and safety, the challenge of maintaining good healthy finances, the challenge of fighting with multiple issues at the same time and finding nothing progressive in its communities cannot flourish at all. In this way, not only does the people, finance or one single institution of the society fall apart, but the society as a whole falls apart into a collapse. Such a society cannot stay integrated and intact.

Covid-19 was a Period of Financial Collapse

The tremendously deadly coronavirus or COVID-19 marked a magnificent impact on the global economies. Such an effect can never be predicted in nature as that of coronavirus. The deadly pandemic bound the people to the limits of their homes. This limitation had a great impact on the daily working, jobs and routine work of people. The effects of COVID-19 cannot be related to those of other pandemics. It had a deadly impact on the economy of not only a single country but of the whole world. COVID-19 was declared a deadly pandemic on 12th March 2020, from China. International and national markets suffered a great loss in response to the spread of the deadly disease throughout the world. The Oil markets crashed and consequently, the economy started getting downward. As a result of the loss and shocks being experienced in the national and international markets, society began to experience a worse downfall (Li et al., 2022).

The other sectors of society were falling. People were confined to the bounds of their homes. They were unable to come out and work at their workplaces. No one was able to do their work properly. The education sector was majorly shifting online. Teachers and students had to struggle hard to cope with these adverse circumstances. The schools were facing numerous issues. Likewise, the labourers were unable to work at their sites. In this way, they were deprived of their wages. It was a period of great economic downfall for them. The hospitals on the other hand were filled with patients. Everyone in the hospital was struggling for life. Not only in the hospital, were people isolated from society in their homes. Everyone was fighting a battle for life and life for everyone was "precarious".

With the onset of lockdown, millions of people lost their jobs and were not able to earn and support their livelihood. Financial stability for them was also precarious. Similarly, the imposition of strict lockdowns across the whole world badly affected the overall market completely, equal to a recession. According to expert economists, the market finance jumped 18 times from low and high in 25 days of March 2020. This thing is shocking for the stability of the market (Shibata, 2021). Apart from this, the decline in the world capital and the increase in the prices of consumer goods, the economy faced a great challenge. The industries that were working at a really good pace began to crash financially.

Just like the whole world, Pakistan also suffered a great financial and social loss with the outbreak of the pandemic. Before the COVID-19 outbreak, the financial sector of Pakistani society was already trying hard to stay intact. It was already at a risk of downfall. However, with the onset of the pandemic, it became evident that something drastic would happen to the finances of the country. The deadly pandemic was not only life-threatening for the people of the society but largely for the finances. Although the pandemic was not especially for Pakistan, all the nations were equally affected by its deadly nature. The economy of Pakistan was already really weak, that's why it had to suffer more as compared to the other nations. Moreover, the society of Pakistan did not have enough capital to cope with the deadly effects of the pandemic. The infrastructure was already weak and inadequate. The situation of emergency was imposed in the country and everything was falling precarious.

Before the onset of the pandemic, Pakistan was preparing to launch new programs to support the financial system of society. Good results were also being marked by the government in their struggle to achieve a sustainable economy. The government was struggling to attain good finance, health, education and other social sectors. With the onset of the pandemic, Pakistan like all the other countries struggled a lot to maintain the integrity of its social institutions. (Sareen, 2020) People were under the imposition of lockdown. No one was able to reach the workplace and get their earnings. Students were facing difficulties in their studies. Education was shifted to the online system. In many areas of Pakistan, there is no technological advancement and similarly no internet infrastructure. Students from poor economic backgrounds had to face a lot of challenges in maintaining their studies. (Sareen, 2020)The academic life of students in Pakistan was precarious.

Due to the lockdown, the shops were shut. Only the medical stores and some of the grocery stores were open. Many people who earned their livelihood from these shops either as owners or as workers, were badly affected. There was a great financial loss for these people. The financial life of rich as well as poor people was becoming precarious with every passing day. In this way, the whole society was under the influence of precarity imposed by the pandemic. This precarity was very hard to deal with as it was natural and there was no predefined time of its ending. Every day every second was precarious for the people.

At higher levels, the industries were getting deprived of the manpower working there. Due to the lockdown, labour was prevented from going to the factories and industries, there was no adequate performance in the work field of these industries and factories. Several textile factories faced a huge financial loss. As they had no income, they had no finance to get their employees paid. As a result of this crisis these factories and industries had to knock out a lot of their employees because they were unable to afford a great number of people. For the fired staff, it became really hard to survive. They lost their source of income and due to the lockdown, they could not find a new one for them. Many people starved to death in these circumstances. Life was precarious. The financial integrity of the factories and industries as well as the social well-being of the workers was really under the influence of precarity(Kasper et al., 2020).

Apart from the financial crisis and financial death of the economy, the state of fear was everywhere. Seeing several people getting infected, seeing hospitals loaded with patients, and having no financial support, it was very hard to deal with this precarity. The precarity was started by the virus, and this precarity in turn was imposing a state of fear among the people in the society. The fear of being the next to be infected, the fear of losing beloved ones, and the fear of having no money were really hard to cope with. The society was really in the lap of precarity. All the lives were precarious matter make or female, rich or poor. In this way we can say that in a way that society and finance empower each other, if by chance, precarity prevails and destroys one of them, the other automatically suffers a loss. If finance goes down the society goes down, and if the society fails the finance also fails.

CONCLUSION

Society is made up of people. People work together to run various institutions for the overall well-being of society. All the institutions of the society need to be integrated in order to maintain it. All of these institutions have to collaborate with one another if precarity prevails in the society. If any precarious element arises, the first victim is always the people and next the finance and then any other institution. We can see the implications of butler's theory of precarity in terms of finance and society. Through this study we can state that, if butler says only the marginalized people are precarious, we can make a novel proposition that every life is precarious depending upon the social circumstances and not only upon that life itself. For a stronger society there must be effective finance. Similarly for effective finance, there must be strong, capable and competent manpower. Manpower is the biggest capital of every society.

References

Abbas, I., Batool, S., & Nawaz, M. A. (2020). Estimating Health Determinants of Two Generations: Evidence from Selected Districts of Pakistan. *Journal of Contemporary Macroeconomic Issues*, 1, 2708–4973. https://www.who.int/about/who-we-are/constitution

Al-Mohammad, H. (2012). A KIDNAPPING IN BASRA: The Struggles and Precariousness of Life in Postinvasion Iraq. *Cultural Anthropology*, 27(4), 597–614. DOI: 10.1111/j.1548-1360.2012.01163.x

Berlant, L., Butler, J., Cvejic, B., Lorey, I., Puar, J., & Vujanovic, A. (2013). Precarity Talk A Virtual. *The Round Table*.

Butler, J. (2009). *Frames of war : when is life grievable?* Verso.

Butler Judith. (2015). Notes Toward a Performative Theory of Assembly - Judith Butler - Google Books. Harvard University Press. https://books.google.com.pk/books?hl=en&lr=&id=tRxUCwAAQBAJ&oi=fnd&pg=PP1&dq=Butler%27s+theory+of+precarity&ots=PBvSj8bVuE&sig=WnQa0tHN_BTOgoaw98xcw2v_oJk&redir_esc=y#v=onepage&q&f=true

During, S. (2015). Choosing precarity. In South Asia: Journal of South Asia Studies (Vol. 38, Issue 1, pp. 19–38). Routledge. DOI: 10.1080/00856401.2014.975901

Ertorer, S. E. (2021). Asylum Regimes and Refugee Experiences of Precarity: The Case of Syrian Refugees in Turkey. *Journal of Refugee Studies*, 34(3), 2568–2592. DOI: 10.1093/jrs/feaa089

Katper, N. K., Tunio, M. N., Hussain, N., Junejo, A., & Gilal, F. G. (2020). COVID-19 crises: Global economic shocks vs Pakistan economic shocks. Advances in Science. *Technology and Engineering Systems*, 5(4), 645–654. DOI: 10.25046/aj050477

Li, Z., Farmanesh, P., Kirikkaleli, D., & Itani, R. (2022). A comparative analysis of COVID-19 and global financial crises: Evidence from US economy. *Ekonomska Istrazivanja*, 35(1), 2427–2441. DOI: 10.1080/1331677X.2021.1952640

Malik, S., Roosli, R., Tariq, F., & Yusof, N. (2020). Policy Framework and Institutional Arrangements: Case of Affordable Housing Delivery for Low-Income Groups in Punjab, Pakistan. *Housing Policy Debate*, 30(2), 243–268. DOI: 10.1080/10511482.2019.1681018

Penny, J. (n.d.). Insecure Spaces, Precarious Geographies: Biopolitics, Security and the Production of Space In Jerusalem and Beyond. www.ucl.ac.uk

Rinaldi, E. E. (2016). The Relationship between Financial Education and Society: A Sociological Perspective Author information. *Italian Journal of Sociology of Education*, 8(3), 126–148. DOI: 10.14658/pupj-ijse

Sareen, S. (2020). COVID-19 and Pakistan: The Economic Fallout.

Shibata, I. (2021). The distributional impact of recessions: The global financial crisis and the COVID-19 pandemic recession. *Journal of Economics and Business*, 115, 105971. Advance online publication. DOI: 10.1016/j.jeconbus.2020.105971

Standing, G. (2019). Meet the precariat, the new global class fuelling the rise of populism | World Economic Forum. Youth Perspectives. https://www.weforum.org/agenda/2016/11/precariat-global-class-rise-of-populism/

Vaia, G., Bisogno, M., & Tommasetti, A. (2017). Investigating the Relationship between the Social and Economic-financial Performance. *Applied Finance and Accounting*, 3(1), 55. DOI: 10.11114/afa.v3i1.2126

Vallejo-Martín, M., Canto, J. M., San Martín García, J. E., & Novas, F. P. (2020). Prejudice and feeling of threat towards Syrian refugees: The moderating effects of precarious employment and perceived low outgroup morality. *International Journal of Environmental Research and Public Health*, 17(17), 1–12. DOI: 10.3390/ijerph17176411

Wacquant, L. (1999). Urban Marginality in the Coming Millennium. In Source. *Urban Studies (Edinburgh, Scotland)*, 36(10), 1639–1647. DOI: 10.1080/0042098992746

Wall, M., Otis Campbell, M., & Janbek, D. (2017). Syrian refugees and information precarity. *New Media & Society*, 19(2), 240–254. DOI: 10.1177/1461444815591967

Chapter 13
Female Governance in COVID-19:
Complex Nexis of Psychology, Society, and Governance in Educational Sector of Pakistan

Asma Kanwal
University of Education, Lahore, Pakistan

Tahir Mehmood
Suncheon National University, South Korea

ABSTRACT

This chapter shines a light on the critical role of women's governance during COVID-19, the Complex nexus of psychology, society, and Governance. The COVID-19 pandemic has dramatically transformed the educational landscape worldwide, Presenting unprecedented challenges and pressure. This pandemic is, no doubt, a threat to humanity (Poon & Peiris, 2020). Female leaders in education sectors across various countries have been instrumental in shaping responses to the pandemic, often demonstrating a unique blend of empathy, resilience, and strategic foresight. This chapter delves into the complex nexus of psychology society and governance, exploring how women's governance has influenced the educational sectors during COVID-19, the societal perceptions and pressures faced by these leaders, and the psychological ramifications of their roles. The COVID-19 pandemic also brought unprecedented challenges to educational systems worldwide, exposing and exacerbating existing inequalities.

DOI: 10.4018/979-8-3693-5733-0.ch013

INTRODUCTION

Female governance refers to the involvement and leadership of women in the decision-making processes and management within organizations, institutions, or governmental bodies. It emphasizes the active participation of women in leadership roles, such as CEOs, board members, ministers, or heads of departments. Female governance aims to foster diversity, equity, and inclusion, recognizing that diverse perspectives can lead to more innovative and effective solutions. It often challenges traditional gender roles and strives to create environments where women can influence policies and practices. This concept is critical in promoting gender equality, enhancing organizational performance, and driving societal progress by ensuring that women's voices and experiences shape decision-making processes.

Female leadership has been critically examined during the COVID-19 pandemic, where governance was put to the test across sectors. From healthcare to education and the commercial sector, women leaders showed remarkable resilience and adaptability in crisis management. In the face of global uncertainty, leaders such as New Zealand's Prime Minister Jacinda Ardern and Germany's Chancellor Angela Merkel stood out for their compassionate leadership, balancing both public health and economic concerns. In contrast, female leaders in Pakistan, such as Dr. Yasmin Rashid and Dr. Shaista Sohail, tackled not only the healthcare challenges but also the technological divide that threatened to derail educational and commercial activities during prolonged lockdowns.

Expansion of Geographical Scope

This study explores female governance in two distinct geographical settings: the West (with a focus on countries like New Zealand, Germany, and Finland) and Pakistan. By contrasting the responses of female leaders in both educational and commercial sectors, the chapter illuminates how women's leadership differed based on cultural, infrastructural, and societal constraints. In the West, more developed economies and educational systems allowed female leaders to innovate and implement policies effectively. However, in Pakistan, where the commercial and educational sectors are often resource-constrained, female leaders face additional challenges.

During the COVID-19 pandemic, female leaders in the West demonstrated notable resilience, empathy, and effectiveness in managing the crisis. Leaders like New Zealand's Prime Minister Jacinda Ardern and Germany's Chancellor Angela Merkel garnered international praise for their proactive and transparent approaches. Ardern's swift implementation of strict lockdown measures and her empathetic communication style were credited with keeping New Zealand's infection rates low. Merkel's scientific background and clear communication helped maintain public trust and compliance with health measures in Germany. In Iceland, Prime Minister Katrín Jakobsdóttir implemented widespread testing and tracing, which significantly curtailed the virus's spread. Finland's Prime Minister Sanna Marin used social media to communicate directly with citizens, particularly the youth, ensuring widespread understanding and adherence to guidelines. These leaders not only prioritized public health but also balanced economic and social impacts, showing a blend of decisiveness and compassion. Their leadership styles highlighted the effectiveness of inclusive and empathetic governance during crises, contrasting with more authoritarian or less transparent approaches observed.

However, in Pakistan, female governance during COVID-19 was exemplified by leaders like Dr. Yasmin Rashid, the Minister of Health for Punjab. Dr Rashid, a trained gynaecologist and a seasoned politician, played a pivotal role in the province's response to the pandemic. She spearheaded efforts to increase testing capacity, establish quarantine centres, and ensure the availability of medical supplies and equipment. Her medical background and commitment to public health were instrumental in managing the crisis in one of Pakistan's most populous regions. Additionally, Senator Sherry Rehman, an advocate for social justice and public health, actively used her platform to raise awareness about the pandemic's impact on vulnerable populations, particularly women and children. She called for more robust health policies and support systems to protect these groups during the crisis. The contributions of these female leaders in Pakistan underscored the importance of having diverse perspectives in governance, particularly in navigating complex public health challenges like the COVID-19 pandemic.

Commercial Sector Context

It refers to the involvement and leadership of women in administrative, managerial, and decision-making roles within educational institutions. This includes positions such as school principals, university deans, department heads, board members, and other leadership roles that influence policy, curriculum, and the overall direction of educational organizations(Ghosh et al., 2020). During the COVID-19 pandemic, female leaders in Western educational sectors played crucial roles in navigating unprecedented challenges. For example, Dr. Jill Biden, the First Lady of the United States and a long-time educator, advocated for the safe reopening of schools and emphasized the importance of addressing educational inequities exacerbated by the pandemic. In the United Kingdom, Amanda Spielman, Ofsted's Chief Inspector, oversaw efforts to assess and mitigate the impact of school closures on children's education and well-being. Female university presidents, such as Dr. Carol Folt of the University of Southern California, implemented strategies to transition to online learning, support students' mental health, and ensure continuity in education despite the disruptions.

These leaders often had to balance public health concerns with educational priorities, making difficult decisions about remote learning, hybrid models, and eventual returns to in-person instruction. They also spearheaded initiatives to support disadvantaged students who were disproportionately affected by the pandemic, such as providing access to technology, internet connectivity, and meal programs. Their leadership highlighted the importance of empathy, resilience, and adaptability in crisis management.

In many cases, female leaders also prioritized staff well-being, recognizing the added pressures on teachers and administrators. By fostering open communication, offering professional development opportunities, and creating support networks, they helped maintain morale and motivation during challenging times. Overall, the contributions of female leaders in Western educational sectors during COVID-19 underscored the vital role of diverse perspectives in effective governance and crisis response. However, in Pakistan, female governance in educational sectors has seen significant progress, with women occupying key leadership roles and driving transformative changes (Sauer, 2022). One notable example is Dr. Nadia Aziz, the Director of the Directorate of Higher Education, Khyber Pakhtunkhwa, who has been instrumental in advancing girls' education and improving institutional frameworks to support female students and staff.

During the COVID-19 pandemic, Dr. Shaista Sohail, the Executive Director of the Higher Education Commission (HEC) of Pakistan, played a pivotal role in managing the transition to online learning across universities (Croft, 2000). Her leadership was crucial in implementing policies that ensured the continuity of education while addressing the digital divide that many students faced. She initiated programs to provide laptops and internet facilities to students from underprivileged backgrounds, ensuring they could continue their studies remotely. Furthermore, the efforts of female educators like Malala Yousafzai have had a profound impact on promoting female education and advocating for gender equality in Pakistan. Although not directly involved in governance, her activism has inspired policies and initiatives that prioritize girls' education and create more opportunities for women to assume leadership roles in the educational sector. These examples reflect the growing influence of female governance in Pakistan's educational landscape, contributing to more inclusive and equitable educational opportunities for all.

There are two kinds of sectors. Public sector and private sectors. Here, we will examine Female governance in public educational sectors during Covid 19, and the challenges that female governance faced during Covid 19 in public sectors. During the COVID-19 pandemic, female leaders in public educational sectors around the world played pivotal roles in addressing the numerous challenges brought about by the crisis (Erbele-Küster & Küster, 2022). These leaders not only managed the transition to remote learning but also focused on ensuring equity and access to education for all students.

In the United States, Dr. Carmen Fariña, former Chancellor of the New York City Department of Education, exemplified strong leadership in one of the largest public school systems. Her initiatives focused on bridging the digital divide by distributing devices and providing internet access to students in need. She also emphasized the importance of mental health support for students and staff, recognizing the heightened stress and anxiety caused by the pandemic. In Finland, Li Andersson, the Minister of Education, played a crucial role in coordinating the national response to school closures. Her leadership ensured that public schools could adapt quickly to remote learning while maintaining educational standards. Finland's existing strong emphasis on teacher autonomy and professional development helped facilitate a smoother transition to online education under her guidance. Andersson also prioritized the well-being of students and teachers, implementing policies that provided psychological support and resources to cope with the new learning environment. In India, Anita Karwal, Secretary of the Department of School Education and Literacy, was instrumental in implementing strategies to minimize learning disruptions. She led efforts to broadcast educational content on television and radio to reach students in rural and remote areas who lacked internet access. This approach ensured that education continued for millions of students despite school closures. Karwal's initiatives also included distributing worksheets and learning materials to students' homes and training teachers to adapt to new modes of instruction. In Pakistan, female leaders in the public educational sector played vital roles during the COVID-19 pandemic, addressing significant challenges to ensure the continuity of education and support for students and staff. Their leadership was crucial in navigating the complex landscape of remote learning, digital access, and educational equity.

Dr. Shaista Sohail, the Executive Director of the Higher Education Commission (HEC) of Pakistan, was instrumental in orchestrating the national response to the pandemic's impact on higher education. She led efforts to transition universities to online learning platforms, ensuring that academic activities could continue despite widespread lockdowns. Under her leadership, the HEC launched several initiatives to bridge the digital divide, including distributing laptops and providing internet connectivity to students in remote and underserved areas. Dr. Sohail also focused on faculty development, offering training programs to help teachers effectively deliver online instruction.

Another notable figure is Dr. Fauzia Khan, the Secretary of the Department of School Education in Sindh. She spearheaded efforts to implement remote learning solutions for primary and secondary students. Recognizing the limitations of digital access in many parts of the province, Dr. Khan promoted alternative learning methods, such as televised lessons and radio broadcasts, to reach students without internet access. Her initiatives included distributing printed learning materials and establishing community learning centres to support students' educational needs during school closures. In Punjab, Dr. Murad Raas, Minister for School Education, worked alongside female leaders and policymakers to develop strategies that ensured educational continuity. Initiatives such as the Taleem Ghar program, which provided educational content through cable TV and online platforms, were critical in reaching a broad student population. Dr Raas emphasized the importance of mental health support, introducing helplines and counselling services for students and teachers grappling with the pandemic's psychological toll.

These female leaders' efforts in the worldwide public education sector during COVID-19 exemplify the critical role of inclusive and empathetic governance. Their actions not only facilitated the continuation of education during an unprecedented crisis but also highlighted the importance of addressing educational inequities opportunities regardless of their circumstances. Their leadership set a foundation for more resilient and adaptable educational systems in the future. These female leaders in public educational sectors demonstrated resilience, innovation, and empathy during the COVID-19 pandemic. Their efforts were crucial in addressing the immediate challenges of remote learning, supporting vulnerable students, and ensuring that public education systems remained resilient in the face of unprecedented disruptions. Through their leadership, they highlighted the importance of inclusive and equitable education, setting a precedent for future crisis management in public education.

Where female governance is a sign of bravery, there she also faced some challenges from society and others. During the COVID-19 pandemic posed a significant challenge to many sectors, including education. For female leaders not only in Pakistan's education sector but also worldwide the stress of job insecurity was compounded by societal expectations and governance responsibilities.

FEMALE LEADERS AND GOVERNANCE

Governance in the West.

The governance models employed by female leaders in the West have been celebrated for their empathy, transparency, and strategic foresight. For example, Jacinda Ardern's swift lockdown measures in New Zealand not only kept the infection rates low but also ensured a balance between public health and economic impacts. Angela Merkel's leadership in Germany, with her background in science, was instrumental in garnering public trust during the pandemic. These leaders demonstrated how female governance can lead to decisive action without compromising on empathy, which is often viewed as a feminine leadership quality.

Governance in Pakistan.

In Pakistan, female leaders like Dr. Yasmin Rashid, Minister of Health for Punjab, were at the forefront of the fight against COVID-19. Beyond healthcare, female leaders in commercial sectors faced the dual burden of managing businesses in a faltering economy while addressing the societal challenges of being women in leadership. This section will further explore how female entrepreneurs and business leaders balanced commercial imperatives with societal expectations during the pandemic.

It refers to the uncertainty surrounding one's employment status, which can significantly impact mental health. Female leaders in public education sectors faced heightened job insecurity during the pandemic due to budget cuts, institutional downsizing, and shifts in educational priorities. This uncertainty led to increased stress and anxiety, affecting their overall well-being and job performance. In many countries, budget cuts in education led to job losses or reduced working hours. For example, in the United States, a significant number of teachers and support staff, many of whom are women, were furloughed or laid off due to decreased funding and lower student enrollment. According to the United Nations Fund for Population Activities (UNFPA) pointed out that disease outbreaks affect women and men differently, and pandemics make existing inequalities for women and girls worse. The effects of COVID-19 on women have been discussed in terms of job losses, intensified care responsibilities, susceptibility to the virus due to concentration in certain occupations, and the potential for domestic violence (VM Moghadam,2021). Similarly, in the UK, temporary contracts and part-time positions, often held by women, were among the first to be cut. In developing nations, the situation was even more precarious. In Pakistan, many female educators in private schools faced salary cuts or job losses as these institutions struggled to stay afloat without tuition fees. Rural areas saw women in informal teaching roles losing their only source of income due to school closures and the lack of digital infrastructure to support remote learning. Furthermore, the increased burden of unpaid care work at home, coupled with the stress of adapting to online teaching, led to heightened job insecurity for women in education. The pandemic highlighted the vulnerability of women in the educational workforce and underscored the need for targeted support and policies to ensure their job security and well-being in future crises. The abrupt shift to online learning exposed and exacerbated the digital divide, particularly in regions with limited technological infrastructure. Female leaders in governance had to address the stark inequalities in access to digital devices and internet connectivity.

In Western countries, while internet penetration and device availability were generally higher, disparities still existed, particularly among low-income families and marginalized communities. Leaders such as Dr. Carmen Fariña in New York City worked to provide devices and internet access, but the initial lag in addressing these needs led to learning losses and increased educational disparities. Feldman (n.d.) while addressing student assessment during this pandemic on how districts can legislate unbiased and evenhanded grading policies based on these recommendations; (i) pandemic-related anxiety will have negative effects on student academic performance, (ii) academic performance of students might be affected by racial, economic and resource differences, and (iii) the larger parts of instructors were not effectively ready to deliver high-quality instruction remotely. The challenges discussed here are limited to the digital transformation of instructional operations during the period of the COVID-19 pandemic. So the sudden shift to an online system was not a problem for Female governance as well as Students. Even in Pakistan, many students in rural and underserved areas lack access to the necessary tools for online education. Dr Shaista Sohail, Executive Director of the Higher Education Commission (HEC) of Pakistan, spearheaded initiatives to provide laptops and internet facilities to students from disadvantaged backgrounds. Despite these efforts, the sheer scale of the problem made it challenging to ensure equitable access for all students. Female leaders had to explore and implement alternative methods, such as televised lessons and radio broadcasts, to reach those without internet access. This multifaceted approach required innovative thinking and extensive coordination with various stakeholders, including government agencies, technology providers, and educational institutions.

The pandemic highlighted in many cases, worsened existing gender inequities. Female leaders had to ensure that the education system continued to support female students, who are often at a higher risk of dropping out during crises. In Western countries, gender inequities were also evident but manifested differently. Gender influences on mental health effects of the COVID-19 pandemic Studies from China, where COVID-19 first surfaced, have found that female gender is significantly associated with higher self-reported levels of stress, anxiety, depression, and post-traumatic stress symptoms, and more severe overall psychological impact (Wang et al. 2020a, b; Liu et al. 2020a, b). Women have a higher prevalence of risk factors known to intensify during a pandemic, including chronic environmental strain (Street and Dardis 2018), preexisting depressive and anxiety disorders (Hao et al. 2020), and domestic violence (Campbell 2020). Female students faced increased domestic responsibilities, violence and mental health challenges, impacting their academic performance. Female leaders worked to provide support and resources to students, but the pandemic's strain on mental health services and increased family responsibilities disproportionately also affected female leaders. In many parts of the world, including Pakistan, girls' education is vulnerable to disruption due to socio-economic factors. Female leaders in governance had to implement targeted interventions to keep girls engaged in their education. This involved not only providing technological support but also addressing cultural and societal barriers that might prevent girls from participating in online learning. Additionally, female leaders themselves often faced increased domestic responsibilities during the pandemic, balancing professional duties with household and caregiving tasks. This dual burden required extraordinary resilience and time management skills.

The transition to remote learning required substantial resources, including technological tools, training programs, and support services. Female leaders often had to operate within tight budgets and face significant resource constraints. In Western countries, while resource constraints were less severe, the sudden demand for digital tools, training, and support services stretched existing budgets. Leaders had to navigate these constraints while ensuring that educational standards were maintained. In Pakistan and other countries with similar economic challenges, securing the necessary funds and resources for a smooth transition to online education was a daunting task. Leaders like Dr. Murad Raas, Minister for School Education in Punjab, had to advocate for additional funding and support from government bodies and international organizations. They had to make strategic decisions on how to allocate limited resources effectively. This often involved prioritizing the most critical needs, such as providing devices to the most disadvantaged students or investing in teacher training programs. The constant balancing act of resource allocation required strong negotiation skills and strategic planning.

FEMALE LEADERS AND PSYCHOLOGY

The pandemic took a significant toll on the mental health and well-being of students, teachers, and administrative staff. Female leaders in public education sectors recognized the importance of addressing these psychological impacts and implemented various support systems. Western countries faced significant mental health challenges, with students and educators experiencing heightened anxiety and stress. Leaders like Amanda Spielman in the UK emphasized the importance of mental health support, introducing counselling services and helplines. However, the unprecedented demand for these services highlighted existing gaps in mental health infrastructure. In Pakistan, Dr Fauzia Khan, Secretary of the Department of School Education in Sindh, Pakistan, and her counterparts globally had to establish mental health support frameworks, such as counselling services and helplines. These services aimed to provide emotional support to students struggling with isolation, anxiety, and the uncertainty of the pandemic. For educators, the shift to remote teaching brought about significant stress and burnout. Female leaders had to ensure that teachers received adequate training and resources to manage online classes effectively while also taking care of their mental health. Balancing the well-being of all members of the educational community became a central aspect of governance during the pandemic.

The governance challenges faced by female leaders were manifold. The sudden shift to online learning and the rapid changes and uncertainties brought about by the pandemic necessitated constant adaptation and decision-making. Female leaders had to implement new policies swiftly, often without the benefit of comprehensive data or clear guidelines. This constant need to make high-stakes decisions contributed to cognitive overload and emotional exhaustion. The psychological effects on female leaders were not confined to their professional lives. The stress of managing educational disruptions, combined with societal expectations, often translated into personal challenges. Many female leaders reported experiencing anxiety, depression, and trauma. According to Cathy Caruth's definition of trauma, it is "too soon, too unexpectedly, to be fully unknown events" at the time of the event (Caruth,1996) although it returns later. Caruth's definition of trauma and loss qualifies the analysis of problems and wounds that women's governance during Covid 19 in education sectors which were exacerbated by the isolation lack of support and societal pressure.

The effects of these challenges were both conscious and unconscious. Consciously, female leaders were aware of their increased stress and the pressure to perform under difficult circumstances. They often struggled with balancing professional responsibilities with personal well-being, which led them to a heightened sense of vulnerability. Unconsciously, the persistent stress and societal pressures lead them to long-term psychological impacts such as anxiety depression and trauma. Unknown trauma arises from the unconscious (Ahmad,2023)Which according to the Substance Abuse And Mental Health Services Administration, Affects the individual's physical, social, emotional or spiritual well-being,(2004).

Continuous exposure to high-stress environments without adequate support contributed to chronic stress disorders and the cumulative impact of these pressures also affected their leadership effectiveness and overall well-being. Cathy Caruth, in her book Unclaimed Experience, introduced the term "trauma theory." She echoes Sigmund Freud in pointing out that trauma should not be understood as bodily injury but as an injury to the consciousness that, for Jon Allen (3), is a wound and creates "a feeling of utter helplessness (4)." The injury is a result of an emotional shock/traumatic event (war, rape, and social discrimination), which affects the mind more than the body and is "accompanied by fear, helplessness, or horror," and the "experience of a trauma repeats itself"(Caruth,1996)which reappears in dreams and memories. Hence, the trauma of the mind is imprinted in the subconscious as a reality or truth and is unavailable to the consciousness at any given moment, which Cathy Caruth called "the unknown."

Despite these significant challenges, women's in public education sectors demonstrated remarkable resilience. They adapted to the rapidly changing education landscape with creativity and determination, implementing innovative strategies to address the needs of students and educators. Their ability to persevere in the face of adversity highlighted their leadership skills and commitment to education. During the pandemic, women in the educational sector also faced unique challenges due to the intersection of societal pressures and the global health crisis. The shift to online learning, economic instability, and heightened domestic responsibilities tested their resilience and even led them to trauma. But, "Once Unknown trauma is spoken and comes to consciousness, it becomes less traumatic. (Ahmad,2023). However, Women's used these kind of psychological strategies to address these issues effectively.

Firstly, psychological resilience became a critical tool. Women employed cognitive restructuring to manage stress and anxiety. By reframing negative thoughts and focusing on achievable goals, they could maintain a positive outlook despite the chaos. This mental shift not only helped them cope but also inspired adaptive strategies for teaching and learning.

Secondly, social support networks played a vital role. Women leveraged connections with colleagues, family, and friends for emotional support and practical assistance. These networks provided a platform for sharing experiences, resources, and coping strategies, which was crucial in navigating the new challenges of remote work and learning. Additionally, mindfulness and self-care practices were embraced to combat burnout. Many women integrated routines such as meditation, exercise, and proper rest into their daily lives. These practices not only improved their mental well-being but also enhanced their capacity to manage stress and maintain productivity. Despite these pressures and limited resources, Pakistani women in education demonstrated remarkable adaptability. By harnessing psychological tools such as resilience, social support, and self-care, they managed to address the multifaceted impacts of COVID-19. Their experience underscores the importance of psychological strategies in overcoming adversity and highlights the critical role of mental health in navigating crises.

CONCLUSION AND IMPLICATIONS

Female leadership during the COVID-19 pandemic proved critical in navigating the global crisis. Whether in the educational or commercial sector, women leaders brought empathy, resilience, and innovation to the forefront, often surpassing societal expectations. Their leadership in both the West and Pakistan demonstrated the importance of diverse perspectives in governance.

The challenges faced by female leaders during COVID-19 highlight the need for policy reforms that ensure gender equality in leadership roles, particularly in commercial sectors. Future governance models should address not only the psychological impact on women leaders but also promote mental health support systems and reduce gendered societal expectations. These implications will be critical in shaping more resilient governance structures in future crises.

References

Ahmad, M. S., Bukhari, Z., Khan, S., Ashraf, I., & Kanwal, A. (2023). No safe place for war survivors: War memory event exposure and migrants' psychological trauma. *Frontiers in Psychiatry*, 13, 966556. DOI: 10.3389/fpsyt.2022.966556

Campbell, A. M. (2020). An increasing risk of family violence during the COVID-19 pandemic: Strengthening community collaborations to save lives. *Forensic Science International. Reports*, 2, 100089. DOI: 10.1016/j.fsir.2020.100089

Caruth, C. (1996). *Unclaimed Experience Trauma, Narrative, and History*. The Johns Hopkins Press Ltd. DOI: 10.1353/book.20656

Croft, W. (2000). *Explaining language change: An evolutionary approach*. Pearson Education.

Erbele-Küster, D., & Küster, V. (2022). *Between Pandemonium and Pandemethics: Responses to Covid-19 from Theology and Religions* (Vol. 27). Evangelische Verlagsanstalt.

Feldman, J. (n.d.). To Grade or Not to Grade? https://filecabinetdublin.eschoolview.com/6D88CF03-93EE-4E59B267B73AA2456ED7/ToGradeorNottoGradearticle.pdf

Ghosh, B., Patgiri, R., & Aparajita, D. (2020). *Digital ethnography during the COVID 10 pandemic*.

Hwangbo, K. (2004). *Trauma, narrative, and the marginal self in selected contemporary American novels*. University of Florida.

Moghadam, V. M. (2021). COVID-19 and MENA: Governance, Geopolitics, and Gender. *Gendered Perspectives on International Development*, 1(1), 45–69. DOI: 10.1353/gpi.2021.0002

Poon, L. L., & Peiris, M. (2020). Emergence of a novel human coronavirus threatening human health. *Nature Medicine*, 26(3), 317–319. DOI: 10.1038/s41591-020-0796-5

Sauer, B. (2022). *Identities Global Studies in Culture and Power ISSN: (Print) (Online) Journal homepage:*https://www.tandfonline.com/loi/gide20*Radical right populist debates on female Muslim body-coverings in Austria. Between biopolitics and necropolitics Radical right populist debates on female Muslim body-coverings in Austria. Between biopolitics and necropolitics*. DOI: 10.1080/1070289X.2022.2071515

Wang, C., Pan, R., Wan, X., Tan, Y., Xu, L., Ho, C. S., & Ho, R. C. (2020a). Immediate psychological responses and associated factors during the initial stage of the 2019 coronavirus disease (COVID-19) epidemic among the general population in China. *International Journal of Environmental Research and Public Health*, 17(5), 1729. DOI: 10.3390/ijerph17051729

Compilation of References

A, A., & N, H. (2005). The reporting of risk in real estate appraisal property risk scoring. *Journal of property investment and finance, 23*(3), 254-68.

Aasad, A. (2010).The role of brand equity in the effects of corporate social responsibility on consumer loyalty. Unpublished master's diss., Universiti Sains Malaysia, Malaysia.

Abbas, I., Batool, S., & Nawaz, M. A. (2020). Estimating Health Determinants of Two Generations: Evidence from Selected Districts of Pakistan. *Journal of Contemporary Macroeconomic Issues*, 1, 2708–4973. https://www.who.int/about/who-we-are/constitution

Abbassi, W., Hunjra, A. I., Alawi, S. M., & Mehmood, R. (2021). The role of ownership structure and board characteristics in stock market liquidity. *International Journal of Financial Studies*, 9(4), 74. DOI: 10.3390/ijfs9040074

Abor, J. (2005). The effect of capital structure on profitability: An empirical analysis of listed firms in Ghana. *The Journal of Risk Finance*, 6(5), 438–445. DOI: 10.1108/15265940510633505

Abu Rumman, A., & Al-Abbadi, L. (2023). Structural equation modeling for impact of Data Fabric Framework on business decision-making and risk management. *Cogent Business and Management*, 10(2), 2215060. Advance online publication. DOI: 10.1080/23311975.2023.2215060

Acharya, V. V., & Agrawal, A. (2013). "Is Out-of-Court Restructuring Really Efficient? An Empirical Examination." *Journal of Financial Economics* 110 (2): 205-230. [Aghion, P., Hart, O., & Moore, J. (1992). The economics of bankruptcy reform. *Journal of Law Economics and Organization*, 8(3), 523–546.

Adam, T., Dasgupta, S., & Titman, S. (2007). Financial constraints, competition, and hedging inIndustry equilibrium. *The Journal of Finance*, 62(5), 2445–2473. DOI: 10.1111/j.1540-6261.2007.01280.x

Adhair, N., & Hutchison, N. (2005). The reporting of risk in real estate appraisal property risk scoring. *Journal of Property Investment & Finance*, 23(3), 254–268. DOI: 10.1108/14635780510599467

Afifah, N., & Asnan, A. (2015). The impact of corporate social responsibility, service experience and intercultural competence on customer company identification, customer satisfaction and customer loyalty (case study: PDAM Tirta Khatulistiwa Pontianak West Kalimantan). *Procedia: Social and Behavioral Sciences*, 211, 277–284. DOI: 10.1016/j.sbspro.2015.11.035

Agarwal, R., & Helfat, C. (2009). Strategic renewal of organizations. *Organization Science*, 20(2), 281–293. DOI: 10.1287/orsc.1090.0423

Agrawal, A., González-Uribe, J. A., & Martínez-Correa, J. (2020). Measuring the Ex-Ante Incentive Effects of Bankruptcy Reorganization Procedures. *The Journal of Finance*, 75(1), 233–271.

Agrawal, N., & Nahmias, S. (1997). Rationalization of the supplier base in the presence of Yield Uncertainty. *Production and Operations Management*, 6(3), 291–308. DOI: 10.1111/j.1937-5956.1997.tb00432.x

Agyei, S. K., & Marfo-Yiadom, E. (2011). Dividend policy and bank performance in Ghana. *International Journal of Economics and Finance*, 3(4), 202–207. DOI: 10.5539/ijef.v3n4p202

Ahmad, A., & Safwan, N. (2011). How demographic characteristics affect the perception of investors about financial risk tolerance. *Interdisciplinary Journal of Contemporary Research in Business*, 3(2), 412–417.

Ahmad, I., & Qayyum, A. (2008). Effect of Goverment spending and macro economic uncertainty on private investment on services sector:evidence from Pakistan. *European Journal of Economics*, 11, 84–96.

Ahmad, M. S., Bukhari, Z., Khan, S., Ashraf, I., & Kanwal, A. (2023). No safe place for war survivors: War memory event exposure and migrants' psychological trauma. *Frontiers in Psychiatry*, 13, 966556. DOI: 10.3389/fpsyt.2022.966556

Aiello, F., Cardamone, P., Mannarino, L., & Pupo, V. (2024). Networks, ownership and productivity does firm age play a moderating role? *Journal of Economic Studies (Glasgow, Scotland)*, 51(9), 212–231. DOI: 10.1108/JES-10-2023-0547

Akerlof, G. A. (1978). The market for "lemons": Quality uncertainty and the market mechanism. In *Uncertainty in economics* (pp. 235–251). Academic Press. DOI: 10.1016/B978-0-12-214850-7.50022-X

Akhtar, S., Hussain, H., & Hussain, R. Y. (2021). Contributing role of regulatory compliance and Islamic operations in bank risk: Evidence from Pakistan. *Nankai Business Review International*, 12(4), 618–635. DOI: 10.1108/NBRI-07-2020-0037

Albert, S. (1985). Research in organizational behavior. *Organizational identity, 7*, 263–295.

Albuquerque, R., Koskinen, Y., & Zhang, C. (2019). Corporate social responsibility and firm risk: Theory and empirical evidence. *Management Science*, 65(10), 4451–4469. DOI: 10.1287/mnsc.2018.3043

Al-Hawari, M., & Ward, T., (2006). The effect of automated service quality on Australian bank's financial performance and the mediating role of customer satisfaction, marketing intelligence and planning, 24(2), 127-147.

Al-Hawari, M., & Ward, T. (2006). The effect of automated service quality on Australian banks' financial performance and the mediating role of customer satisfaction. *Marketing Intelligence & Planning*, 24(2), 127–147. DOI: 10.1108/02634500610653991

Ali, A., Jan, F. A., & Atta, M. (2015). The impact of dividend policy on firm performance under high or low leverage; evidence from Pakistan. *Journal of Management*, 2(4), 16–25.

Ali, N., Rehman, M. Z. U., Ashraf, B. N., & Shear, F. (2022). Corporate dividend policies during the COVID-19 pandemic. *Economies*, 10(11), 263. DOI: 10.3390/economies10110263

Almaida, H., & Campello, M. (2007). Financial constraints, asset tangibility, and corporate investment. *Review of Financial Studies*, 20(2), 1429–1460. DOI: 10.1093/rfs/hhm019

Almeida, H., Campello, M., Cunha, I., & Weisbach, M. S. (2014). Corporate liquidity management: A conceptual framework and Survey. *Annual Review of Financial Economics*, 6(1), 132–145. DOI: 10.1146/annurev-financial-110613-034502

Al-Mohammad, H. (2012). A KIDNAPPING IN BASRA: The Struggles and Precariousness of Life in Postinvasion Iraq. *Cultural Anthropology*, 27(4), 597–614. DOI: 10.1111/j.1548-1360.2012.01163.x

Altman, E. I. (1983). A Further Empirical Investigation of the Bankruptcy Cost Question. *The Journal of Finance*, 38(2), 203–218.

Altman, E. I. (1983). Measuring the ex-ante incentive effects of bankruptcy reorganization procedures. *The Journal of Finance*, 39(4), 1067–1089. DOI: 10.1111/j.1540-6261.1984.tb03893.x

Altman, E. I., & Hotchkiss, E. (2006). *Corporate financial distress and bankruptcy* (3rd ed.). John Wiley & Sons.

Amidu, M. (2007). How does dividend policy affect performance of the firm on Ghana stock Exchange. Investment management and financial innovations, 4(2), 103-112.

Amran, A., Manaf Rosli Bin, A., & Che Haat Mohd Hassan, B. (2008). Risk reporting: An exploratory study on risk management disclosure in Malaysian annual reports. *Managerial Auditing Journal*, 24(1), 39–57. DOI: 10.1108/02686900910919893

Andayani, W., & Wuryantoro, M. (2023). Good Corporate Governance, Corporate Social Responsibility and Fraud Detection of Financial Statements. *International Journal of Professional Business Review: Int.J. Prof. Bus. Rev.*, 8(5), 9.

Anderson, Eugene W., Fornell, C., and Mazvancheryl S., K. (2004). Customer Satisfaction and Shareholder Value, *Journal of Marketing*, 68, 172-85.

Anderson, R. L., DAHLQUIST, S. H., & GARVER, M. S. (2018). MILLENNIALS'PURCHASING RESPONSE TO CSR BEHAVIOR. *Marketing Management Journal, 28*(1).

Anderson, E. W. (1998). Customer satisfaction and word of mouth. *Journal of Service Research*, 1(1), 5–17. DOI: 10.1177/109467059800100102

Anderson, E. W., Fornell, C., & Rust, R. T. (1997). Customer satisfaction, productivity, and profitability: Differences between goods and services. *Marketing Science*, 16(2), 129–145. DOI: 10.1287/mksc.16.2.129

Anderson, E. W., & Sullivan, M. W. (1993). The antecedents and consequences of customer satisfaction for firms. *Marketing Science*, 12(2), 125–143. DOI: 10.1287/mksc.12.2.125

Andrade, R. (2011). A construção do conceito de incerteza: Uma comparação das contribuições de Knight, Keynes, Shackle e Davidson. *Nova Economia*, 21(2), 171–195. DOI: 10.1590/S0103-63512011000200001

Annabi, A., Breton, M., & François, P. (2012). Resolution of financial distress under chapter 11. *Journal of Economic Dynamics & Control*, 36(12), 1867–1887. DOI: 10.1016/j.jedc.2012.06.004

Anserson, E. W., & Mittal, V. (2000). Strengthening the satisfaction-profit chain. *Journal of Service Research*, 3(2), 107–120. DOI: 10.1177/109467050032001

Apple. (2020). Apple's Environmental Progress Report. Retrieved from https://www.apple.com/environment/pdf/Apple_Environmental_Progress_Report_2020.pdf

Arıkan, E., & Güner, S. (2013). The impact of corporate social responsibility, service quality and customer-company identification on customers. *Procedia: Social and Behavioral Sciences*, 99, 304–313. DOI: 10.1016/j.sbspro.2013.10.498

Arlow, P., & Gannon, M. (1982). Social responsiveness, corporate structure, and economic performance. *Academy of Management Review*, 7(2), 235–241. DOI: 10.2307/257302

Arrow. (1971). *Essays on Theory of Risk-Bearing Chicago,* . Illusions: Markham Publishing Company.

Aslan, H., & Öztekin, Ö. (2019). The Effect of Out-of-Court Restructuring on Post-Restructuring Financial Performance: Evidence from Emerging Markets. *Emerging Markets Review*, 38, 100618.

Aupperle, K., Carroll, A., & Hatfield, J. (1985). An empirical examination of the relationship between corporate social responsibility and profitability. *Academy of Management Journal*, 28(2), 446–463. DOI: 10.2307/256210

Aydin, S., & Özer, G. (2005). The analysis of antecedents of consumer loyalty in the Turkish mobile telecommunication market. *European Journal of Marketing*, 39(7/8), 910–925. DOI: 10.1108/03090560510601833

Baker, M. (2017). NotPetya cyber-attack cost TNT at least $300m. Retrieved from https://www.bbc.com/news/technology-40870928

Baker, M., Bergstresser, D., Serafeim, G., & Wurgler, J. (2018). Financing the Response to Climate Change: The Pricing and Ownership of U.S. Green Bonds. NBER Working Paper No. 25194.

Banker, R. D., Potter, G., & Srinivasan, D. (2000). An empirical investigation of an incentive plan that includes non-financial performance measures. *The Accounting Review*, 75(1), 65–92. DOI: 10.2308/accr.2000.75.1.65

Barnett, E. A., & Clark, R. C. (1996). The Determinants of Successful Turnarounds During Bankruptcies and Out-of-Court Workouts. *Journal of Economic Behavior & Organization*, 29(3), 459–489.

Baron, R. M., & Kenny, D. A. (1986). The moderator-mediator variable distinction in social psychological research: Conceptual, strategic, and statistical considerations. *Journal of Personality and Social Psychology*, 51(6), 1173–1179. DOI: 10.1037/0022-3514.51.6.1173

Barry, T., Lepetit, L., & Tarazi, A. (2011). Ownership structure and risk in publicly held a privately owned banks. *Journal of Banking & Finance*, 35(5), 1327–1340. DOI: 10.1016/j.jbankfin.2010.10.004

Baum, C., Canglayan, N., Ozkan, N., & Talavera, O. (2006, January). The impact of macroeconomic uncertaintyonnon-financial firms 'demandforliquidity. *Review of Financial Economics*, 15(4), 289–304. DOI: 10.1016/j.rfe.2006.01.002

Bebchuk, L. A., & Fried, J. (2004). Executive Compensation and the Choice Between Bankruptcy and Out-of-Court Debt Restructuring. *The Journal of Finance*, 59(5), 2049–2082.

Becchetti, L., Ciciretti, R., & Hasan, I. (2015). Corporate social responsibility, stakeholder risk, and idiosyncratic volatility. *Journal of Corporate Finance*, 35, 297–309. DOI: 10.1016/j.jcorpfin.2015.09.007

Becker-Olsen, K. L., Cudmore, B. A., & Hill, R. P. (2006). The impact of perceived corporate social responsibility on consumer behavior. *Journal of Business Research*, 59(1), 46–53. DOI: 10.1016/j.jbusres.2005.01.001

Bedenk, S., & Mieg, A. (2018). Failure in innovation decission making. *Strategies in failure mangement: Scintific insight, case stuudies and tools*, 95-106.

Ben Fatma, H., & Chouaibi, J. (2024). The mediating role of corporate social responsibility in good corporate governance and firm value relationship: Evidence from European financial institutions. *Meditari Accountancy Research*, 32(4), 1084–1105. DOI: 10.1108/MEDAR-08-2022-1762

Ben-Ari, D., Frish, Y., Lazovski, A., & Eldan, U.. (2017). "Artificial Intelligence in the Practice of Law: An Analysis and Proof of Concept Experiment" 23 (2). *Rich. J. L. & Tech*, 3, 53.

Bennett, M., & James, P. (2017). *The Green Bottom Line: Environmental Accounting for Management*. Routledge. DOI: 10.4324/9781351283328

Bergman, B., & Klefsjoe, B., (2003).Quality: From customer needs to customer satisfaction (2nded.). Lund: Student literature

Bergman, B., & Klefsjoe, B. (2003). *Quality:Fromcustomerneedstocustomersatisfaction(2nded.)*. Studentlitteratur.

Berkovitch, E., & Israel, R. (1999). Optimal bankruptcy laws across different economic systems. *Review of Financial Studies*, 12(2), 347–377. DOI: 10.1093/rfs/12.2.347

Berlant, L., Butler, J., Cvejic, B., Lorey, I., Puar, J., & Vujanovic, A. (2013). Precarity Talk A Virtual. *The Round Table*.

Bernanke, B. (2004). Speech at the Bond Market Association Annual Meeting. *the Economic Outlook and Monetary Policy*.

Bernstein, S., Colonnelli, E., Giroud, X., & Iverson, B. (2019). Bankruptcy spillovers. *Journal of Financial Economics*, 133(3), 608–633. DOI: 10.1016/j.jfineco.2018.09.010

Betker, B. L. (1997). The administrative cost of debt restructurings: Some recent evidence. *Financial Management*, 26(4), 56–68. DOI: 10.2307/3666127

Bharath, S. T., & Denis, D. I. (2010). Do Secured Debtholders Dictate the Choice of Bankruptcy Procedures? An Empirical Investigation. *Journal of Financial Economics*, 95(1), 103–120.

Bharath, S. T., & Hertzel, M. G. (2005). The Choice Between Out-of-Court Debt Restructurings and Chapter 11 Bankruptcy: A Test of Competing Theories. *The Journal of Finance*, 60(2), 639–668.

Bilawal Khaskheli, M., Wang, S., Hussain, R. Y., Jahanzeb Butt, M., Yan, X., & Majid, S. (2023). Global law, policy, and governance for effective prevention and control of COVID-19: A comparative analysis of the law and policy of Pakistan, China, and Russia. *Frontiers in Public Health*, 10, 1035536. DOI: 10.3389/fpubh.2022.1035536

Birch, D. G., & McEvoy, M. (1992). 'Risk analysis for information systems. *Journal of Information Technology*, 7(1), 44–53. DOI: 10.1177/026839629200700107

Biresaw, S. (2022). "The Impacts of Artificial Intelligence on Research in the Legal Profession". SSRN *Electronic Journal*. 1-29.

Bloomberg, N. E. F. (2020). Electric Vehicle Outlook 2020. Retrieved from https://about.bnef.com/electric-vehicle-outlook/

Bollapragada, S., & Morton, T. (1999). Myopic heuristics for the random yield problem. *Operations Research*, 47(5), 713–722. DOI: 10.1287/opre.47.5.713

Bolton, P., & Scharfstein, D. S. (1996). Optimal debt structure with multiple creditors. *Journal of Political Economy*, 104(1), 1–25. DOI: 10.1086/262015

Bolton, R. N., & Drew, J. H. (1991). A Longitudinal Analysis of the Impact of Service Changes on Customer Attitudes. *Journal of Marketing*, 55(1), 1–9. DOI: 10.1177/002224299105500101

Bontis, N., Booker, L. D., & Serenko, A. (2007). The mediating effect of organizational reputation on customer loyalty and service recommendation in the banking industry. *Management Decision*, 45(9), 1425–1445. DOI: 10.1108/00251740710828681

Boubaker, S., Cellier, A., Manita, R., & Saeed, A. (2020). Does corporate social responsibility reduce financial distress risk? *Economic Modelling*, 91, 835–851. DOI: 10.1016/j.econmod.2020.05.012

Boyle, G., & Guthrie, G. (2003). Investment,uncertainty,andliquidity. *The Journal of Finance*, 58(5), 2143–2166. DOI: 10.1111/1540-6261.00600

Brammer, S., Jackson, G., & Matten, D. (2012). Corporate social responsibility and institutional theory: New perspectives on private governance. *Socio-economic Review*, 10(1), 3–28. DOI: 10.1093/ser/mwr030

Bris, A., Deroose, C., & De Schutter, O. (2004). The Impact of Out-of-Court Restructurings on Post-Bankruptcy Performance: Evidence from France. *Journal of Business Finance & Accounting*, 31(5-6), 875–912.

Bris, A., Welch, I., & Zhu, N. (2006). The costs of bankruptcy: Chapter 7 liquidation versus chapter 11 reorganization. *The Journal of Finance*, 61(3), 1253–1303. DOI: 10.1111/j.1540-6261.2006.00872.x

Broadie, M., Chernov, M., & Sundaresan, S. (2007). Optimal debt and equity values in the presence of chapter 7 and chapter 11. *The Journal of Finance*, 62(3), 1341–1377. DOI: 10.1111/j.1540-6261.2007.01238.x

Brown, S., & Eisenhardt, B. (1997). The art of continous change:Linking complexity theory and time paced evaluation in relentlessly shifting organnization. *Administrative science Quaterly, 42*(1), 1-34. DOI: 10.2307/2393807

Brown, D. T., James, C. M., & Mooradian, R. M. (1993). The information content of distressed restructurings involving public and private debt claims. *Journal of Financial Economics*, 33(1), 93–118. DOI: 10.1016/0304-405X(93)90026-8

Brown, R. V., & Vari, A. (1992). Towards a research agenda for prescriptive decision science: The normative tempered by the descriptive. *Acta Psychologica*, 80(1-3), 33–47. DOI: 10.1016/0001-6918(92)90039-G

Bugg-Levine, A., & Emerson, J. (2011). *Impact Investing: Transforming How We Make Money While Making a Difference*. Jossey-Bass.

Buhmann, A., & Fieseler, C. (2023). Deep learning meets deep democracy: Deliberative governance and responsible innovation in artificial intelligence. *Business Ethics Quarterly*, 33(1), 146–179. DOI: 10.1017/beq.2021.42

Butcher, J., & Beridze, I. (2019). What is the state of artificial intelligence governance globally? *RUSI Journal*, 164(5–6), 88–96. DOI: 10.1080/03071847.2019.1694260

Butler Judith. (2015). Notes Toward a Performative Theory of Assembly - Judith Butler - Google Books. Harvard University Press. https://books.google.com.pk/books?hl=en&lr=&id=tRxUCwAAQBAJ&oi=fnd&pg=PP1&dq=Butler%27s+theory+of+precarity&ots=PBvSj8bVuE&sig=WnQa0tHN_BTOgoaw98xcw2v_oJk&redir_esc=y#v=onepage&q&f=true

Butler, H. N., & Mahoney, M. J. (1997). The Effect of Pre-Bankruptcy Restructuring on Debt Renegotiations. *The Journal of Finance*, 52(4), 1541–1570.

Butler, J. (2009). *Frames of war : when is life grievable?* Verso.

Cadbury, A. (1992). Report of the committee on the financial aspects of corporate governance, Gee.

Cai, H. (2000). Delay in multilateral bargaining under complete information. *Journal of Economic Theory*, 93(2), 260–276. DOI: 10.1006/jeth.2000.2658

Cai, L., Cui, J., & Jo, H. (2016). Corporate environmental responsibility and firm risk. *Journal of Business Ethics*, 139(3), 563–594. DOI: 10.1007/s10551-015-2630-4

Cain, M., & McKeon, S. (2016). CEO personal risk-taking and corporate policies. *Journal of Financial and Quantitative Analysis*, 51(1), 139–164. DOI: 10.1017/S0022109016000041

Calomiris, C. W., & Carlson, M. (2016). Corporate governance and risk management at unprotected banks: National banks in the 1890s. *Journal of Financial Economics*, 119(3), 512–532. DOI: 10.1016/j.jfineco.2016.01.025

Camilleri, M. A. (2019). Measuring the corporate managers' attitudes towards ISO's social responsibility standard. *Total Quality Management & Business Excellence*, 30(13–14), 1549–1561. DOI: 10.1080/14783363.2017.1413344

Camilleri, M. A. (2023). *Artificial intelligence governance: Ethical considerations and implications for social responsibility.* John Wiley & Sons Ltd., DOI: 10.1111/exsy.13406

Campbell, A. M. (2020). An increasing risk of family violence during the COVID-19 pandemic: Strengthening community collaborations to save lives. *Forensic Science International. Reports*, 2, 100089. DOI: 10.1016/j.fsir.2020.100089

Campello, M., Gao, J., Qiu, J., & Zhang, Y. (2018). Bankruptcy and the cost of organized labor: Evidence from union elections. *Review of Financial Studies*, 31(3), 980–1013. DOI: 10.1093/rfs/hhx117

Campello, M., Lin, C., Ma, Y., & Zou, H. (2011). The real and financial implications of corporate hedging. *The Journal of Finance*, 66(5), 1615–1647. DOI: 10.1111/j.1540-6261.2011.01683.x

Cane, P. (2013). *Atiyah's accidents, compensation and the law*. Cambridge university press. DOI: 10.1017/CBO9781139548885

Cao, M., & Zhang, Q. (2011). Supply chain collaboration: Impact on collaborative advantage and firm performance. *Journal of Operations Management*, 29(3), 163–180. DOI: 10.1016/j.jom.2010.12.008

Caprio, G., Laeven, L., & Levine, R. (2007). Governance and bank valuation. *Journal of Financial Intermediation*, 16(4), 584–617. DOI: 10.1016/j.jfi.2006.10.003

Carapeto, M. (1999). Does debtor-in-possession add value? (IFA Working Paper No. 294-1999). Retrievefrom https://papers.ssrn.com/sol3/papers.cfm?abstract_id=161428

Carr, N. (2014). Reassessing the assessment: exploring the factors that contribute to comprehensive financial risk evaluation.

Carroll, A. B. (2016). "Carroll's pyramid of CSR: taking another look." International journal of corporate social responsibility**1**: 1-8.

Carroll, A. B. (2016). Carroll's pyramid of CSR: taking another look. *International journal of corporate social responsibility, 1*(1), 1-8.

Carroll, A. B. (1991). Corporate social performance measurement: A comment on methods for evaluating an elusive construct. In Post, L. E. (Ed.), *Research in corporate social performance and policy, 12, 385-401*. JAI Press.

Carroll, A. B. (1991). The pyramid of corporate social responsibility: Toward the moral management of organizational stakeholders. *Business Horizons*, 34(4), 39–48. DOI: 10.1016/0007-6813(91)90005-G

Carroll, A. B., & Shabana, K. M. (2010). The business case for corporate social responsibility: A review of concepts, research and practice. *International Journal of Management Reviews*, 12(1), 2010. DOI: 10.1111/j.1468-2370.2009.00275.x

Caruth, C. (1996). *Unclaimed Experience Trauma, Narrative, and History*. The Johns Hopkins Press Ltd. DOI: 10.1353/book.20656

Carvalho, A., Levitt, A., Levitt, S., Khaddam, E., & Benamati, J. (2019). Off-the-shelf artificial intelligence technologies for sentiment and emotion analysis: A tutorial on using IBM natural language processing. *Communications of the Association for Information Systems*, 44, 918–943. DOI: 10.17705/1CAIS.04443

Chan, F., & Qi, H. (2003). An innovative performance measurement method for supply chain management. *Supply Chain Management*, 8(3), 209–223. DOI: 10.1108/13598540310484618

Chatterjee, S., Dhillon, U. S., & Ramírez, G. G. (1996). Resolution of financial distress: Debt restructurings via chapter 11, pre-packaged bankruptcies, and workouts. *Financial Management Association*, 25(1), 5-18.

Chatterjee, S., Dhillon, U. S., & Ramirez, G. G. (1995). Coercive tender and exchange offers in distressed high-yield debt restructurings: An empirical analysis. *Journal of Financial Economics*, 38(3), 333–360. DOI: 10.1016/0304-405X(94)00815-I

Cheng, B., Ioannou, I., & Serafeim, G. (2014). Corporate social responsibility and access to finance. *Strategic Management Journal*, 35(1), 1–23. DOI: 10.1002/smj.2131

Cheng, S. (2008). Board size and the variability of corporate performance. *Journal of Financial Economics*, 87(1), 157–176. DOI: 10.1016/j.jfineco.2006.10.006

Chen, H. J., & Lin, K. T. (2016). How do banks make the trade-offs among risks? The role of corporate governance. *Journal of Banking & Finance*, 72, S39–S69. DOI: 10.1016/j.jbankfin.2016.05.010

Cheruiyot, F. K. (2010)., The relationship between corporate social responsibility and financial performance of companies listed at the Nairobi Stocks Exchange, *Unpublished MBA Thesis*, University of Nairobi.

Chin, W. (2010). How to write up and report PLS analyses. In C. W. W. EspositoVinzi V, Henseler, J. & Wang, H. (Eds.), *Handbook of partial least squares: concepts, methods and applications* (pp. 655 – 690). Heidelberg: Springer. DOI: 10.1007/978-3-540-32827-8_29

Chin, M. (2019). Be the opportunity: The heart and soul of corporate social responsibility. *Journal of Fair Trade*, 1(1), 27–35. DOI: 10.13169/jfairtrade.1.1.0027

Chiou, J. S., & Droge, C. (2006). Service quality, trust, specific asset investment, and expertise: Direct and indirect effects in a satisfaction-loyalty framework. *Journal of the Academy of Marketing Science*, 34(4), 613–627. DOI: 10.1177/0092070306286934

Choffray, J. M., & Johnson, P. (1977). 8). Measuring perceived pre-purchase risk for a new industrial product'. *Industrial Marketing Management*, •••, 333–334.

Choi, Y., & Yu, Y. (2014). The influence of perceived corporate sustainability practices on employees and organizational performance. *Sustainability (Basel)*, 6(1), 348–364. DOI: 10.3390/su6010348

Chopra, S., & Meindl, P. (2020). *Supply Chain Management: Strategy, Planning, and Operation*. Pearson.

Christensen, H. B., Hail, L., & Leuz, C. (2021). Mandatory CSR and sustainability reporting: Economic analysis and literature review. *Review of Accounting Studies*, 26(3), 1176–1248. DOI: 10.1007/s11142-021-09609-5

Christopher, M. (2016). *Logistics & Supply Chain Management*. Pearson.

Christopher, M., & Peck, H. (2004). Building the Resilient Supply Chain. *International Journal of Logistics Management*, 15(2), 1–14. DOI: 10.1108/09574090410700275

Chung, K. H., Yu, J. E., Choi, M. G., & Shin, J. I. (2015). The effects of CSR on customer satisfaction and loyalty in China: The moderating role of corporate image. *Journal of Economics. Business and Management*, 3(5), 542–547. DOI: 10.7763/JOEBM.2015.V3.243

Chung, K. N.. (2021). Debt Restructuring, Operating Efficiency, and Long-Term Growth: Evidence from Distressed Firms. *Strategic Management Journal*, 42(1), 159–189.

Climate Bonds Initiative. (2020). 2019 Green Bond Market Summary. Retrieved from https://www.climatebonds.net/resources/reports/2019-green-bond-market-summary

Climate Bonds Initiative. (n.d.). Green Bonds. Retrieved from https://www.climatebonds.net/resources/green-bonds

Cohen, M., & Moon, S. (1990). Measuring supply chain performance. *International Journal of Operations & Production Management*, 19(3), 275–292.

Contrafatto, M. (2014). Stewardship theory: Approaches and perspectives. Accountability and social accounting for social and non-profit organizations, Emerald Group Publishing Limited: 177-196.

Cooper, T., & Faseruk, A. (2011). Strategic risk, risk perception and risk behavior: Meta-analysis. *Journal of Financial Management and Analysis*, 2, 20–29.

Cordell, D. (2001). Risk PACK: How to evaluate risk tolerance. *Journal of Financial Planning*, 14(6), 36–40.

Corea, F., Fossa, F., Loreggia, A., Quintarelli, S., & Sapienza, S. (2022). A principle-based approach to AI: The case for European Union and Italy. *AI & Society*, 38(2), 521–535. DOI: 10.1007/s00146-022-01453-8

Costantino, N., & Pellegrino, R. (2010). Choosing between single and multiple sourcing based on supplier default risk: A real options approach. *Journal of Purchasing and Supply Management*, 16(1), 27–40. DOI: 10.1016/j.pursup.2009.08.001

Croft, W. (2000). *Explaining language change: An evolutionary approach*. Pearson Education.

Cucchiella, F., & Gastaldi, M. (2006). Risk management in supply chain: A real option approach. *Journal of Manufacturing Technology Management*, 17(6), 700–720. DOI: 10.1108/17410380610678756

Dahiya, S., John, K., Puri, M., & Ramirez, G. (2003). The dynamics of debtor-in-possession financing: Bankruptcy resolution and the role of prior lenders. *Journal of Financial Economics*, 69, 259–280. DOI: 10.1016/S0304-405X(03)00113-2

Damaraju, N. L., Barney, J. B., & Makhija, A. K. (2015). Real options in divestment alternatives. *Strategic Management Journal*, 36(5), 728–744. DOI: 10.1002/smj.2243

Danone. (2020). Danone issues a €2bn sustainability-linked bond to support climate goals. Retrieved from https://www.danone.com/media/press-releases-list/2020/green-bond-2020.html

Daub, C. H., & Ergenzinger, R. (2005). Enabling sustainable management through a new multi-disciplinary concept of customer satisfaction. *European Journal of Marketing*, 39(9/10), 998–1012. DOI: 10.1108/03090560510610680

Davis, J. H., Schoorman, F. D., & Donaldson, L. (1997). Toward a stewardship theory of management. *Academy of Management Review*, 22(1), 20–47. DOI: 10.2307/259223

DeAngelo, H., & Stark, R. W. (1986). Bankruptcy Reorganization and Stockholder-Bondholder Conflicts. *The Journal of Finance*, 41(2), 347–364.

Dellaportas, S., Gibson, K., Alagiah, R., Hutchinson, M., Leung, P., & Homing, D. V. (2005). *Ethics Governance and Accountability* (1st ed.).

Demir, F. (2009). Financializatiion and manufacturing firm profitability under uncertainty and macroeconomics volatility:ecidence from emerging market. *Review of Devellopment Economics, 13*(9), 592-609. doi:org/DOI: 10.1111/j.1467

Demir, E., & Danisman, G. O. (2021). Banking sector reactions to COVID-19: The role of bank-specific factors and government policy responses. *Research in International Business and Finance*, 58, 101508. DOI: 10.1016/j.ribaf.2021.101508

DeStefano, A., & Gottlieb, D. (1997). Out-of-Court Workouts vs. Formal Bankruptcy: An Empirical Investigation of Distressed Real Estate Ventures. *Real Estate Economics*, 25(2), 297–330.

Dick, A., & Basu, K. (1994). Customer loyalty: Toward an integrated conceptual framework. *Journal of the Academy of Marketing Science*, 22(2), 99–113. DOI: 10.1177/0092070394222001

DiMaggio, P. J., & Powell, W. W. (1983). The iron cage revisited: Institutional isomorphism and collective rationality in organizational fields. *American Sociological Review*, 48(2), 147–160. DOI: 10.2307/2095101

Dixit, A. K., & Pindyck, R. (1995). The options approach to capital investment. *Harvard Business Review*, 73(3), 105–115.

Djebali, N., & Zaghdoudi, K. (2020). Testing the governance-performance relationship for the Tunisian banks: A GMM in system analysis. *Financial Innovation*, 6(1), 1–24. DOI: 10.1186/s40854-020-00182-5

Doherty, B., Haugh, H., & Lyon, F. (2014). Social Enterprises as Hybrid Organizations: A Review and Research Agenda. *International Journal of Management Reviews*, 16(4), 417–436. DOI: 10.1111/ijmr.12028

Donaldson, K., Brown, G. M., Brown, D. M., Bolton, R. E., & Davis, J. M. (1989). Inflammation generating potential of long and short fibre amosite asbestos samples. *Occupational and Environmental Medicine*, 46(4), 271–276. DOI: 10.1136/oem.46.4.271

Donaldson, T., & Preston, L. E. (1995). The stakeholder theory of the corporation: Concepts, evidence, and implications. *Academy of Management Review*, 20(1), 65–91. DOI: 10.2307/258887

Dossi, A., & Patelli, L. (2010). You learn from what you measure: Financial and non-financial performance measures in multinational companies. *Long Range Planning*, 43(4), 498–526. DOI: 10.1016/j.lrp.2010.01.002

Ducháček, M., & Schőnlaub, M. (2015). Restructuring and Resolution of Distressed Banks: Lessons from the Great Financial Crisis. *Journal of Banking & Finance*, 57, 30–41.

During, S. (2015). Choosing precarity. In South Asia: Journal of South Asia Studies (Vol. 38, Issue 1, pp. 19–38). Routledge. DOI: 10.1080/00856401.2014.975901

Du, S., Bhattacharya, C. B., & Sen, S. (2010). Maximizing business returns to corporate social responsibility (CSR): The role of CSR communication. *International Journal of Management Reviews*, 12(1), 8–19. DOI: 10.1111/j.1468-2370.2009.00276.x

Du, S., Xu, X., & Yu, K. (2020). Does corporate social responsibility affect auditor-client contracting? Evidence from auditor selection and audit fees. *Advances in Accounting*, 51, 100499. DOI: 10.1016/j.adiac.2020.100499

Easterbrook, F. H. (1984). Two agency-cost explanations of dividends. *The American Economic Review*, 74(4), 650–659.

Eberhart, A. C., Altman, E. I., & Aggarwal, R. (1999). The equity performance of firms emerging from bankruptcy. *The Journal of Finance*, 54(5), 1855–1868. DOI: 10.1111/0022-1082.00169

Eccles, R. G., Ioannou, I., & Serafeim, G. (2014). The Impact of Corporate Sustainability on Organizational Processes and Performance. *Management Science*, 60(11), 2835–2857. DOI: 10.1287/mnsc.2014.1984

El Ghoul, S., Guedhami, O., Kwok, C. C. Y., & Mishra, D. R. (2011). Does corporate social responsibility affect the cost of capital? *Journal of Banking \& Finance*, 35(9), 2388–2406.

El-Garaihy, W., Mobarak, A., & Albahussain, S. (2014). Measuring the Impact of Corporate Social Responsibility Practices on Competitive Advantage: A Mediation Role of Reputation and Customer Satisfaction. *International Journal of Business and Management*, 9(5), 109–124. DOI: 10.5539/ijbm.v9n5p109

Elkington, J. (1997). "The triple bottom line." Environmental management: Readings and cases 2: 49-66.

Ellen MacArthur Foundation. (2019). Completing the Picture: How the Circular Economy Tackles Climate Change. Retrieved from https://www.ellenmacarthurfoundation.org/assets/downloads/Completing_The_Picture_How_The_Circular_Economy-_Tackles_Climate_Change_V3_26_September.pdf

El-Sayed Ebaid, I. (2009). The impact of capital-structure choice on firm performance: Empirical evidence from Egypt. *The Journal of Risk Finance*, 10(5), 477–487. DOI: 10.1108/15265940911001385

Engel, C., Ebel, P., & Leimeister, J. M. (2022). Cognitive automation. *Electronic Markets*, 32(1), 339–350. DOI: 10.1007/s12525-021-00519-7

Erbele-Küster, D., & Küster, V. (2022). *Between Pandemonium and Pandemethics: Responses to Covid-19 from Theology and Religions* (Vol. 27). Evangelische Verlagsanstalt.

Erdem, A., & Özekici, A. (2002). Inventory models with random yield in a random environment. *International Journal of Production Economics*, 78(3), 239–253. DOI: 10.1016/S0925-5273(01)00165-7

Ertorer, S. E. (2021). Asylum Regimes and Refugee Experiences of Precarity: The Case of Syrian Refugees in Turkey. *Journal of Refugee Studies*, 34(3), 2568–2592. DOI: 10.1093/jrs/feaa089

European Commission. (2018). Action Plan: Financing Sustainable Growth. Retrieved from https://ec.eu.eu/info/publications/180308-action-plan-sustainable-growth_en

European Commission. (2018). Action Plan: Financing Sustainable Growth. Retrieved from https://ec.europa.eu/info/publications/180308-action-plan-sustainable-growth_en

Farber, D. B. (2005). Restoring trust after fraud: Does corporate governance matter? *The Accounting Review*, 80(2), 539–561. DOI: 10.2308/accr.2005.80.2.539

Fehr, R., & Hari, J. (2014). Assessing the risk attitudes of private investors using the implicit association test. *Journal of Financial Service Professionals*, 68(6), 50–62.

Feldman, J. (n.d.). To Grade or Not to Grade? https://filecabinetdublin.eschoolview.com/6D88CF03-93EE-4E59B267B73AA2456ED7/ToGradeorNottoGradearticle.pdf

Felicio, J. A., Rodrigues, R., Grove, H., & Greiner, A. (2018). The influence of corporate governance on bank risk during a financial crisis. *Ekonomska Istrazivanja*, 31(1), 1078–1090. DOI: 10.1080/1331677X.2018.1436457

Feng, J., Han, P., Zheng, W., & Kamran, A. (2022). Identifying the factors affecting strategic decision-making ability to boost the entrepreneurial performance: A hybrid structural equation modeling – artificial neural network approach. *Frontiers in Psychology*, 13, 1038604. Advance online publication. DOI: 10.3389/fpsyg.2022.1038604

Feng, J., Pan, Y., & Zhuang, W. (2022). Measuring the Enterprise Green Innovation Strategy Decision-Making Quality: A Moderating—Mediating Model. *Frontiers in Psychology*, 13, 915624. Advance online publication. DOI: 10.3389/fpsyg.2022.915624

Fernando, S. (2014, Fall). Lawrence & Stewart, (2014), "A Theoretical Framework for CSR Practices: Integrating Legitimacy Theory, Stakeholder Theory And Institutional Theory. *The Journal of Theoretical Accounting*, 10(1), 149–178. https://www.researchgate.net/profile/Susith-Fernando/publication/290485216_A_theoretical_framework_for_CSR_practices_Integrating_legitimacy_theory_stakeholder_theory_and_institutional_theory/links/5a8629ee458515b8af890861/A-theoretical-framework-for-CSR-practices-Integrating-legitimacy-theory-stakeholder-theory-and-institutional-theory.pdf

Finch, P. (2004). Supply chain risk management. *Supply Chain Management*, 9(2), 183–196. DOI: 10.1108/13598540410527079

Fitzpatrick, M. (1983). The definition and assessment of political risk in international business: A review of the literature. *Academy of Management Review*, 8(2), 249–254. DOI: 10.2307/257752

Fombrun, C., & Shanley, M. (1990). What's in a name? Reputation building and corporate strategy. *Academy of Management Journal*, 33(2), 233–258. DOI: 10.2307/256324

Fornell, C, & Larcker, D. F. (1981). Evaluating structural equation models with unobservable

Fornell, C. (1992). A national customer satisfaction barometer: The Swedish experience. *Journal of Marketing*, 56(1), 6–21. DOI: 10.1177/002224299205600103

Fornell, S., Mithas, S., Morgeson, F. V.III, & Krishnan, M. S. (2006). Customer Satisfaction and Stock Prices: High Returns, Low Risk. *Journal of Marketing*, 70(1), 3–14. DOI: 10.1509/jmkg.70.1.003.qxd

Freeman, R. B., & Medoff, J. L. (1984). What do unions do. *Indus. & Lab. Rel. Rev.*, 38, 244.

Freeman, R. E. (1984). *Strategic Management: A Stakeholder Approach*. Pitman.

French, S. (2000). Statistical Decision Theory.

Friede, G., Busch, T., & Bassen, A. (2015). ESG and financial performance: Aggregated evidence from more than 2000 empirical studies. *Journal of Sustainable Finance & Investment*, 5(4), 210–233. DOI: 10.1080/20430795.2015.1118917

Friedman, A. L., & Miles, S. (2002). Developing stakeholder theory. *Journal of Management Studies*, 39(1), 1–21. DOI: 10.1111/1467-6486.00280

Froot, K. A., & Shleifer, A. Y. (2000). Financial Crises and Restructuring: Some Lessons from East Asia. *The Journal of Law & Economics*, 43(2), 249–294.

Froot, K., Scharfstein, D. S., & Stein, J. C. (1993). Risk management: Coordinating corporate investment and financing policies. *The Journal of Finance*, 48(5), 1629–1658. DOI: 10.1111/j.1540-6261.1993.tb05123.x

Fruth, M., & Teuteberg, F. (2017). Digitization in Maritime Logistics—What is there and what is missing? *Cogent Business & Management*, 4(1), 1411066. DOI: 10.1080/23311975.2017.1411066

Fu, X. M., Lin, Y. R., & Molyneux, P. (2014). Bank efficiency and shareholder value in Asia Pacific. *Journal of International Financial Markets, Institutions and Money*, 33, 200–222. DOI: 10.1016/j.intfin.2014.08.004

Galaz, V., Centeno, M. A., Callahan, P. W., Causevic, A., Patterson, T., Brass, I., Baum, S., Farber, D., Fischer, J., Garcia, D., McPhearson, T., Jimenez, D., King, B., Larcey, P., & Levy, K. (2021). Artificial intelligence, systemic risks, and sustainability. *Technology in Society*, 67, 101741. DOI: 10.1016/j.techsoc.2021.101741

Gallardo-Vázquez, D., & Sanchez-Hernandez, M. I. (2014). Measuring Corporate Social Responsibility for competitive success at a regional level. *Journal of Cleaner Production*, 72, 1422. DOI: 10.1016/j.jclepro.2014.02.051

Garaya, L., & Font, X. (2011). Doing good to do well? Corporate social responsibility reasons, practices and impacts in small and medium accommodation enterprises'. *International Journal of Hospitality Management*, 30, 1–9.

Garrido, J. M. Out-Of-Court Debt Restructuring, World Bank Study, World Bank (2012)

Garriga, E., & Mele´, D. (2004). Corporate Social Responsibility Theories: Mapping the Territory. *Journal of Business Ethics*, 53(1/2), 51–71. DOI: 10.1023/B:BUSI.0000039399.90587.34

Gertner, R., & Scharfstein, D. (1991). A theory of workouts and the effects of reorganization law. *The Journal of Finance*, 46, 1189–1222.

Gertner, R., Scharfstein, D., & Stein, J. (2013). Internal and External Governance and the Choice Between Out-of-Court Restructuring and Bankruptcy. *The Journal of Finance*, 68(5), 1911–1944.

Gertner, R., & Skeel, D. (1999). The Dynamics of Out-of-Court Workouts. *The Journal of Finance*, 54(6), 1559–1579.

Ghahramani, Z. (2015). "Probabilistic Machine Learning and Artificial Intelligence" 521. *Nature*, 452, 459.

Ghosh, B., Patgiri, R., & Aparajita, D. (2020). *Digital ethnography during the COVID 10 pandemic*.

Giammarino, R. M. (1989). The resolution of financial distress. *Review of Financial Studies*, 2(1), 25–47. DOI: 10.1093/rfs/2.1.25

Gianfrate, G., & Peri, M. (2019). The Green Advantage: Exploring the Convenience of Issuing Green Bonds. *Journal of Cleaner Production*, 219, 127–135. DOI: 10.1016/j.jclepro.2019.02.022

Gilovich, T. (2002). *Heuristics and Biases: The Psychology of Intuitive Judgement*.

Gilson, R. J. (2003). A Model of Out-of-Court Debt Restructuring. *The Journal of Finance*, 58(3), 1145–1162.

Gilson, S. C., & Murphy, K. J. (1998). Troubled debt restructurings: An efficient approach to corporate workouts. *Journal of Applied Corporate Finance*, 10(3), 84–97.

Gilson, S., John, K., & Lang, L. (1990). Troubled Debt Restructurings - An Emperical Study Of Private Reorgination Of Firms In Default. *Journal of Financial Economics*, 27(2), 315–353. DOI: 10.1016/0304-405X(90)90059-9

Gleason, K. C., Mathur, L. K., & Mathur, I. (2000). The interrelationship between culture, capital structure, and performance: Evidence from European retailers. *Journal of Business Research*, 50(2), 185–191. DOI: 10.1016/S0148-2963(99)00031-4

Global Impact Investing Network. (n.d.). What is Impact Investing? Retrieved from https://thegiin.org/impact-investing/what-is-impact-investing

Godfrey, P. C. (2005). The relationship between corporate philanthropy and shareholder wealth: A risk management perspective. *Academy of Management Review*, 30(4), 777–798. DOI: 10.5465/amr.2005.18378878

Gołaszewska-Kaczan, U. (2009). *Corporate social commitment*. Publishing House of the Bialystok University of Technology.

Gordon, M. J. (1963). Optimal investment and financing policy. *The Journal of Finance*, 18(2), 264–272.

Gourinchas, P. O., & Obstfeld, M. (2012). Stories of the Twentieth Century for the Twenty-First. *American Economic Journal. Macroeconomics*, 4(1), 226–265. DOI: 10.1257/mac.4.1.226

Governance, C. (2015). What is corporate governance.

Grable, J. E. (2000). Financial risk tolerance and additional factors that affect risk taking in everyday money matters. *Journal of Business and Psychology*, 14(4), 625–630. DOI: 10.1023/A:1022994314982

Grable, J., & Lytton, J. (1999). Financial risk tolerance revisited: The development of a risk assessment instrument. *Financial Services Review*, 8(3), 163–181. DOI: 10.1016/S1057-0810(99)00041-4

Graham, J., & Harvey, C. (2001). the theory and practice of corporate finance: Evidence from the field. *Financial Econom*, 187–243.

Green, T., & Peloza, J. (2011). How does corporate social responsibility create value for customers? *Journal of Consumer Marketing*, 28(1), 48–56. DOI: 10.1108/07363761111101949

Gregory, H. J., & Simms, M. E. (1999). Corporate governance: what it is and why it matters. *9th International Anti-Corruption Conference*, Kuala Lumpur.

Gulzar, U., Khan, S. N., Baig, F. J., Ansari, M. A. A., Akram, R., & Kamran, M. (2021). The Impact Of Corporate Governance On Risk Management: Evidence From The Banking Sector Of Pakistan. [BBE]. *Bulletin of Business and Economics*, 10(3), 196–207.

Gunn, J. L., Li, C., Liao, L., Yang, J., & Zhou, S. (2024). Audit firms' corporate social responsibility activities and auditor reputation. *Accounting, Organizations and Society*, 113, 101569. DOI: 10.1016/j.aos.2024.101569

Guo, J., Sun, L., & Li, X. (2009). Corporate social responsibility assessment of Chinese corporation. *International Journal of Business and Management*, 4(4), 54–57. DOI: 10.5539/ijbm.v4n4p54

Guo, S., Zhao, L., & Xu, X. (2016). Impact of supply risks on procurement decisions. *Annals of Operations Research*, 241(1-2), 411–430. DOI: 10.1007/s10479-013-1422-4

Gupta, S. K. (2020). Performance Analysis of Electrosteel Steels Ltd. Pre, During and Post CIRP: A Case Study. *The Management Accountant Journal*, 55(2), 91–95. DOI: 10.33516/maj.v55i2.91-95p

Gurney, J., Humphries, D., & Newton, D. (2020). Brexit and the Automotive Industry: A Supply Chain Perspective. *The Journal of Supply Chain Management*, 56(3), 45–61.

Guthrie, J., & Parker, L. D. (1989). Corporate social reporting: A rebuttal of legitimacy theory. *Accounting and Business Research*, 19(76), 343–352. DOI: 10.1080/00014788.1989.9728863

Hair, J., Ringle, C. M., & Sarstedt, M. (2011). PLS-SEM: Indeed a Silver Bullet. *Journal of Marketing Theory and Practice*, 19(2), 139–151. DOI: 10.2753/MTP1069-6679190202

Hamed, R. S., Al-Shattarat, B. K., Al-Shattarat, W. K., & Hussainey, K. (2022). The impact of introducing new regulations on the quality of CSR reporting: Evidence from the UK. *Journal of International Accounting, Auditing & Taxation*, 46, 100444. DOI: 10.1016/j.intaccaudtax.2021.100444

Handfield, R., & Nichols, E. (1999). (P.-H. upply Chain Management, Ed.)

Hanna, S. (2013). Assessing risk tolerance. *Theory and Management*, 99-120.

Hansen, S. D., Dunford, B. B., Boss, A. D., & Angermeier, I. (2011). Corporate social responsibility and the benefits of employee trust: A cross disciplinary perspective. *Journal of Business Ethics*, 102(1), 29–45. DOI: 10.1007/s10551-011-0903-0

Haraguchi, M., & Lall, U. (2015). Flood risks and impacts: A case study of Thailand's floods in 2011 and research questions for supply chain decision making. *International Journal of Disaster Risk Reduction*, 14, 256–272. DOI: 10.1016/j.ijdrr.2014.09.005

He, F., Chen, L., Hao, J., & Wu, J. (2024). Financial market development and corporate risk management: Evidence from Shanghai crude oil futures launched in China. *Energy Economics*, 129, 107250. DOI: 10.1016/j.eneco.2023.107250

He, H., & Li, Y. (2011). CSR and service brand: The mediating effect of brand identification and moderating effect of service quality. *Journal of Business Ethics*, 100(4), 673–688. DOI: 10.1007/s10551-010-0703-y

Hilman, A. J., & Keim, G. D. (2001). Shareholder Value, Stakeholder Management, Social Issues: What's the Bottom Line. *Strategic Management Journal*, 22(2), 125–139. DOI: 10.1002/1097-0266(200101)22:2<125::AID-SMJ150>3.0.CO;2-H

Hirsch, J., Parry, I., Coady, D., & Shang, B. (2020). The fiscal and welfare impacts of reforming energy subsidies in emerging market and developing economies. *IMF Economic Review*, 68(3), 586–635.

Höhne, N., Khosla, S., Fekete, H., & Gilbert, A. (2012). Mapping of Green Finance Delivered by IDFC

Holder-Webb, L., Lopez, T., & Regier, P. (2005). The Performance Consequences of Operational Restructurings. *Review of Quantitative Finance and Accounting*, 25(4), 319–339. DOI: 10.1007/s11156-005-5458-7

Holz, C. A. (2002). The impact of the liability–asset ratio on profitability in China's industrial state-owned enterprises. *China Economic Review*, 13(1), 1–26. DOI: 10.1016/S1043-951X(01)00054-2

Hora, M., & Klassen, R. (2013). Learning from others' misfortune: Factors influencing knowledge acquisition to reduce operational risk. *Journal of Operations Management*, 31(1-2), 52–61. DOI: 10.1016/j.jom.2012.06.004

Hortovanyi, L., Szepesi, B., & Pogacsas, P. (2024). Navigating crisis: SME strategies for risk mitigation through strategic upgrading. *Cogent Business and Management*, 11(1), 2392043. Advance online publication. DOI: 10.1080/23311975.2024.2392043

Hoskisson, R., & Chirico, F. (2017). Managerial risk taking: a multitheoretical review and future research agenda. *43*(1), 137-169.

Hotchkiss, E. S. (1995). Post-bankruptcy performance and management turnover. *The Journal of Finance*, 50(1), 3–21. DOI: 10.1111/j.1540-6261.1995.tb05165.x

Hotchkiss, E. S., John, K., Mooradian, R. M., & Thorburn, K. S. (2008). Bankruptcy and the resolution of financial distress. In Eckbo, B. E. (Ed.), *Handbook of Empirical Corporate Finance* (Vol. 2, pp. 235–287). North Holland: Elsevier. DOI: 10.1016/B978-0-444-53265-7.50006-8

Hotchkiss, E., John, K., Thornbern, K., & Mooradian, R. (2008). *Bankruptcy and The resolution of Financial Distress* (Vol. 2). Handbook Of Emperical Corporate Finance.

Hsu, K. (2012). The advertising effects of Corporate Social Responsibility on corporate reputation and brand equity: Evidence from the life insurance industry in Taiwan. *Journal of Business Ethics*, 109(2), 189–201. DOI: 10.1007/s10551-011-1118-0

Huang, Q., Xiong, M., & Xiao, M. (2022). Does managerial ability affect corporate financial constraints? Evidence from China. *Ekonomska Istrazivanja*, 35(1), 3731–3753. DOI: 10.1080/1331677X.2021.2004186

Hummel, K., & Jobst, D. (2024). An overview of corporate sustainability reporting legislation in the European Union. *Accounting in Europe*, 1-36.

Hunjra, A. I., Hanif, M., Mehmood, R., & Nguyen, L. V. (2021). Diversification, corporate governance, regulation and bank risk-taking. *Journal of Financial Reporting and Accounting*, 19(1), 92–108. DOI: 10.1108/JFRA-03-2020-0071

Hunjra, A. I., Jebabli, I., Thrikawala, S. S., Alawi, S. M., & Mehmood, R. (2024). How do corporate governance and corporate social responsibility affect credit risk? *Research in International Business and Finance*, 67, 102139. DOI: 10.1016/j.ribaf.2023.102139

Hunjra, A. I., Tayachi, T., Mehmood, R., & Hussain, A. (2022). Does economic risk affect corporate cash holdings? *Journal of Economic and Administrative Sciences*, 38(3), 471–484. DOI: 10.1108/JEAS-05-2020-0069

Hunjra, A. I., Zureigat, Q., Tayachi, T., & Mehmood, R. (2020). Impact of non-interest income and revenue concentration on bank risk in South Asia. *Banks and Bank Systems*, 15(4), 15–25. DOI: 10.21511/bbs.15(4).2020.02

Hunter, D. (2002, Septembe). Risk perception and risk tolerance in aircraft pilots. *Risk_Perception_and_Risk_Tolerance_in_ Aircraft Pilots*. Retrieved from www.researchgate.net

Hussain, R. Y., Bajaj, N. K., Kumari, S., & Al-Faryan, M. A. S. (2023). Does economic policy uncertainty affect foreign remittances? Linear and non-linear ARDL approach in BRIC economies. *Cogent Economics & Finance*, 11(1), 2183642. DOI: 10.1080/23322039.2023.2183642

Hussain, R. Y., Wen, X., Butt, R. S., Hussain, H., Ali Qalati, S., & Abbas, I. (2020). Are growth led financing decisions causing insolvency in listed firms of Pakistan? *Zagreb International Review of Economics & Business*, 23(2), 89–115. DOI: 10.2478/zireb-2020-0015

Hussain, R. Y., Wen, X., Hussain, H., Saad, M., & Zafar, Z. (2022). Do leverage decisions mediate the relationship between board structure and insolvency risk? A comparative mediating role of capital structure and debt maturity. *South Asian Journal of Business Studies*, 11(1), 104–125. DOI: 10.1108/SAJBS-05-2020-0150

Hussain, R. Y., Xuezhou, W., Hussain, H., Saad, M., & Qalati, S. A. (2021). Corporate board vigilance and insolvency risk: A mediated moderation model of debt maturity and fixed collaterals. *International Journal of Management and Economics*, 57(1), 14–33. DOI: 10.2478/ijme-2020-0032

Husted, B. W. (2000). Contingency theory of corporate social performance. *Business & Society*, 39(1), 24–48. DOI: 10.1177/000765030003900104

Hwangbo, K. (2004). *Trauma, narrative, and the marginal self in selected contemporary American novels*. University of Florida.

IKEA Group. (2020). Sustainability Report FY20. Retrieved from https://www.ikea.com/us/en/this-is-ikea/sustainability-report-pub0159a43b

Ittner, C., & Larcker, D. F. (1998). Are non-financial measures leading indicators of financial performance? An analyses of customer satisfaction. *Journal of Accounting Research*, 36(supplement), 1–35. DOI: 10.2307/2491304

Ivanov, D. (2020). *Predicting the impacts of epidemic outbreaks on global supply chains: A simulation-based analysis on the coronavirus outbreak (COVID-19/SARS-CoV-2) case.* Transportation Research Part E: Logistics and Transportation Review.

Ivanov, D., & Das, A. (2020). *Coronavirus (COVID-19/SARS-CoV-2) and supply chain resilience: A research note.* International Journal of Integrated Supply Management.

J. S. Ang, J. H. Chua and J. Mconnel, (1982). *The Administrative Costs Of Corporate Bankruptcy- A Note,* Journal Of Finance, vol. XXXVii, no.1

Jackson, I., Ivanov, D., Dolgui, A., & Namdar, J. (2024). Generative artificial intelligence in supply chain and operations management: A capability-based framework for analysis and implementation. *International Journal of Production Research*, 62(17), 6120–6145. Advance online publication. DOI: 10.1080/00207543.2024.2309309

Janiesch, C., Zschech, P., & Heinrich, K. (2021). Machine learning and deep learning. *Electronic Markets*, 31(3), 685–695. DOI: 10.1007/s12525-021-00475-2

Jeffery, S. (2009). Goal attainment as a resource: The cushion effect in risky choice above a goal. *Journal of Behavioral Decision Making*, 23(2), 191–202. DOI: 10.1002/bdm.645

Jensen, M. C. (1989). Active investors, LBOs, and the privatization of bankruptcy. *The Bank of America Journal of Applied Corporate Finance*, 2(1), 35–44. DOI: 10.1111/j.1745-6622.1989.tb00551.x

Jensen, M. C., & Meckling, W. H. (2019). Theory of the firm: Managerial behavior, agency costs and ownership structure. In *Corporate governance* (pp. 77–132). Gower.

Jessop, D. (1994). Purchasing management, analysis, planning and practice: A J van Weele Chapman & Hall London (1994). *European Journal of Purchasing & Supply Management*, 3(1), 194–195. DOI: 10.1016/0969-7012(94)90010-8

Ji, M., You, X., Lan, J., & Yang, S. (2011). The impact of risk tolerance, risk perception and hazardous attitude on safety operation among airline pilots in China. *Safety Science*, 49(10), 1412–1420. DOI: 10.1016/j.ssci.2011.06.007

Jiménez, D., Delerce, S., Dorado, H., Cock, J., Muñoz, L. A., Agamez, A., & Jarvis, A. (2019). A scalable scheme to implement data-driven agriculture for small-scale farmers. *Global Food Security*, 23, 256–266. DOI: 10.1016/j.gfs.2019.08.004

Jin, Y. (2017). The impact of the Hanjin Shipping bankruptcy on global supply chains. *International Journal of Physical Distribution & Logistics Management*, 47(6), 500–518.

Kache, F., & Seuring, S. (2014). Linking collaboration and integration to risk and performance in supply chains via a review of literature reviews. *Supply Chain Management*, 19(5/6), 664–682. DOI: 10.1108/SCM-12-2013-0478

Kahneman, D., & Tversky, A. (1979). Prospect theory: An analysis of decision under risk. *Econometrica*, 47(2), 263–292. DOI: 10.2307/1914185

Kalay, A., Sighal, R., & Tashjian, E. (2007). Is Chapter 11 costly? *Journal of Financial Economics*, 84(3), 772–796. DOI: 10.1016/j.jfineco.2006.04.001

Katper, N. K., Tunio, M. N., Hussain, N., Junejo, A., & Gilal, F. G. (2020). COVID-19 crises: Global economic shocks vs Pakistan economic shocks. Advances in Science. *Technology and Engineering Systems*, 5(4), 645–654. DOI: 10.25046/aj050477

Keasey, K. and M. Wright (1993). "Issues in corporate accountability and governance: An editorial." Accounting and business research 23(sup1): 291-303.

Keeney, R. L. (1992). On the foundations of prescriptive decision analysis. *Utility theories: Measurement and applications.*

Keynes, J. (1936). the General Theory of Employment. *Interest, and Money.*

Kinzer, I. (1982). Uncertainty, Discovery and human action: A study of enterprenurial Profile in the Misesian System. *Method, Process and Austrian Economics:Eassays in Honor of Ludwing Von Mises.*

Kitces, M. (2006, March). Rethinking risk tolerance. *Financial Planning*, 51-59.

Klatt, S., Noël, B., Schwarting, A., Heckmann, L., & Fasold, F. (2021). Adaptive Gaze Behavior and Decision Making of Penalty Corner Strikers in Field Hockey. *Frontiers in Psychology*, 12, 674511. Advance online publication. DOI: 10.3389/fpsyg.2021.674511

Kleindorfer, P.R, & Saad, G. (2005). Production and Operations Management. *Managing disruption risks in supply chains,* 14(1), 53-58.

Knight, F. (1921). (B. M. Houghton Mifflin Company, Ed.) *Risk, Uncertainty, and Profit.*

Kogut, B. (1991). Joint ventures and the option to expand and acquire. *Management Science*, 37(1), 19–33. DOI: 10.1287/mnsc.37.1.19

Kölbel, J. F., Heeb, F., Paetzold, F., & Busch, T. (2020). Can Sustainable Investing Save the World? Reviewing the Mechanisms of Investor Impact. *Organization & Environment*, 33(4), 554–574. DOI: 10.1177/1086026620919202

Koniakou, V. (2023). From the "rush to ethics" to the "race for governance" in artificial intelligence. *Information Systems Frontiers*, 25(1), 71–102. DOI: 10.1007/s10796-022-10300-6

Kotler, P., & Lee, N. (2005). *Corporate Social Responsibility: Doing the Most Good for Your Company and Your Cause*. John Wiley & Sons, Inc.

Kovács, G., & Spens, K. M. (2007). Humanitarian logistics in disaster relief operations. *International Journal of Physical Distribution & Logistics Management*, 37(2), 99–114. DOI: 10.1108/09600030710734820

Kovak, D., & Srhoj, S. (2022). The Impact of Bargaining Failures in Out-of-Court Restructuring: Evidence from a Novel Dataset. *Journal of Corporate Finance*, 78, 102664.

Kraljic, P. (1983). Purchasing must become supply management. *Harvard Business Review*, 61(5), 109–117.

Kramer, M. R., & Porter, M. E. (2006). Strategy and society: The link between competitive advantage and corporate social responsibility. *Harvard Business Review*, 84(12), 78–92.

Kraus, A., & Litzenberger, R. H. (1973). A state-preference model of optimal financial leverage. *The Journal of Finance*, 28(4), 911–922.

Kremic, T., Icmeli Tukel, O., & Rom, W. O. (2006). Out sourcing decision support: A survey of benefits, risks, and decision factors. *Supply Chain Management*, 11(6), 467–482. DOI: 10.1108/13598540610703864

Krieger, K., Mauck, N., & Pruitt, S. W. (2021). The impact of the COVID-19 pandemic on dividends. *Finance Research Letters*, 42, 101910. DOI: 10.1016/j.frl.2020.101910

Krychowski, C., & Quélin, B. (2010). Real options and strategic investment decisions: Can they be of use to scholars? *The Academy of Management Perspectives*, 24(2), 65–78. DOI: 10.5465/AMP.2010.51827776

KsiężaK, P. and B. Fischbach (2017). "Triple bottom line: The pillars of CSR." Journal of corporate responsibility and leadership**4**(3): 95-110.

Kumar, P., & Yerramilli, V. (2017). Optimal capital structure and investment with real options and end ogenous debt costs. *Review of Financial Studies*, 31(9), 3452–3490. DOI: 10.1093/rfs/hhx093

Langlois, R., & Cosgel, M. (1993). Frank knight on risk, uncertainty, and the firm: A new interpretation. *Economic Inquiry*, 31(3), 456–465. DOI: 10.1111/j.1465-7295.1993.tb01305.x

Lantos, G. P. (2001). The boundaries of strategic corporate social responsibility. *Journal of Consumer Marketing*, 18(7), 595–630. DOI: 10.1108/07363760110410281

Lantos, G. P. (2002). The ethicality of altruistic corporate social responsibility. *Journal of Consumer Marketing*, 19(3), 205–230. DOI: 10.1108/07363760210426049

Larcker, D. F.. (2005). "How important is corporate governance?" Available at SSRN 595821.

Larrán Jorge, M., Herrera Madueño, J., Martínez-Martínez, D., & Lechuga Sancho, M. P. (2015). Competitiveness and environmental performance in Spanish small and medium enterprises: Is there a direct link? *Journal of Cleaner Production*, 101, 26–37. DOI: 10.1016/j.jclepro.2015.04.016

Larsen, K. L., & Stanley, E. A. (2021). Leaders' Windows of Tolerance for Affect Arousal—And Their Effects on Political Decision-making During COVID-19. *Frontiers in Psychology*, 12, 749715. Advance online publication. DOI: 10.3389/fpsyg.2021.749715

Latif, W., Islam, M. A., Mohamad, M., Sikder, M. A. H., & Ahmed, I. (2015). A conceptual framework of brand image on customer-based brand equity in the hospitality industry at Bangladesh: Tourism management and advertisement as moderators. *Journal of Scientific Research and Development*, 2(11), 1–16.

LeCun, Y., Bengio, Y., & Hinton, G. (2015). Deep learning. *Nature*, 521(7553), 436–444. DOI: 10.1038/nature14539

Lee, S., Seo, K., & Sharma, A. (2013). Corporate social responsibility and firm performance in the airline industry: The moderating role of oil prices. *Tourism Management*, 38, 20–30. DOI: 10.1016/j.tourman.2013.02.002

Leroy, S., & Singel, L. (1987). Knight on risk and uncertainty. *Journal of Political Economy*, 95(2), 394–406. DOI: 10.1086/261461

Lestari, P., Pratiwi, U., & Irianto, B. S. (2023). The moderating effects of gender on managerial performance assessment and dysfunctional behaviour: Evidence from Indonesia. *Cogent Business and Management*, 10(1), 2193207. Advance online publication. DOI: 10.1080/23311975.2023.2193207

Li, H., Meng, L., Wang, Q., & Zhou, L. A. (2008). Political connections, financing and firm performance: Evidence from Chinese private firms. *Journal of Development Economics*, 87(2), 283–299. DOI: 10.1016/j.jdeveco.2007.03.001

Lins, K. V., Servaes, H., & Tamayo, A. (2017). Social capital, trust, and firm performance: The value of corporate social responsibility during the financial crisis. *the Journal of Finance,* 72(4), 1785-1824.

Liu, W., Lin, G., & He, Q. (2024). Enhanced management information disclosure responsibilities and corporate risk-taking: Evidence from the accountability system for errors in China. *International Review of Economics & Finance*, 89, 511–531. DOI: 10.1016/j.iref.2023.10.028

Li, X. (2017). Optimal procurement strategies from suppliers with random yield and all-or-nothing risks. *Annals of Operations Research*, 257(1-2), 167–181. DOI: 10.1007/s10479-015-1923-4

Li, Z., Farmanesh, P., Kirikkaleli, D., & Itani, R. (2022). A comparative analysis of COVID-19 and global financial crises: Evidence from US economy. *Ekonomska Istrazivanja*, 35(1), 2427–2441. DOI: 10.1080/1331677X.2021.1952640

Lomuscio, A.. (2015). Debt Restructuring in Distress: Out-of-Court vs. In-Court Workouts. *Journal of Financial Transformation*, 34(3), 207–242.

Luo, X., & Bhattacharya, C. B. (2006). Corporate social responsibility, customer satisfaction, and market value. *Journal of Marketing*, 70(4), 1–18. DOI: 10.1509/jmkg.70.4.001

MacCrimmon, K. R. (1986). Taking Risks. *The Management of Uncertainty*.

MacCrimmon, K., Wehgur, D., & Stanbury, W. (1986). *Taking Risks: The Management of Uncertainty*.

MacCrimmon, K., & Wehgur, D. (1990). Characteristics of Risk Taking Executives. *Management Science*, 36(4), 422–435. DOI: 10.1287/mnsc.36.4.422

Mahapatra, S., Levental, S., & Narasimhan, R. (2017). Market price uncertainty, risk aversion and procurement's combining contracts and open market sourcing alternatives. *International Journal of Production Economics*, 185(3), 34–51. DOI: 10.1016/j.ijpe.2016.12.023

Maignan, I., Ferrell, O. C., & Ferrell, L. (2005). A stakeholder model for implementing social responsibility in marketing. *European Journal of Marketing*, 39(9/10), 956–977. DOI: 10.1108/03090560510610662

Maignan, I., Ferrell, O. C., & Hult, G. T. M. (1999). Corporate citizenship: Cultural antecedents and business benefits. *Journal of the Academy of Marketing Science*, 27(4), 455–469. DOI: 10.1177/0092070399274005

Malik, S., Roosli, R., Tariq, F., & Yusof, N. (2020). Policy Framework and Institutional Arrangements: Case of Affordable Housing Delivery for Low-Income Groups in Punjab, Pakistan. *Housing Policy Debate*, 30(2), 243–268. DOI: 10.1080/10511482.2019.1681018

Margolis, J. D., & Walsh, J. P. (2003). Misery Loves Companies: Rethinking Social Initiatives by Business. *Administrative Science Quarterly*, 48(2), 268–305. DOI: 10.2307/3556659

Marin, L., Ruiz, S., & Rubio, A. (2009). The role of identity salience in the effects of corporate social responsibility on consumer behavior. *Journal of Business Research*, 84(1), 65–78.

Markowitz, H. (1952). Portfolio selection. *The Journal of Finance*, 7(1), 77–91.

Marquis, C., Toffel, M. W., & Zhou, Y. (2014). Scrutiny, Norms, and Selective Disclosure: A Global Study of Greenwashing. *Organization Science*, 25(2), 483–504. DOI: 10.1287/orsc.2015.1039

Martel, A., Diaby, M., & Boctor, F. (1995). Multiple items procurement under stochastic nonstationary demands. *European Journal of Operational Research*, 87(1), 74–92. DOI: 10.1016/0377-2217(94)00019-9

Mateti, J. K. (2013). R.S and G. Vaudevan, *Resolution of financial distress: A theory of the choice between Chapter 11 and workout. Journal of Financial Stability*, 9(2), 196–209. DOI: 10.1016/j.jfs.2013.03.004

Matzler, K., & Hinterhuber, H. H. (1998). How to make product development projects more successful by integrating Kano's model of customer satisfaction into quality function deployment. *Technovation*, 18(1), 25–38. DOI: 10.1016/S0166-4972(97)00072-2

McGuire, J., Sundgren, A., & Schneeweis, T. (1988). Corporate social responsibility and firm financial performance. *Academy of Management Journal*, 31(4), 854–872. DOI: 10.2307/256342

McGrath, R., & MacMillan, I. (2009). *Discovery driven growth. A break through process to reduce risk and seize opportunity.*

McGrath, R. G., & Nerkar, A. (2004). Real options reasoning and a new look at the R&D investment strategies of pharmaceutical firms. *Strategic Management Journal*, 25(1), 1–21. DOI: 10.1002/smj.358

McKinsey & Company. (2020). How COVID-19 has Pushed Companies over the Technology Tipping Point—and Transformed Business Forever. Retrieved from https://www.mckinsey.com/business-functions/strategy-and-corporate-finance/our-insights/how-covid-19-has-pushed-companies-over-the-technology-tipping-point-and-transformed-business-forever

McWilliams, A., & Siegel, D. (2001). Corporate Social Responsibility: A Theory of the Firm Perspective. *Academy of Management Review*, 26(1), 117–127. https://www.jstor.org/stable/259398. DOI: 10.2307/259398

McWilliams, A., Siegel, D. S., & Wright, P. M. (2006). Corporate social responsibility: Strategic implications. *Journal of Management Studies*, 43(1), 1–18. DOI: 10.1111/j.1467-6486.2006.00580.x

Meckling, W. H., & Jensen, M. C. (1976). *Theory of the Firm.* Managerial Behavior, Agency Costs and Ownership Structure.

Medina-Serrano, R., González, R., Gasco, J., & Llopis, J. (2022). Do risk events increase supply chain uncertainty? A case study. *Ekonomska Istrazivanja*, 35(1), 4658–4676. DOI: 10.1080/1331677X.2021.2016462

Meena, P., Sarmah, S. P., & Sarkar, A. (2011). Sourcing decisions under risks of catastrophic event disruptions. *Transportation Research Part E, Logistics and Transportation Review*, 47(6), 1058–1074. DOI: 10.1016/j.tre.2011.03.003

Mehmood, R., Hunjra, A. I., & Chani, M. I. (2019). The impact of corporate diversification and financial structure on firm performance: Evidence from South Asian countries. *Journal of Risk and Financial Management*, 12(1), 49. DOI: 10.3390/jrfm12010049

Mehmood, R., Khan, M. A., Khan, M. M., & Javed, N. (2023). The influence of board attributes and gender diversity on risk-taking in banking sector. *Journal of Namibian Studies: History Politics Culture*, 35, 4565–4585.

Mentari, S., ... (2019). Effectiveness of the Board of Commissioners Role: Review of Resources Dependence Theory. 3rd International Conference on Accounting, Management and Economics 2018 (ICAME 2018), Atlantis Press.

Messick, S. (1988). Validity. In Linn, R. L. (Ed.), *Educational Measurement* (3rd ed.). Macmillan.

Metaxas, T., & Tsavdaridou, M. (2010). Corporate social responsibility in europe: Denmark, Hungary and Greece. *Journal of Contemporary European Studies*, 18(1), 25–46. DOI: 10.1080/14782801003638679

Meyer, B. H., Prescott, B., & Sheng, X. S. (2022). The impact of the COVID-19 pandemic on business expectations. *International Journal of Forecasting*, 38(2), 529–544. DOI: 10.1016/j.ijforecast.2021.02.009

Miller, K. (2007). Risk and rationality in entrepreneurial processes. *Strategic Entrepreneurship Journal*, 1(1-2), 57–74. DOI: 10.1002/sej.2

Mittal, R. K., Sinha, N., & Singh, A. (2008). An Analysis of Linkage between Economic Value Added and Corporate Social Responsibility. *Management Decision*. 46 (9), 1437-1443 available on line. www.emeraldinsight.com/journals.htm?articleid =1747817 accessed.

Modigliani, F., & Miller, M. H. (1958). The cost of capital, corporation finance and the theory of investment. *The American Economic Review*, 48(3), 261–297.

Modigliani, F., & Miller, M. H. (1958). The cost of capital, corporation finance, and the theory of investment. *The American Economic Review*, 48(3), 261–275.

Moghadam, V. M. (2021). COVID-19 and MENA: Governance, Geopolitics, and Gender. *Gendered Perspectives on International Development*, 1(1), 45–69. DOI: 10.1353/gpi.2021.0002

Mohamed, M. B., & Sawandi, N. B. (2007). Corporate Social Responsibility (CSR) activities in mobile telecommunication industry: case study of Malaysia. *Paper presented at theEuropean Critical Accounting Conference*

Mohamed, I. M. A., & Salah, W. (2016). Investigating corporate social responsibility disclosure by banks from institutional theory perspective. *Journal of Administrative and Business Studies*, 2(6), 280–293.

Mohr, L., Webb, D., & Harris, K. (2001). Do consumers expect companies to be socially responsible? The impact of corporate social responsibility on buying behavior. *The Journal of Consumer Affairs*, 35(1), 45–72. DOI: 10.1111/j.1745-6606.2001.tb00102.x

Mooradian, R. M. (1994). The effect of bankruptcy protection on investment: Chapter 11 as a screening device. *The Journal of Finance*, 49(4), 1403–1430. DOI: 10.1111/j.1540-6261.1994.tb02459.x

Morais-Storz, M., Stoud Platou, R., & Berild Norheim, K. (2018). Innovation and metamorphosis towards strategic resilience. *International Journal of Entrepreneurial Behaviour & Research*, 27(7), 1181–1199. DOI: 10.1108/IJEBR-11-2016-0369

Moussa, F. B. (2019). The influence of internal corporate governance on bank credit risk: An empirical analysis for Tunisia. *Global Business Review*, 20(3), 640–667. DOI: 10.1177/0972150919837078

Mumtaz, M., & Pirzada, S. S. (2014). Impact of corporate social responsibility on corporate financial performance. *Research on Humanities and Social Sciences*, 4(14), 7–15.

Mutamimah, M., Tholib, M., & Robiyanto, R. (2021). Corporate governance, credit risk, and financial literacy for small medium enterprise in Indonesia. *Business: Theory and Practice*, 22(2), 406–413. DOI: 10.3846/btp.2021.13063

Myers, S. C. (1984). Finance theory and financial strategy. *Interfaces*, 14(1), 126–137. DOI: 10.1287/inte.14.1.126

Naumann, E. (1995). *Customer satisfaction measurement and management: Using the voice of the customer*. Thomson Executive Press.

Negri, E., Fumagalli, L., & Macchi, M. (2017). A review of the roles of digital twin in CPS-based production systems. *Procedia Manufacturing*, 11, 939–948. DOI: 10.1016/j.promfg.2017.07.198

Nelson, E. C., Rust, R. T., Zahorik, A., Rose, R. L., Batalden, P., & Siemanski, B. A. (1992). Do Patient Perceptions of Quality Relate to Hospital Financial Performance? [December.]. *Journal of Health Care Marketing*, •••, 6–13.

Ngo, H. T., & Duong, H. N. (2024). Covid-19 pandemic and firm performance: Evidence on industry differentials and impacting channels. *International Journal of Social Economics*, 51(4), 569–583. DOI: 10.1108/IJSE-02-2023-0072

Nguyen, A. H., Pham, C. D., Doan, N. T., Ta, T. T., Nguyen, H. T., & Truong, T. V. (2021). The effect of dividend payment on firm's financial performance: An empirical study of Vietnam. *Journal of Risk and Financial Management*, 14(8), 353. DOI: 10.3390/jrfm14080353

Nicholson, N. (2005). Personality anddomain-specific risk taking. *Journal of Risk Research*, 157-176. Nobre, L., & Grable, J. (20155). The role of risk profiles and risk tolerance in shaping client investment decisions. *Journal of Financial Service Professionals*, 69(3), 18–21.

Nissim, D., & Ziv, A. (2001). Dividend changes and future profitability. *The Journal of Finance*, 56(6), 2111–2133. DOI: 10.1111/0022-1082.00400

O'Brien, J., & Folta, T. (2009). Sunk costs, uncertainty and market exit: A real options perspective. *Industrial and Corporate Change*, 18(5), 807–833. DOI: 10.1093/icc/dtp014

Öberseder, M., Schlegelmilch, B. B., Murphy, P. E., & Gruber, V. (2014). Consumers' perceptions of corporate social responsibility: Scale development and validation. *Journal of Business Ethics*, 124(1), 101–115. DOI: 10.1007/s10551-013-1787-y

OECD. (2019), "Artificial Intelligence in Society". *OECD Publishing*, Paris, 20. https://www.oecd-ilibrary.org/science-and-technology/artificial-intelligence-in-society_eedfee77-en

Oecd, O. (2004). The OECD principles of corporate governance. *Contaduría y Administración*, •••, 216.

Orlitzky, M. (2013). Corporate social responsibility, noise, and stock market volatility. *The Academy of Management Perspectives*, 27(3), 238–254. DOI: 10.5465/amp.2012.0097

Otero, L., Alaraj, R., & Lado-Sestayo, R. (2020). How corporate governance and ownership affect banks' risk-taking in the MENA countries? *European Journal of Management and Business Economics*, 29(2), 182–198. DOI: 10.1108/EJMBE-01-2019-0010

Özdamar, K. (2017). *Olcek ve test gelistirme yapisal esitlik modellemesi IBM SPSS, IBM SPSS AMOS ve MINTAB uygulamali* [Scale and test development Structural equation modeling IBM SPSS, IBM SPSS AMOS and MINTAB applied]. Nisan Kitabevi.

Pagell, M., & Shevchenko, A. (2014). Why research in sustainable supply chain management should have no future. *The Journal of Supply Chain Management*, 50(1), 44–55. DOI: 10.1111/jscm.12037

Pagkalou, F. I., Galanos, C. L., & Thalassinos, E. I. (2024). Exploring the Relationship between Corporate Governance, Corporate Social Responsibility and Financial and Non-Financial Reporting: A Study of Large Companies in Greece. *Journal of Risk and Financial Management*, 17(3), 97. DOI: 10.3390/jrfm17030097

Pakseresht, A. (2010). Brand equity and corporate responsibility: A review of brand valuation methods. https://www.essays.se/essay/9e20739689/ (accessed 23 January 2011).

Panda, B. and N. M. Leepsa (2017). "Agency theory: Review of theory and evidence on problems and perspectives." Indian journal of corporate governance **10**(1): 74-95.

Patagonia. (n.d.). Our Footprint. Retrieved from https://www.patagonia.com/our-footprint.html

Paul, K. (2024). Why corporate social responsibility should be recognized as an integral stream of international corporate governance. *Green Finance*, 6(2), 348–362. DOI: 10.3934/GF.2024013

Penny, J. (n.d.). Insecure Spaces, Precarious Geographies: Biopolitics, Security and the Production of Space In Jerusalem and Beyond. www.ucl.ac.uk

Pérez, A., Salmones, M. M. G., & Bosque, I. R. (2013a). The effect of corporate associations on consumer behaviour. *European Journal of Marketing*, 47(1/2), 218–238. DOI: 10.1108/03090561311285529

Pfeffer, J., & Salancik, G. (2015). External control of organizations—Resource dependence perspective. Organizational behavior 2, Routledge: 355-370.

Phillips, W., Roehrich, J. K., & Kapletia, D. (2023). Responding to information asymmetry in crisis situations: Innovation in the time of the COVID-19 pandemic. *Public Management Review*, 25(1), 175–198. DOI: 10.1080/14719037.2021.1960737

Piercy, N. F., & Lane, N. (2009). Corporate social responsibility: Impacts on strategic marketing and customer value. *The Marketing Review*, 9(4), 335–360. DOI: 10.1362/146934709X479917

Pokorny, G. (1995) Building brand equity and customer loyalty. Retrieved January 23, 2019, from http://findarticles.com/p/articles/mi_qa3650/is_199505/ai_n8728762/pg_3/?tag=content;col1

Poon, L. L., & Peiris, M. (2020). Emergence of a novel human coronavirus threatening human health. *Nature Medicine*, 26(3), 317–319. DOI: 10.1038/s41591-020-0796-5

Porter, M. E., & Kramer, M. R. (2011). Creating Shared Value. *Harvard Business Review*, 89(1/2), 62–77.

Post, C., Rahman, N., & Rubow, E. (2011). Green governance: Boards of directors' composition and environmental corporate social responsibility‖. *Business & Society*, 50(1), 189–223. DOI: 10.1177/0007650310394642

Rahman, M. J., Zhu, H., & Chen, S. (2023). Does CSR reduce financial distress? Moderating effect of firm characteristics, auditor characteristics, and covid-19. *International Journal of Accounting \&. Information & Management*, 31(5), 756–784.

Ram Singh and Hitesh kumar Thakkar (2021). Settlements and Resolutions Under the Insolvency and Bankruptcy Code: Assessing the Impact of Covid-19. Journal of Business Ethics, 197(3), 607-626.

Raman, M., Lim, W., & Nair, S. (2012). The impact of corporate social responsibility on consumer loyalty. *Kajian Malaysia: Journal of Malaysian Studies, 30*(2).

Rampini, A., Sufi, A., & Viswanathan, S. (2014). Dynamic risk managemen. *Journal of Financial Economics*, 111(2), 271–296. DOI: 10.1016/j.jfineco.2013.10.003

Ram, S., & Sheth, J. (1989). Consumer resistance to innovations: The Market problem and its solutions. *Journal of Consumer Marketing*, 6(2), 5–14. DOI: 10.1108/EUM0000000002542

Rashid, M. M., & Kabir, M. R. (2024). Corporate governance and corporate sustainability performance: The mediating role of CSR expenditure. *Asian Review of Accounting*. Advance online publication. DOI: 10.1108/ARA-12-2023-0350

Renieris, E. M., Kiron, D., & Mills, S. (2022). "Should organizations link responsible AI and corporate social responsibility? It's Complicated". *MIT Sloan*https://sloanreview.mit.edu/article/should-organizations-link-responsible-ai-and-corporate-social-responsibility-its-complicated/

Renn, O., & Benighaus, C. (2013). Perception of technological risk: Insights from research and lessons for risk communication and management. *Journal of Risk Research*, 16(3-4), 293–313. DOI: 10.1080/13669877.2012.729522

Rinaldi, E. E. (2016). The Relationship between Financial Education and Society: A Sociological Perspective Author information. *Italian Journal of Sociology of Education*, 8(3), 126–148. DOI: 10.14658/pupj-ijse

Ringle, C. M, Wende, S., & Becker, J., M., (Producer) (2015). SmartPLS 3. Retrieved from http://www.smartpls.com

Rinta-Kahila, T., Someh, I., Gillespie, N., Indulska, M., & Gregor, S. (2022). Algorithmic decision-making and system destructiveness: A case of automatic debt recovery. *European Journal of Information Systems*, 31(3), 313–338. DOI: 10.1080/0960085X.2021.1960905

Ritchie, B., & Marshall, D. (1993). Business. *Risk Management*.

Roberta, C., & Christopher, P. (2014). Achieving supply chain resilience: The role of procurement. *Supply Chain Management*, 19(5/6), 19. DOI: 10.1108/SCM-09-2013-0346

Rodrıguez de las Heras Ballell, T. (2019). "Legal Challenges of Artificial Intelligence: Modeling the Disruptive Features of Emerging Technologies and Assessing their possible Legal Impact" 24. *University of Florida Law Review*, 302, 314.

Roeser, S. (2010). Intuitions, emotions and gut reactions in decisions about risks: Towards a different interpretation of "neuroethics. *Journal of Risk Research*, 13(2), 175–190. DOI: 10.1080/13669870903126275

Roger Strand, D. O. (2009). Risk and Uncertainty as a Research Ethics Challenge. Norway: The National Committee for Research Ethics in Science and Technology (NENT).

Rowe, W. (1977). *Anatomy of Risk*.

Ruiz-Torres, A., & Mahmoodi, F. (2007). The optimal number of suppliers considering the costs of individual supplier failures. *Omega*, 35(1), 104–115. DOI: 10.1016/j.omega.2005.04.005

Saam, N. J. (2007). Asymmetry in information versus asymmetry in power: Implicit assumptions of agency theory? *Journal of Socio-Economics*, 36(6), 825–840. DOI: 10.1016/j.socec.2007.01.018

Salmones, M. M. G., Crespo, A. H., & del Bosque, I. R. (2005). Influence of corporate social Responsibility on loyalty and valuation of services. *Journal of Business Ethics*, 61(4), 369–385. DOI: 10.1007/s10551-005-5841-2

Sambala, G. L. (2015). *The role of company's corporate social responsibility in community development: The case of Morogoro Municipality* (Doctoral dissertation, Mzumbe University).

Sareen, S. (2020). COVID-19 and Pakistan: The Economic Fallout.

Sarkis, J.. (2020). Sustainable supply chain management and the transition towards a circular economy: Evidence and some applications. *Omega*.

Sauer, B. (2022). *Identities Global Studies in Culture and Power ISSN: (Print) (Online) Journal homepage:*https://www.tandfonline.com/loi/gide20*Radical right populist debates on female Muslim body-coverings in Austria. Between biopolitics and necropolitics Radical right populist debates on female Muslim body-coverings in Austria. Between biopolitics and necropolitics.* DOI: 10.1080/1070289X.2022.2071515

Schein, E. (1992). *Organizational Culture and Leadership*.

Scholtens, B. (2009). Corporate social responsibility in the international banking industry. *Journal of Business Ethics*, 86(2), 159–175. DOI: 10.1007/s10551-008-9841-x

Shackle, G. (1966). Policy, poetry and success. *Economic Journal (London)*, 76(304), 755–767. DOI: 10.2307/2229081

Shapira, Z. (1995). Risk taking: a managerial perspective.

Sheffi, Y. (2021). *The Power of Resilience: How the Best Companies Manage the Unexpected*. MIT Press.

Shevlin, P., & Skeel, D. (2005). Out-of-Court Workouts, Formal Bankruptcy, and Value Maximization. *The American Bankruptcy Law Journal*, 79(3), 489–545.

Shibata, I. (2021). The distributional impact of recessions: The global financial crisis and the COVID-19 pandemic recession. *Journal of Economics and Business*, 115, 105971. Advance online publication. DOI: 10.1016/j.jeconbus.2020.105971

Shi, Y., Wu, F., Chu, L. K., Sculli, D., & Xu, Y. H. (2011). A portfolio approach to managing procurement risk using multi-stage stochastic programming. *The Journal of the Operational Research Society*, 62(11), 1958–1970. DOI: 10.1057/jors.2010.149

Shleifer, A., & Vishny, R. W. (1992). Liquidation values and debt capacity: A market equilibrium approach. *The Journal of Finance*, 47(4), 1343–1366. DOI: 10.1111/j.1540-6261.1992.tb04661.x

Shleifer, A., & Vishny, R. W. (1997). A survey of corporate governance. *The Journal of Finance*, 52(2), 737–783. DOI: 10.1111/j.1540-6261.1997.tb04820.x

Silbermayr, L., & Minner, S. (2014). A multiple sourcing inventory model under disruption risk. *International Journal of Production Economics*, 149(3), 37–46. DOI: 10.1016/j.ijpe.2013.03.025

Simon, H. (1955). A behavioral model of rational choice. *The Quarterly Journal of Economics*, 69(1), 99–118. DOI: 10.2307/1884852

Singleton, K. (2013). Investor flows and the 2008 boom/bust in oil prices. *Management Science*, 60(2), 300–318. DOI: 10.1287/mnsc.2013.1756

Sitkin, S., & Wiengart, L. (1995). Determinants of risky decision-making behavior: A test of the mediating role of risk perceptions and propensity. *Academy of Management Journal*, 38(6), 1573–1592. DOI: 10.2307/256844

Slovic, P., Finucane, M., Peters, E., & Mecregor, D. (2004). Risk as analysis and risk as feelings: Some thoughts about affect, reason, risk, and rationality. *Risk Analysis*, 24(2), 311–322. DOI: 10.1111/j.0272-4332.2004.00433.x

Sodhi, M. S., & Tang, C. S. (2012). *Managing supply chain risk*. Springer Science & Business Media.

Soh, C.. (2014). Corporate social responsibility (CSR) implementation in South Korea: Lessons from American and British CSR policies. *Journal of International and Area Studies*, •••, 99–118.

Solomon, R., & Hansen, K. (1985). *It's good business*. Atheneum.

Srhoj, S., Kovač, D., Shapiro, J. N., & Filer, R. K. (2023). The Impact of Delay: Evidence from Formal Out-of-Court Restructuring. *Journal of Corporate Finance*, 78, 102626. DOI: 10.1016/j.jcorpfin.2022.102319

Srivastava, R. K., Shervani, T. A., & Fahey, L. (1998). Market-based assets and shareholder value: A framework for analysis. *Journal of Marketing*, 62(1), 2–18. DOI: 10.1177/002224299806200102

Stanaland, A. J. S., Lwin, M. O., & Murphy, P. E. (2011). Consumer perceptions of the antecedents and consequences of corporate social responsibility. *Journal of Business Ethics*, 102(1), 47–55. DOI: 10.1007/s10551-011-0904-z

Standing, G. (2019). Meet the precariat, the new global class fuelling the rise of populism | World Economic Forum. Youth Perspectives. https://www.weforum.org/agenda/2016/11/precariat-global-class-rise-of-populism/

Stanwick, P. A., & Stanwick, S. D. (1998). The relationship between corporate social performance and organizational size, financial performance, and environmental performance: An empirical examination. *Journal of Business Ethics*, 17(2), 195–204. DOI: 10.1023/A:1005784421547

Staw, B. M. (1981). The escalation of commitment to a course of action. *Academy of Management Review*, 6(4), 577–587. DOI: 10.2307/257636

Stobierski, T. (2021), *Online Harvard Business School*, https://online.hbs.edu/blog/post/types-of-corporate-social-responsibility

Story, J., & Neves, P. (2015). When corporate social responsibility (CSR) increases performance: Exploring the role of intrinsic and extrinsic CSR attribution. *Business Ethics (Oxford, England)*, 24(2), 111–124. DOI: 10.1111/beer.12084

Suchman, M. C. (1995). Managing Legitimacy: Strategic and Institutional Approaches. *Academy of Management Journal*, 20(3), 571–610.

Sureshchandar, G. S., Rajendran, C., & Anantharaman, R. N. (2002). The relationship between service quality and customer satisfaction—A factor specific approach. *Journal of Services Marketing*, 16(4), 363–379. DOI: 10.1108/08876040210433248

Swaen, V., & Chumpitaz, R. C. (2008). Impact of Corporate social responsibility on consumer trust. *Recherche et Applications en Marketing*, 23(4), 7–33. DOI: 10.1177/076737010802300401

Sydow, J. (2009). Academy of Management Review. *Organizational path dependence: Opening the black box, 34*(4), 689–709.

Talluri, S., Narasimhan, R., & Chung, W. (2010). Manufacturer cooperation in supplier development under risk. *European Journal of Operational Research*, 207(1), 165–173. DOI: 10.1016/j.ejor.2010.03.041

Tang, C. (2006). Perspectives in supply chain risk managemen. *International Journal of Production Economics*, 103(2), 451–488. DOI: 10.1016/j.ijpe.2005.12.006

Tang, C. S., & Musa, S. N. (2011). Identifying risk issues and research advancements in supply chain risk management. *International Journal of Production Economics*, 133(1), 25–34. DOI: 10.1016/j.ijpe.2010.06.013

Tang, D. Y., & Zhang, Y. (2020). Do shareholders benefit from green bonds? *Journal of Corporate Finance*, 61, 101427. DOI: 10.1016/j.jcorpfin.2018.12.001

Tashjian, E., Lease, R. C., & McConnell, J. J. (1996). Prepacks: An empirical analysis of Pre-packaged bankruptcies. *Journal of Financial Economics*, 40(1), 135–162. DOI: 10.1016/0304-405X(95)00837-5

Tayachi, T., Hunjra, A. I., Jones, K., Mehmood, R., & Al-Faryan, M. A. S. (2023). How does ownership structure affect the financing and dividend decisions of firm? *Journal of Financial Reporting and Accounting*, 21(3), 729–746. DOI: 10.1108/JFRA-09-2021-0291

Toyota. (n.d.). Toyota Global Vision. Retrieved from https://global.toyota/en/vision

Tricker, R. L. "Part 1—The Concept of Corporate Governance."

Tricker, R. I. (2015). *Corporate governance: Principles, policies, and practices.* Oxford University Press.

Tripsas, B., & Gavetti, G. (2000). Capabilities, condition and inertia: Evidence from digital imaging. *Strategic Management Journal*, 21(10/11), 1147–1161. DOI: 10.1002/1097-0266(200010/11)21:10/11<1147::AID-SMJ128>3.0.CO;2-R

Turban, E. (2008). A Managerial Perspective. *Electronic Commerece 2008*.

Unilever. (n.d.). Sustainable Living. Retrieved from https://www.unilever.com/sustainable-living/

Usakli, A., & Baloglu, S. (2011). Brand personality of tourist destinations: An application of self-congruity theory. *Tourism Management*, 32(1), 114–127. DOI: 10.1016/j.tourman.2010.06.006

Vaia, G., Bisogno, M., & Tommasetti, A. (2017). Investigating the Relationship between the Social and Economic-financial Performance. *Applied Finance and Accounting*, 3(1), 55. DOI: 10.11114/afa.v3i1.2126

Valentine, S., & Godkin, L. (2016). Ethics policies, perceived social responsibility, and positive work attitude. *Irish Journal of Management*, 35(2), 114–128. DOI: 10.1515/ijm-2016-0013

Vallejo-Martín, M., Canto, J. M., San Martín García, J. E., & Novas, F. P. (2020). Prejudice and feeling of threat towards Syrian refugees: The moderating effects of precarious employment and perceived low outgroup morality. *International Journal of Environmental Research and Public Health*, 17(17), 1–12. DOI: 10.3390/ijerph17176411

Vătavu, S. (2015). The impact of capital structure on financial performance in Romanian listed companies. *Procedia Economics and Finance*, 32, 1314–1322. DOI: 10.1016/S2212-5671(15)01508-7

Vintilă Georgeta and Elena Alexandra Nenu (2016) " Liquidity and Profitability Analysis on the Romanian Listed Companies", *Journal of Eastern Europe Research in Business & Economics*, Vol. 2016 (2016).

Vlachos, P. A. (2012). Corporate social performance and consumer- retailer emotional attachment: The moderating role of individual traits. *European Journal of Marketing*, 46(11/12), 1559–1580. DOI: 10.1108/03090561211259989

Wacquant, L. (1999). Urban Marginality in the Coming Millennium. In Source. *Urban Studies (Edinburgh, Scotland)*, 36(10), 1639–1647. DOI: 10.1080/0042098992746

Wagner, S., Bode, C., & Koziol, P. (2009). Supplier default dependencies: Empirical evidence from theautomotiveindustry. *European Journal of Operational Research*, 199(1), 150–161. DOI: 10.1016/j.ejor.2008.11.012

Wagner-Tsukamoto, S. (2019). In search of ethics: From Carroll to integrative CSR economics. *Social Responsibility Journal*, 15(4), 469–491. DOI: 10.1108/SRJ-09-2017-0188

Wahjudi, E. (2020). Factors affecting dividend policy in manufacturing companies in Indonesia Stock Exchange. *Journal of Management Development*, 39(1), 4–17. DOI: 10.1108/JMD-07-2018-0211

Walker, W., Harremoës, P., Rotmans, J., van der Sluijs, J. P., van Asselt, M. B. A., Janssen, P., & Krayer von Krauss, M. P. (2003). Defining Uncertainty: A Conceptual Basis for Uncertainty Management Model base Decision Support. *Integrated Assessment*, 4(1), 5–17. DOI: 10.1076/iaij.4.1.5.16466

Walk, J. G., & Shapira, Z. (1987). Managerial perspectives on risk and risk taking. *Management Science*, 33(11), 1404–1418. DOI: 10.1287/mnsc.33.11.1404

Wall, M., Otis Campbell, M., & Janbek, D. (2017). Syrian refugees and information precarity. *New Media & Society*, 19(2), 240–254. DOI: 10.1177/1461444815591967

Wang, C., Pan, R., Wan, X., Tan, Y., Xu, L., Ho, C. S., & Ho, R. C. (2020a). Immediate psychological responses and associated factors during the initial stage of the 2019 coronavirus disease (COVID-19) epidemic among the general population in China. *International Journal of Environmental Research and Public Health*, 17(5), 1729. DOI: 10.3390/ijerph17051729

Wang, J.. (2016). Financial Restructuring, Operational Turnaround, and Firm Performance: Evidence from China. *Strategic Management Journal*, 37(12), 2507–2532.

Warner, J. B. (1977). Bankruptcy costs: Some evidence. *The Journal of Finance*, 32(2), 337–347. DOI: 10.2307/2326766

Warner, J. T., & Tortellini, R. E. (1997). Financial reconstructing under different legal systems: Evidence from out-of-court restructures. *The Review of Economics and Statistics*, 79(4), 612–625.

Weber, E., Blais, A.-R., & Betz, N. E. (2002). A domain-specific risk-attitude scale: Measuring risk perceptions and risk behaviors. *Journal of Behavioral Decision Making*, 15(4), 263–290. DOI: 10.1002/bdm.414

Weber, M. (1947). The theory of economic and social organization. In *Trans. AM Henderson and Talcott Parsons*. Oxford University Press.

Weill, L. (2008). Leverage and corporate performance: Does institutional environment matter? *Small Business Economics*, 30(3), 251–265. DOI: 10.1007/s11187-006-9045-7

Welford, R. (Ed.). (2005). *Corporate environmental reporting and disclosure in China*. CSR Asia.

Westin, L., & Parmler, J. (2020). Inclusion of CSR in the extended performance satisfaction index–new development. *Total Quality Management & Business Excellence*, •••, 1–12. DOI: 10.1080/14783363.2020.1856651

White, M. J. (1994). Corporate bankruptcy as a filtering device: Chapter 11 reorganizations and out-of-court debt restructurings. *Journal of Law Economics and Organization*, 10(2), 268–295.

Whittlestone, J., Nyrup, R., Alexandrova, A., Alexandrova, A., Dihal, K., & Cave, S. (2019). "Ethical and societal implications of algorithms, data, and artificial intelligence: A roadmap for research" *London* [Ethical-and-Societal-Implications-of-Data-and-AI-report-Nuffield-Foundat.pdf] [nuffieldfoundation.org]. *Nuffield Foundation*, 1, 59.

William, T. M. (1994). Using a risk register to integrate risk management in project definition. *International Journal of Project Management*, 12(1), 17–22. DOI: 10.1016/0263-7863(94)90005-1

WIPO "Technology Trends 2019 Artificial Intelligence", 39.

Wiseman, R., & Gomez-Mejia, L. R. (1998). A behavioral agency model of managerial risk taking. *Academy of Management Review*, 23(1), 133–153. DOI: 10.2307/259103

Wooster, R. B., Blanco, L., & Sawyer, W. C. (2016). Equity commitment under uncertainty: A hierarchical model of real option entry mode choices. *International Business Review*, 25(1), 382–394. DOI: 10.1016/j.ibusrev.2015.07.006

Xie, F. (2009). Managerial flexibility, uncertainty, and corporate investment. *The real options effect.International Review of Economics & Finance*, 18(4), 643–655. DOI: 10.1016/j.iref.2008.11.001

Xuezhou, W., Hussain, R. Y., Hussain, H., Saad, M., & Qalati, S. A. (2022). Analyzing the impact of board vigilance on financial distress through the intervention of leverage structure and interaction of asset tangibility in the non-financial sector of Pakistan. *International Journal of Financial Engineering*, 9(02), 2150004. DOI: 10.1142/S2424786321500043

Xuezhou, W., Hussain, R. Y., Salameh, A. A., Hussain, H., Khan, A. B., & Fareed, M. (2022). Does firm growth impede or expedite insolvency risk? A mediated moderation model of leverage maturity and potential fixed collaterals. *Frontiers in Environmental Science*, 10, 841380. DOI: 10.3389/fenvs.2022.841380

Yang, A. S., & Baasandorj, S. (2017). Exploring CSR and financial performance of full-service and low-cost air carriers. *Finance Research Letters*, 23, 291–299. DOI: 10.1016/j.frl.2017.05.005

Yano, C., & Lee, H. (1995). Lot sizing with random yields: A review. *Operations Research*, 43(2), 311–334. DOI: 10.1287/opre.43.2.311

Yeoh, P. (2019). "Artificial Intelligence: Accelerator or Panacea for Financial Crime?" 26 (2). *Journal of Financial Crime*, 634(2), 646. DOI: 10.1108/JFC-08-2018-0077

Yoe, C. E. (2019). *Principles of risk analysis: decision making under uncertainty*. Taylor & Francis Group, LLC. DOI: 10.1201/9780429021121

Yuniarti Hidayah Suyoso Putra, Sri Yati, Nanik Wahyuni, (2015) "Acting Green: Theoretical Framework on Corporate Social Responsibility". *Australian Journal of Basic and Applied Sciences*, 9(7) A, pp. 248-250.

Yusif, S., & Hafeez-Baig, A. (2024). Impact of stakeholder engagement strategies on managerial cognitive decision-making: The context of CSP and CSR. *Social Responsibility Journal*, 20(6), 1101–1121. DOI: 10.1108/SRJ-05-2023-0295

Zarghami, S. A. (2024). 'There are also unknown unknowns': A resilience-informed approach for forecasting and monitoring management reserve in projects. *International Journal of Production Research*, 1–21. Advance online publication. DOI: 10.1080/00207543.2024.2359044

Zhang, Y., & Kajikawa, Y. (2021). Editorial: Advanced Analytics and Decision Making for Research Policy and Strategic Management. In *Frontiers in Research Metrics and Analytics* (Vol. 6). Frontiers Media SA. DOI: 10.3389/frma.2021.778622

Zsidisin, G. (2003). Managerial perceptions of supply risk. *The Journal of Supply Chain Management*, 39(4), 14–26. DOI: 10.1111/j.1745-493X.2003.tb00146.x

Zsidisin, G. A., Panelli, A., & Upton, R. (2000). Purchasing organization involvement in risk assessments, contingency plans, and risk management: An exploratory study. *Supply Chain Management*, 5(4), 187–198. DOI: 10.1108/13598540010347307

About the Contributors

Rana Yassir Hussain did his PhD from Jiangsu University China. Currently, he is serving as an assistant professor at University of Education Lahore, Pakistan. He possess a vast research and teaching experience of almost seventeen years to graduate and post graduate level students. Till now he has published 58 articles and book chapters in many of the internationally acknowledged journals. He is also serving as member editorial board of couple of journals.

Ali Qalati is a well known researcher with over 70 publications till date. Currently, he is serving as associate professor at Liaocheng University of China. He is serving as part of editorial team in various web of science and scopus indexed journals. He also handle various special issues of very reputed publishers including sage, springer, MDPI and frontiers.

Haroon Hussain is serving as professor at Malik Firoze Khan Noon Business School, University of Sargodha. He has very vast research as well as teaching experience of over 15 years. He completed his doctorate from University Utara Malaysia. He is well versed with the corporate governance theory and practice. His competence as a researcher in risk mitigation of both financial and non-financial firms exemplary.

***

Yasir Aleem has done Phd from UUM Malaysia and LL.M form University of Sargodha, Sargodha, Pakistan. Before That he completed LL.B(Hons) from International Islamic University, Islamabad, Pakistan.

Mohsin Altaf is professionally seasoned with more than 14 years of expertise of teaching, research and managerial roles. He is serving as Lecturer Global Banking School with the affiliation of Canterbury Christ Church University, UK.

Saifullah Hassan is a distinguished legal scholar, educator, and a researcher, currently serving as a Lecturer in Law at Sargodha University. He holds a Gold Medal in LL.M International Trade Law from International Islamic University, Islamabad, and has a strong academic background in law. His research expertise includes commercial law, corporate law, international business law, and intellectual property law, with publications in HEC-recognized journals.

Hammad Hassan Mirza has been a member of the University of Sargodha's faculty, contributing significantly to the academic community. He is an academic professional with a rich and extensive career spanning nearly two decades. Dr. Mirza earned his Doctor of Philosophy (PhD) in Management Sciences from COMSATS University Islamabad in 2015. Currently, Dr. Mirza holds the position of Professor of Finance at Malik Firoz Khan Noon Business School. In this role, he imparts his extensive knowledge and expertise to the next generation of business graduates, shaping the future of the financial world. Dr. Mirza's influence extends beyond the classroom. He is the Editor of the HEC Recognized Journal titled "Advances in Business and Commerce (ABC)," underscoring his commitment to the advancement of business and commerce through scholarly research and publication.

Saqib Muneer is teaching in University of Ha'il. He has diversify research experience in field of finance and economics.

Naveed Mushtaq is an Associate Professor of Management at Malik Firoz Khan Noon Business School, University of Sargodha, Pakistan. He has done Ph.D. in Operation Management From the University of Sains, Malaysia. Before that, he completed MBA in Business Management From Texas A&M Commerce, USA. He also holds a degree in Industrial Engineering from, EMU, Turkey, TRNC. Previously he served as Assistant Manager MIS at CSBIL.

Muhammad Bilal Mustafa is working in Birmingham City University as Lecturer and perusing PhD. He published many research papers in well reputed research journals.

Geoffrey Norman Tumwine is my name. I was born and raised in rural area in Uganda where families had strong ties, and each viewed the other as a family member, unlike in urban areas where families existed in isolation. This shocked me when I first arrived . I have remained social despite my location. Educationally, I hold BSC (Maths/Economics) and MA economics from Makerere university . PhD in economics was studied at the university of Dar es Salaam, Tanzania. I have worked in educational institutions since I graduated and have had enjoyable experiences in education and research.

Index

A

Accountability 13, 15, 23, 99, 104, 105, 106, 109, 110, 111, 119, 127, 133, 134, 138, 139, 144, 146, 148, 149, 216, 218
Agency Theory 98, 131, 132, 134, 135, 136, 137, 143, 150, 205, 218
Auditors 105, 106, 107, 108, 109, 110, 111, 112

B

banks 5, 51, 63, 81, 86, 94, 143, 150, 205, 215, 216, 217, 218, 219, 222, 223, 224, 225, 229, 230
board meetings 215, 220, 222
Business Development 120, 177, 179, 180, 189, 190, 192, 195
Butler 85, 227, 231, 232, 236, 237

C

Capital Structure 171, 201, 202, 203, 204, 205, 206, 207, 208, 210, 211, 212, 224
CEO duality 215, 219, 220, 222
Corporate governance 91, 92, 98, 100, 113, 122, 131, 132, 133, 134, 138, 139, 144, 145, 146, 147, 148, 149, 150, 151, 211, 215, 216, 217, 218, 219, 221, 222, 223, 224, 225
Corporate Social Responsibility 20, 22, 31, 32, 33, 34, 35, 36, 42, 43, 44, 45, 46, 47, 48, 49, 50, 51, 52, 53, 54, 55, 56, 57, 58, 59, 99, 100, 102, 104, 105, 106, 107, 108, 109, 110, 111, 112, 113, 115, 118, 119, 121, 127, 128, 129, 131, 132, 138, 139, 140, 141, 144, 145, 146, 147, 148, 149, 150, 151, 224
COVID-19 2, 4, 7, 28, 52, 88, 114, 198, 199, 201, 202, 206, 208, 210, 211, 212, 218, 223, 224, 234, 237, 238, 239, 240, 241, 242, 243, 244, 245, 246, 249, 250, 251, 252
credit risk 7, 159, 215, 216, 217, 218, 219, 220, 221, 222, 224, 225
CSR 22, 31, 32, 33, 34, 35, 36, 37, 38, 42, 43, 44, 45, 46, 47, 48, 49, 50, 51, 53, 54, 55, 57, 59, 60, 100, 103, 105, 106, 107, 108, 109, 110, 111, 112, 113, 114, 115, 116, 118, 119, 120, 121, 122, 123, 124, 125, 126, 128, 131, 132, 138, 139, 140, 141, 142, 143, 144, 145, 146, 147, 148, 149, 150, 151
Customer Satisfaction 32, 33, 34, 35, 36, 37, 38, 42, 43, 44, 45, 46, 47, 48, 49, 50, 51, 52, 53, 54, 55, 56, 57, 59

D

Decision Making 27, 34, 92, 98, 131, 144, 154, 156, 158, 160, 164, 166, 170, 175, 178, 180, 182, 183, 186, 189, 192, 193, 194, 196, 197, 198, 199, 222
Disclosure and Transparency 91, 98
Disclosure Regulations 97
Dividend Policy 201, 202, 203, 205, 206, 207, 208, 210, 212

E

Ethical Practices 23, 105, 109, 146

F

Female Governance 239, 240, 241, 242, 244, 245, 246
Finance 1, 2, 11, 12, 13, 14, 15, 16, 19, 20, 24, 25, 27, 28, 29, 31, 40, 41, 55, 60, 84, 85, 86, 87, 88, 89, 100, 104, 113, 134, 143, 148, 150, 151, 156, 157, 160, 167, 168, 169, 170, 172, 173, 175, 201, 202, 203, 210, 211, 212, 223, 224, 227, 228, 229, 230, 231, 232, 233, 234, 235, 236, 238
financial decision making 131, 144
Financial Policies 201, 202, 208
Financial Risk Management 1
Fixed Effect 203, 207, 208

G

gender diversity 215, 219, 220, 222, 225
Ghana 31, 32, 33, 34, 38, 49, 50, 204, 205, 210
GMM 203, 207, 208, 215, 221, 223

I

IBC 61, 62, 63, 64, 65, 66, 69, 70, 71, 73
Information Asymmetry 68, 96, 97, 98, 99, 199
Insolvency 55, 62, 63, 65, 66, 69, 72, 73, 88, 202, 211, 213, 224

M

managerial Economics 153, 177, 178, 179, 180, 181, 182, 184, 186, 187, 188, 189, 191, 192, 193, 195, 196, 197
Manufacturing Sector 203
Mediation 45, 46, 47, 48, 54

N

NCLT 65, 66, 71
non-financial sector 60, 202, 225

O

Organization 2, 25, 28, 32, 33, 34, 35, 37, 45, 47, 48, 49, 84, 89, 92, 93, 94, 95, 98, 99, 100, 110, 111, 122, 133, 136, 137, 138, 142, 143, 145, 151, 155, 157, 160, 163, 166, 167, 175, 180, 181, 182, 183, 184, 186, 190, 192, 193, 194, 195, 196
Organizational Performance 19, 31, 32, 33, 34, 35, 36, 37, 38, 42, 44, 45, 46, 47, 48, 49, 50, 53, 123, 134, 240
Out of Court Settlement 61, 63, 64, 65, 66, 67, 69, 70, 71, 73, 79, 80, 81, 83
ownership structure 104, 135, 150, 210, 211, 212, 216, 223, 225

P

Pakistan 1, 52, 55, 60, 91, 105, 115, 131, 167, 201, 202, 203, 205, 206, 210, 211, 215, 218, 223, 224, 225, 227, 232, 233, 234, 235, 237, 238, 239, 240, 241, 242, 243, 244, 245, 246, 247, 250
Pakistan Stock Exchange 201, 203, 206
precariousness 231, 232, 233, 237
precarity 227, 231, 232, 233, 235, 236, 237, 238
Psychology 52, 136, 170, 198, 239, 247

R

Restructuring 61, 62, 63, 64, 65, 66, 67, 68, 69, 70, 73, 74, 75, 76, 77, 78, 79, 80, 81, 82, 83, 84, 85, 86, 87, 88, 89, 249
Risk 1, 3, 4, 5, 6, 7, 9, 10, 11, 12, 14, 17, 18, 19, 21, 22, 27, 29, 54, 55, 91, 92, 93, 94, 95, 98, 99, 100, 102, 104, 106, 107, 108, 110, 113, 115, 116, 136, 146, 147, 150, 153, 154, 155, 156, 157, 158, 159, 160, 161, 162, 163, 164, 166, 167, 168, 169, 170, 171, 172, 173, 174, 175, 179, 180, 184, 185, 186, 187, 188, 189, 192, 193, 194, 196, 197, 198, 199, 202, 205, 207, 209, 210, 211, 212, 213, 215, 216, 217, 218, 219, 220, 221, 222, 223, 224, 225, 234, 246, 251
Risk Management 1, 3, 9, 10, 11, 12, 17, 18, 19, 29, 91, 92, 93, 94, 99, 100, 102, 104, 106, 107, 108, 113, 146, 156, 159, 160, 161, 162, 169, 173, 175, 179, 180, 184, 185, 187, 188, 189, 192, 193, 196, 198, 216, 217, 222, 223, 224
Risk Management Practices 93, 102

S

SEM 43, 54
Socially Responsible Governance 100
Society 31, 32, 34, 35, 36, 50, 55, 58, 100, 105, 113, 118, 119, 120, 121, 122, 123, 125, 126, 127, 128, 133, 134, 138,

139, 140, 141, 142, 146, 149, 174, 227, 228, 229, 230, 231, 232, 233, 234, 235, 236, 238, 239, 244

Structural Equation Modeling 43, 57, 198

Supply Chain 1, 2, 3, 4, 5, 6, 7, 8, 9, 10, 11, 12, 13, 14, 15, 16, 17, 18, 19, 20, 21, 22, 23, 26, 27, 28, 29, 68, 142, 160, 161, 168, 169, 171, 173, 174, 175, 184, 192, 196, 198, 199

Sustainable Financing 1, 2, 4, 5, 10, 11, 12, 13, 14, 17, 18, 19, 20, 24, 25

Sustainable Performance 4, 133, 201, 202, 204, 205, 206, 207, 208, 209

T

Transparency 11, 13, 21, 22, 23, 91, 92, 97, 98, 99, 102, 105, 106, 109, 111, 124, 134, 138, 143, 144, 146, 218, 244

U

Uncertainty 8, 13, 22, 55, 96, 98, 99, 104, 153, 154, 155, 156, 157, 158, 159, 160, 161, 162, 163, 164, 167, 168, 169, 171, 172, 173, 175, 178, 179, 180, 184, 197, 199, 231, 240, 245, 247